David Rohl is the author of the best-selling history book *A Test of Time: The Bible – From Myth to History* (1995, published in the USA as *Pharaohs and Kings*) and presenter of the internationally acclaimed three-part documentary series 'Pharaohs and Kings: A Biblical Quest' which was first broadcast in September 1995. His second best-seller, *Legend: The Genesis of Civilisation* (1998), has since formed the basis of documentary programmes entitled 'In Search of Eden' and 'The Egyptian Genesis'.

David holds a degree in Ancient History and Egyptology (University College London) and was awarded the prestigious W. F. Masom History Research Scholarship by the University of London. He is currently President of the Institute for the Study of Interdisciplinary Sciences (ISIS), Editor of the *Journal of the Ancient Chronology Forum* (JACF) and Honorary President of the Sussex Egyptology Society (SES). He excavated at Kadesh-on-the-Orontes (Tell Nebi Mend) in Syria during the 1990s for the Institute of Archaeology, London, and is currently co-Field Director of the Eastern Desert Survey in Egypt, as well as being Editor of the Eastern Desert Survey Report.

D0910702

From Eden to Exile

The Epic History of the People of the Bible

First published in hardback as
*The Lost Testament: From Eden to Exile – The
5000-year History of the People of the Bible*

David M. Rohl

arrow books

Published by Arrow Books in 2003

3 5 7 9 10 8 6 4 2

Copyright © David Rohl 2002

David Rohl has asserted his right under the Copyright, Designs and
Patents Act, 1988, to be identified as the author of this work

First published in the United Kingdom in 2002 by Century with the
title *The Lost Testament*

Arrow Books Limited
The Random House Group Limited
20 Vauxhall Bridge Road, London SW1V 2SA

Random House Australia (Pty) Limited
20 Alfred Street, Milsons Point, Sydney,
New South Wales 2061, Australia

Random House New Zealand Limited
18 Poland Road, Glenfield
Auckland 10, New Zealand

Random House South Africa (Pty) Limited
Endulini, 5a Jubilee Road, Parktown 2193, South Africa

Random House Group Limited Reg. No. 954009

www.randomhouse.co.uk

A CIP catalogue record for this book
is available from the British Library

Papers used by Random House UK are
natural, recyclable products made from wood grown in
sustainable forests. The manufacturing processes conform to the
environmental regulations of the country of origin

ISBN 0 09 941566 6

Typeset by
Ditas Rohl

Printed and bound in Great Britain by
Bookmarque Ltd, Croydon, Surrey

For my brother and sisters

Professor John C. G. Röhl
Angela Kingsford Röhl
Nora Smith

Contents

Part Four
Legendary Kings

Part Five
The Two Kingdoms

Part Six
Reference Section

INTRODUCTION

The book you are about to read is a true story. It is the epic tale of a people, as handed down through their own traditions, and through the legends and epics of other cultures making up the ancient world within which they lived. The story of these people can also be told through the more recent scholarly disciplines of Middle Eastern archaeology and the study of ancient texts. All these sources – legendary and archaeological – have been synthesised in *From Eden to Exile* to bring you an epic narrative focusing on a small tribe which became a people and then a nation through exploration, challenge and adversity – a nation known to us from the Bible as the Israelites. But who were they? Where did they come from? And what was so special about their one 'true god' – Yahweh – which set him apart from the plethora of gods worshipped by all the other nations?

By telling their amazing story, I hope to reveal the real geographical and historical background of the Children of Yahweh, setting the great events and personalities of the Old Testament in their proper political and cultural context.

If you are a committed Christian, Jew or Muslim you can choose to read this book as a companion to the Bible, TANAAKH or Koran. It will hopefully cast new and fascinating light on what each of you may regard as the most

1

important literary work humanity has produced. For those who do not hold to any particular religious beliefs, this book offers an explanation for the early development of Yahwism (the foundation of Judaeo-Christian theology) and puts the origins of this powerful faith into an illuminating extra-biblical setting. I trust you will take what you want from this wonderful story – the first of all stories – told here in a very different way and from an entirely new 'historical' perspective.

What makes *From Eden to Exile* different to all those other works dedicated to the task of 'explaining' the Bible through archaeology and modern scholarship? The answer is a single word – 'chronology'. Those of you who have watched the television documentary series 'Pharaohs and Kings' or read *A Test of Time: The Bible – From Myth to History* and *Legend: The Genesis of Civilisation* will be aware of the fact that a group of scholars, made up of specialists from many different scientific and historical disciplines, have been developing a radical alternative chronology for the ancient world. This 'New Chronology' proposes that scholars of the last two centuries inadvertently reconstructed the ancient timeline of the pre-Christian era in such a way that it has become artificially over-extended by some two hundred to three hundred and fifty years. What this means is that the civilisations of the ancient Near East have been misaligned with biblical history, so that the events described in the Old Testament can no longer be found in the archaeological record and are therefore seen as 'unhistorical' inventions of the biblical writer(s) or redactor(s). The New Chronology has readjusted the timeline, removing the extra years introduced by modern scholarship, and, as a result, has demonstrated that it is perfectly feasible to fit the biblical story into a workable archaeological framework. The Israelites were always there – it is just that we have not been looking for them at the correct place in the historical timeline.

* * *

The Bible remains the most published, translated and read literary work in the world. But what is this most famous of books? Is it a history? Is it a fairy tale? Is it fact or fiction? Are the people of The Book real historical figures or simply the literary invention of the storytellers? And why does any of this matter anyway? It matters because many of the world's greatest religions look to the stories contained in the Old Testament (the Tanaakh of Judaism) and the Koran for their moral and theological teaching. In that respect the narratives have formed the basis or foundation of both Western and Middle-Eastern culture for the past two thousand years and more.

The key question, then, is whether that foundation has been laid on solid rock or drifting sand. If we are dealing with a 'glorified mirage' – as some scholars believe – then the Old Testament is quite useless as an historical source. There were no Israelites in Egypt; no Moses and Exodus; no Conquest of the Promised Land; no mighty warrior David; no merchant prince Solomon; no history of Israel, as such, before the first mention of Israelite rulers in the ninth-century annals of the Assyrian kings. This is not a question of faith or theology; it is simply a matter of whether the stories and people of the Bible were real.

Is the Old Testament history or myth? The only way to answer that question is to investigate the biblical stories using the archaeological evidence, combined with a study of the ancient texts of the civilisations which had a role to play in the Bible story. But this has to be done with an open mind. In my view the biblical text – just like any other ancient document – should be treated as a *potentially* reliable historical source until it can be demonstrated to be otherwise.

It is true to say that, until recently, much of the Old Testament was believed to be inconsistent with the archaeo-logical record. The views of earlier scholars such as Albright (1891–1971) and Wright (1909–1974) – both advocates of the historicity of the biblical narratives – have become more and more unfashionable since, from the 1950s onwards, excavations began to undermine their 'maximalist' inter-pretation of the biblical text. Major turning points in Israelite history were simply not evidenced in the remains found at the sites. There were no Israelite settlements in Egypt to correspond with the bondage years; no consistent pattern of burning and destruction to match Joshua's con-quest of Canaan; no magnificent buildings to reflect the 'golden age' of Solomon. The picture coming out of the ground was almost entirely negative. Small wonder that a number of respected academics who actually teach Bible exegesis in the universities have become sceptics or even biblical 'minimalists' during the last few decades.

But then, recently, a new group of researchers (including myself) began to highlight the inconsistencies and mistakes made in the last two centuries which have resulted in an artificially extended chronology for the ancient world. We realised that, because this stretched timeline detached the historical narrative of the Bible from its true archaeological setting, archaeologists had been searching for evidence of the Old Testament stories in the right places but in entirely the wrong time. If you look for the fallen walls of Jericho in the levels of the Late Bronze Age at Tell es-Sultan (the modern Arabic name of the ruin mound of Jericho) you will not find them. But if you dig several metres deeper, the fallen walls of Joshua's Jericho are there to be unearthed. Indeed, they have already been partially excavated but simply remain unrecognised for what they are. Similar stories can be told for the eras of Joseph and Solomon, and even back to the time of Nimrod and the Tower of Babel.

The New Chronology, developed by this younger generation of scholars, initially came to the general public's attention through a series of popular books published dur-ing the 1990s. The first, *Centuries of Darkness* by Peter James *et al.*, exposed the flaws in the conventional chronology of the Old World, highlighting the artificial 'dark ages' which scholars had created to fill out their overstretched timeline.

Next came my own book, *A Test of Time: The Bible – From Myth to History*, which dealt specifically with the problems of Egyptian chronology and how those problems were behind the impression that the Bible could never be treated as an historical work. *A Test of Time* then went on to show how a revised chronology might be capable of re-establishing the Old Testament as an historical narrative based on real events and personalities. Archaeological and chronological settings were found for the Israelites in Egypt, the conquest of the Promised Land and rise of the United Monarchy in Israel. The television series 'Pharaohs and Kings: A Biblical Quest' brought these ideas to a huge international audience and was the catalyst of considerable controversy (some would say notoriety) within academia.

Next came *Legend: The Genesis of Civilisation* in which I attempted to reconstruct a history for the book of Genesis within this new chronological framework. By its very nature this was a more speculative enterprise than the historical analysis covered in *A Test of Time*. The legendary age of Genesis is a fascinating era for study, but is dependent on epic literature and only limited archaeological resources for its reconstruction. Nevertheless a great deal can be gleaned about the primeval age of Man's early history from such sources – if they are studied and interpreted from within the landscapes in which those stories were set.

Aside from these books and related TV programmes, the Institute for the Study of Interdisciplinary Sciences (ISIS) has published nine volumes of the *Journal of the Ancient Chronology Forum* (*JACF*), now established as a recognised forum for debate on the New Chronology thesis and other chronological and historical issues raised by Old World archaeology. There is even a lively internet discussion group devoted to New Chronology research and debate (www.group.yahoo.com/group/NewChronology). Several PhD research projects are underway which cover different aspects of the New Chronology thesis in more detail, whilst a dedicated team of NC researchers are working on areas not so far fully covered in the books or academic papers. These include Mesopotamian chronology, astronomical dating, Iron Age stratigraphy in the Levant and a re-examination of the various scientific dating methods.

In spite of all this published research and willingness to debate the issues, advocates of the New Chronology have met either apathy or intense resistance from the conservative academic community. I myself have been labelled 'a charlatan', 'a TV chronologist' and 'an absolute crank', whilst the New Chronology thesis has been described as 'one hundred per cent rubbish'.

Sir Mortimer Wheeler once said that 'Archaeology is not a science – it is a vendetta.' Things haven't changed very much since his day. Such invective speaks volumes about scholarly paranoia and only serves to illustrate the innate conservatism which pervades *some parts* of the academic community. I stress 'some parts' because not all of my colleagues show Luddite tendencies. Physicist Professor Max Planck's famous quote from the 1940s pointedly sums up the reality which confronts many revolutionary ideas:

A new scientific truth does not triumph by convincing its opponents and making them see the light, but rather because its opponents eventually die, and a new generation grows up which is familiar with it.

Where does all this leave us in respect of biblical scholarship? In my opinion it leaves us with a potential cure for the malaise but with a patient stubbornly refusing to take his medicine because he doesn't like the taste.

As I was finishing the last few chapters of *From Eden to Exile* I watched a new television documentary series with considerable interest (and, it has to be said, some amusement). It was entitled 'It Ain't Necessarily So' and was presented by Beirut hostage victim John McCarthy. The book upon which the series was based bears the same title and was written by historian Matthew Sturgis.* The subtitle of this rather thin volume (read in a day) is 'Investigating the Truth of the Biblical Past'. That truth, according to both TV series and book, is once again that the Bible is almost entirely worthless as an historical source. McCarthy interviewed the leading archaeologists of today digging in what we call the Holy Land. The conclusions of these eminent scholars (many of whom I met during the filming of 'Pharaohs and Kings' and at various conferences) is stark (and even more so for its virtual unanimity). Here are just a few examples of their views, combined with Sturgis and McCarthy's conclusions about the historicity of the biblical narratives.

- **Sturgis on the Exodus** – 'For them (the majority of scholars) – in the absence of archaeological evidence – the Exodus – like the story of Joshua's conquest – remains an exploded myth.'

- **Ze'ev Herzog on the Exodus** – 'a history that never happened.'

- **McCarthy on the Conquest** – 'When the site at Jericho was reworked in the 1950s for example, it was discovered that the walls had fallen down long before Joshua and his people were supposed to have arrived – and that at that time Jericho was almost certainly unoccupied. ... the conquest of the Promised Land by the Children of Israel began to evaporate into the thin, hazy air ... The fact that the archaeological evidence at Jericho – and other sites mentioned in the Bible – refutes the conquest story, came as a shock. ... Archaeologist after archaeologist told me that ... not

---

* M. Sturgis: *It Ain't Necessarily So: Investigating the Truth of the Biblical Past* (London, 2001).

only was there no conquest of Canaan by Joshua and the Children of Israel (that was all a later invention) but that the Israelites were, in fact, Canaanites.'

- **Bill Dever on Jericho** – 'Joshua destroyed a city that wasn't even there.'

- **Sturgis on the Conquest** – 'According to the latest count (carried out by Bill Dever and Lawrence Stager) of the thirty or so cities Joshua is said to have conquered, almost all of them were found to have been uninhabited during the thirteenth century BCE (the conventional date for the conquest) or destroyed by other agents or not destroyed at all. … If the children of Israel did not sweep into Canaan and conquer it, did they ever escape out of Egypt and cross the wilderness? Indeed, were they ever in Egypt?'

- **Sturgis on the book of Judges** – 'The notion that the early Israelites did not arrive as conquerors from outside the country, but emerged as settlers from within the indigenous Canaanite population, is arresting. It seems – at first acquaintance – rather shocking. And, as it sinks in, it seems more shocking. A God-given conquest of the Promised Land and a distinct racial identity as God's Chosen People: these are the two great planks of Jewish tradition. Take them away and it seems to realign radically the accepted story of the Old Testament. It undermines the entire dynamic of the biblical narrative. And it suggests that extreme caution must be exercised in attempting to use the book of Judges as an historical source.'

- **Sturgis on Davidic Jerusalem** – 'After a century and a half of surveying, digging and sifting, almost no clear archaeological evidence for King David's capital has come to light.'

- **McCarthy on tenth-century Jerusalem** – 'There is no archaeological evidence whatsoever that Jerusalem was a great city of palaces and temples at the time of Kings David and Solomon. Archaeologists have found much material from earlier periods, and much from later, but from the tenth century BC there is nothing.'

- **Israel Finkelstein on United Monarchy Jerusalem** – 'There is almost no evidence for the tenth century. There is almost no evidence for Solomon. Jerusalem at this time was probably a very small village, or a very poor town.'

- **Sturgis on David** – 'some commentators … doubt the very existence of King David. They have suggested that he was perhaps a complete and late fabrication. Or, at best, a mythical figure like King Arthur, blown up to magnificent proportions from very modest beginnings, an heroic champion created by later generations as the symbol of a long-vanished golden age that never actually existed.'

- **Sturgis on Solomon** – 'For most scholars the compass and character of Solomon's kingdom has dwindled. For some it has vanished to nothingness. … Solomon's grandeur remains stubbornly and disconcertingly mythical.'

And so it goes on. Journalist McCarthy concludes his introduction to the book with the immortal line 'The creation of the Bible history is one of the finest examples of spin ever spun.'

When you read a book like *It Ain't Necessarily So*, it really brings home the massive psychological problems surrounding 'Biblical Archaeology' (a phrase which is itself now taboo amongst archaeologists working in the region). The frustrating thing is that the solution to all their problems has been staring scholars in the face for decades – but they simply can't see the wood for the trees. They have observed clear archaeological evidence which matches the biblical narrative – but it is at the wrong point in the historical timeline for them so cannot be linked with the Israelites. When they believe they are at the correct point in the historical timeline they turn up no archaeological evidence to match the biblical narrative. So, the Bible *must* be wrong.

Then I come along and have the temerity to suggest that we should perhaps take another look at that timeline to see if it can't be made to synchronise better with the archaeological evidence. And for that heresy I am labelled a charlatan and crank. As a result, writers like Matthew Sturgis dare not contemplate a radical revision such as that offered by the New Chronology thesis. Why? For fear of condemnation. It is not that Sturgis is unaware of a potential solution to all the issues raised in his book. He simply has to dismiss the New Chronology in a few sentences when dealing with the dilemma of Jericho before wandering back into his forest of problems.

> In an effort to overcome this difficulty some popular publications on the topic have prescribed a resort to drastic measures. In his book *A Test of Time* David Rohl, for instance, has recently suggested that the currently accepted Egyptian chronology needs to be drastically revised by almost 350 years. Not the least significant effect of his proposal would be to place Joshua once more amid the ruins of Jericho – at least in theory. Such hypotheses hold little sway with academics in the field. [*It Ain't Necessarily So*, p. 49]

Ask most scholars to articulate why they are not prepared to take the New Chronology seriously and they will tell you that, although they themselves are not experts in this field or that, 'so and so' has told them that the New

Chronology is 'one hundred per cent rubbish'. 'So and so' invariably turns out to be Professor Kenneth Kitchen, formerly of Liverpool University, who has taken it upon himself to be the Witchfinder General of the New Chronology. Ask Israeli archaeologists why Pharaoh Hedjkheperre Shoshenk I is dated to 945–925 BC (the time of the biblical Shishak) and they will tell you because Kenneth Kitchen says so. The fact that Shoshenk is dated solely by identifying him with Shishak – and therefore entirely through biblical chronology – comes as a bit of a shock to them. You explain that the Egyptian and overseas archaeological evidence, on the other hand, points to a later date for Shoshenk I (*c.* 820 BC) and that he cannot, therefore, be identified with Shishak (*c.* 925 BC). It is not an exaggeration to say that Professor Kitchen, in spite of the mounting evidence against the equation, stubbornly refuses to sever the link between Shoshenk and the biblical Shishak – a link which lies at the heart of all the problems for Holy Land archaeology. These Israeli archaeologists – mostly fine intellectuals – look puzzled, scratch their heads, go back to their digs and continue to use Kitchen's dating – in spite of what you have said. But who can blame them? After all, the New Chronology really is a radical idea – too radical for most to contemplate. It overturns two centuries of historical reconstruction. It flies in the face of everything that they were taught at university. It can't possibly be right because they know that the Egyptian dates – supplied by their Egyptological colleagues – are accurate to within a decade or so … aren't they?

On the other hand, millions of ordinary people – people without qualifications in Egyptology and archaeology – watched 'Pharaohs and Kings', read *A Test of Time*, and took a different view. They saw the common sense of the argument. They were drawn to the new discoveries which added so much to the biblical story. Daylight was suddenly penetrating the dim forest of biblical scholarship and they could finally see the wood, in spite of the academic trees.

So now we have an interesting situation: a popular hypothesis lies on the table which explains so much but which, for all intents and purposes, has been ignored by the academic establishment. Scholarship says that the Bible is almost entirely mythological fiction. The New Chronology proposes that, far from being a myth, the Old Testament is essentially historical – not, perhaps, in every detail but certainly in its major events and personalities.

* * *

The book you are about to read is quite simply the biblical story set in its proper chronological context. It is not written for an academic audience. It is basically the narrative history of a people who worshipped a powerful god with many names, whom we know today as Yahweh or Jehovah. The story of these people begins in a place called Eden in the sixth millennium BC and ends with the destruction of Jerusalem by the Babylonians in the sixth century BC. It is a wonderfully rich story of immense diversity and complexity – the epic of epics – the book of books – here narrated in a straightforward and uncompromising way. If you want to read the story of the Children of Yahweh in its classic form, then by all means choose the King James translation of the Bible with all its 'thees' and 'thous', but if you would also like to read what really happened as a modern historian might write it – when and where, and with which famous historical figures from outside the Bible – then this is the book for you. I hope you find it stimulating and intellectually challenging. It was assuredly that to write – and ceaselessly rewarding to research.

This book will undoubtedly generate considerable gnashing of teeth within many academic furrows (most grindingly in one study of a certain leafy Liverpool suburb), but that is to be expected. I just have to do what my conscience dictates and keep bashing away at the foundations of conservative academe. You never know, one day its walls may actually come tumbling down, just like Jericho, and it will finally be accepted that 'Joshua destroyed a city *that really was there'*.

* * *

Traditionally, the authorship of the first five books of the Bible – what scholars refer to as the Pentateuch – is attributed to Moses. And, indeed, this is apparently what Jesus and the apostles believed (John 5:45–47). But it is not the general academic consensus today. Within biblical scholarship an alternative view, known as the 'Documentary Hypothesis', has held sway for the last one hundred years. This theory, famously articulated by J. Wellhausen (1844–1919), proposes that the Pentateuch is made up of four separate documents which had been combined into a single work in order to tell the story of the Israelites from the Creation down to the death of Moses, just before the Conquest of the Promised Land. Moreover, these four documents were written many centuries after Moses. This would, of course, considerably reduce their value as historical sources since they would not be remotely close in time to the events being described.

However, more recent research, evolving out of our better understanding of ancient civilisations through the translation of thousands of cuneiform and hieroglyphic texts, has demonstrated that many elements of the Pentateuch contain parallels to extra-biblical texts of much 'earlier' times. For instance, Professor Kenneth Kitchen himself has highlighted the similarity in structure between law codes from the Old Babylonian period (OC – *c.* 1894–1595 BC or NC – *c.* 1667–1362 BC) and the laws of Moses (OC – *c.* 1240 BC or NC – *c.* 1440 BC). You will note from the dates that the Orthodox Chronology (OC) has Moses writing his laws several centuries after Hammurabi's Law Code was composed, whilst the New Chronology (NC) has Moses following soon after Hammurabi, thus explaining the obvious similarities in common law within the two documents.

Kitchen has also shown that the slave prices mentioned during different eras in the Old Testament correspond to the purchase prices of domestic servants in independently dated documents from Mesopotamia. Thus Joseph was sold into slavery in Egypt for the price of twenty shekels [Genesis 37:28] which corresponds to the 'going rate' in the ancient world during the era from the Isin-Larsa period to the Old Babylonian Dynasty of Hammurabi (collectively spanning OC – c. 2025–1595 BC or NC – c. 1805–1362 BC). If the story of Joseph had been written as late as the second century BC (as argued by the minimalist Copenhagen School) when the slave price was one hundred and twenty shekels, then it would be surprising that the author was aware of the true price of Joseph's bondage more than a millennium earlier. Again, in the New Chronology, we find Joseph living in the seventeenth century BC when the contemporary records from Mesopotamia confirm that an appropriate slave price was paid for the young Israelite by Midianite caravaneers.

As a result of such research, some scholars are now arguing for a less rigid understanding of how the Old Testament story was constructed. It is reasonable to assume that oral recitation played a part. In other words, some elements were told and retold – passed from generation to generation as oral epics which were only written down fairly late in the process of compiling the biblical texts. Other sections were indeed written in the form of manuscripts (or tablets) but then later copied and edited, either before or at the time of the compilation.*

* * *

As you can imagine, the task of retelling the biblical story in a modern archaeo-historical way is fraught with difficulty. Indeed, from the Bible's very first page this writer was confronted with dilemmas. How should I treat the issue of the Creation? How can I accept Adam as literally the first human on Earth? Why does the book of Genesis refer to 'gods' (plural) 'making Man in our own likeness' when the rest of the Bible seems to be a monotheistic work? Who were the 'giants' (Hebrew *nephilim*) born of the sons of gods by the daughters of men? How can I accept, without question, the extraordinary ages of the antediluvian patriarchs? Methuselah lived for 969 years? And what about the later patriarchs, such as Abraham and Isaac, living to over a hundred? Is this really credible?

So many questions that must be broached and answered – or perhaps, better, interpreted – in as honest a way as possible. Of course, we could simply dismiss ninety per cent of Genesis as myth. This magnificent opening book of the Bible is, after all, by its very nature, epic and legendary. But we have to begin at the beginning where all stories start. So I have resorted to a degree of 'poetic licence', telling the story of Adam and the Garden of Eden in a way which is at least consistent with the archaeological, anthropological and geographical evidence but, at the same time, trying to retain the colour and character of the original tale of Man's departure from the Earthly paradise.

* * *

Not every aspect and incident in the biblical narrative has a place in this reworking of the story. Where details are not obviously relevant to the historical narrative, or where I simply have no historical explanation for them (certain

---

* Some of this editing resulted in chronological anachronisms. For example, no-one believes that Jacob and the Israelites settled 'in the Land of Ramesses' as stated in Genesis 47:11 because pharaohs called Ramesses did not rule in Egypt until several centuries after the time of Jacob and Joseph – on any chronology. Clearly the location 'in the Land of Ramesses' has been added into the text to clarify the place of the Israelite sojourn for an audience/readership of the editor's own time when Goshen was currently identified with the delta region around the city of Pi-Ramesse. The ruins of the city of Ramesses were still known by that name in the time of Abbess Etheria (also known as Egeria) who travelled to Egypt in the fourth century AD.

'miraculous' events come to mind here), I have chosen to pass them by, leaving the reader to add his own perspective on such matters. My personal views are not important here. I am simply telling the story within a revised chronological and archaeological framework for others to overlay their own belief-systems or theological interpretations.

You will occasionally be confronted by names that are not familiar to you – especially Egyptian and Meso-potamian names, some of which can be fairly obscure. However, they all have their place in the story and bring each episode into clearer historical focus. So, don't let them put you off.

The crucial new element is, of course, the dating. Throughout I have employed New Chronology dates and only identified them as such when comparing those new dates with the older conventional dating used in the vast majority of works on ancient history. Where dates are being compared they are given as NC (New Chronology) and OC (Orthodox Chronology).

It would be quite impossible to include all the detailed arguments and evidence here in this book simply for lack of space. Such an all-inclusive volume would be thousands of pages long! So, if you want to study a topic more deeply, I suggest you take a look at the chapters in *A Test of Time* and *Legend* (where further references can be found), and the various papers by other scholars and New Chronology researchers which have been published in academic journals (some of which are otherwise available at the website www.Nunki.net).

The first part of this book deals with the antediluvian age of prehistory where the dates are necessarily speculative and imprecise. However, I think we can now say that the chronology of the 'Dynastic Age' of kingdoms and empires has been determined to a fair degree of accuracy. The dates of the kings and dynasties – stretching from Mesopotamia to Egypt – span the period from the flood in *c.* 3113 BC down to the fall of Jerusalem in 587 BC. These dates vary slightly from those proposed in *A Test of Time* and *Legend* in order to accommodate more recent research, but the historical synchronisms are essentially the same as those put forward in the first two volumes of the New Chronology thesis. But please remember that this is all 'work in progress' and is not set in stone like the conventional chronology. What makes the New Chronology so exciting is that it is not stuck in its own dogma. Flexibility and a willingness to adjust are a hallmark of NC endeavour – not a weakness.

I hope you will enjoy delving a little more deeply into this fascinating field of research which has been described as 'a Sherlock Holmes mystery with four-thousand-year-old clues'.

Part One

Origins

Chapter One

ADAM AND THE
GARDEN OF EDEN

(Genesis 2:8 to Genesis 4:16)

*The Land of Eden – The Garden of Eden – Adam and
the Adamites – The Mountain of God – Eve, Mother of
All the Living – Cain and Abel – Exile from Eden –
The Land of Nod*

n the beginning – the beginning of memory – there
was once a luxuriant land called Eden with a paradisal
garden set towards its eastern limits. Eden lay beyond
the broad mountain range which separates the Mesopotamian plain from the steppes of central Asia, its heartland located in the area of the two great salt lakes of Van
and Urumiya. The lush primeval valleys and plains of Eden
were hemmed in by tall snowcapped peaks, their slopes
covered in a dense canopy of pine (*erini*) and cedar (*survan*)
forest. Later, the Persians would simply know the place as
pairidaeza – Paradise.

Four of the ancient world's great rivers flowed from
Eden. The headwaters of the Hiddekel (Tigris) and Perath

(Euphrates) were located in the west, whilst those of the Gihon (Gaihun-Aras), flowing through the land of Cush, and Pishon (Kezel Uzun), winding through the land of Havilah, rose in its eastern part.

Eden was the place which gave birth to civilisation – the womb of the great earth-goddess and the mother of the Neolithic Revolution. This was the time when Stone Age Man finally gave up the wandering hunter-gatherer way of life, settled in villages and began to raise crops and domesticate animals.

Located in the eastern part of the sparsely populated region of Eden was a long east–west valley, protected by high mountains on three sides. The sun rose at one end and set at the other. To the north stretched the Mountains of Cush beyond which lay the land of the same name, through which flowed the River Gihon. At its eastern end, the range culminated in the rocky volcanic pinnacle of Mount Savalan, guarding the eastern entrance into Eden. To the south the snow-topped Bazgush ridge separated the valley from the Land of Havilah with its fast-flowing streams, rich in gold, which joined to form the meandering

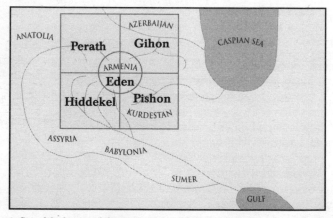

1. Simplified map of the four rivers of Eden, showing their sources in Classical Armenia (eastern Turkey and western Iran).

River Pishon. At the western end of this southern range rose the mountain massif of Sahand – an icy world of glistening volcanic peaks. The valley was bounded on its west side by salty Lake Urumiya beyond a broad area of inhospitable marshland and salt flats.

It was here in this lush valley 'in the east of Eden' [Genesis 2:8] that Adam and his people settled. The epic story of the Children of Yahweh begins here in this first of all gardens – the Bible's Earthly paradise.

The 'garden' (Hebrew *gan*) into which the Adamites had arrived was sheltered on three sides – a haven from the worst of the highland climate and a refuge from nomadic bands moving through the surrounding mountains along the major communication routes. Westerly winds brought warm rain from the Mediterranean, creating a microclimate in the long narrow valley. This extra moisture encouraged dense vegetation growth and an amazing variety of fruit-bearing trees 'enticing to look at and good to eat' [Genesis 2:9]. In deep red soil covering the foothills, orchards of apple, apricot, pistachio and almond grew in abundance. Intermingled with the fruit- and nut bearing trees, wild vines entwined the natural sloping terraces, heavily laden with bunches of sweet green grapes. The vine was the Tree of Life at the heart of Eden.

Scattered across the valley floor Adam's people found bubbling hot springs which watered meadows carpeted in wild flowers. And through the centre of this idyll flowed a river, the numerous sources of which originated atop the summits of the surrounding peaks. The river of the Garden flowed westwards before disgorging into the swamps of Urumiya. Today this river is called the Adji Chay – the 'bitter waters' – because of the high mineral content washed down from the metal-rich mountains. Its more ancient name was Maidan, meaning 'Royal Garden'.

Here was a place that had everything. Adam and his followers established their roots in this virginal landscape – the legendary Garden of Eden.

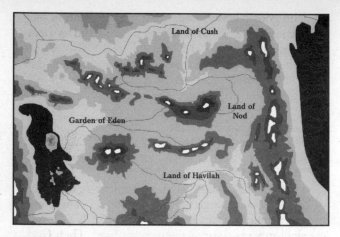

2. A simplified relief map of the eastern part of Eden with the Garden of Eden at its centre. The river valleys north of the Savalan and Kusheh-Dagh ridge were known to the biblical writer as Cush and by the later Classical geographers as Cossaea. To the south of the Sahand and Bazgush ridge lay the biblical land of Havilah through which the gold-bearing Pishon (Uzun) flowed. To the west is Lake Urumiya and to the east the land of Nod (Noqd), beyond which lies the Caspian Sea.

The Red Earth Man

Adam was both the ruler and high priest of his community. He was in tune with the voices of nature which spoke to him in vision and trance. Adam *knew* the power of the plants and the animals.

He was also well aware of the harsh realities of life and its inevitable end. The great MOTHER EARTH regularly took back the bodies of the creatures she had created, leaving only bleached bones as witness to their brief existence. Earth to earth, dust to dust – or, more correctly, clay to clay [Genesis 3:19]. Just as the potter produced vessels on his potter's wheel, so the gods (Hebrew *elohim*, Sumerian *igigi*) made Man in their likeness from the clay of Mother Earth on a potter's wheel.

The gods (elohim) said, 'Let us make Man in our own image, in the likeness of ourselves, and let them be masters of the fish and the sea, the birds of heaven, the cattle, all the wild animals, and all the creatures that creep along the ground.' [Genesis 1:26]

They (the gods) summoned the goddess, the midwife of the gods, wise Mami ('mummy' = Ninhursag), and asked: 'You are the womb-goddess, creator of Mankind! Create a mortal, that he may bear the yoke!' ... Enki ('Lord of the Earth') made his voice heard and spoke to the great gods: '... Then one god should be slaughtered. ... NINTU ('Lady of Birth') shall mix clay with his flesh and blood. Then God and Man shall be mixed together in clay'. [*Atrahasis Epic* 1:4]

Yahweh shaped Man from the clay of the ground and blew the breath of life into his nostrils, and Man became a living being. Yahweh planted a garden in the east of Eden and there he put the man he had fashioned. [Genesis 2:7–8]

Yahweh took the man and settled him in the Garden of Eden to cultivate and take care of it. [Genesis 2:15]

In the creation mythology of ancient Mesopotamia Man was made in the likeness of the gods by combining the clay of the earth with the blood of a sacrificed god. So it was that Adam received his own traditional name meaning 'red earth' – the red earth or clay taken from the Red Mountain overlooking the Garden. Excavations in Eden have revealed that red ochre was used to paint the walls of the houses, decorate clay figurines and cover the bones of the dead as 'replacement blood' or as a substitute for the flesh stripped from the bones by carrion.* Adam *knew* the earth because he was of the earth.

Mountain of God

To the south of the settlement a narrow, steep-sided valley rose up in the direction of the most prominent mountain at the western end of the Garden. The great snow-covered dome of the mountain towered above the orchards, its summit often shrouded in clouds. One day Adam decided to follow the stream up the valley. The fast-flowing brook, charged with ice-cold waters from the spring thaw, led him higher and higher until he found himself within sight of the mountain top. There, immersed in the clouds, the landscape began to take on a supernatural form.

The fruit-bearing trees, heavy with blossom, had dwindled away soon after Adam had begun his climb. He had then crossed a barren moorland which spread out before the mountain. Following a bend in the gorge, made by the fast-flowing stream, he was now confronted by an amazing sight. The source of the stream was a shimmering pool, bubbling with hot gases. Enclosing the spring were conical towers of volcanic tephra. The reflection of these huge molars appeared as a gaping jaw in the water, at the centre of which lurked utter darkness. Above this entrance into the underworld the icy dome of the mountain stood sentinel.

Just as with Abraham and Moses, thousands of years later, Adam first came face to face with his god here in this 'high place' above the Garden of Eden. This was a crucial turning point in Man's journey through time; the moment which transformed Adam – the red earth man – into the genealogical fount of Judaeo, Christian and Islamic lineage.

---

* Primitive man most likely daubed his skin with ochre to ward off insects. In the valley of the Garden the swarms of mosquitoes which bred in the marshes of the great lake were a constant irritant, but the tribe soon learnt that red ochre was an effective insect repellent.

It was what distinguished the great ancestor of Yahweh's children from all who had gone before him. Here, and at this moment, the age of the Mother Goddess gave way to the era of the Lord of the Earth – the god recognised throughout the ensuing primeval age as the 'Friend of Man'.

Later tradition (in the form of the books of Ezekiel and Isaiah) would refer to a mysterious 'mountain of God', the 'exalted throne' and the 'mountain of the assembly (or heavenly host)'. By the time of the prophets Ezekiel and Isaiah, this holy mountain lay 'far away to the north' of Israel [Isaiah 14:13]. It became synonymous with the place of Man's fall. From these heights humanity (in its manifestation as the Phoenician King of Tyre) fell from grace to suffer mortal existence, forever beyond the protection of the Earthly paradise.

> Son of Man, raise a lament for the King of Tyre. Say to him 'The Lord Yahweh says this: "You were in Eden, in the Garden of God … you were upon the holy Mountain of God, where you walked amongst the red hot coals. … I have cast you down from the Mountain of God and destroyed you … Of the nations, all who know you are stunned at your fate. You are an object of terror gone forever."' [Ezekiel 28:11–19]

The primitive, innocent world came to an end with Adam. The symbolic metaphor of the Tree of Knowledge of Good and Evil and the incident of the Temptation mark the second crucial turning point in Adam's lifetime when Man began to seek the unknown. That all too human quest for knowledge became the 'mortal sin' which ignited Mortal Man's struggle and suffering in the descendants of primeval Adam. Our story of the Children of Yahweh really begins with that first step beyond the domain of the sacred mountain and its fabulous garden, the descent or 'fall' from heaven and the ceaseless wanderings which culminated in bondage on the banks of the River Nile over three and a half thousand years later.

The Mountain of God is still there to this day. You will find it marked on maps of western Iran as the 3,700-metre (10,500 ft) mountain massif of Sahand. The sacred pool – the primeval and original 'abyss' (Sumerian *ab.zu*) – has gone, as have the 'red-hot coals'. But, if you climb Sahand today, following in Adam's footsteps, you will come across the ancient troglodyte village of Kandovan, hewn out of the old volcanic towers beside the bubbling spring. Time stands still in this place where humanity first communicated with the god of the Bible.

A Marriage Made in Heaven

Not long after the establishment of their village at the foot of Mount Sahand, the Adamites came into contact with

3. Here, in this 4,000-year-old cylinder seal impression from Meso-potamia, we see Adam (right, wearing a horned helmet, the symbol of deification) and Eve (left) seated before the Tree of Knowledge of Good and Evil, heavily laden with fruit. The tree has seven branches, just as the *menorah* candelabra which represents the tree in the Garden of Eden. Adam and Eve gesticulate to each other to take the fruit of the tree. Behind Eve is the serpent. The seal is on display in the British Museum Mesopotamian galleries. At first labelled as the 'temptation seal', in more recent times the seal has been redesignated as a 'banqueting scene'.

other people settled in the region. To the south, beyond the Mountain of God in Eden, lay the Land of Havilah, 'rich in gold', where the Huwawa tribe lived. The chieftain of that tribe had a daughter – a priestess of the goddess Ninhursag – the 'mistress of the mountain peaks' and the 'mother of all the living' – whom he now offered in marriage to Adam. The union of Adam and Eve (Hebrew *Hawwah*) produced three sons and several daughters. In the biblical tradition Eve was given the epithet 'mother of all the living' because of her role as the great female ancestor of the Hebrew line. But there was also a ritual significance to this epithet. Adam, chieftain of the Eden clan, and Eve, priestess of the birth-goddess of Havilah, performed the annual union of the Sacred Marriage in which Eve took on the persona of the great Mother Goddess. Three thousand years later, Adam's successor rulers would still be practising this most ancient sexual rite in the 'dark chambers' atop the great ziggurats of Mesopotamia so as to create an heir to the sacred throne and ensure the fertility of the land at the birth of each year.

The first-born of Eve's sons was CAIN, followed by ABEL, his younger brother by three years. The two boys grew up together, learning not only to domesticate wild sheep, goats and cattle, but also to cultivate the land. In adulthood, Cain became a farmer whilst Abel took to shepherding in the hills. Their contrasting and conflicting ways of life – the tilling of soil versus pastoralism – would eventually be responsible for a great tragedy, shattering the unity of the village and leading to the exile of one group from Eden. This conflict between sedentary farming and nomadic pastoralism still simmers in the Iranian highlands today – the eternal curse of Cain and Abel.

Chapter Two

ENOCH
THE CITY BUILDER

(Genesis 4:17 to Genesis 6:4)

The Cherubim – Enoch – The foundation of Eridu –
Journey to Shinar – Yahweh's oldest name –
Uanna-Adapa

The Adamite tribe was split asunder. One faction –
the Cainites – had migrated eastwards into the
land of Noqd (biblical Nod, modern Ardabil
province). The rest of the clan, still under the leadership of
Adam, had also soon after left the Garden of Eden to begin
their difficult trek southwards through the Zagros mountains and on into northern Mesopotamia. Eve had given
birth to a third son named SETH who, in adulthood, was to
replace the murdered Abel as leader of the pastoralists.
The story of these nomadic shepherds and their descendant,
Abraham, continues a thousand years later but, first, we
must travel with the Cainites on their journey from heaven
(Sumerian AN) – the mountain paradise – down to earth
(Sumerian KI) and the beginnings of history. The year is
now 5245 BC.

Guardians of Paradise

Following their exile from Eden, Cain's tribe found themselves constantly harassed by the local inhabitants of Noqd – a wild nomadic people known as the Kheruba. These fearsome hunters roamed the landscape in search of game which they killed both for food and for their shamanistic rites. The appearance of the Kheruba, clad in animal skins and wearing horned headdresses, filled the people of the region with fear. The enemy chieftains wore magnificent cloaks covered in vulture's feathers woven into coarse fabric. In later tradition, these shaman priests were magically transformed into the winged guardians of paradise and the holy places – the biblical cherubim, fearsome protectors of the eastern gateway into Eden.

That eastern gateway is still there today. It is the barren mountain pass which leads from the Ardabil basin westwards into the long valley of the Adji Chay – the valley of the Garden. Its southern pillar is the Bazgush mountain range; its northern pillar the craggy volcanic peak of Mount Savalan, one of the traditional birth places of the later prophet and sage Zoroaster. In the local language Savalan means '[place of] toll' suggesting a long-standing tradition that this was a gateway or frontier point. The pass which separates Noqd from Eden is bleak and desolate in the winter months when thunder storms crackle with lightning as they roll down from the clouded summit of Savalan. The cherubim, guardians of paradise, were possessors of the 'fiery flashing sword' – the lighting bolts of 'toll mountain'.

> He (God) banished the man and, in front of the Garden of Eden, he posted the mighty winged creatures (Hebrew *kerubim*) and the fiery flashing sword to guard the way to the Tree of Life. [Genesis 3:24]

The cherubim of the Bible are known from AKKADIAN texts where the word for the great winged creatures is *kuribu.* They protect the holy places just as the biblical cherubim protect paradise and the holy of holies in the Temple of Jerusalem. They are often represented as winged lions but are part of a larger family of demonic hybrid creatures, including winged bulls and griffins (lions with birds' heads and wings), which stand sentinel as the gatekeepers of temples and palaces throughout Mesopotamia.

Descent from Heaven

Within a generation the Cainites decided to leave Noqd behind and head south-eastwards across the River Pishon, flowing down to the southern shore of the Caspian Sea, and along the wide vale of Zanjan. Some of the tribe chose to settle in this valley where they established a village, the ruins of which are now located at Ismailabad. The rest moved on to the Iranian plateau where they found themselves standing before a huge inland sea surrounded by marshes. Today, that sea has disappeared leaving behind a vast expanse of salt – the DASHT-É KAVIR. The tribe settled down close to the western shore of the lake, building a village of reed and brushwood huts which were later rebuilt in sun-dried mudbricks. This small settlement became the foundation of a large town now known as Tepe Sialk. Excavations, undertaken here and at Ismailabad, have produced some of the Middle East's earliest pottery – thin-walled vessels of extraordinary quality decorated with black designs on a red background (Sialk II). They also learnt to work metal (by hammering), extracting copper from the Talmessi malachite mines of nearby Anarak. This is how Cain ('metal-smith') inherited his traditional name.

Again, after several generations, the people moved on, leaving behind some of the rapidly growing tribe to continue the community at Sialk. Drawn ever southwards towards the warmer climate of the Gulf, the wanderers entered the central Zagros mountains and reached the vale of Kangavar. Again, part of the tribe set down roots here as the rest continued southwards, following the course of the Saidmarreh river through steep-sided gorges which eventually brought them down onto the Susiana plain. This whole process, from leaving Eden to arriving in the broad flatlands south of the Zagros mountains, had taken over four centuries. In that time the dynasty of Cain had come to an end and the mantle of leadership had passed into new hands. The third great leader and dynastic head of the Children of Yahweh was Enoch.

The Anunnaki

This eponymous founder of the third dynasty of the Adamites would be remembered by his distant descendants as the first builder of cities. Apocryphal works (the Books of Enoch) would be written about him, portraying this legendary figure as the first 'holy man' in history. So worthy was this man of God and sage that the angels took him away from Mankind and carried him up to heaven. His name – Enoch (Hebrew *Hanok* = 'founder') – was given to the pre-eminent Sumerian city of Uruk (biblical Erech) in its original Sumerian form *Unuk*. The Mesopotamian civilisations of later centuries elevated Enoch and the 'mighty men' of the primeval age who followed him to the status of gods whom they called Anunnaki or Anunna ('founders'). The name Anunnaki can also be understood as 'the ones of heaven and earth' – in other words those who came from heaven (*an*) to settle on earth (*ki*) or from the mountains to the alluvial plain. They were mortal men who became gods.

When the gods were Man … [*Atrahasic Epic*, line 1]

They were Earthbound gods who, being of flesh and blood, passed from the mortal world to govern the underworld of the dead. They did not dwell amongst the Igigi gods of heaven. The Egyptians also knew them as the mythological founders of civilisation, known as the Shebtiu.

> These are the great gods, the Senior Ones, the revered Shebtiu, ... They are (among) the twenty gods who proclaimed the Earth upon its foundation since the time of the primaeval age of gods unto the completion of eternity. ... the offspring of the Creator, Glorious Spirits of the Early Primaeval Age of Gods, Brethren of the (Seven) Sages and the Builder Gods ... [*Shebtiu Text* from Edfu]

Enoch, the original 'founder', named the very first city in Mesopotamia after his eldest son Irad – the city which historians and archaeologists know as Eridu and which the Sumerians gave a second name – Nun.ki (the 'mighty place'). The word *ki* is a determinative employed in cuneiform to denote 'city' and so Eridu's Sumerian name may simply be read as Nun – 'mighty'.

> None of the cloud-people had established a king. Until then, no diadem or crown had been set upon a head; no sceptre inlaid with lapis-lazuli. Not one of the shrines had been built. ... Sceptre, crown, diadem, and (shepherd's) crook still lay deposited before Anu in heaven ... Then kingship descended from heaven. [*Etana Epic*]

Enoch and his people had entered the lowlands by following the course of the Saidmarreh river which now joined other streams to form the River Kerkeh. At its southern outlet into the Persian Gulf the Kerkeh divided into numerous branches which made up a swampy delta, thick with tall clumps of reeds. These proved to be an excellent material for building not only reed houses but boats. The *berdi* reed is still used for that purpose today by the Marsh Arabs of southern Iraq. Enoch's tribe were the first to build boats by this method which they used to gradually explore the open sea of the northern Gulf (archaeologically speaking during the early Ubaid period, c. 4800–4000 BC). The clan chief himself and his entourage sailed westwards along the coast to discover the mouths of the Tigris and Euphrates rivers. The biblical tradition is that their antediluvian ancestors entered Shinar (historical Sumer in southern Iraq) from the east.

> Now, as the people came from the east, they found
> a valley in the land of Shinar where they settled.
> [Genesis 11:2]

At the marshy estuary of the Euphrates they came upon a circular island of clean sand surrounded by a freshwater lake and more of the berdi reeds ideal for building. Enoch witnessed a falcon alight on a perch of reeds growing along the shore of the island. He took this as a favourable omen and went ashore to lay the foundations of what was to become Eridu's holiest shrine – the E-Abzu ('house of the abyss') where the god of the Adamites would reside for two thousand years.

In the Egyptian tradition the Shebtiu-gods planted the reed upon which the falcon-god Horus alighted and, in doing so, established the foundation of the primeval temple upon the island of creation.

> … they planted a slip of reed in the Waters of Nun;
> then the falcon came and the reed raised him up …
> and so the great primeval mound came into being.
> [*Shebtiu Text* from Edfu]

The Name of God

It is only now, at this crucial point in human prehistory, that we can identify the god of the antediluvian patriarchs of the 'first time'. The ancients knew him by several names and epithets. The Sumerians refer to the god of Eridu as Enki ('lord of the earth') and Nudimud ('maker of man') whereas the East Semitic-speaking peoples of Mesopotamia (the Babylonians and Assyrians) knew him simply as EYA. This name is probably not Semitic and may have been borrowed from the original settlers in the Sumerian marshes who introduced their god to Mesopotamia from the eastern mountains. Thus the Sumerian epithet *en.ki* ('lord of the earth') is merely the principal title of the god of Eden whose personal name was Eya. The Hittites and Hurrians of the Late Bronze Age called him Aya. The West Semitic Israelites from a thousand years later referred to this same god as Yah (pronounced Ya), as well as by his longer formal name – Yahweh (pronounced Yawé). The shortened form of Yahweh's name is the most commonly used, occurring in numerous Israelite/Judaean names (e.g. Jeremiah [Heb. Yirmeyah 'Yah raises up'], Amaziah ['Yah is strong'], Josiah ['Yah supports'], Jedidiah ['beloved of Yah'], etc.) and in well-known biblical expressions such as halleluiah ('exalted is Yah'). Yah was undoubtedly the most popular name of God in late biblical times.

The Egyptians referred to this deity of the sacred island of the 'first Time' (*sep tepi*) as Tanen who, in later times, was known as Ptah (principal god of the first capital of unified Egypt – Memphis). Tanen/Ptah resided in the primeval temple in the Waters of Nun (the abyss) as a sacred falcon alongside the sun-god Atum/Re.

In his earliest manifestation – as the Sumerian deity Enki – Eya/Ya/Tanen was the god of the life-giving waters. These were the sweet water springs and rivers as opposed to the salt water seas. He was also the god of wisdom. He, in consort with the great Earth Mother Goddess Ninhursag (also known as Nintu 'Lady of Birth'), created Mankind from clay. He was acknowledged as the 'Friend of Man' – the god who warned the Mesopotamian flood hero of the impending catastrophe destined to destroy all humanity. In this part of our story we will mainly refer to the god of the antediluvian patriarchs by his Sumerian epithet Enki (except where quoting from an Akkadian source where Eya is used).

Holy Island

With Enoch's arrival upon the island of Nun (Eridu) at the mouth of the Euphrates river, the Lord of the Earth, god of the fresh water springs, had a new home made for him, where generations of holy men (Sumerian *en.si*) could communicate with their god in the 'dark chamber'. At first the temple of Enki was a simple reed shrine surrounded by a reed enclosure wall. But, over the centuries, this little shrine would grow into a huge platform temple, later to symbolise the arrogance of Man in his quest to be as great as the gods. The famous Sumerian King List (SKL) refers to this crucial moment in history when the Anunnaki (Egyptian *Shebtiu*) arrived in the southern marshlands of Sumer and founded the first city in Mesopotamia.

> When kingship was lowered from heaven, the (first) kingship was in Eridu. [*SKL*, column I, line 1]

The sandy mound upon which Enki's shrine was built rose out of a reed swamp bordering on the Persian Gulf. The swamp was fed by the sweet waters of the Euphrates and an underground spring which bubbled up in front of the mound. Yet the salt waters of the sea lay close by. The Sumerians called this swamp the Abzu or 'abyss' because they believed that one of the entrances to the underworld ocean was located here. Eridu was also known as the 'bolt of the sea' because it kept the dangerous waters of the gulf at bay, along with any foreign invaders it might bring. Eridu was the gateway into Mesopotamia from the great southern ocean known to the ancients as the Lower Sea.*

As I have already hinted, the event of the first 'foundation' also lies at the heart of Egyptian mythology. But that story belongs in a later chapter of this epic tale. In the meantime, we will follow Enoch in another disguise as he turns the barren and unpopulated swamps of southern Mesopotamia into rich farming lands and the home of the first true civilisation on the planet.

Uanna-Adapa

The Akkadian legends (as well as the Mesopotamian historian BEROSSUS) tell of a great sage, the first of the seven *apkallu* (Sumerian *ab.gal*) sent by Eya to bring the arts of civilisation to Mankind. He came from the east in the company of the Anunnaki gods. On islands in the marshlands of Sumer the Anunnaki established the first cities in Mesopotamia, and their spiritual leader – the first of the apkallu – set up kings to rule over the settlers. This sage's name was UANNA-ADAPA** – the biblical Enoch.

The Bible is almost silent when it comes to the settlement of Uanna/ Enoch and the legendary Anunnaki in the primeval land of Sumer. Little if any

4. Uanna-Adapa represented as a fish-man coming up out of the sea.

---

* Later known as the Erythrean or 'Red' Sea. What we today call the Red Sea was, in fact, previously known as the Arabian Sea whilst the Persian Gulf was the original Red Sea named after the mythical hero Erythreas – the 'red man'.

** Uanna was the *pashishu*-priest of Enki/Eya's sacred shrine at Eridu. His name is written in Hebrew (i.e. West Semitic) in the form Hanok but which in the Semitic language of Mesopotamia (i.e. East Semitic) would have been transcribed Anok or Unuk (without the initial aspirate so typical of West Semitic which, although written, was unpronounced). In Sumerian, the final 'k' of this name is what is called an amissible consonant which was only voiced when followed by a grammatical element which began with a vowel. The original Sumerian version of Enoch's name was therefore pronounced something like Anna, Unu or Uanna.

historical information can be gleaned about their descendants either. We are told of Cain's exile but then, after listing the 'generations' of antediluvian patriarchs who followed Cain, the Genesis narrative leaps forward to the flood, missing out one thousand years of ancestral history. We subsequently hear, in chapter 11 of Genesis, that 'the people came from the east and found a valley in the land of Shinar where they settled'.

The Island of Nun

At first the villages of Shinar were constructed on sandy turtlebacks rising out of the freshwater swamps fed by the river Euphrates. At the heart of the holy precinct of Eridu the reed shrine, dedicated to the god of Eden, was soon rebuilt in mudbrick. Archaeologists have found the first pottery in the region, associated with this earliest building activity, which they have called Ubaid (after the site of its initial discovery not far from Eridu). The Ubaid archaeological era has four phases, the last of which coincides with the Flood date proposed by Sir Leonard Woolley who unearthed a thick layer of water-borne sediment at the city of Ur. We will hear more about this in the next chapter but, for now, let us continue with our story of the tiny mudbrick shrine standing on the sandy island of Eridu.

Uanna/Enoch, descendant of Adam and priest of Enki, erected an offering table at the centre of the single chamber, before the niche where the symbol of his god had been placed. On this table worshippers offered fish to the Lord of the Abyss, the bones of which have been unearthed by the archaeologist's trowel. The Sumerian legends tell that Uanna went out into the marshes to catch these fish himself.

> At that time, in those years, he (Uanna-Adapa) was a sage, a son of (the city of) Eridu. Eya created him as a protecting spirit amongst Mankind. A sage – nobody rejects his word – clever, extra-wise. He

was one of the Anunnaki – holy, pure of hands, the
pashishu-priest who always tends to the rituals. He
does the baking with the bakers of Eridu. He pre-
pares the food and water of Eridu every day and
sets up the offering table with his pure hands.
Without him no offering table is cleared away. He
takes the boat out and does the fishing for Eridu.
[*Adapa Legend*]

The small sandy island of Nun was expanded for the
construction of buildings by laying cut reeds at the water's
edge to form a dense mat. Gradually the island of Nun
expanded as the reed collar solidified and turned to soil.
All around Nun more sandbanks were inhabited and
expanded in the same way. The Egyptian mythological
texts refer to these islands as the '*pay*-lands' of the primeval
world. Larger islands became the sites of other major settlements, eventually to become towns and great cities in their
own right. The names of these cities are synonymous with
early Mesopotamian civilisation – Uruk (Unuk), Ur ('city'),
Ubaid, Larsa, Girsu, Lagash and Bad-Tibira ('settlement
of the metalworkers').

The swamplands were gradually drained, and water
from the great rivers diverted along old abandoned water-
courses. A network of such channels was created to both
reduce the water flow into the southern marshes and create
fertile zones in the dry, dusty plain to the north. Over the
fourth millennium BC southern Mesopotamia was transformed into a paradise land of agricultural fields and date-
palm groves. The cities of Sumer became extremely prosperous and, as a result, their political influence expanded
dramatically.

Allies and Trade

The Anunnaki had come into contact with the indigenous
population of the Susiana plain prior to their move west-

wards and expansion into the southern marshes of Sumer. The newcomers from the mountains had been received with friendship – after all, there was little competition for land and resources in this vast area capable of sustaining a far greater population. The two groups intermarried and in effect became one.

When Uanna and some of his people moved on by reed boat into the land of Shinar, they maintained close ties with their kinfolk back in Susiana. Contact was maintained via the Persian Gulf as the direct land route across the marshes was slow and dangerous. Sea trade thus became the key to the expansion of the Anunnaki in the region. They journeyed south, along the shore of the Arabian peninsula at least as far as Bahrain and Qattar, establishing temporary trading outposts for the exploitation of mineral resources from the desert interior.

In Kuwait, near the head of the Gulf (and not far from Eridu), a British team of archaeologists from the Institute of Archaeology, London, have recently unearthed fragments of bitumen bearing the imprint of reed bundles. It seems clear that this bitumen once coated reed ships because the exterior faces of the bitumen slabs are covered in barnacles. It is well known that early Mesopotamian watercraft were waterproofed with bitumen to increase buoyancy by preventing the reeds from getting saturated. Associated with this remarkable find are pottery sherds from the Middle Ubaid period (Ubaid III) and obsidian. The latter has been analysed for its chemical signature and identified as originating from western Arabia or the Yemen. Such evidence is proof positive of wide-ranging (possibly seagoing) trade in the Middle Ubaid period (*c.* 3800 BC) – far earlier than had previously been thought.

The black reed ships (coated in bitumen) also sailed north, up the Euphrates and Tigris, to make contact with settlements in what would later become Agade (Akkad), Babylonia and Assyria. The people they met in the north spoke a different language – Semitic – but, once again, the two cultures cemented close ties through mutual trade. The Anunnaki bartered grain (which they were able to grow in abundance) for wool, cloth and metal tools, all of which were products of the northern plains and hill country. Semitic-speaking people also moved into the new agricultural land created by the Anunnaki in the south and so Sumer became a multicultural and multilingual land.*

---

* A thousand years later, following the great flood, a third language group would arrive in the region to become the dominant political force for the next five hundred years until the rise of the Semitic dynasty of Sargon of Agade. These were the Sumerians, or rather the Sumerian-speaking peoples, who also came down from the mountains of the north just as the Anunnaki had done all those generations earlier.

Chapter Three

NOAH AND THE FLOOD

(Genesis 6:5 to Genesis 9:17)

Home of the Flood Hero – Building the Ark –
The Deluge Catastrophe – Mountain of the Ark

The year is now 3113 BC. According to the earliest
Old Testament text (the Greek translation of Genesis, known as the Septuagint, written by seventy
Jewish scholars for Pharaoh Ptolemy Soter I in *c.* 300 BC)
a grand total of 2,262 summers and winters had come and
gone since Adam and his people first set foot in the Garden
of Eden and it was 1,687 years since Enoch/Uanna had
brought the Anunnaki down from the mountains to settle
in the Mesopotamian alluvial plain. Over that long period
of time the villages of Shinar had grown into sprawling
towns of mudbrick houses with their own vast tracts of
agricultural land. By digging canals and draining the
standing water away into the marshes, the people of the
mountains had succeeded in turning their once inhospitable
new homeland into a paradisal garden – a second, urban
Eden more than a thousand kilometres away from the original garden of the gods beyond the mountains of heaven.

45

At the heart of each settlement stood the cult centre and earthly residence of the deity adopted by the people as their protector.* The descendants of Cain had begun to worship numerous deities, each city possessing its own temple complex dedicated to the local deity. Enki/Eya remained the principal god of Eridu, but there were powerful cults to the sun-god (Utu/Shamash), the moon-god (Nanna/Sin) and the atmosphere-god Enlil ('lord wind'), the god of heaven (Anu) and the queen of heaven (Inanna/Ishtar).

In one of Shinar's larger settlements – the city of Shuruppak, a little over one hundred kilometres to the north of Eridu – the local ruler, son of Ubartutu, was a devout worshipper of Enki, even though the main city temple was dedicated to Enlil. The later Sumerians remembered this pious man by the epithet Ziusudra. The name is formed by two elements – 'long-lived' (*ziu*) combined with the epithet 'the far-distant' (*sudra*), because of the tradition (later passed down in the Gilgamesh Epic) that the flood hero and his wife were the only humans to be granted eternal life by the gods in a far-off land where the sun rose. To the Semitic-speaking peoples of early Mesopotamia Ziusudra was known as Atrahasis 'exceedingly devout', often accompanied by the epithet *ruku* ('the far-distant').

> Noah was a good man, an upright man among his contemporaries, and he walked with God. [Genesis 6:9]

The later Babylonians gave him the name Utnapishtim, which means something like 'he found (eternal) life', whereas Berossus, the famous Babylonian historian of the third century BC, called him Xisuthros after the original

---

* Thus Nippur had become the home of Enlil ('lord wind'); Uruk adopted both An ('heaven') and, later, Inanna ('lady of heaven'); Ur belonged to the moon-god Sin; Sippar and Larsa housed temples dedicated to the sun-god Utu; and, of course, Enki ruled over the Abzu Temple at Eridu.

Sumerian epithet Ziusudra. Of course, we know the flood hero as Noah – the name given to him in the biblical tradition and which possibly derives from the second element of Ut-na-pishtim (sometimes written Ut-na'-ishtim where the *na'* may have been vocalised *nua*).*

Preparing for Destruction

One day Noah (as we shall call him) had a vision. He was standing in a shrine within the city of Shuruppak, deep in prayer. The breeze from the Southern Sea, which made the hot and sticky afternoons a little more bearable, was whispering through the reed walls of the shady hut. In his heightened state of awareness, Noah began to hear a voice carried on the gentle wind. His god was calling him.

> Reed house, reed house! Wall, wall! Hear, O reed house! Understand, O wall! O man of Shuruppak, son of Ubartutu, tear down your house and build a boat! [*Gilgamesh Epic*, tablet XI, col. 1]

The Lord of the Earth (Enki) had come to warn Noah that 'lord wind' (Enlil) was about to send a terrible rainstorm which would wipe out Mankind.

Now because the people of Shuruppak were worshippers of Enlil, Noah kept the warning of their god's impending destruction of humankind to himself for fear of angering the population. Instead he assembled the council of elders to inform them that he was leaving on a pilgrimage to Eridu where the Temple of the Abzu and Enki's cult centre were located.

> He gathered the elders at his door. Atrahasis (Noah) made his voice heard and spoke to the elders, 'My

---

* On the other hand earlier scholars such as C. J. Ball read the Babylonian name as Nuh-napishtim where, of course, Nuh would also be the equivalent of Hebrew Noah.

god is out of favour with your god. Enki and Ellil (Enlil) have become angry with each other. They have driven me out of my house. Since I always stand in awe of Enki, he told me of this matter. I can no longer stay in Shuruppak. I cannot set my foot on Ellil's territory again. I must go down to the Abzu at Eridu and stay with my god. This is what he told me.' [*Atrahasis Epic*]

Having arrived in Eridu, and acting upon the instructions of his god, Noah and his family set about building a huge vessel made out of berdi reeds which they partly obtained from the local marshes but also from materials salvaged out of the dismantling of the king's own residence in Enki's city of Eridu.

For eighteen months Noah and his three sons laboured to build the ark (Hebrew *tjeba*). The final act was to daub the whole vessel with bitumen in order to make it watertight. The great black ship was ready for its task by the summer of 3114 BC, standing proud and erect in the ruins of the royal compound. It was then launched into the waters of the Abzu and tethered to the shore. Noah then began to gather the creatures of the Earth to save each species from their impending extinction.

Everything that there was [growing in the earth], everything that there was [grazing off the land], the pure ones [of the animals], the fat ones [of the herds and flocks] – all of these he selected [and put on board]. [The birds] that fly in the sky, the cattle of Shakkan, the wild animals [roaming] the open country – [all of these he selected and] put on board. [*Atrahasis Epic*]

Noah and his family waited whilst the rest of the world went about their daily business. They did not have to wait long.

The Great Flood

All the windstorms, exceedingly powerful, attacked as one. At the same time the flood swept over the cult-centres. [*Ziusudra Epic*]

The waters rose, swelling higher above the land, and the ark drifted away over the waters. The waters continued to rise above the land until all of the highest city mounds under the whole of heaven were drowned. The waters finally reached their peak of fifteen cubits (seven metres), and the mounds were submerged. [Genesis 7:18–20]

The downpour, the tempest and the flood overwhelmed the land ... [*Gilgamesh Epic*]

For seven days (and) seven nights the flood swept over the land (and) the huge boat was tossed about by the windstorms on the mighty waters. [*Ziusudra Epic*]

Yahweh sent a wind across the land and the waters began to subside. The springs of the deep and the sluices of heaven were stopped up and the heavy rain from heaven was held back. Little by little the waters ebbed from the land. [Genesis 8:1–3]

(Finally) Utu (the sun-god) came forth – the one who sheds light on heaven and earth. Ziusudra (Noah) opened a window of the huge boat and the hero Utu brought his rays into the giant boat. Ziusudra, the king, prostrated himself before Utu. [*Ziusudra Epic*]

Utnapishtim (Noah) opened a window and light fell upon his face. He looked down upon the sea – all

was silence. All Mankind had returned to clay.
[*Gilgamesh Epic*]

Aftermath

After one hundred and fifty days the waters receded
and in the seventh month, on the seventeenth day
of the month, the ark came to rest on the mountains
of Ararat. [Genesis 8:3–5]

The land was emerging everywhere. The boat came
to rest on Mount Nimush. The mountain of Nimush
held the boat fast and did not let it budge. [*Gilgamesh
Epic*]

The water abated and the matter was ended. The
ark rested on Mount Judi. [Koran, Sura XI:44]

Ziusudra, the king, prostrated himself before Anu
and Enlil. Anu and Enlil cherished Ziusudra. Life,
like a god, they gave him. Breath eternal, like a god,
they brought down for him. [*Ziusudra Epic*]

Then Ziusudra, the preserver of the name of vegetation and of the seed of Mankind, they caused to
dwell in the land of crossing – Mount Dilmun – the
place where the sun rises. [*Ziusudra Epic*]

I have let the ancient texts themselves relate the story of
the great flood catastrophe. But perhaps you would like to
know *how* it happened?

The Mesopotamian flood plain is extremely flat, rising
only a few metres in hundreds of kilometres from the Lower
Sea. The rivers Tigris and Euphrates flow within levees or
banks which are higher than the surrounding land. As a
result, in the past they constantly burst their banks to find
new routes to the sea. Hundreds of ancient water courses

have been detected during surveys of the region. The most dangerous time of year was always in spring when the snows of the Zagros and Taurus mountains melted, swelling the rivers as they descended onto the plain.

In the fourth millennium BC there was another factor which added to the problems of the settlers in the southern Mesopotamian plain. The waters of the Gulf were also steadily rising as the ice caps continued to melt following the end of the last ice age. At this time Sumer was mostly a vast marshland which had been tamed and planted by the Enochite settlers of what archaeologists call the Ubaid period (c. 5000–3100 BC). For more than a thousand years the descendants of Adam had been busy cutting canals and irrigation ditches to divert the excess waters and drain the land. By the end of this period they were managing successfully to produce large surpluses of grain which they traded with their neighbours to the north for wool and metals. But it had always been a struggle. Over the fourth millennium a number of devastating floods had swept the land. The people simply picked themselves up and got back to their daily routines. Nothing on the scale of what was about to happen to them had ever occurred before.

For the previoust five years the winters had been particularly fierce. The mountains to the north had gradually become heavily laden with snow, choking the alpine valleys. The summers had not been warm either. As a result, the mountain ice had failed to melt and drain into the Southern Sea. What was the cause of this bleak weather pattern? Well, these unusual conditions were not just happening over the Middle East. The whole planet had been suffering from a global climate change brought on by a major volcanic eruption in the Aleutian Islands. We know today how certain types of volcanic explosion can bring about rapid and severe weather conditions, but the 3119 BC event was a massive eruption on a scale which has not been witnessed in the succeeding five millennia of Earth-history. Millions of tons of ash and sulphuric acid had been thrown up into the atmosphere, blotting out the sunlight and causing a mini ice age. All over the world people were enduring cold winters and only slightly warmer summers, living in a twilight world of hazy darkness, crops failing and livestock dying through lack of fresh feed.

In the Mesopotamian lowlands things were a little better for a while because of the well-organised agricultural system and large grain surpluses. Even so, famine soon began to bite, gradually becoming more severe with every failed harvest. The spring flood-waters were not arriving in the plain due to the fact that the snow and ice in the mountains was not thawing. The land in Sumer was becoming dry and salty.

> When the second year arrived, they (the people) had depleted the store-house. When the third year arrived, the people's looks were changed by starvation. ... When the sixth year arrived, they served up a daughter for a meal, then served up a son for food. [*Atrahasis Epic*]

Things were desperate. The people who were still alive had resorted to cannibalism. This was why the ruler of Shuruppak – the biblical Noah – was praying for guidance in his reed shrine when Eya came to warn his pious devotee of the even greater catastrophe to come.

After six long years the sun finally started to penetrate the grey clouds of sulphuric acid crystals enveloping the Earth. By April the air above the uplands was warming up and the ice began to melt. At first the thaw was a trickle – but then it became a torrent. All the 'waters of the deep' (the abyss or fresh water ocean beneath the Earth's surface) poured into the swollen streams, tearing away the soil of the banks and turning the rivers dark red. The hundreds of sources for the mighty Tigris and Euphrates joined the main channels as the flood charged south and then eastwards towards the lowlands of Mesopotamia. In the text known as 'the Lamentations Over the Destruction of Sumer and Ur', an invasion from the mountains by the barbaric Gutian hordes which brought an end to the Dynasty of Agade in 1937 BC was likened to the coming of Enlil's great flood which had descended from the mountains a thousand years earlier.

At the same time as the northern onrush of the river flood, the sudden heating up of the atmosphere had triggered a great electrical storm as the thick mantle of frozen sulphuric acid crystals began to dissolve and fall to earth. Strong winds drove dark clouds from the southern ocean northwards towards the Land of the Two Rivers. The sea began to rise.

This was nature at its most violent. Nothing like this had been witnessed before. The acid rain lashed the land. As if acting out some perverse battle strategy, the gods of nature threw all their combined forces into this campaign to destroy humanity and wipe their own creation from the landscape.*

The south wind tore at the reed dwellings; lightning crashed and danced upon the waters as thunder rolled down from the mountains; the mighty rivers joined the attack upon those who had dared to tame them, pouring the blood-red waters of the deep over a flat and helpless landscape. The meagre crops which had been planted just weeks before were destroyed, the animals abandoned to their fate. The people who had survived the years of famine fled to the towns in a desperate attempt to find refuge … but the waters continued to rise, dissolving their mudbrick houses and literally washing away any last vestige of sanctuary from this terrible onslaught of the gods – gods who were now themselves terrified by what they had unleashed.

---

* These gods are the Elohim of Genesis who made Man in their own likeness. The first part of the first book in the Bible is not a purely monotheistic work. There are hints of other 'false' gods hidden within the text who Man worshipped at this time (and, indeed, later).

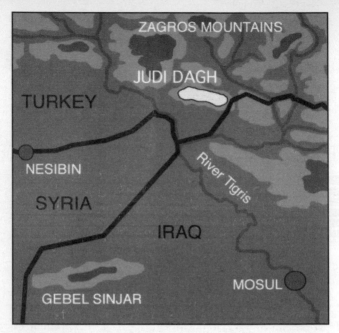

5. Simplified map of the Judi Dagh region showing the location of the 'mountain of the heights' (Judi Dagh) in relation to Mosul and Nesibin (Nusaybin).

> Even the gods were afraid of the flood-weapon. They withdrew and took themselves up to heaven. The gods cowered, like dogs crouched by an outside wall. ... The gods, humbled, sat there weeping. [*Gilgamesh Epic*]

The rain poured down and the flood swept over the land until all the city mounds were submerged and the cries of the people ceased. Finally, the storm abated. Everywhere was silence.

The ark drifted northwards, carried by the southerly wind which had now become a gentle breeze. Days and days passed until the great black ship shuddered to a halt, grounded on one of the first hills bordering the 'mountains of Ararat'. The ancient Babylonians called this place Mount Nimush but its modern name is Judi Dagh – 'mountain of the heights' – rising a short distance north of the city of Mosul on the Tigris. The Arabs (and the Koran) call it Gebel Judi ('Mount Judi').

The Place of the Descent, from which the offspring of Noah went out to rebuild the cities and re-establish civilisation, was venerated for millennia before the thirteenth century AD when European travellers first passed by Agri Dagh in north-east Turkey and decided to identify *that* lofty volcanic peak with 'Mount Ararat'. But the Nestorian Christians of the first millennium AD and the followers of Islam knew otherwise. They continued to accept the ancient tradition which located the Place of Descent on Judi Dagh in the 'mountains of Ararat' (that is the general area of the Zagros mountains in Urartu, and including Kurdistan). There, on the slopes of Mount Judi, fragments of the black bitumen, which once coated Noah's ark, are still collected today by the local tribal communities as they climb the Mountain of the Heights to make sacrifice for the deliverance of Mankind.

Chapter Four

NIMROD AND THE
TOWER OF BABEL

(Genesis 9:18 to Genesis 11:9)

Cush and the Sea – The Mighty Hunter – Enmerkar/
Nimrod – Inanna – Quarrels between Uruk and
Aratta – Dumuzi/Ashur/Osiris – Inanna/Ishtar/Isis –
Ninurta, the hunter god – The Tower of Babel

The generations which followed the flood witnessed far-reaching changes. Later generations would perceive this time as a rebirth of humankind – a second creation which heralded the heroic age of ancient Sumer. The devastation and destruction of the deluge seemed to spark a new resolve to ensure stronger and more resilient communities which could better protect themselves from the powerful forces of nature.

The original cities of Sumer were rebuilt on an even grander scale. Lavish temples were constructed on high mudbrick platforms – artificial mountains which could also serve as refuges from any future flooding of the Meso-potamian plain. Lines of powerful warlord rulers sprang up from the leading élites of the main population centres –

kings who were to become legendary representatives of a 'Golden Age'. The book of Genesis refers to them as the Nephilim – the 'giants' or 'mighty ones', the offspring of certain gods who had slept with the daughters of men. The greatest of these heroic dynasties was that of Uruk, founded by Meskiagkasher in 3000 BC. The book of Genesis identifies MeskiagKASHer as Cush, 'son' of Ham and 'grandson' of Noah.

After ruling for several decades, during which time a number of trading colonies were founded in northern Mesopotamia along the banks of the Upper Euphrates, Cush and his merchants ventured out into the ocean beyond the Lower Sea (Persian Gulf), in search of new resources on distant continents. The large reed ships which had been employed to ferry trading produce up and down the Euphrates (bringing grain from Sumer to the north, returning with copper and wool from northern Mesopotamia to Sumer) were plying the still waters of the gulf, exploiting the islands of Bahrain (ancient historical Dilmun) for dates and the peninsula of Oman (ancient Magan) for copper ore.

Contact further afield with the Indus valley peoples of Meluhha had been established, and exotic woods and stones (such as lapis-lazuli) were finding their way back to the cities of southern Mesopotamia where they were employed in the decoration of the cult centres. All this exploration of the Lower Sea by the high-prowed reed ships of Sumer had instilled in the merchant-sailors of Uruk a taste for adventure and a sense of wonderment at what Mother Earth could provide beyond their ever-expanding horizon of knowledge.

The king of Uruk himself was very much a man of his time and he too felt the desire to venture into the unknown. After all, this was the first age of sea adventure in human history. So, just as the Phoenicians and Greeks would do in the Mediterranean two thousand years later, Cush set out from Eridu into the Lower Sea, leading his fleet of

black ships on an epic journey around the Arabian peninsula to colonise the African continent. We shall hear more
about this remarkable adventure in the next chapter …
but, for now, our story remains rooted here in the Land of
the Two Rivers, as we find ourselves, a century later, in the
presence of one of Cush's greatest successors.

The Mighty Hunter

> Cush fathered Nimrod who was the first potentate
> on Earth. He was a mighty hunter before Yahweh,
> hence the saying, 'Like Nimrod, a mighty hunter
> before Yahweh'. [Genesis 10:8–9]

Enmerkar ('Enmer the hunter'), the historical figure behind
the legendary hero Nimrod the 'mighty hunter' (later
deified as the Mesopotamian hunter-god NINURTA), was
the first great conqueror of lands. The Bible calls him 'the
first potentate on Earth' [Genesis 10:8]. King Enmer/
Nimrod claimed descent from a people who had arrived
in southern Mesopotamia from the Zagros mountains, for
he was a descendant of Noah whose clan had returned to
the plains from the mountains of Ararat (Urartu) following
the retreat of the flood waters. Having established his
authority as ruler of Uruk, one of Nimrod's first acts was to
adopt the goddess Inanna as patron deity of a great religious
complex being built in the city – the E-anna or 'house of
heaven'. The year is 2852 BC and it is 2,523 years since
Enmer's great ancestor Adam had arrived in the Garden
of Eden.

Inanna was a mountain goddess who would soon
become one of Sumer's most favoured deities because she
represented fertility – the fertility of domesticated animals,
the crops in the fields, and of human procreation – the key
factors in successful sedentary life. These characteristics
suggest that Inanna was in reality the great earth-mother-
goddess NINHURSAG in a new guise.

6. During the Uruk period the statues, reliefs and glyptic art (cylinder seals) show a royal male figure who has become known as 'the Priest-King of Uruk'. He is shown in acts of piety or in prayer, usually before the shrine or image of Inanna, fertility-goddess of Uruk. The king sports a full beard and a chignon (cloth band) around his head. The upper torso is usually naked. The lower part of his body is clothed in a long tunic which extends below his knees. This distinctive figure appears on the Gebel el-Arak knife handle (from Egypt) where, as the 'Master of Animals' he controls two large lions. On the Uruk Hunter's Stela (from southern Mesopotamia) the king is depicted killing lions with spear and bow. Are they all representations of a single figure? Could the Priest-King of Uruk be none other than King Enmer/Nimrod – the mighty hunter?

The First Letter

In the time of Nimrod and the 1st Dynasty of Uruk a fabulous country existed beyond the Zagros mountains. The Sumerians knew it as the kingdom of Aratta – a name which has come down to us through the Bible in the form 'the mountains of Ararat' [Genesis 8:4] and through the royal annals of first-millennium-BC Assyria as the land of Urartu. The heartland of Aratta lay in the Mannean plain (Sumerian *edin*, biblical Eden) south of Lake Urumiya, entered through a mountain pass which was the southern entrance into Eden. Across this fertile upland plain flowed the River Aratta – now known as the Simineh Rud or 'silver river'. We know this from the Year 8 campaign of the Assyrian king Sargon II (721–705 BC) who, having marched over seven mountain ranges, crossed the River Aratta as he entered the district of Surikash in the land of the Manneans. Ancient Surikash is buried under the Kurdish town of Sakkez.

Surrounding the plain of Aratta were mineral-rich mountains bearing gold, silver, malachite (copper) and semi-precious stones, including a seam of lapis-lazuli. The slopes of the mountains were covered in pine forests and the great plain scattered with stands of tall poplars, ideal for construction. The capital of this ancient 'Eldorado' (as one scholar has called Aratta) stood on a hill, its red-painted city walls dominating the plain. Not far to the east, the red mountain (from which the ochre used to paint the houses and fortification walls of the city was obtained) protected a small plateau where Aratta's most sacred shrine was located. At the heart of a ring of volcanic mountains a single tall cone of rock rose up to dominate the plateau. But this was no volcano. It was rather a powerful spring so rich in minerals that, over the millennia, the solubles which saturated the water had gradually built up around the rim of the pool until a one-hundred-metre cone had formed. In effect it was a volcano of water – perhaps the most spectacular of Eden's primeval abzus (ab = water; zu = gushing forth).

Today the ZENDAN-É SULEIMAN, as it was dubbed by the invading Arabs in the seventh century AD, remains an impressive sight to behold. As you round the red mountain on the way to the Zoroastrian fire temple at TAKHT-É SULEIMAN, the perfect cone rises up in front of you. Even though the spring itself has dried up, revealing a deep and jagged crater, the scale of this majestic work of Mother Nature cannot but impress. It must have been a truly amazing place when the crater was overflowing with ice-cold water which poured down the slopes of the cone on all sides. This spring was one of the sources of the Gold River (Zarineh Rud) which flows down into the plain of Aratta to partner the Silver River as both head northwards into the great salt lake of Urumiya. The streams flowing down from the plateau of Takht-é Suleiman, in all directions, carry gold in their beds. The most famous is the biblical PISHON which winds eastwards from here towards the Caspian Sea; for this is the biblical Land of Havilah, 'rich in gold'.

Around the cone of the sacred spring the priests had built a small sanctuary dedicated to the great goddess of Aratta – Inanna. The later Babylonians knew her as Ishtar and the Canaanites as Astarte. She is the Ashtaroth of the Bible and the Egyptian Iset – better known by the Greek pronunciation Isis. Here, in the mountains of Eden and Havilah, she was worshipped in her early incarnation as the 'Lady of Heaven' ... but all that was to change when King Enmer appropriated the goddess for his new sacred precinct in Uruk.

In order to give his patron deity the most beautiful cult centre in Sumer, Enmer intended to lavish the courts and sanctuary of the E-anna complex with fine timber, precious metals and stones, all of which had to be brought down from the mountain kingdom of Aratta. The epic of 'Enmerkar and the Lord of Aratta' informs us that the king of Uruk also devoted the same attention to the much older shrine of the Abzu at Eridu.

> Let the people of Aratta artfully fashion gold and silver. ... Let them bring down precious stone and pure lapis-lazuli. Let the people of Aratta, having brought down the stones of the mountains from their highland, build for me a great temple, set up for me a great shrine of the gods. ... Fashion for me the Abzu like a holy highland. Purify for me Eridu like a mountain. [*Enmerkar and the Lord of Aratta Epic*]

But, in order to accomplish his desires, Enmer/Nimrod first needed to make Aratta subservient to Uruk. Thus begins history's first recorded diplomatic negotiations between independent states. I use the word 'diplomatic' advisedly here as the communications from the king of Uruk to Ensukushsiranna, ruler of Aratta, were more akin to threats than trade negotiations. Enmer was certainly not averse to bullying tactics to get what he wanted. He had already effectively stolen Aratta's goddess and now, to add insult to injury, he was demanding that the kingdom of Aratta supply all its exotic products to furnish her new home down in the alluvial plain. It is hardly surprising, therefore, to find that the ruler of Aratta resisted for as long as he could.

Over a number of years Enmer's patient envoy trekked up into the mountains with messages from his king, insisting that the lord of Aratta accede to his master's wishes or risk an invasion of Aratta. In the end the messages became so long and complicated that Enmer resorted to writing his demands on a clay tablet which the envoy delivered to its bemused recipient. According to tradition, these were the very first words to be written down on a tablet and so mark the beginning of writing in Mesopotamia.

> The herald was heavy of mouth and could not repeat it (the king's message). So, because the herald was heavy of mouth and could not repeat it, the Lord of Kullab (one of the two districts of Uruk) patted a lump of clay and set up the words like a tablet. Formerly there had been no-one who set words on clay. Now, as Utu is [Lord of Justice], it was so. The Lord of Kullab set up words like a tablet and it was so. [*Enmerkar and the Lord of Aratta Epic*]

As a result, Enmer's envoy appears to have been the first postman in history – and with one of the longest postal rounds on record (a four-month journey out through seven 'gates' (i.e. mountain passes) following the spring thaw and four months back before the snows of winter closed the route).

> Going to the mountain-land of Aratta: 'Emissary, by night, like the stormy south wind, drive on! By day, like the dew, be up!' … The emissary journeying to Aratta covered his feet with the dust of the road and stirred up the pebbles of the mountains. Like a huge serpent prowling about the *edin* (plain) he was unopposed. [*Enmerkar and the Lord of Aratta Epic*]

Eventually, after decades of acrimonious argument, Enmer ran out of patience and invaded Aratta in an effort to seize what was needed to decorate Inanna's sacred precinct at Uruk and the Abzu temple of Enki in Eridu. The king personally led the expedition, accompanied by his élite companions-at-arms, including his 'son' and future successor to Uruk's throne, Lugalbanda. In the epic 'Lugalbanda and Mount Hurrum' we read of Enmer's forces crossing Mount Hurrum as they marched towards Aratta. Hurrum has long been recognised as the region from where the Hurrians of later times originated – that is to say the Zagros mountains of Kurdistan. This confirms that Aratta lay to the north of Kurdistan in the vicinity of western Iran's Azerbaijan province.

The conquest of resource-rich Aratta was the culmination of Enmer's expansionist policy. By the end of his long reign the king of Uruk controlled much of Mesopotamia and had greatly enriched the cult centres of Sumer. He also controlled the donkey trade routes through the Zagros mountains and sea trade via the Persian Gulf. To the north, large heavily fortified colonies were established close to the main waterways and therefore connected to the heart of the empire by means of fast-moving ships. Exotic goods and metals were pouring into the capital city of Uruk and, of course, Enmer's palace coffers. This really does make him the first potentate on Earth, just as the Genesis tradition states. In his guise of the warrior-hero, Enmer/Nimrod is remembered as the founder of the mightiest cities in Assyria and Babylonia, as well as a great builder in the old religious centres of Sumer.

No wonder, then, that he was represented as both semi-divine hero and god. The Babylonians knew him as Nin-urta, the hunter-god armed with bow, and linked him with Marduk, warrior-god and the lord of vegetation. The Sumerians of Eridu themselves elevated the mortal King Enmerkar ('Enmer the hunter') to godhood as Asar, 'son' of Enki. The Sumerians of the Early Dynastic times named him Ningirsu, god of war and agriculture. In the city of Lagash they built the House of Ninnu (*E-Ninnu*) as Nin-girsu's temple and gave him the epithet Enmersi after his ancient and original name. The Assyrians recognised Enmer/Asar as their state deity, Ashur. When the author of Genesis calls him Nimrod, this is a play on words in which the name Enmer is Hebraised into *nmrd* ('we shall rebel') because this king rebelled against Yahweh by building the Tower of Babel.

> Cush fathered Nimrod who was the first potentate on Earth. He was a mighty hunter in opposition to (previously read 'before') Yahweh, hence the saying, 'Like Nimrod, a mighty hunter in opposition to Yahweh'. The mainstays of his empire were Babel, Erech and Accad, all of them in the land of Shinar. From that country he went forth to Assyria and built Nineveh, that vast city, and Calah, which is (also) a great city, and the canal between Nineveh and Calah. [Genesis 10:8–12]

To all these nations the ruler known variously as Enmerkar/Ninurta/Nimrod/Asar was the founding father of kingship in all its awesome power. He was later adopted into the western world as the hero Ninus (from Ninurta – 'lord plough') of Greek legend, the husband of Semiramis 'Queen of Heaven' (in other words Inanna – 'Lady of Heaven') and founder of the Assyrian empire.* The Phoenicians and Syrians worshipped him as Rashap, god of war. New Kingdom Egypt too adopted him in this Canaanite persona where he appears as the warrior-god Reshpu, lord of eternity, wearing the white crown of Upper Egypt, carrying a shield and spear in the left hand and a club in the right. You see him every night as he crosses the sky, arm raised as if to smite his enemy or let loose his mighty bow. He is the constellation of Orion.

The Tower of Babel

King Enmer of Uruk is also infamous as the ruler who ordered the building of the Tower of Babel in direct affront to Eya/Enki, lord of Eridu. The great platform temple, built in the place the Bible calls Babel, was not constructed in the holy precinct of Babylon (alternatively written in its Sumerian name of *Nun.ki*) but rather on the holy island of Eridu (the *original* Sumerian *Nun.ki*). Over the centuries, the tiny shrine dedicated to Enki/Eya by Uanna/Enoch (referred to in Chapter Two) had been superseded by mudbrick temples of increasing grandeur. By Enmer's time the seventeenth temple building stood several metres directly above Enoch's little buried shrine with all the temples inbetween acting as the foundation for the latest edifice. This was the sacred cult centre of the Abzu which Enmer of Uruk wished to rebuild and adorn with the wondrous products of Aratta.

---

* In addition, there are legendary associations between Ninurta and the Sumerian deity Dumuzi (the biblical Tammuz), god of death and resurrection. Further afield, the Egyptians remembered him as the mythical king Asar (Osiris), god of the dead and husband of the fertility-goddess Iset (Isis/Ishtar/Inanna). The name Asar has been translated as 'the mighty one' and is written with the hieroglyph of a king's throne and an all-seeing eye.

Let the people of Aratta artfully fashion gold and silver. … Let them bring down precious stone and pure lapis-lazuli. Let the people of Aratta … build for me a great temple, set up for me **a great shrine of the gods**. … Fashion for me the Abzu like **a holy highland**. Purify for me Eridu **like a mountain**. [*Enmerkar and the Lord of Aratta Epic*]

But Enmer was not simply intending to renovate the ancient shrine of Eridu's patron deity, as had been done on countless occasions before. Instead he wanted to build 'a great temple … a great shrine of the gods'. And so the people of Sumer began to erect a huge mudbrick platform which rose up above the surrounding marshes like a mighty tower. This was the first ziggurat in Mesopotamia – 'a mountain' home for all the gods, constructed down in the flat alluvial plain. But, according to Genesis 11:1–9, as well as Josephus and the Sumerian myth known as 'Ninurta's Pride and Punishment', Yahweh/Eya/Enki thwarted Nimrod/Ninurta/Enmer's ambitions and humbled the proud hero. The massive building effort was brought to a sudden and a premature end. Enki had seen through the 'ambitious god who made secret, hostile plans against him'. He knew that 'the hero Ninurta had set his face towards the entire world' and that he needed to be punished for his arrogant challenge to the authority of the god of the abyss. This was Enki's holy city and the worship of other gods was not going to be allowed in Eridu, the 'mighty place' (Sumerian *Nun.ki*), the first city on Earth where the Mesopotamian creation began.

The people were dispersed and the huge platform was left to be enveloped by the drifting sands. We hear no more of Nimrod the rebel against God. The temple of the Abzu – Sumer's most ancient holy site – lay abandoned and forlorn for a thousand years before its reconstruction at the time of the Sumerian revival during the Third Dynasty of Ur (1900–1793 BC).

The Tower of Nun.ki

> Now, as the people came from the east they found
> a valley in the land of Shinar where they settled.
> They said to one another, 'Come, let us make bricks
> and bake them in the fire.' For stone they used bricks,
> and for mortar they used bitumen. 'Come,' they
> said, 'let us build ourselves a city and a tower with
> its top reaching heaven.' [Genesis 11:2–4]

The scribes of the Old Babylonian period (1667–1362 BC)
were highly educated men who spoke and read at least
two languages – AKKADIAN and SUMERIAN. It was their
regular practice to write certain names and words in
Sumerian in what were otherwise predominantly Akkadian
texts. This was rather like educated monks and state officials
mixing both English and Latin during the British medieval
age (or barristers in a court of law today for that matter).
So, when a scholar reads an Old Babylonian tablet written
in Akkadian cuneiform, he will come across a number of
Sumerian 'logograms' which he must transcribe into
Akkadian before translating into English. We have already
seen this practice in words such as *kar* (Sumerian) = *habilum*
(Akkadian) meaning 'hunter', and *nun* (Sumerian) = *rubum*
(Akkadian) meaning 'mighty'. Many places retained their
ancient Sumerian names as well as their contemporary
Akkadian names. Thus the sacred precinct of the city of
Babylon – BAB-ILU in Akkadian – was also identified by its
Sumerian name NUN.KI.

Now imagine the author or editor of the book of Genesis
attempting to incorporate the tradition of the Tower of Babel
into his story about the origins of civilisation. He has before
him an Akkadian cuneiform tablet containing an epic tale
about the building of a mighty temple tower. He reads the
name of the place where the tower was built in its Sumerian
logogram form – Nun.ki – and quite naturally interprets
this as the sacred precinct of the city he knows as Bab-Ilu

(Babylon). And so the incident of Nimrod's rebellion against his god, described in Genesis, is passed down to us as the saga of the building of the 'Tower of Babel' (actually the tower 'in' Babel).

What the Genesis author clearly did not appreciate was that Babylon had no ziggurat or temple tower before the Old Babylonian period when Hammurabi's Amorite capital first became a great city. The earliest mention of Babylon* occurs in the reign of Sharkalisharri (2000–1976 BC), descendant of Sargon the Great (2117–2062 BC), founder of the Dynasty of Agade. However, the Tower of Babel story originated from a much older incident which had taken place not long after the flood – a thousand years *before* the first mention of Babylon.

What the author of Genesis seems not to have realised is that a much older Sumerian city had existed which bore the *original* name Nun.ki – the 'mighty place'. This city is otherwise known as Eridu – the very first royal capital in Sumer and the residence of the god of the abyss, Enki. Indeed, it seems that the sacred precinct at Babylon was named after that original Nun.ki, even going so far as to call the temple dedicated to Marduk, E-sagila or the 'lofty house' and also known as the 'mooring post of heaven and earth', after the original tower temple at Eridu. So, the biblical Tower of Babel/Nun.ki was not the second millennium Old Babylonian ziggurat at Babylon but rather the prototype third-millennium ziggurat built at Eridu/Nun.ki in the Late Uruk period. It is the Jewish historian Josephus who informs us that the builder of the Tower of Babel was the legendary Nimrod.

> Now it was Nimrod who excited them (the people) to such an affront and contempt of God. He was the grandson of Ham son of Noah – a bold man, and of

---

* Written as *Ka-dingir.ki* – another Sumerian name for the Ammorite city of Babylon.

great strength of hand. He persuaded them not to ascribe their prosperity and happiness to God as if it was through his means they were happy, but to believe that it was their own courage which procured that happiness. He also gradually changed the government into tyranny – seeing no other way of turning men from the fear of God but to bring them into a constant dependence upon his power. He also said he would be revenged on God, if he should have a mind to drown the world again. For that he would build a tower too high for the waters to be able to reach! And so (by that method) he would avenge himself on God for destroying their forefathers! [*Antiquities of the Jews*, Book I:iv:2]

And we also learn from the epic tale 'Enmerkar and the Lord of Aratta' that the rebuilding of the Abzu temple at Eridu was Enmerkar's principal reason for seeking the wealth of Aratta. So it seems that Enmer 'the hunter' (whom we have identified with the biblical Nimrod) was the king who began the construction of the last great phase of the platform temple on the island of Nun.ki. Let me remind you of Enmerkar's command.

> Let the people of Aratta ... build for me the great temple, set up for me the great shrine of the gods. ... Fashion for me the Abzu **like a holy highland**. Purify for me Eridu **like a mountain**. [*Enmerkar and the Lord of Aratta Epic*]

Temple I at Eridu (the last of seventeen buildings erected on the same site, one on top of the other), excavated in the 1940s by archaeologists from Iraq (led by Fuad Safar), was a massive structure. It consisted of a huge, steeply sloping platform of mudbrick, on top of which the builders intended to erect the temple proper. The bricks of the platform were pointed with bitumen just like the biblical Tower of Babel.

In the beginning God created heaven and earth. And the earth was without form. For there was darkness over the deep with a divine wind sweeping over the waters. Then God said, 'Let there be light' – and there was light. [Genesis 1:1-3]

Plate 1: Lake Urumiya at the heart of Eden and due west of the Garden of Eden (Azerbaijan Province, western Iran).

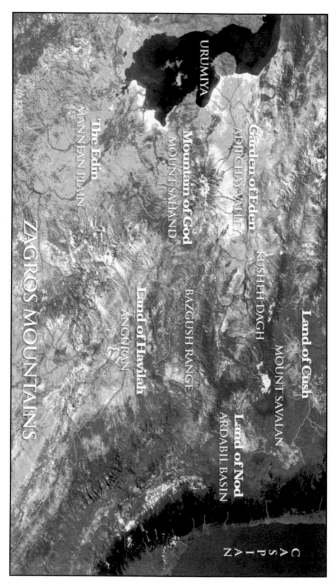

Plate 2: Satellite image of the Garden of Eden.

Plate 3: Here, in this 4,000-year-old cylinder seal impression from Mesopotamia, we see Adam (right, wearing a horned helmet, the symbol of deification) and Eve (left) seated before the Tree of Knowledge of Good and Evil, heavily laden with fruit. The tree has seven branches, just as the menorah candelabra which represents the tree in the Garden of Eden. Adam and Eve gesticulate to each other to take the fruit of the tree. Behind Eve is the serpent. The seal is on display in the British Museum Mesopotamian galleries. At first labelled as the 'temptation seal', in more recent times the seal has been redesigned as a 'banqueting scene'.

Plate 4: The Shebtiu scene from Edfu temple with the sacred falcon perched upon the reeds and, behind him, the founders seated upon their thrones on the Island of Creation.

'Your brother's blood is crying out to me from the earth. Now be cursed and banned from the ground that has opened its mouth to receive your brother's blood at your hands. When you till the ground it will no longer yield up its strength to you. A restless wanderer you will be on this earth.' ... And so Cain left Yahweh's presence and settled in the land of Nod to the east of Eden. [Genesis 4:10–12]

Plate 5: The Zagros Mountains separating heaven from earth.

Plate 6: *Tablet XI of the Gilgamesh Epic, containing the Babylonian version of the deluge story where Utnapishtim is the name of the flood hero.*

Plate 7: *Gustave Doré's image of Noah's Ark coming to rest on the Mountains of the Descent.*

Plate 8: A colossal statue of Gilgamesh carrying a lion cub, from the palace of Sargon II at Khorsabad (Louvre Museum).

God blessed Noah and his sons and said to them, 'Breed, multiply and fill the Earth. Be the terror and the dread of all the animals on land and all the birds of heaven. Of everything that moves on land and all the fish of the sea – they are given into your hands.' [Genesis 9:1–2]

Plate 9: The Hunter Stela showing Nimrod/Enmerkar slaying lions with spear and bow (Baghdad Museum).

Plate 10: Detail from the Narmer palette showing the king smiting an enemy with his pear-shaped mace. Note the rosette and hem-vessel behind the head of the royal sandal-bearer and compare these with the same symbols behind the king wearing a white crown from Susa (p. 92).

Now the multitude were very ready to follow the will of Nimrod, ... and they built a tower, neither sparing any pains nor being in any degree negligent about the work. ... It was built of burnt brick, cemented together with mortar made of bitumen that it might not be liable to admit water. [Josephus: *Antiquities of the Jews*, Book I:iv:3]

On the platform's south side, a smaller temple was completed, the attached columns of which were lavishly decorated in colourful clay cone mosaics. This type of decoration was also found in the temple precinct at Uruk. As you can see from the archaeologist's reconstruction, the Enki temple building was an impressive structure. So just imagine what the main temple on the great platform might have looked like if it had ever been finished.

7. Eridu Temple I, built at the end of the Uruk period (at the time of Nimrod/Enmerkar).

71

However, just as in the biblical story, the evidence from the excavations of Eridu suggests that the structure on top of the tower was abandoned not long after the foundations were laid and the whole complex was soon covered in windblown sand.

Before that abandonment, the great platform at Eridu rose majestically above the waters of the abyss which surrounded it and, as Josephus remarks, was an amazing sight to behold. Remember that no building on this scale had even been attempted before. It was literally Man's first attempt at building an artificial mountain – intended to recreate the high throne for the gods down in the Sumerian marshes. The gods of the highlands (heaven) had been brought down to the lowlands (earth) by the Anunnaki – the original mountain people who worshipped them. It was therefore quite understandable (once the technology and resources were available) for the descendants of those first settlers to desire to replace the natural mountain home of their gods with a man-made structure upon which a new house of the heavenly assembly could be built – the Tower of Nun.ki/Babel.

8. Typical cone mosaic columns of the late Uruk period (these from the Pillared Hall at Uruk), similar to the Eridu temple of Nun.ki.

A Babble of Tongues

> Now Yahweh came down to see the city and the
> tower that the people had built. 'So they are all a
> single people with a single language!' said Yahweh.
> 'This is only the start of their undertakings! Now
> nothing they plan to do will be beyond them. Come,
> let us go down and confuse their language there, so
> that they cannot understand one another.' Yahweh
> scattered them thence all over the world, and they
> stopped building the city. That is why it was called
> Babel, since there Yahweh confused the language of
> the whole world; and from there Yahweh scattered
> them all over the world. [Genesis 11:5–9]

This passage makes it clear that the Tower of Babel was so
named because of the confusion of tongues which came
about as a consequence of its construction and God's
punishment for the arrogance of Mankind. Here the play
on words is between the original Akkadian *Bab-Ilu* ('Gate
of the God') and the Hebrew verb *balal* meaning 'to con-
fuse'. This aspect of the Babel story is also part of the
Sumerian tradition surrounding the city of Eridu and its
principal deity.

> Then Enki, lord of abundance, whose commands
> are trustworthy, the lord of wisdom who understands
> the land, the leader of the gods endowed with
> wisdom, the lord of Eridu, changed the speech in
> their mouths, bringing contention into the speech
> of Man which until then had been one. [Ashmolean
> Museum fragment of *Enmerkar and the Lord of Aratta
> Epic*]

We can now also understand much better Nimrod's building activities, once he is identified with Enmerkar and the
original Tower of Nun.ki/Babel.

9. Seal impression depicting the priest-king of Uruk being transported in his sledge palanquin.

> The centres of his (Nimrod's) empire were Babel, Erech and Akkad, all of them in the land of Shinar. [Genesis 10:10]

As I have stated, current knowledge indicates that Babylon was not founded until a thousand years after the time of Nimrod and the immediate post-flood epoch. Its ziggurat was built in the Old Babylonian period of Hammurabi. Babylon simply doesn't fit the story. However, once we realise that the original 'Gate of the God' was the first city of Sumerian civilisation, the principal entry-point into the underworld realm of Enki, and the entry point of the original Anunnaki (the earth-bound gods) as they came from the east in their reed ships, then the biblical text can be amended to read:

> The centres of his (Enmer's) empire were Bab-Ilu (Nun.ki = Eridu), Erech (Uruk) and Akkad (location unknown), all of them in the land of Shinar (Sumer). [Genesis 10:10]

The epic of Enmerkar and the Lord of Aratta confirms the activities of 'Enmer the hunter' in both Eridu and Uruk whilst Sumerian remains have been found in the lowest strata of several cities in northern Mesopotamia dated to the Uruk period when Enmerkar ruled. There can be little doubt that this king – 'the first potentate on Earth' according to Genesis 10:8 – was long remembered by the ancients.

Chapter Five

THE SONS OF HAM

(Genesis 10:6–7)

Migration to Africa – Crossing the Eastern Desert – The
Dynastic Race – Horus and Seth – The Dispersing of
the Nations – Cush and Mizraim – The Shebtiu

And Yahweh scattered them all over the world.
[Genesis 11:9]

With this single, bland statement the author of the
book of Genesis dismisses one of the most important events in prehistory – the colonisation of
Arabia, north-east Africa, the Levant, Anatolia, Greece and
the Aegean islands by the people of early Mesopotamia.
However, in Genesis chapter 10 we find ourselves reading
a list – the so-called 'Table of Nations' – of just about every
civilisation and tribal grouping known from the Bible and
ancient texts. In effect, this table is a summary of how the
ancient world ended up following the scattering or 'dis-
persement' of the people who built the Tower of Babel.

The list is broken down into three main sections described as the Sons of Japheth (the Indo-European group), the Sons of Ham (the African and Canaanite group) and the Sons of Shem (the Semitic group). Was this list merely an attempt on the part of the Bible writer(s) to explain the three principal language groups of the ancient world? ... or is there some historical reality to the tradition that the people who lived in Sumer in the centuries following the flood began to colonise other, far-reaching parts of the world?

> The sons of Noah who came out of the ark were Shem, Ham and Japheth – Ham being the father of Canaan. These three were Noah's sons, and from these the whole Earth was peopled. [Genesis 9:18–19]

Josephus, the great Jewish historian of the first century AD, explains this 'dispersion of the Nations' in much more detail.

> After this (the abandonment of the Tower of Babel) they (the descendants of Noah) were dispersed abroad, on account of their languages, and went out by colonies everywhere; and each colony took possession of that land which they came upon, and to which God led them. So that the whole continent was filled with them – both the inland and maritime countries. There were some who also passed over the sea in ships and inhabited the islands. And some of these nations still retain the names given to them by their first founders. [Josephus: *Antiquities of the Jews*, Book I]

We have seen in the previous chapter how archaeology has revealed clear evidence of the 'inland' colonisation of upper Mesopotamia (at sites such as Habuba Kabira and Jebel Aruda) but what of the colonists who 'passed over the sea in ships'? Where did they go? And who did they become? The answer to these questions is both startling and highly controversial. But the archaeological evidence and ancient traditions unquestionably point us towards Africa and the world's most glorious ancient civilisation – Egypt of the pharaohs.

Before we board the high-prowed boat of Cush as he leads his fleet of colonists to their new homeland by the banks of the Nile, let us try to understand the motives for setting out on such a challenging adventure.

A Great Migration

For centuries the people of Eridu and the neighbouring cities of Shinar had been exploring the Lower Sea (Persian Gulf) in search of mineral resources to make their tools and weapons and exotic produce to lavish upon their city temples and palaces. In the nearly two-millennia-long archaeological era which scholars have dubbed the Ubaid period (c. 4800–3000 BC, named after the mound where the culture was first discovered), colonies of Ubaidian traders were established along the Arabian shore of the Gulf. Their fine, highly decorated pottery has been found everywhere from the towns on the upper Euphrates to the Qatar peninsula. It was during this period that the people of southern Mesopotamia gained their sea-legs, gradually learning how to construct stronger and more ocean-worthy sailing craft out of the berdi reeds growing in the Sumerian marshes.

The reach of Mesopotamian sea trade was extending with every journey. The people of Sumer soon penetrated the Lower Sea as far as Oman to obtain copper ore. Another leap took them along the southern coast of the Iranian plateau to the Indus valley (modern Pakistan) where they traded for scented woods and precious stones, including the much sought after lapis-lazuli of Badakhshan in Afghanistan.

Eventually, by the time of the Early Uruk period (*c.* 3100–2900 BC – commencing a century after the flood which effectively brought an end to the Ubaid period), the southern coast of Arabia was mapped and our Mesopotamian adventurers were exploring up the Red Sea coast of Africa. Here they found wondrous resources to take back to Sumer, including exotic animal skins (leopards, cheetahs and panthers), plentiful supplies of ivory, incenses, fine-grained hardwoods such as ebony, the shiny black stone known as obsidian and, above all, gold in abundance. North-east Africa and the Nile valley had become the new Eldorado of the Mesopotamians, eclipsing the majestic mountain kingdom of Aratta in Eden which was so very difficult to reach. The journey to Africa could be done by boat in a few weeks, letting the winds and currents do all the work. The trek over the seven mountain ranges to Aratta took three to four months, during which time every painful step was fraught with danger. Aratta and Eden slipped slowly into legend. Only heroes such as Gilgamesh dared to journey there on his epic adventure to the 'Land of the Living'. The primeval world beyond the eastern mountains had been transformed into the legendary realm of the gods – the 'heaven' (*an*) from which the Anunnaki had 'descended' to found the first cities on Earth (*ki*).

The First African Colonies

And so it is time to follow the progeny of Noah, through his eldest son Ham, as the latter's descendants journey to their new homes in Africa and Canaan. Understandably, the book of Genesis principally concerns itself with the historical progress of the 'sons of Shem' from whose line Abraham eventually descended. To learn the fate of the 'sons of Ham' we need to turn to extra-biblical sources such as Josephus and the Egyptian mythological texts, as well as the archaeological evidence from Egypt's late predynastic period.

First, I will let Josephus summarise the wide-ranging explorations undertaken by Ham's 'sons' during the first colonisation period prior to the construction of the Tower of Babel and the second migration phase.

> The children of Ham possessed the land from Syria and Amanus, and the mountains of Libanus (Lebanon), seizing upon all that was on its seacoasts and as far as the ocean, and keeping it as their own. Some, indeed, of its names are utterly vanished away, others of them being changed, and another sound given them, are hardly to be discovered. Yet only a few have kept their names intact. Of the four sons of Ham, time has not at all hurt the name of Chus (Cush), for the Ethiopians – over whom he reigned – are even at this day, both by themselves and by all men in Asia, called Chusites (Kushites).
> [Josephus: *Antiquities of the Jews*, Book I]

The followers of Cush, having shore-hopped all along the Arabian coast, found themselves at the gates (Bab el-Mandeb) of the Arabian Sea (the modern Red Sea). For some years Persian Gulf sea traders had been in contact with the indigenous peoples of Ethiopia, bargaining for the exotic produce of the African hinterland and obtaining obsidian from Yemen in south-west Arabia. They had already established a trading colony on the coast of what is today called Eritrea. This entrepôt was named Poen after its founding clan – adventurers from the Persian Gulf island which the Arabs call BAHRAIN but which was earlier known as Dilmun. These Poenite pioneers were the pathfinders of the Lower Sea – fearless seafarers who could supply experienced navigators to the colonising expeditions from Mesopotamia. In the three millennia which followed this initial spreading of Mesopotamian culture the POENI would retain their renown as the ancient world's greatest navigators. The classical writers knew them as the Phoenicians

(*Phoenike*) whilst the Egyptians maintained contact with the original colony of Poene(t) which they called 'God's Land' and which is known to Egyptology as the Land of Punt.

In 2980 BC Cush and his followers came ashore north of Poen at the place where the port of Suakin is today (just south of Port Sudan). From there they journeyed inland, through the wadis of the Nubian highlands, to the great Dongola Bend of the upper Nile where the kingdom of Kush was established. There they peacefully settled alongside and married into the indigenous population which archaeologists have called the Nubian A-Group culture. This newly created civilisation, in its various guises (first as the A-Group, then later as the Kushites and finally as the Napatan and Meroitic dynasties), endured for nearly three thousand five hundred years – beyond even the pharaonic state of Egypt which came to an end with the death of Cleopatra and the rise of the empire of the Caesars. In fact, the kingdom of the 'black pharaohs' survived along the upper reaches of the Nile for centuries into the Christian era. The civilisation of Meroe was still building its royal pyramids into the fifth century AD when time finally caught up with this last vestige of pharaonic power.

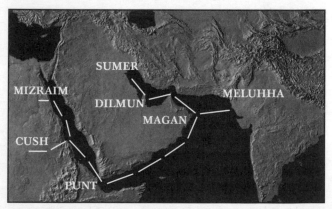

10. The sea route around the Arabian peninsula to Africa taken by the sons of Ham.

Meanwhile, Cush's younger brother, Masri (the biblical Mizraim of Genesis 10:6 & 13–14), who had accompanied the colonists to Africa with his own fleet of boats, sailed on up the western coast of the Red Sea in search of a new home for his followers. Masri's fleet of a dozen black ships, large and small, came ashore where the little town of Mersa Alam hugs the beach today. Again, this area had been visited many times before by the Poenite traders of Dilmun and Punt. But here the attraction was not ivory, animal skins and choice hardwoods, but gold ore, mined in limited quantities by the local population from the mountains of the Eastern Desert.

If truth be known, the followers of Masri were well aware of the riches of this part of Africa even before they set sail from Mesopotamia. Gold – that prized commodity above all others – was in short supply in the Land of the Two Rivers and news had quickly spread of the abundant seams of the precious metal in Egypt's Red Sea hills. Masri had wisely brought a Poenite scout with him who had traversed the Eastern Desert during earlier trading missions. The later Egyptians of pharaonic times deified this scout as the wolf-god Wepwawet – the 'opener of the ways' who had escorted the demigods – the bringers of civilisation – to the Nile valley.

Wepwawet, as we shall also call him (for his actual name is lost to us), had briefed Masri on the miracle of the Nile river which flooded annually during the summer months. In these early times that inundation – caused by heavy spring rains in the Ethiopian highlands – was much greater than in modern times (or for the last four thousand years for that matter). As much as four times the modern volume of water began to arrive in the Nile valley towards the end of the month of July. As a result, the broad, flat wadis of Upper Egypt became flooded to a distance approximately one third of the way (some sixty kilometres) to the Red Sea. Masri's strategy was to haul his fleet of reed ships out of the Red Sea, load them onto palm-log sledges and have

11. The rock-art boat from site ER–1 in Wadi el-Atwani. I believe that the boats carved in Egypt's Eastern Desert give us an insight into the colonisation of the Nile valley by Mesopotamians from Uruk and Susiana.

their crews drag the vessels through the mountain canyons until they eventually arrived at the point where the inundation reached. His people would then sail the fleet the rest of the way to the Nile valley where they would be able to dominate the local population who only possessed smaller and much inferior papyrus riverine craft. This stratagem, hard as it was to achieve, plus a new development in warfare – the pear-shaped mace – were the keys to establishing the Mesopotamian colony at Hierakonpolis – the 'city of the hawk' from which the Horus kings of Upper Egypt would eventually succeed in conquering the whole of Egypt. Josephus also briefly refers to the eponymous founder of Musri (the Semitic name of Egypt) and the followers of Masri whom he calls the Mesraites. This is clearly a late (first century AD) garbled version of the Mizraim of Genesis – in other words the followers or tribe of Mizra.

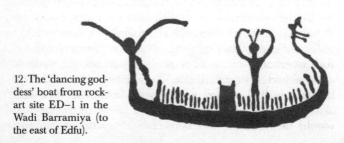

12. The 'dancing god-dess' boat from rock-art site ED–1 in the Wadi Barramiya (to the east of Edfu).

82

The memory also of the Mesraites is preserved in their name, for all we who inhabit this country (of Judaea) call Egypt 'Mestre' and the Egyptians 'Mestreans'. [Josephus: *Antiquities of the Jews*, Book I, Chapter VI:2]

From Hunters to Gold Prospectors

The indigenous population of the Nile valley and desert margins (known as the HAMMAMAT) had long ventured into the Red Sea hills on hunting expeditions and in search of schist for their slate make-up palettes. These two activities were interrelated. In primeval times the hunters daubed their faces and bodies with 'war paint' decoration in pre-hunt rituals which were designed to propitiate a successful mission into the desert. During the predynastic period the Eastern Desert was semi-fertile savannah with open watering holes and perennial streams. The Neolithic Wet Phase of higher rainfall, which began in around 6000 BC, was gradually coming to an end, heralding the much drier climate phase of the pyramid age and beyond. However, during the three-hundred-year transition between the two climatic eras, the Eastern Desert mountains were still teeming with wild cattle, asses, antelopes, ibexes, elephants, giraffes and ostriches.

For generations the Nile valley hunters had made regular forays eastwards to their favoured hunting grounds where the desert sandstone ridge formed canyon bottlenecks along the migration routes of the wild herds. There the hunters would wait with their packs of trained hunting hounds, armed to the teeth with bows, lassoes, throw-sticks, staffs and clubs. They encamped beneath favourite shady rock overhangs or in caves until the unwitting creatures approached to meet their fate. The herds were corralled in the narrow, high-walled wadis, lassoed, shot with bow and arrow and savaged by the hounds. Some of the bovids would be hobbled and herded back to the valley for

13. Hunting scenes from the Eastern Desert (DR–1) showing the use of hunting hounds and bows.

domestication; other less fortunate beasts were tethered for ritual slaughter. When it was all over, the hunters decorated their own bodies with the symbols of the animals they had conquered. Upon the canyon walls of the sacred hunting grounds they carved images of themselves, wearing tall twin ostrich plumes or antelope and ibex horns on their heads. These 'masters of the animals' finally returned in triumph to their villages hugging the alluvium of the Nile valley, the mission to dominate the powerful forces of nature successfully accomplished.

It was through this age-old activity that the complex wadi terrain was explored and even mapped. Several rock-carved maps have been found at crucial locations in the Red Sea hills. Stones were examined and brought back for carving and the grey schist of the WADI HAMMAMAT selected as the medium for the make-up palettes upon which green malachite and GALENA were ground and mixed with fat for the skin-painting rituals. It was during these years of exploration in the sandstone hills that the hunters began to notice the glint of gold in stream beds flowing through the Wadi Barramiya and Hammamat areas during the winter rains. Exposed seams were soon being exploited and the Egyptian gold mining industry was born.

Small wonder the Mesopotamian colonists were drawn to this region. Coming from the wide alluvial plain of the two rivers, Tigris and Euphrates, where few animals roamed and where the settlements were almost entirely deprived of valuable minerals and stone, the Eastern Desert must have seemed like a treasure house. And beyond to the west was a magnificent river flowing through a lush narrow valley – a river moreover which conveniently flooded after harvest time and before the planting season, washing clean the soils and depositing rich silt as a natural fertiliser. This perfect gift of nature was in stark contrast to the Tigris and Euphrates which disgorged their flood waters during the last weeks before the harvest, regularly destroying the grain crop. The new Nile valley homeland of the 'sons of Ham' was everything that the Mesopotamian plain was not. It was a new Eden 'rich in gold' and with everything 'good to eat'.

The Followers of Horus

Masri's tribe had managed to bring their reed ships safely through the coral reef which hugs the western shore of the Red Sea to beach them on the soft sand at the entrance to a wide wadi mouth leading into the Eastern Desert mountains. The narrow strip of coastal plain was dotted with sycamores and palms which the boat-people felled to build strong log sledges, strapped together with palm-frond and reed ropes. The black ships were then carefully manhandled onto their land transport and the Herculean task of dragging the boats to the Nile began.

At first the task was a struggle. Some of the larger craft, capable of carrying more than eighty crew, were of tremendous weight. But then these vessels had proportionately larger dragging teams to pull them. Gradually the best technique and rhythm was established and the convoy of high-prowed ships slowly moved westwards at a rate of a little over one kilometre per day. Scouting parties, led by Wepwawet, were sent ahead to clear the route and to hunt herds of antelopes, ibexes and wild cattle in order to feed the convoy. Water was ferried by pack-animals from the watering holes and small oases dotted about the landscape.

Four long winter months passed as the ships drew ever

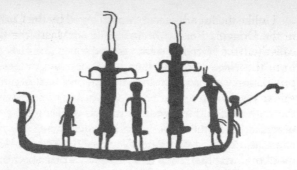

14. The main boat at rock art site DR–2 in Wadi Abu Markab el-Nes (discovered by Hans Winkler in 1938). The two tall figures wear twin plumes and carry bows; the three smaller figures may be the children of the larger figures. This remarkable image might therefore be a representation of a 'holy family' or the 'royal family' of the incoming migrants from Mesopotamia.

nearer to their destination in the Wadi Abbad. The crews of the black ships had hauled the precious craft more than one hundred and thirty kilometres and now took their rest in the shade of the southern cliffs of the valley, waiting for the annual miracle of the flood. Weeks passed. Some of the men went on hunting expeditions whilst others repaired the boats. Like the Hammamat, they too carved images of themselves and their boats on the smooth sandstone rocks where the indigenous hunters had already decorated the surfaces with elephants, giraffes, bovids, wild donkeys, antelopes, ibexes, hippos, crocodiles and ostriches. They waited ... and waited ... as the temperature steadily rose. Finally, at the beginning of the month we call August in 2979 BC, a glistening silver thread began to appear on the western horizon of the wide, flat wadi. In a couple of days the waters of the Nile inundation were lapping at the hulls of the high-prowed ships. Within a week the craft were buoyant, and could be dragged and punted down the wadi at ten kilometres per day. Soon the water was deep enough to deploy the oars and the fleet raced towards their final destination – the Nile.

Unlike the friendly reception received by the Cushites in the Dongola Reach, the followers of Masri (the Bible calls them the Mizraim) were met with sustained resistance from the Nile valley dwellers. Although the indigenous population were in no position to take on a well-organised military expedition, hardened by a year of adventure on the high seas and exploration in desert mountains, they organised themselves to fight the newcomers. The clash came at a spot on the great Kena Bend just north of the modern town of LUXOR. The fighting took place both along the shore and in the river itself. The Mizraim were successful in the land battle principally because of their use of the pear-shaped mace which proved far more effective than the disc-shaped maces carried by the local warriors. Many of the latter were slaughtered and their chieftains captured, soon to meet a sorry end in smiting rituals at the hands of the foreigners. The small crescent-shaped papyrus riverine craft of the Nile dwellers were rammed and utterly crushed by the great black ships of the Mesopotamian boat-people. Lifeless bodies floated northwards with the current – a stark message to all who dwelt along the banks of the great river. There was a new order in the valley and things would never be the same again.

With the bloody suppression of the local chieftainships accomplished, the Masri clan turned to building their settlement and temple precinct on the west bank of the river at a site later known to the Egyptians as Nekhen and to the Greeks as HIERAKONPOLIS. In the later early-dynastic period a second settlement was established on the east bank, at the mouth of the wadi leading back to the Red Sea. This place was known as Nekheb – the city of the vulture-goddess Nekhbet.

Masri had chosen the falcon as his standard and the *har* emblem had been carried at the head of the expedition ever since it had landed on the African shoreline. So came into being the kingdom of the hawk and, with it, the legend of the *Shemsa-Har* – the Followers of Horus – the élite warriors of the Horus kings of Upper Egypt who would eventually go on to conquer the whole length of the Egyptian Nile valley and unify the country under the pharaohs of the 1st Dynasty.

Put and Canaan

> These are the descendants of Noah's sons – Shem, Ham and Japheth – to whom sons were born after the flood. … **Ham's sons were Cush, Mizraim, Put and Canaan.** Cush's sons were Seba, Havilah, Sabtah, Raamah and Sabteca. Raamah's sons were Sheba and Dedan. [Genesis 10:1 & 6–7]

A substantial number of Masri's people, led by his younger brothers Paut and Kanaan (biblical Put and Canaan), chose to explore the valley further northwards, to see where the river current might take them. Little is known about their adventures, but they went on to establish a port near the mouth of the Canopic branch of the Nile in the western delta, from where they ventured out into the eastern Mediterranean. This port became the capital of the Lower Egyptian kingdom of the delta marshes – PER WADJET, known to the classical world as Buto. As with the twin settlements of Nekhen and Nekhbet, in time Buto consisted of two centres opposite each other on either side of the Nile river, known as Pe and Dep, the former being the royal residence. Later tradition would remember the first rulers of Lower Egypt as the 'Souls of Pe', whilst the first rulers of Upper Egypt were known as the jackal-headed 'Souls of Nekhen'.

Acting in much the same way as ancient Eridu at the mouth of the Euphrates, Buto opened up the Mediterranean to the black ship traders and adventurers. The traditions inform us that Paut founded settlements along the north African coast of Libya, whilst Kanaan and his Poenite navigators sailed on north along the Levantine coast

15. The Gebel el-Arak knife handle. Left (obverse): the Mesopotamian 'Master of Animals'. Right (reverse): a battle scene with high-prowed boats typical of the early Mesopotamian period. The knife was found near the entrance to the Wadi Hammamat in Upper Egypt.

to make contact with the Mesopotamian colonies in northern Syria and the upper Euphrates valley through their newly established ports of Byblos (Egyptian *Kebny*) and UGARIT. It was these colonial trade links with the eastern Mediterranean coastal region (later known as Kanaan or Canaan after the settlers' eponymous ancestor) which provided Lower Egypt with Lebanese cedar to ignite the technological innovation of wooden ship construction and the use of high-quality timber in Egyptian architectural design. These early developments in Buto and the Poenite ports of the northern Levant would lead to three thousand years of Phoenician seafaring dominance in the Mediterranean Sea.

The Dynastic Race

The Horus kings of Egypt were descended from Ham and therefore the Mesopotamian flood hero himself. The common epithet for the man who survived the great disaster to re-establish human civilisation in the Mesopotamian plain was 'the far distant' because he departed from his people to live out his eternal existence with the gods on Mount Tilmun or Dilmun – not the historical and later island of Dilmun now called Bahrain but the original home of Enki and Ninhursag, the Dilmun of Eden.

Noah's descendants had rebuilt the drowned cities. The new settlements had rapidly grown into large metropoli with their own city gods. Indeed, the worship of deities had proliferated to such a degree that the legendary founders and 'mighty men' of those cities were soon themselves being deified. Following his death, Ham ('hot')

16. This cylinder seal from Mesopotamia depicts a ruler (wearing a kilt and carrying what appears to be a ceremonial club), approaching a shrine, above which are two crude representations of birds (probably falcons – compare to early Egyptian art). Behind the king follow two court officials carrying standards. The symbols on top of the standard poles appear to be the hieroglyphic signs for *meh* (left) and *ka* (right). The scene is stylistically Mesopotamian (and the seal originates from southern Iraq) but the symbols are all Egyptian motifs.

17. This cylinder seal impression depicts the priest-king of Uruk standing before a niched-façade building. This type of recessed panelling also appears in Egypt around the beginning of the 1st Dynasty (especially in tomb architecture). Scholars have determined that this complex form of architecture was first invented in Mesopotamia and then subsequently exported to Egypt where it became a royal motif associated with the king's Horus name (known as the *serekh*).

was identified with the sun-god Utu/Shamash; centuries after the reign of Enmerkar/Nimrod, the 'mighty hunter' and first empire builder was elevated to godhood as the popular patron deity of hunting and warfare, Ninurta; and the flood hero himself was remembered by the later Egyptians as the original Horus king from whom the pharaohs had descended. The Egyptian word *Har* (Greek 'Horus') means 'the far distant'.

The legendary Egyptian Followers of Horus claimed descent from the greatest of Mesopotamian heroes and each succeeding ruler of that clan carried the epithet 'Horus' before his name in much the same way as the later Roman emperors bore the title Caesar after the man who inaugurated Rome's imperial age. It is clear that the Followers of Horus were thought of as the legendary ancestors of Pharaoh's courtiers – an élite which distinguished itself from the rest of the population in the Nile valley by maintaining a class-structure similar to the Hindu caste system. At the top of the social and political pyramid was the pharaoh and the royal family; then came the Iry-Paut ('the ones who belong to the Pat clan'), claiming direct descent from the first Horus kings. Below this élite clan were the state officials who were not Iry-Paut. Then came the descendants of the ancient indigenous population of Upper Egypt – the Hammamat – and finally the indigenous delta dwellers – the Rekhyt – whose name was adopted as the collective term for the peasant population of Egypt as a whole during the pharaonic era. The Iry-Paut nobility jealously guarded their status as members of the royal entourage and continued to marry within the clan in order to maintain their pure bloodline. They were Egypt's 'Dynastic Race', descended from the Anunnaki and the sun-god himself. They were the biblical Sons of Ham.

The Contendings of Horus and Seth

With their great ocean-going vessels plying the waters of the Nile, the Shemsa-Har of Nekhen dominated Upper Egypt, establishing a second power base at ONBET near the modern village of Nakada, north of Luxor, twinned with GEBTU, on the east bank opposite Onbet. These two

18. Details from a damaged cylinder seal discovered at Susa, depicting a battle. The 'ruler', wearing an Upper Egyptian white crown (compare with the Egyptian hieroglyphic version on the left) stands between two *hem* hieroglyphs (the symbol of Egyptian royalty often translated as 'his majesty'). Behind the king is a crude rosette (again associated with early Egyptian royalty and the hieroglyph *netjer* meaning 'god' or 'divinity'). Behind the rosette a member of the king's entourage carries the crescent-moon standard (typically Mesopotamian). In the lower register a princess or wife of the king is being transported in a palanquin. This rare form of glyptic art (showing a specific battle) has both Egyptian and Mesopotamian motifs, yet its provenance is south-western Iran (the region later known as Elam).

settlements were located at the western end of a great transverse wadi leading to the Red Sea and, of course, serviced the gold mines of the Wadi Hammamat. Onbet has been described as the 'Klondyke' of predynastic Egypt. Things were peaceful for the best part of a century (spanning the archaeological phase known as Nakada II) as the new-comers set to the task of building towns and establishing their cult centres. They quickly adapted to the new environ-ment, enthusiastically exploiting the deep rich soil and instigating Mesopotamian basin irrigation techniques to cultivate their grain crops, as well as domesticating herds of cattle rounded up in the Eastern Desert. However, they also maintained contact with their homeland, sending gold ore back to Mesopotamia via the Arabian peninsula sea route and the ports of Buto and Byblos. In return, the Nile valley colonists received lapis-lazuli and finished tools and weapons brought back in the returning ships. This con-tinuing link with Sumer, especially via the southern route, eventually proved to be dangerous.

A Second Migration

During the reign of Enmer of Uruk (c. 2830 BC) a new wave of Mesopotamian colonisers began to arrive in Upper Egypt. These city-dwellers had long been witness to the wealth of the African colonies, manifest in the heavily laden ships docking in Eridu and sailing up the rivers Euphrates, Tigris and Karun. In addition, large numbers of foreigners were also arriving in the Land of the Two Rivers – both Sumerian-speaking tribes from the eastern mountains and Semitic-speaking tribes from the west. This massive influx was beginning to stretch the resources of the region to its limits. War and skirmish was rife. This was the era the biblical text refers to as 'the confusion of tongues'.

All this had been triggered and then inflamed, at least in part, by the political ambitions and military successes of King Enmer himself. Towards the end of his long reign the colonial empire, created by over forty years of conquest, was beginning to fragment. Sumer became ripe for incursion by foreign raiders, speaking several different tongues. This instability, in turn, created its own refugee crisis with many Mesopotamians seeking a better future overseas – in particular alongside their 'brethren' in Africa. We will follow one convoy of ships which departed from the south-eastern alluvial plain – the region archaeologists have called Susiana, after its principal city – SUSA.

Susa's fleet of black ships sailed south from Susiana and out through the River Karun's marshy delta. But, instead of heading west for Eridu and the gateway to Sumer as the ships of the great ancestor Uanna/Enoch had done, they kept right on heading south, past Dilmun/Bahrain and through the Strait of Hormuz into the Indian Ocean. For two weeks they hugged the eastern shore of the Arabian peninsula, regularly going ashore for food and water. Finally the fleet reached the Bab el-Mandeb and the trading centre of Poene (Punt), where the colonists rested.

Patiently the boat captains waited for the northerly winds of the Red Sea to change. Then in July, as had been discovered over the years, the expected reversal of the air pattern took hold and the winds began to blow steadily from the south. The people reboarded their vessels, sails were unfurled and the fleet set off on the last leg of its sea journey along the east coast of the African continent.

The people of Susiana (archaeologists call them the Proto-Elamites) had long since maintained strong ties with Kushite traders from both Punt and the early kingdom of Kush centred on the Sudanese Nile valley. They themselves claimed descent from King Meskiagkasher (biblical Cush) of Uruk who, shortly after his death, had been deified both in the Nile valley kingdom and in Susiana. He, after all, was the hero who had adventured out into the sea and established the first of the African colonies, bringing new wealth to the Mesopotamian homelands and instigating the rebirth of civilisation following the catastrophic deluge.

The author of Genesis knew him as Cush, son of Ham; the Sumerian king list recorded the first antediluvian ruler of Uruk by the eponym Meskiagkasher, which translates as 'Kash, the hero who divided the Earth (amongst his followers)'; the later Egyptians also remembered him through the name of their southern neighbour, the kingdom of Kash (which Egyptologists refer to as Kush); and, through the Greeks, we derive our own word 'chaos' (i.e. division) from this same hypocoristicon. But Cush is also known to us by his second and more infamous Egyptian name – Seth, Lord Chaos.

The fleet from Susiana sailed up the Red Sea as far as Kuseir and, in a repetition of the earlier Followers of Horus expedition, successfully transported their ships across the desert, this time along the Wadi Hammamat route. As with their forerunners, the newcomers had been drawn to the rich gold supplies of the Eastern Desert Hammamat region. With the influx of the colonists from Susiana, the population of Onbet and Gebtu trebled overnight.

It was not long before the new foreign element – the Followers of Seth (as we shall now call them) – had superimposed themselves over the whole area of the Nile valley from Luxor in the south to Assiut in Middle Egypt. The original clan Masri settlers in this region were driven south to seek refuge with their kin in Nekhen, bringing tales of harsh treatment and usurpation by these unwelcome neighbours. A clash between the two groups – The Followers of Horus of Nekhen in southern Upper Egypt and The Followers of Seth of Onbet (Egyptological 'Seth the Ombite', Greek *Ombos*) in northern Upper Egypt – was inevitable … and it came sooner rather than later.

Whilst the ruler of Nekhen, the Horus king Scorpion, was on an expedition to expand his kingdom southwards beyond the sandstone narrows in the river at Gebel es-Silsila, the ruler of Onbet led his fleet on a raid southwards into the territory of the Horus clan. On hearing the news, Scorpion turned his fleet around and sailed north to con-

19. Map of Upper Egypt showing the kingdoms of Nekhen (Hierakonpolis), Nubt (Nakada) and Tjenu (Thinis/Abydos) in relation to the two main west–east wadis and principal rock-art sites.

front his enemy. A chaotic river battle took place opposite the site where the temple of Edfu stands today, resulting in a convincing victory for the Followers of Horus. The Sethite ruler was harpooned and drowned in the Nile, his men slaughtered and their ships taken. Seizing the moment, Scorpion sailed north and captured Onbet. The head of the Sethite king was severed from his body, the headless corpse dragged by its feet through the streets of the Upper Egyptian towns as a warning to all those who might dare to challenge the power of the Horus king.

In a single week of fighting the Followers of Horus had regained their former territory and Scorpion determined never to lose it again. A new capital of the re-unified Upper Egyptian kingdom was established at the settlement of TJENU north of the Kena Bend. The original burial site of the town, in the western desert beneath the limestone cliffs of Abydos, continued to be used and became the place of interment for three dynasties of Horus kings. Scorpion was the first of the Upper Egyptian kings to be buried there in his large mudbrick sepulchre known today as Tomb Uj. The royal burial ground endured intermittently for two hundred years, starting with the last predynastic period which archaeologists call Nakada III (sometimes given the historical designation 'Dynasty 0') and ending with the last king of the 2nd Dynasty and the inauguration of the pyramid age at Sakkara.

From this time on Abydos was to be regarded as the most sacred necropolis in Egypt, being closely associated with the cult of Osiris/Asar and the burial place of the early Horus kings. The name Abydos is itself a Greek version of Egyptian *Abdju* which would have been pronounced Abzu – the Sumerian word for the watery entrance to the underworld. In later years the pharaohs would stage mock battles on the Abzu lake at Abydos to commemorate the legendary naval victory of the Followers of Horus over the Followers of Seth.

The Unification of Egypt

Meanwhile, in the far north of Egypt, the delta kingdom of the breakaway colony founded by Put had been flourishing in semi-isolation from its southern counterpart. Its success lay securely founded in Mediterranean trade, even though the very produce offered in barter with the western Sumerian colonies of Canaan came from Upper Egypt. In effect, the two royal houses of Upper and Lower Egypt, with their different sea-route connections to the old homeland, became trading rivals and contenders for the Eastern Desert's resources. Expeditions by river into Upper Egypt to acquire minerals and stone by the ships of Buto created tensions which eventually exploded into full-blown conflict.

During the next fifty years the rulers of Upper Egypt gradually expanded their kingdom northwards by military force until they finally conquered the delta and unified the country under the founder of the 1st Dynasty proper – King Horus Aha ('the fighter'), known to history as Menes after his Nebty ('two ladies') name, Meni. The Two Ladies were the vulture-goddess Nekhbet of Nekheb and the cobra-goddess Wadjet of Buto. The Horus king Aha Meni was the first to bear a Nebty name as king over both predynastic kingdoms.

Aha founded yet another royal capital just south of modern Cairo which was called ANBU-HAZ after the great white plastered defensive wall surrounding the royal residence. It later acquired the designation Men-nefer – the name of Pharaoh Pepi I's 6th Dynasty pyramid looking down upon the city from the Sakkara desert escarpment. It was this name which came down to us in its Graecised form of Memphis (Coptic *Menfè*). The great religious complex of the god Ptah at Memphis was known as *Hiku–Ptah* ('temple of Ptah'), from which came the Greek *Aegyptos* and our modern name for the Land of the Pharaohs – Egypt.

Part Two

Wandering Years

Chapter Six

ABRAHAM
THE AMORITE

(Genesis 11:10 to Genesis 25:18)

*Abram's Ancestors – From Harran to Egypt – Conflict
with Mesopotamia – The Destruction of Sodom –
Ishmael and Isaac – Burial in Hebron*

The story of the Children of Yahweh leaps forward
ten 'generations' or generations of dynasties (in this
case a thousand years) to the time of the patriarchs
and the great wanderer Abraham – the man regarded as
Israel's progenitor. We have reached 1900 BC and a new
beginning. We are at the dawn of the Patriarchal Age.

The Mesopotamian era in this story of the Children of
Yahweh has come to an end as our focus now moves south
into Middle-Bronze-Age Canaan and First-Intermediate-
Period Egypt, bringing us to our first sight of the Promised
Land. The Sumerian Early Dynastic period (*c.* 2600–2100
BC) and the mighty Egyptian Old Kingdom (*c.* 2554–2062
BC) are in the past. Khufu's Great Pyramid has already
been standing on the Giza plateau for nearly six hundred
years. The great Early Bronze Age city states of the Fertile

Noah to Abraham
(according to the begettings data supplied in the Septuagint)

Noah (Last pre-flood Generation/Dynasty)	c. 3713–3213 BC
Shem (1st Generation/Dynasty)	c. 3213–3011 BC
Arpachshad (2nd Generation/Dynasty)	c. 3011–2876 BC
Kenan (3rd Generation/Dynasty)	c. 2876–2746 BC
Shelah (4th Generation/Dynasty)	c. 2746–2616 BC
Eber (5th Generation/Dynasty)	c. 2616–2482 BC
Peleg (6th Generation/Dynasty)	c. 2482–2352 BC
Reu (7th Generation/Dynasty)	c. 2352–2222 BC
Serug (8th Generation/Dynasty)	c. 2222–2090 BC
Nahor (9th Generation/Dynasty)	c. 2090–1970 BC
Terah (10th Generation/Dynasty)	c. 1970–1900 BC
Abraham (11th Generation/Dynasty begins)	c. 1900 BC

Crescent have recently been destroyed by a cataclysmic series of earthquakes and abandoned, the refugees of the disaster disappearing into the countryside. Nomadic tribes wander the hills and deserts scratching out a living with their meagre flocks.

The Intervening Centuries

Following the building of the Tower of Babel and the period of Sumerian colonisation, the great civilisations of Mesopotamia and Egypt had begun to develop independently of each other. The pharaohs of the Archaic Period (1st and 2nd Dynasties – c. 2770–2554 BC) soon ceased to have contact with their original homeland. As a result, exotic goods from the southern ocean trade routes – such as lapis-lazuli – no longer found their way to the Nile valley on Poenite ships. Instead the focus of Egyptian trade switched to the Mediterranean. Lebanese cedar and pine was regularly transported by ship from the cities of the Levantine coast – especially Byblos, one of the Sumerian colonies founded in the time of Enmerkar by Poenite traders. These prized woods were used in royal architecture (palaces, temples and tombs) and to build the great funerary boats of the pharaohs. Turquoise was also beginning to be mined in the mountains of western Sinai around the Wadi Maghara region. With strong agricultural and state administration in place to exploit the natural wealth of the Nile valley and Eastern Desert, Egypt was becoming richer with every year that passed. All this wealth manifested itself in the famous Pyramid Age or Old Kingdom (3rd to 6th Dynasties), first with the construction of the world's oldest stone building – the Step Pyramid of Sakkara (*c.* 2554 BC) – and then culminating in the mighty Pyramids of Giza (the building of Khufu's pyramid commencing in *c.* 2475 BC).

Whilst all this was going on in Egypt, the Sumerians of the Mesopotamian plain continued to expand their sprawling mudbrick cities, surrounded by vast tracts of agricultural land. These cities were interconnected by the rivers Tigris and Euphrates and a complex network of canals, facilitating intercity trade and helping to distribute the irrigation water which was so vital to the region. Over the years the Sumerians had turned the partly dry and partly swampy alluvial plain between the two rivers into a veritable paradise. This was the age of the epic hero Gilgamesh (*c.* 2500–2450 BC) of Uruk (ED I) and the magnificent royal burials of Ur (ED III) excavated by Sir Leonard Woolley in the 1920s and 30s. Archaeologists call it the Early Dynastic period – an era of Sumerian dominance which lasted for half a millennium (*c.* 2600–2100 BC). Indeed, this was a high point in both of the great Early Bronze Age civilisations, with Gilgamesh erecting the mighty mudbrick wall of Uruk in Sumer at the same time as Sneferu (*c.* 2499–2475 BC) and Khufu (*c.* 2475–2452 BC) were building their stone pyramids above the western escarpment of the Nile valley.

But then came dramatic change in the affairs of the peoples of the Two Rivers. During the Early Dynastic Period Mesopotamia had, by and large, been ruled by

Sumerian-speaking kings. Now, in 2117 BC, a dynasty of Semitic-speaking monarchs came to the fore under the mighty conqueror Sargon of Agade (2117–2062 BC). Once he had taken over the throne from Ur-Zababa, a ruler of the 4th Dynasty of Kish (for whom he served as cup-bearer), Sargon set about carving himself a huge empire, even greater than that of Nimrod/Enmerkar. Over his fifty-year reign he fought many battles, defeating the Sumerian dynasties of the south, led by Lugalzaggesi of Uruk, and establishing an Agadean hegemony from the Upper Sea to the Lower Sea.

The Sumerian dominance of Mesopotamia came to an end as the mighty wall of Uruk, built by Gilgamesh in Early Dynastic I, was overthrown and Lugalzaggesi captured. The king of Uruk was dragged off like a beast of burden in a wooden yoke to be brought before the storm-god Enlil at Nippur for sacrifice. The rest of the Sumerian city-dynasts fell one after the other as Sargon's forces swept through the land.

As a consequence of this dramatic political change, the East Semitic language known as Akkadian, spoken by Sargon's dynasty, came to predominate in the region whilst classical Sumerian was reduced to the status of an archaic language employed by educated scribes. For one hundred and eighty years the kings of Agade ruled in Mesopotamia (2117–1937 BC) whilst the Egyptian Old Kingdom withered and collapsed in the Nile valley (late-6th, 7th and 8th Dynasties). Then, towards the end of the Agadean period, disaster descended upon the whole Middle East.

A series of powerful earthquakes rocked the cities to their foundations, bringing fire and destruction. Plague soon followed. The climate became much hotter and there was little rain to quench the dry soil. The broad plains gradually began to turn into desert. Warlike tribes descended from the mountains to the north of Mesopotamia, raiding the weakened settlements of the plain. The Gutians, in particular, struck at the heart of the Agadean homeland (near modern Baghdad) and Sargon's great empire slowly disintegrated. The death of the last great emperor of Agade, Sharkalisharri (2000–1976 BC), was presaged by a celestial event – a lunar eclipse – a dark omen recorded by the soothsayer priests.

> In this year the king will die. An eclipse of the moon and the sun will occur. A great king will die. [Tablet RME-192]

> The omen is given for Agade. The king of Agade will die, but his people will be well. The reign of Agade will fall into anarchy, but its future will be good. [*Enuma Anu Enlil*, Tablet 20]

The date of that lunar eclipse was 15th March 1977 BC – the last year of Sharkalisharri. The great king of Agade died soon after and his long reign was indeed followed by a short period of anarchy when no fewer than four rival kings appear to have claimed hegemony over the ailing empire within the space of three years.

> Who was king? Who was not king? Was Igigi king? Was Nanum king? Was Imi king? Was Elulu king? Their tetrad was king and reigned three years! [*Sumerian King List*]

Following the brief interregnum in Agade, Sargon's dynasty continued for another thirty-nine years under its last two kings, Dudu (1972–1952 BC) and Shu-Durul (1951–1937 BC), but, by then, the legacy of Sargon the Great was just an echo of its former glory.

Governments and monarchies fell across the ancient world as the city folk abandoned their homes, driven by hunger and in search of respite from the plague. The prosperous era of the great Early Bronze Age cities collapsed back into a semi-nomadic existence of living from hand to mouth. Archaeologists call this period either the Middle Bronze I period (MB I) or the Intermediate Early-Middle Bronze Age (EB-MB) – the time of the Amorite incursions.

The Amorites (the word is best translated as 'western-ers') comprised a large population of semi-nomadic herds-men whose homeland centred on the north-Mesopotamian plain or steppe-land bordering on and including the foot-hills of the Zagros mountains. In fact, their original tribal territory seems to have been located close to the Mountain of Descent where folklore claims Noah's Ark came to rest. Now, at the beginning of the second millennium BC, with the gradual desiccation of their traditional grazing grounds through drought, the Amorites were on the move south in search of new pasture-lands for their large flocks. But they were not just peaceful pastoralists – these were fierce tribal clansmen who would not hesitate to use force to establish their territorial claims on other people's land.

In Egypt the Old Kingdom had given way to the First Intermediate Period when the unified pharaonic state fragmented into petty kingdoms ruled once more by minor dynasties. The ancient world had slipped into its first post-empire dark age.

The 'barbaric' Gutian Dynasty held sway in Mesopota-mia for ninety-one years before its last king, Tirigan, was defeated in battle by Utuhegal, sole ruler of the Uruk V dynasty. On the night before Utuhegal's great victory there was another eclipse of the moon – always regarded as an important omen in the ancient world.

> The omen is given for the king of the Gutians. There will be a downfall of Guti in battle. The land will be totally laid waste. [*Enuma Anu Enlil*, Tablet 21]

In his own account of the war against the Gutians, Utuhegal describes being encamped near Muru on the eve of battle when 'In the midst of the night [an eclipse of the moon took place]'. The moon-god Sin was the special deity of the Gutian tribes and so this shaming of the moon presaged a political eclipse of the Gutian Dynasty. The date of that lunar eclipse was 28th June 1908 BC.

During Utuhegal's short reign of ten years (1910–1901 BC) Ur-nammu was governor/ruler of the city of Ur. When the king of Uruk died Ur-nammu became master of the entire region of Sumer, inaugurating the Ur III Dynasty and what has become known as the 'Sumerian Revival'. Over the reigns of Ur-nammu (1900–1883 BC) and his successor, Shulgi (1882–1835 BC), the Sumerian kingdom greatly expanded until it dominated the whole of Mesopotamia. Assyria, Elam and the Zagros mountain tribes all became subservient to the Ur III dynasts. Even Byblos on the Mediterranean coast of Canaan had a governor loyal to Ur. In Cappadocian central Anatolia Sumerian colonies thrived. All these lands paid tribute into the coffers of the Sumerian bureaucratic empire based at Ur. Outwardly this was a period of wealth and stability – but, in reality, the empire teetered on the edge of disaster for much of the era. A new threat was surfacing from the west.

Enter the Martu or Amorites onto the stage of world history. The Amorites were another unruly group of semi-nomadic tribes living in the upper Euphrates and Tigris valleys around Gebel Bishri, and in the Balikh and Harran regions. Like the Gutians, they worshipped the moon-god Sin, as well as a much older mountain-god – EL-SHADDAI (also known as Il-Amurru – 'El of the Amorites'). Indeed, Sin and EL were often closely related, but the latter was also the Amorite name of Eya, whose original home lay atop the Mountain of God beyond the Zagros mountains in the now legendary land of Eden. In a sense, the principal god of the Amorite people was an amalgam of the ancient gods worshipped by the Mesopotamians of Noah's time.

Here, with these Amorite people, we begin to see for the first time an ancestral link to the biblical Israelites. The Martu spoke a West Semitic dialect from which the Hebrew, Ugaritic and Arabic languages were to descend.

These scattered tribes were hardly a confederacy at this time but, despite their fragmentary political structure, they at first managed to inflict regular irritation upon the Ur III empire and finally undermine it to such a degree that the dynasty's tenuous control over its subject lands was irrevocably broken. Ur III's last king, Ibbi-Sin (1816–1793 BC), was defeated by his former subjects, the Elamites, and carried off to Susa where he died in captivity. The Ur III empire had lasted one hundred and eight years (1900–1793 BC), its ignominious end recorded in another lunar eclipse omen dated to 19th April 1793 BC.

> The omen is given for the King of the World. The destruction of Ur. The city walls will fall. … Devastation for the city and its lands. [*Enuma Anu Enlil*, Tablet 21]

It was right in the middle of this Ur III 'Sumerian Revival' that the life and wanderings of the Amorite chieftain, Abraham, have their setting.

Migration South

> Yahweh said to Abram, 'Leave your country, your kindred and your father's house for a country which I shall show you. For I shall make you a great nation, I shall bless you and make your name famous. You are to be a blessing!' [Genesis 12:1–2]

At his birth ABRAHAM was named Abram, meaning 'the father is exalted'. He was the son of Terah and the eldest brother of Nahor and Haran. For the previous several centuries, the ancestral tribe had been settled in a region of Upper Mesopotamia bordering the mountains of Kurdistan (i.e. ancient Kaldu/Kardu) where the towns of UR and Harran are located. The latter settlement is attested in contemporary documents of precisely this period. However, even though it is an attractive idea, the town of Harran is unlikely to have been named after Terah's youngest son because, in Semitic writing, the spelling of the two Harans is not the same (possessing different aspirates). Terah's youngest son died after fathering Lot, Iscah and Milcah. MILCAH became Nahor's wife. Abraham married Sarai who later took the name SARAH.

The traditional oral genealogy of Abraham's tribe claimed descent from the great ancestor Shem, son of Noah, via the 'generations' of Arpachshad, Kenan (only recorded in the Septuagint), Shelah, Eber (eponymous ancestor of the Hebrews), Peleg, Reu, Serug, Nahor and, finally, Terah the father of Abraham. The Bible intimates that these ten 'generations' span just two hundred and ninety-two years but, as with the ten pre-flood 'generations', I believe these names actually represent the most significant figures in a much longer line of descent. They are, in fact, dynastic heads – leading personalities in a now lost list of over forty true generations.

Terah and his family had set off from UR OF KALDU with the intention of migrating southwards into Canaan. But Terah managed only to get as far as Harran, where he once more established his home, dying there at a ripe old age. It was his son Abram who, in 1855 BC, took up the calling of the tribal god El (associated in this region with the moon) to shepherd his people towards their promised new home in the hill country of Palestine. So Abram, Sarai and their nephew, Lot, migrated across the Syrian plain with their followers and flocks, passing through the oases of Tadmor and Damascus before reaching Shechem (i.e. modern Nablus), nestled in the hills south of the Jezreel valley. There Abram built an altar to El near the sacred oak tree of Moreh, before continuing down the spine of hills which separate the coastal plain from the Jordan valley and on into the broad expanse of the Negeb arid region bordering on Sinai.

The journey from Harran to the border of Egypt had

taken two years. Each time Abraham's tribe pitched their tents, intending to settle for a while, they were forced to move on because of the severe famine conditions which continued to prevail across the land. There was barely enough food to feed the local Canaanite and Perizite populations, let alone the hordes of nomadic newcomers to the region migrating from the semi-deserts to the north, east and south.

For the past half millennium the climate in the Levant had gradually become more and more arid. But the fifty years following the earthquakes had been far worse. The level of the Dead Sea, fed by the River Jordan and the highland streams, had dropped considerably. The desert sands were encroaching on the pasture lands and the world had become a hard place in which to survive. Only in the heartland of Sumer, with its well organised state agricultural system, and in Egypt, with its beneficent Nile and lush vegetation, was the land managing to sustain its people.

The Amorites of northern Syria were not welcome in the Sumer of Ur III dynasty times and so, as would happen on many occasions in the future, the hungry people of Syria and Palestine headed for refuge from the famine into the Land of the Pharaohs – Abram and his tribe amongst them.

They (Abram's tribe) set off for the land of Canaan, and arrived there. Abram passed through the country as far as the holy place of Shechem, beside the oak of Moreh. The Canaanites were in the country at that time. Yahweh appeared to Abram and said, 'I shall give this country to your progeny.' And there, Abram built an altar to Yahweh who had appeared to him. From there he moved on to the mountainous district east of Bethel, where he pitched his tent, with Bethel to the west and Ai to the east. There he built an altar to Yahweh and invoked the name of Yahweh. Then Abram made his way stage by stage to the Negeb. There was a famine in the country and so Abram went down to Egypt to stay there for a time, since the famine in the country was severe. [Genesis 12:5–10]

Abraham in Egypt

Abram's people crossed northern Sinai, driving their flocks before them, and entered the eastern delta in 1853 BC. There they found a rich, fertile land of deep alluvium, dissected by the main Pelusiac and Tanitic Nile branches and numerous canals. This was the district of Kesen (the biblical Goshen of the Massoretic text and 'Gesem of Arabia' of the Septuagint), where the summer palace of Pharaoh was located at *Hat-Rowaty-Khety* ('the house of the two ways of King Khety'). This small royal estate would later grow into the vast Asiatic city of Avaris – the place where the events of Exodus would be played out to their dramatic conclusion. But in 1853 BC all that was here was the summer palace of Pharaoh Nebkaure Khety IV, sixteenth ruler of the 10th (Heracleopolitan) Dynasty which had originated from the Faiyum region.

As a foreign tribal chieftain of some stature, Abram, the Hebrew leader, was expected to pay his respects to the Egyptian king upon the latter's arrival from the dynastic capital at EHNAS to spend the summer months at his delta residence. At the audience, Pharaoh was immediately struck by the beauty of the woman accompanying the foreign dignitaries. Abram, in fear for his own safety, did not divulge that the woman was none other than his own wife. Instead he informed the king that Sarai was his sister and soon found himself caught in a trap of his own making. Over the weeks that followed, Pharaoh's interest in the Hebrew beauty failed to wane as Abram had hoped. In the end Khety proposed that Sarai be given to him in marriage by way of a diplomatic gift. Abram could hardly refuse the wishes of the Egyptian sovereign, the gracious host to his beleaguered people, and so his wife was taken to the royal harem to be prepared for her new role as queen of Egypt.

As the months passed, Egypt too began to suffer from a series of climatic disasters beyond anything experienced before. The Egyptians themselves referred to these times as 'painful years of distress' and 'years of misery'. First the summer was blisteringly hot and prolonged. Animals and people succumbed in their thousands as a shroud of suffocating air clung to the Nile valley. The winter months provided little relief. The burning sun continued to oppress the population. Royalty and commoner suffered in equal measure. Then the Asiatic plague reached Egypt and began to sweep through the land.

> But Yahweh inflicted severe plagues on Pharaoh and his entire household because of Abram's wife Sarai.
> [Genesis 12:17]

Finally, the following year, the spring rains in Ethiopia failed and, as a result, the Nile inundation was the lowest in memory. Famine and insurrection loomed.

King Khety summoned his advisers to counsel him on a remedy for the plague and to seek ways to appease the gods who had clearly been angered by something. With some trepidation, one of the palace courtiers hesitatingly informed his master that he had heard a disturbing rumour. Sarai, Pharaoh's new queen, was not what she appeared to be. Ever since the marriage, her reticence to share Pharaoh's bed had been a cause for concern but the king was so much in love with his Hebrew queen that he found it difficult not to accept her every excuse. But now the courtier offered a damning reason for the behaviour of Khety's reluctant bride. She was already the wife of the tribal chieftain of the Hebrew refugees. The priests were quick to suggest that the continuing displeasure of the gods might be due to Pharaoh's dishonour in taking another man's wife as his own. Khety was mortified at the sin he had unwittingly committed. Sarai was brought before the court and commanded to deny the rumour. She could not. Abram was then arrested and, realising all was revealed, confessed to his deception, pleading that he had only acted out of fear of Pharaoh's power and majesty.

Khety was no violent despot. Indeed, he was one of the wisest and most venerated rulers of his age – as the famous surviving words of advice to his son and successor, Merykare, testify.

> May you be justified before God, that people may say that you punish to suit the crime. To be of good nature is heavenly, whilst cursing brings only pain. … Do not be evil. Kindness is good. Make the remembrance of you last through the love of you. … A fool is he who covets what others possess. Life on Earth passes – it is not long. … Is there anyone who lives forever?
>
> Strong is the king who has councillors. And wealthy is he who is rich in nobles. Speak the truth in your palace, so that the administrators of the land respect you. … Beware of punishing wrongfully. Do not kill – it does not serve you. … Do not take the life of a man whose virtues you know – a man who was brought up before God.
>
> Do not execute one who is close to you, whom you have favoured. … Make yourself loved by everyone. A person who is good of character is remembered long after his time on Earth has passed.
> [*Instructions to Merykare*]

Realising that to execute Abram and the much-loved Sarai would do nothing to placate God, and instead might well anger him further by compounding the sin, the king wisely, and with some compassion, chose to banish his deceivers from Egypt, returning the Hebrews to the famine-torn northern lands whence they had come.

So Pharaoh summoned Abram and said, 'What is this you have done to me? Why did you not tell me she was your wife? Why did you say, 'She is my sister' so that I took her to be my wife? Now, here is your wife. Take her and go!' And Pharaoh gave his people orders concerning him and they sent him on his way with his wife and all his possessions. [Genesis 12:18–20]

And so the Children of Yahweh left Egypt – for the first time – and re-entered the Promised Land, once more in search of a place to settle amongst the multitudes struggling for existence in the parched hills of the southern Levant.

Behold the impotent Asiatic, he is wretched because of the situation in which he finds himself: short of water, without wood, whose paths are many and painful because of mountains. He does not dwell in one place because the search for food forces him to move on. He has been in conflict since the time of Horus, not conquering nor being conquered. ... Do not concern yourself with him. [*Instructions to Mery-kare*]

Throughout the time since the Hebrews had left Harran and migrated southwards into Egypt and then the hill country, Abram had been accompanied by his nephew, Lot. He had brought with him his own extended family and followers amounting to a small tribe in their own right. Both tribes had large herds of sheep and goats which began to be the cause of friction as the animals competed for the limited grazing land in the hill country. And so Lot's clan chose to separate from Abram and create a new life for themselves in the rich landscape of the Jordan valley. Abram's tribe remained on the plateau centred on the small village of Hebron, thirty kilometres south of the fortified town of Shalem.

Lot and his followers eventually pitched their tents in the vale of Siddim – a fertile stretch of coastline bordering the west side of the Salt Sea (today's Dead Sea), near the oasis of EN-GEDI and where the city of Sodom was located.

War Against the Five Kings

Some years after Abram had resettled in the hill country he was sitting beneath the oak of Mamre, near Hebron, when a group of exhausted refugees brought news of a great battle in the Jordan valley. Four powerful rulers of Mesopotamia had led a mighty army on a raid to subdue the Amorite and Amalekite cities around the southern shore of the Salt Sea. For twelve years the city rulers of the Arabah (to the south of the Salt Sea) and the Negeb had paid tribute to the Elamite king Kutir-Lagamar, the loyal vassal and 'tax collector' of Amar-Sin (1834–1826 BC), third monarch of the Ur III Dynasty, son of Shulgi, and supreme ruler of Mesopotamia at this time. But the cities and tribes of the south then decided that they would no longer pay tribute to their distant overlords. As one they revolted. A year later they found themselves facing annihilation before the weapons of a great Mesopotamian expeditionary force.

Amar-Sin (biblical Amraphel, king of Shinar) was not the first in line to succeed to the throne of Ur. There had been much unrest in the land because of famine. One of Amar-Sin's ambitious brothers saw his opportunity to grab the reins of power whilst the people blamed the king for bringing the wrath of the gods upon them. The scheming prince had his father, Shulgi, murdered whilst the old king was praying at the tomb of the dynasty founder, Ur-nammu. But Amar-Sin quickly put an end to his sibling rival and seized the throne. Again this bloody palace coup was recorded in a lunar eclipse omen.

> The omen is given for Ur and its king. The king of Ur will experience famine. There will be many

deaths. The king of Ur will be wronged by his son. Shamash (the sun-god) will catch him. The king will die in the place of his father's mourning. The king's son who was not named for the kingship will seize the throne. [*Enuma Anu Enlil*, Tablet 20]

The date of the lunar eclipse was 31st July 1835 BC.

Amar-Sin could call upon his vassal rulers for military assistance at any time. Indeed, the Elamites of Susa were commissioned to police the empire on behalf of their Sumerian overlord in Ur. The unruly Amorite tribes of the north had long been threatening the stability of the Ur III empire. This blatant refusal by their southern cousins to pay tribute turned out to be the final insult. The new Sumerian emperor decided to put an end to the irritation once and for all. Preparations were set in train to gather together the largest military force the ancient world had yet seen. In addition to the five-thousand-strong standing army of Sumer, Zariku governor of Ashur (biblical [Z]arioch of Ellasar), despatched a thousand troops, Kutir-Lagamar of Susa (biblical Chedor-La[g]omer of Elam) brought with him a thousand spearmen and five hundred archers, and Tishadal of Urkish (biblical Ti[sha]dal, king of the nations) supplied two thousand five hundred of his fiercest warriors from the Hurrian tribal confederacy of the Zagros mountains [Genesis 14:1–3].

In 1833 BC this powerful invading army of ten thousand marched down the King's Highway along the heights of Transjordan, through the land of Moab, and descended, via the deep gorge of the River Karak, onto the south-east shore of the Salt Sea and into the great rift valley of the Arabah. The four kings and their confederate forces then fell upon the city of Bela (later called Zoar), leaving its walls toppled and the houses burnt to the ground. The panic-stricken rulers and citizens of the other cities of the northern Arabah fled westwards, around the southern shore of the Salt Sea, to the vale or plain of Siddim, where they pleaded to be taken into the strong-walled city of Sodom. In the meantime the Mesopotamian army went on a protracted rampage of death and destruction in the Negeb before turning north and heading for the rebel kings holed up in their last remaining stronghold. The five rulers of the plain marched their remaining forces out to meet the four rulers of Mesopotamia for the decisive battle.

The two armies met on the west shore of the Salt Sea just to the south of Sodom and fought a prolonged and bloody battle amidst the bitumen pits of the Salt Sea basin. King Bera of Sodom and King Birsha of Gomorrah were slain and cast into the bitumen pits; the rulers of Admah, Zeboim and Bela fled into the hills via the rock cleft at En-Gedi and reached Abram in Mamre by nightfall. Amongst the refugees were some of Lot's kinfolk who had seen Abram's nephew and their tribal chieftain taken captive by Mesopotamian soldiers. It was common practice for prisoners of war to be taken home by the victors for selling into chattel slavery. Abraham knew that he had to save Lot and, that night, summoned three hundred and eighteen of his best fighting men to the oak tree near Hebron.

For several days Abram's guerrilla force shadowed the Mesopotamian army on its victorious return march north up the Jordan valley. Then, one night, when the rearguard marshalling the captives of war was camped near the town of Laish (later renamed Dan), Abram made his move. A daring raid by his small band of followers took the guards completely by surprise. The latter had been celebrating victory over the cities of the plain for days and, as a consequence, were in no fit state to resist a determined assault in the dead of night. The Mesopotamian soldiers, in their drunken stupor, were quickly despatched and the captives released. Abram and the rescued deportees slipped back into the darkness before the alarm could be raised in the main army camp a few kilometres to the north.

On his return to Hebron Abram passed by Mount Moriah and the city of Shalem at its foot. There, in the valley of Shaveh, he was met by the son and successor of Sodom's unfortunate ruler who had succumbed in the slime pits and Melchizedek, king of Shalem. This is our first introduction to the place which would become the heart of the Israelite nation – the city of Jerusalem – for Uru-Shalem means the 'city of Shalem'.

The Destruction of Sodom

Following his rescue by Abram from deportation to Mesopotamia, Lot returned to the land he had chosen as his home in the great Jordan rift valley. But recent events had left him feeling insecure. Living the nomadic way of life out in the fields and open pasture lands was no longer safe in a world of marauding armies and intercity conflicts. His clan had survived one attempt to enslave them in a distant foreign land and he was not about to make the people vulnerable to capture again. Lot and his tribe therefore chose to give up their pastoralist ways and start a new life as city-dwellers, acquiring houses within the strong walls of the city of Sodom.

Sodom was situated on the west shore of the Salt Sea, just south of the spring at En-Gedi. Here a small, fertile plain extended out into the waters where the deep gorge of the Nahal Hever brings winter rainwater down from the high plateau (which we know today as the hill country of Palestine). Sodom was a prosperous, well-fortified settlement which gained its wealth by mining black pitch from the local bitumen quarries. Like many a mining town, the population was tough and resilient. The men worked hard in stifling conditions and played hard at night between their shifts in the slime pits.

There had been a settlement here in the vale of Siddim for centuries. The magnificent copper hoard found in the cave at Nahal Mishmar came from the temple of Sodom dated to late Chalcolithic times (*c.* 2800 BC). It had been buried during an earlier crisis when the city was attacked and destroyed, the priests no longer alive to retrieve their hidden treasure. Sodom had risen from the ashes to be rebuilt on an even grander scale. It was this Early Bronze Age city which provided protection for Lot and his kin.

Even in the driest periods, when the climate in the rest of the southern rift valley was so harsh that life was almost impossible to sustain, the vale of Siddim enjoyed oasis-like conditions. The En-Gedi spring, just a couple of kilometres away, provided ample fresh water, year round, and succulent dates from its thick canopy of palms. Many wild animals congregated near the spring and were a constant supply of fresh meat for the Sodomites, whilst the valuable bitumen was traded for any other material comforts, such as linen and wool garments, which the people desired. Even after the fall of its king, at the hands of the four kings of Mesopotamia, Sodom continued to prosper. Then in the summer of 1830 BC disaster struck once more. This time the outcome would see the final end of the city of Sodom.

For days there had been warnings of what was to come. Minor earth tremors had shaken the town. Men had been killed in the slime pits as quarry walls collapsed. The level of the Salt Sea had suddenly dropped several metres. Most of the townsfolk ignored the signs, having experienced similar things before in this land of shifting earth. They took great comfort in the belief that their strong city, built on its deep stone foundations, would survive the shaking ground as it had always done in the past. How misguided this overconfidence would turn out to be.

Lot, on the other hand, was a newcomer to Sodom and his pastoralist instinct was to escape the confines of the city and seek refuge in the hills of Transjordan. Lot's immediate family left Sodom and headed for Zoar (a small settlement rebuilt on the ruins of Bela) – today the archaeological site of Bab ed-Drah, located at the foot of the gorge through which the River Karak flows. The decision to leave Sodom was made just in time. As they hurried across the salt basin of the Lisan peninsula, south of the Salt Sea, the

Earth let out a mighty roar to herald the onslaught of the infamous and legendary cataclysm.

The great geological rift which extends along the Jordan valley, through the Arabah and on down the Gulf of Akaba into the Red Sea, convulsed in a final terrifying spasm. Giant fissures opened up, swallowing the cultivated fields and orchards. Liquid sulphur from the bowels of the Earth was ejected a thousand feet into the air, raining down as 'fire and brimstone' onto the cities of Sodom and Gomorrah. The citizens were either asphyxiated or burnt alive in their tightly packed homes. Sulphur balls from this awe-inspiring fireworks display can still be picked up in the region today. The vale of Siddim collapsed as its earthly foundations disappeared from under the fertile soil. The earth literally dissolved as subterranean water was sucked up to the surface (the modern geological term for this phenomenon, commonly associated with earthquakes, is liquefaction). The Salt Sea rushed over the land and engulfed Sodom's burning ruins. This infamous place, whose very name is synonymous with acts of debauchery, slid beneath the bubbling waters where it remains to this day, just a little over one hundred metres beneath the surface of the Dead Sea, which is itself – at four hundred metres below sea level – the lowest spot on this Earth.

The Sons of Abram

During all their years together, Abram and Sarai had been childless as a couple. But then, when she was believed to be past childbearing, Sarai gave birth to a healthy boy. This was very much regarded as a gift from God. The child was named ISAAC. However, Isaac was not Abram's first or only son. Whilst Abram had been in Egypt he acquired a female servant as part of the gift exchange with Pharaoh Khety. This girl had been given the name Hagar by her new master and assigned to Sarai's service when the Hebrews departed from Egypt.

> Thus after Abram had lived in the land of Canaan for ten years, Sarai took Hagar, her Egyptian servant, and gave her to Abram as his wife. He went to Hagar and she conceived. [Genesis 16:3-4]

So, in 1842 BC, several years before the birth of Isaac, Hagar had become Abram's concubine and had borne him a son, named ISHMAEL. But, with the birth of Sarai's son in 1829 BC, there was a new heir to Abram's property who, as the child of the tribal chieftain's principal wife, outranked Ishmael both in status and inheritance. Over the ensuing years tension between the two mothers grew to such a degree that an open conflict was inevitable.

Eventually, Sarai concluded that, whilst Ishmael and his Egyptian mother remained in the camp, her own son's inheritance was under threat. She went to Abram and, in a fit of jealousy, demanded that Hagar and Ishmael be banished from the tribe and sent as far away as possible. No-one was going to undermine her position as principal wife and her son's status as heir. With a heavy heart, Abram agreed to Sarai's wishes and sent his eldest son away.

Hagar and Ishmael headed south via Beer-Sheba to the Desert of Paran in Sinai where they settled. Ishmael married an Egyptian wife and went on, as tradition has it, to father twelve sons who, in turn, became the eponymous founders of twelve tribes (just as would happen later with Jacob and the twelve tribes of Israel). Ishmael is recognised in Arabian folklore as the founder of the 'Arab nation'.

This episode of the banishment of Isaac's half-brother would soon repeat itself as Sarai once again ruthlessly chose to eliminate her son's perceived rivals. Abram had a second concubine named Keturah who bore him six sons. At Sarai's insistence, she too was sent away with all her sons. Supplied with provisions, and under the protection of a loyal band of retainers, this second group of exiles from the Abramic inheritance headed eastwards into Transjordan, where they became the ancestral tribal heads of

Midian in north-west Arabia. These Midianites were to play a major role in re-establishing the cultural heritage of Israel following the period of bondage in Egypt – but that is still in the distant future when they become part of the story surrounding the life of Moses. Here, in the time of the first great patriarch, Abram, the heritage of the sons of Hagar and Keturah was taken from them because of the ambitions of a jealous mother for her only son. The schism between those traditional, lifelong enemies – the Arabs and Jews – began here with a family squabble over the division of property.

A Sacrifice Too Far

Life in the ancient Bronze Age was often brutal and bloody. Nature itself reigned blow after blow down on the unfortunate inhabitants of the Earth – violent storms, floods, prolonged heat waves, plagues, famines, earthquakes. The way the people chose to deal with this violent world in which they lived was constantly to placate the gods with sacrifices in the hope that the series of disasters would abate. As we have witnessed, the time of Abram was particularly fraught with widespread famine and plague. And, in this desperate atmosphere, drastic measures were often called upon to ensure survival. To convince your god that you were unwavering in your loyalty and devotion, only a great personal sacrifice would suffice. And the greatest sacrifice of all was to offer your god the thing that meant most to you – your eldest son and heir. So the institution of the sacrifice of the firstborn came into being during these difficult times.

This truly misguided practice, originally born out of desperation, continued in use for more than a thousand years. During city sieges, eldest sons would be tossed from the battlements in the vain hope that the local god would witness this ultimate act of allegiance and come to the aid of his city [Ashkelon Wall at Karnak and 2 Kings 3:27]. In

Phoenician Late Bronze Age Ugarit the sacrifice of children by fire (the 'molok-sacrifice') was a form of El and Baal worship. The Israelite Judge Jephthah sacrificed his daughter to the fire in honour of Yahweh [Judges 11:30–31]. The kings of Judah – Ahaz and his grandson Manasseh – burnt their sons in a place of *molok*-sacrifice located in the Hinnom valley, just south of Jerusalem. In the time of the Israelite prophets Jeremiah and Ezekiel the same valley continued in use as the place where young children were assigned to the flames in the name of Yahweh and other idols – much to the prophets' abhorrence.

> Yes, the people of Judah have done what displeases me … and have built the high places of *tophet* in the valley of Ben-Hinnom, in order to burn their sons and daughters – a thing I [Yahweh] never commanded and which had never entered my thoughts. [Jeremiah 7:30–31]

Phoenician Carthage (founded in 825 BC) contains a large cemetery, also known as the *tophet*, which was entirely dedicated to the immolated remains of thousands of small children. In the palace of Knossos on Crete archaeologists even found the bones of children which clearly showed cut-marks from knives – the telltale signs of ritual sacrifice and cannibalism. And, of course, we all recollect the sacrifice of Agamemnon's beautiful daughter, Iphigenia, before the Achaean fleet set off across the Aegean Sea to Troy. The story of how the Israelites were supposed to have given up this practice of human sacrifice in its early days is related in Genesis chapter 22.

One day, when Isaac was in his teenage years, Abram had a vision in which El demanded the ultimate sacrifice of him. The next day, with heavy heart, he loaded up donkeys with wood for the burnt offering and set off northwards to the designated place of sacrifice on Mount Moriah – a rocky outcrop overlooking the city of Shalem where

Abram's spiritual mentor, Melchizedek, ruled. After three days Abram, Isaac and their escort were standing on the ridge of Silwan with Mount Moriah before them across the vale of Kidron. The servants were instructed to wait there whilst Abram and Isaac went ahead to perform the offering to El. When father and son reached the stone altar where the sacrifice was to be made, Isaac realised that he was to be the burnt offering. There was no sign of sacrificial sheep or goat tethered at the summit. In an act of total devotion to his beloved father, Isaac allowed his hands to be bound and then quietly prepared himself by lying across the altar. No words were spoken between the sacrificer and his intended sacrifice. No words could express how either felt at this moment of supreme test of the loyalty of a devout worshipper to his only god and the loyalty of a son to his beloved father.

Just as Abram raised his bronze dagger above his head to perform the deed, he heard the sound of rustling nearby. Looking up, the old man saw a young ram caught by his horns in a thicket. Abram took this as a sign that the sacrifice of his son was no longer required. El had provided him with a substitute offering – a scapegoat. Isaac was released from his bonds and assisted his father in bringing the ram to the altar for sacrifice.

From this day forward the Children of Yahweh forbade the taking of human life on the sacrificial altar and only the firstborn of the animals were chosen for offering to the god of the mountains.

The Burial Cave of Machpelah

Soon after Isaac had attained his manhood, his mother, Sarai, died. Abram purchased a cave in Kiriath-Arba (later called Hebron) from Ephron, an Anatolian migrant who owned the field known as Machpelah, and there he buried his wife. The cave of Machpelah, today, lies beneath the ancient mosque at the heart of Hebron.

In the two centuries following Sarai's burial, her tomb became the final resting place of the leading figures in Abram's patriarchal family. Abram himself was laid to rest in the cave. Many years later the tomb was opened twice again, to receive the bodies of Isaac and Rebecca. Finally, the third 'generation' of Abram's line – in the form of the mummified body of the patriarch Jacob – was brought out of Egypt for burial in the family tomb at Kiriath-Arba. There Jacob joined his first wife Leah, whom he had buried, twenty years earlier, before departing for Egypt. With the burial of Jacob, the cave of Machpelah was sealed for the final time. But that was all in the unknown and distant future as we find Abram's servant heading back to the Hebrews' original homeland in search of a wife for his master's son and heir.

A Bride for Isaac

The loyal servant arrived at the town of Harran in the land of ARAM-NAHARAIM. There he visited the household of Bethuel – Abram's nephew, the son of Nahor (Abram's brother) and Milcah. Negotiations were conducted between Abram's representative and Bethuel's eldest son, Laban, for his sister's hand in marriage to Isaac. In due course, Rebecca, daughter of Bethuel, and her female servants set off south into Canaan to join her uncle's tribe.

So, as would be the custom in years to come, the heir to the Hebrew inheritance married a daughter of the city of Harran in north Syria. These close ties to Abram's native land were only to break down during the years of bondage in the Nile valley when Hebrew males were forbidden to leave the Black Land by their Egyptian masters.

The Death of Abraham

Finally, after a long and fruitful life, Abram breathed his last and was laid to rest in the cave which he had purchased from Ephron, son of Zohar, many years earlier for the burial of Sarai. The stone blocking the tomb entrance was removed and Isaac gathered up the bones of his mother, placing them at the side to make room for his father's burial. In the year 1815 BC Abram's body was carried into the cave by his two sons Isaac and Ishmael, assisted by those sons of Keturah who were close enough to attend the funeral. The tomb was then resealed to await the next Hebrew leader destined to sleep with his ancestors.

Chapter Seven

THE ROAD TO BONDAGE

(Genesis 25:19 to Genesis 37:36)

*Esau and Jacob – Jacob in Mesopotamia – The Return
to Canaan – Joseph and his Brothers*

The death of Abraham heralded yet another period
of uncertainty for the Children of Yahweh, with
further hardship brought on by famine and disputes over the tribal heritage. The stories of the lives of
Isaac and Jacob were set in an era of political transition
throughout the Fertile Crescent.

In the Land of the Two Rivers the picture was one of
collapse and slow recovery. The Ur III empire of Abraham's time had slowly disintegrated under hyperinflation
and revolt amongst its subject nations. The reign of the ill-
starred Ibbi-Sin, fifth ruler of Ur, had come to an ignominious end with the king's deportation to Elam. The
Sumerian dynasty of Ur was succeeded by two royal houses
bearing Semitic names, ruling contemporaneously from
the cities of Isin and Larsa. The Amorites of northern Mesopotamia were becoming ever more powerful. To the south

127

of Canaan, in the valley of the Nile, a new dynasty – the 12th – was beginning its 163-year rule.*

Beyond Egypt's borders, to the north, a contest of rights and inheritance was taking place amongst the Amorite Hebrew clans and, in particular, within the family nucleus of Abraham's descendants.

Birthright

Isaac, now head of the clan, had fathered twin sons – Esau and Jacob – through his principal wife, Rebecca, the sister of Laban of Harran. The elder twin, Esau, was a strong, muscular man whose great passion was hunting and adventuring. Jacob, on the other hand, was very close to his mother, Rebecca, and tended to remain in the tribal encampment. The contrast between the two brothers was marked, and their parents' affections gradually gravitated to the two personalities, Isaac favouring the gregarious Esau and Rebecca mothering the reserved Jacob. Isaac himself had gone blind as old age took its hold. He loved both his sons (now in their late thirties) but, following tradition, intended the older Esau as his heir. Rebecca, on the other hand, had quite different ambitions. She plotted to have her favourite son succeed to the chieftainship and therefore the tribal inheritance. Her plan was to fool her blind husband into proclaiming Jacob as his heir. In the ancient world

---

* The 12th Dynasty founder, Sehetepibre Amenemhat (Manetho's Ammanemes I), was not directly connected by blood to the preceding line of pharaohs – most of which had carried the birth-name Montuhotep. He had been the vizier of Nebtawyre Montuhotep IV – the best that could be said of whom was that he was the 'nominal ruler' during a seven-year period of anarchy and political turmoil. The last of the 11th Dynasty Montuhoteps passed away without heir in 1804 BC. Amenemhat's powerful position in the royal court ensured that he was the candidate best placed to succeed to the throne. The Black Land had a strong, new pharaoh and a fresh royal bloodline which would be responsible for overseeing a remarkable renaissance in Egyptian civilisation following the impoverished decades of the post Old Kingdom collapse.

a promise was a promise and could not be broken. If Isaac chose Jacob to succeed him – even under false pretences – then this would become set in stone and Esau would forfeit his birthright to his younger brother.

Realising that he was nearing his end, Isaac asked Esau to hunt down a gazelle and serve the game to him as he had done many times before. It was Isaac's favourite meal and he wanted to use the occasion to give Esau the blessing which would formally recognise his eldest son as his successor. The carefree Esau happily set off into the hills to do his father's bidding. In the meantime Rebecca dressed Jacob in Esau's clothes and instructed her son to go to Isaac's tent with the kid-goat stew which she had already prepared. The pretender served the meal to the blind old man and, thinking that it was Esau before him, Isaac conferred the tribal inheritance upon his younger son.

Upon Esau's return the deceit was uncovered but, by then, it was too late. Once again a Hebrew mother had manipulated her powerful husband into ensuring her favourite son's status in the tribe. Isaac's chieftainship had been the product of his mother Sarah's ambitions and now Rebecca had connived to raise her younger son to Jacob's inheritance above that of her elder son and rightful heir. It was not a fortunate thing to be a Hebrew patriarch's eldest son – none became tribal leader. Ishmael's rights were superseded by the birth of Isaac; Esau was usurped by Jacob; and, as we will soon see, Jacob's eldest son, Reuben, relinquished his leadership of the Hebrew tribe to a much younger half-brother named Joseph.

In Search of Wives

As one might imagine, his own brother's trickery in seizing the inheritance did not go down well with Esau. Needless to say, Isaac was also very disenchanted with his younger son. The old man dismissed Jacob from the camp and bade him go north, back to the ancestral homelands in Paddam-

Aram (the region around Harran). This exile from the tribe was not only to punish him for his deceit but also for Jacob to find himself a wife from within his mother's family.

When Jacob eventually reached the house of Laban (son of Nahor and brother of his mother Rebecca) he was immediately attracted to Laban's youngest daughter, Rachel. But, as custom required, the eldest daughter in the household must be married before her younger siblings. So, after living and working for the Harran tribe for a number of years, Jacob married Leah ('cow') and then, soon after, took Rachel ('sheep') as his second wife.

All in all Jacob remained in Paddam-Aram for fourteen years, in which time Leah bore him six sons – Reuben, Simeon, Levi, Judah, Issachar and Zebulun. As was the custom at that time, the wives of tribal leaders and heads of households usually possessed maid servants or slave girls to help them with the chores. Leah's servant-girl, given to her by her father Laban, was named Zilpah. She, as Jacob's chattel and concubine, also bore him two sons – Gad and Asher. Rachel on the other hand gave birth to just two sons – Joseph and Benjamin, whilst her slave-girl, Bilhah, provided Jacob with another two – Dan and Naphtali. So, Leah's side of the tribe consisted of eight sons and Rachel's four. Twelve sons whose names would be forever remembered as the eponymous ancestors of the tribes of Israel.

After all the years of exile had passed, Jacob, his wives and sons, left Laban's tribe and headed back south to Canaan and Isaac's encampment.

Rape and Revenge

On the way Jacob's caravan passed through the territory of SHECHEM just as Abraham had done many years earlier. The people of the town were friendly towards their guests and so Jacob bought the piece of land outside the city wall where he had set up his tent. The Hebrews remained in Shechem for a month and Jacob built a stone altar dedicated to EL-SHADDAI which he enclosed in an open courtyard. At the heart of the plot he had acquired was the old oak tree under which Abraham had rested. Centuries later this same spot would witness the erecting of a mighty white stone before which Joshua and the victorious Israelite tribes would swear their covenant with Yahweh following the conquest of the Promised Land. Nearby, the patriarch Joseph, having been removed from his Egyptian tomb, would be buried by his descendants.

Now Jacob also had a daughter by Leah named Dinah. She was a pretty teenager who turned many a male head. Shechem, the son of the local chieftain Hamor, was immediately captivated by the Hebrew girl and began to court her in secret. Shechem's passion soon led to sexual relations which came to the attention of Dinah's father Jacob. The patriarch's sons were away in the hills tending to their flocks and so the aged Jacob could do nothing immediately to avenge the dishonour to his household. In the meantime, Shechem went to Hamor and begged his father to ask Jacob for Dinah's hand in marriage. The two went to Jacob's tent following the return of the Hebrew men to the town and, together, they parleyed. But Jacob's sons were just biding their time. Having learnt of Shechem's infidelity with their virgin sister, they only had bloody revenge on their minds.

The price demanded of Hamor for their consent to the marriage was that all the Canaanite men of the town should be circumcised so that they were ritually clean and therefore able to take Hebrew women as their wives. That way the two tribes could join and prosper.

> To give our sister to an uncircumcised man would be a disgrace for us. We can only agree on one condition – that you become like us by circumcising all of your males. Then we will give you our daughters, taking yours for ourselves, and we will stay with you to make one nation. [Genesis 34:14–16]

Hamor, accepting these words in good faith, conveyed the proposal to the elders at the city gate where such matters were discussed. The Canaanites agreed to the terms and all their young men, including Shechem, underwent the painful operation. Three days later, when the Shechemites were still weak and recovering from their ordeal, the sons of Jacob went into the town and slaughtered them all. Hamor and his son were put to the sword and Dinah removed from the household of her murdered husband. The town was pillaged and all the animals seized. Every house was systematically looted and the women and children taken into slavery. Overnight the Hebrews became hated and feared by the local population in the northern hill country – an enmity which lasted for centuries and even survives today in the hearts and minds of the modern Shechemites of what is now the town of Nablus.

The bloodstained clothes of the Hebrew executioners were burnt before they left the scene of the crime and moved on southwards to Luz. There Jacob erected a standing stone to his god El-shaddai, and so the name of the place was changed to Bethel – the 'House of God'. Jacob himself also took another name. From now on he was to be known as Isra-El – 'may El be strong' – the epithet by which the Israelite nation would identify itself down to the present day.

As yet Jacob's last son was still in his mother's womb. Soon after leaving Bethel Rachel went into labour and died giving birth to Benjamin. She was buried on the road to Ephrath, subsequently renamed BETHLEHEM – the birth-place, seventeen centuries later, of Joshua, son of Joseph and Mary, the Christian Messiah now known as Jesus.

Finally, having reconciled with his brother Esau, who had settled and made a new life for himself in the land of Edom, Jacob arrived home in Kiriath-Arba (Hebron) and made peace with his dying father Isaac. The old man was laid to rest by his two sons in the cave of Machpelah alongside the bones of Isaac's father, Abraham.

A Coat of Many Colours

Joseph was the eleventh of Jacob's twelve sons and, to all intents, a rather precious and arrogant teenager. He was his father's favourite because he was the eldest of Rachel's two sons and, following her death, the living reminder of the patriarch's beloved wife. Joseph's elder brothers were constantly reminded of this when they witnessed their sibling sporting the fabulous multicoloured coat which Jacob had presented to Joseph when the boy had reached his sixteenth birthday.

The 'coat-of-many-colours' is legendary – instantly recognised and instantly associated with Joseph. There was no other garment like it – not in value, for it was neither richly adorned in jewels nor interlaced with golden twine. It was a straightforward woollen overcoat but elaborately woven in dyed threads of red, black and cream. Dazzling to the eye it may have been, but this prized possession was also the visible symbol of jealousy and rivalry amongst the third 'generation' descended from Abraham.

One day, in Joseph's seventeenth year, the teenager was sent from his father's camp in Hebron to the territory surrounding the town of Shechem where his elder brothers had returned to pasture their flocks. When the brothers heard that Joseph was on his way to them, they decided to rid themselves of him once and for all. They argued amongst themselves as to what they should actually do with their obnoxious sibling. Some wanted Joseph to meet with an unfortunate accident, but Reuben could not bring himself to kill the boy and persuaded the rest to sell him to a passing band of Midianite traders who were on their way down into Egypt. With Joseph heading off into a life of slavery in the land of the pharaohs, Jacob's sons returned to their father to break the terrible news that his favourite son had disappeared. Jacob was handed Joseph's multi-coloured coat, torn and soaked in blood.

Jacob mourned for many weeks, inconsolable at his

loss and distraught at not being able to bury his beloved son. The rest of the tribe continued to eke out a meagre existence in the dry hills around Hebron, but their leader was no longer the man he had been, remaining for the most part in his tent, reluctant to attend to the daily affairs of the tribe or have any dealings with his other sons.

> Tearing his clothes and putting sackcloth around his waist, Jacob mourned his son for many days. All his sons and daughters tried to comfort him, but he refused to be comforted. 'No,' he said 'I will go down to the underworld (Sheol) in mourning and join my son.' Thus his father wept for him. [Genesis 37:34–35]

Chapter Eight

JOSEPH
VIZIER OF EGYPT

(Genesis 39:1 to Genesis 50:26)

*Enslavement in Egypt – Joseph's Pharaoh –
The Egyptian Famine – Hebrews in Goshen – Joseph's
Palace – Joseph's Egyptian Tomb*

e now come to what is perhaps the richest and most detailed biography in the Old Testament – the life and times of Joseph son of Jacob – the Hebrew slave who rose to the exalted status of vizier and right-hand man to the Egyptian pharaoh, Amenemhat III, greatest ruler of the 12th Dynasty.

Joseph the Slave

In the hill country of Canaan Jacob remained in seclusion within his tent, looking after his youngest child, Benjamin, whilst his older sons ranged over the inhospitable terrain in search of grazing ground for their flocks. In the meantime, the Midianites had crossed northern Sinai and arrived in the eastern delta of Egypt. There they sold Joseph on – to the country estate of Podipare (biblical Potiphar), a military commander in the army of Re (the sun-god) based at the city of IONA. He was also the high priest of the temple of the Ben Ben stone in the same city and governor of the state prison in Memphis. Joseph became a domestic servant in Podipare's summer mansion where, by gaining the trust and admiration of his owner through displays of wisdom and loyalty, he quickly rose to the position of senior steward.

The lady of Podipare's household, Nofret, was much younger than her husband and, as is often the case with young women who marry wealthy older men, she had become bored and self-indulgent. Over the next three years, Nofret developed an infatuation for the handsome Hebrew slave and eventually began to pursue him. But, always loyal to his master, Joseph rejected her advances and the scorned woman's passion soon turned to calculating hate. Nofret went to her husband, accusing Joseph of attempted rape. Podipare, knowing his wife well, was not convinced of his servant's guilt, but an Egyptian lady's honour had been besmirched and justice had to be seen to be done.

Normally, the punishment for such crime was execution, however Podipare ensured that Joseph's life was spared. Even so, the young man was incarcerated in the Great Prison in Memphis. There he stayed for nine years, once again gaining the trust of the guards and so being placed in charge of the work details. In the seventh year of his jail sentence he befriended two disgraced court officials who had been sent to prison by Pharaoh for a period of 'correction'. Like Podipare before them, the baker Ankhtify and cup-bearer Meketre immediately recognised the wisdom and talent in the young Hebrew. And so they came to Joseph with stories of dreams which they asked him to interpret for them. The interpretation of dreams was commonly practised in the ancient world, for it was believed that each man's destiny was written in the stars and in the twilight world of dreams. The two courtiers soon recognised that Joseph was a master of the art.

The Hebrew soothsayer predicted that the cup-bearer would be released from prison and restored to his position as trusted servant of Pharaoh but that the baker would meet his end at the orders of this same pharaoh. And so, in due course, it happened. Unfortunately, Meketre soon forgot the friend who had interpreted his dream so favourably and Joseph continued to languish in the Great Prison for a further two years.

Interpreting Pharaoh's Dream

Meketre's lord and master was Pharaoh Nimaatre Amenemhat III (1678–1635 BC). But Amenemhat was not the only pharaoh on the throne at this time. For twelve years he had been the coregent of his father, Khakaure Senuseret III, who had begun his reign thirty-one years earlier in 1698 BC. It had become royal policy during the 12th Dynasty for the senior pharaoh to take his son in coregency ever since the assassination of the dynasty founder, Amenemhat I (1803–1774 BC). The latter had been murdered by members of his own court whilst the crown prince (subsequently Senuseret I) was campaigning in Libya. The prince rushed back to Memphis just in time to put down the attempted *coup d'état* and secure his throne ... but it was a close-run thing.

From that day forth, the Middle Kingdom pharaohs ensured a smooth succession by the expediency of dual monarchy. After the king had ruled for a number of years and established his credentials as an able monarch, he would crown his eldest son as joint ruler, handing over the duties of supreme commander of the army and administrator of the affairs of state following a period of transition. The senior king (in age) would then quietly pass into what can only be described as semi-retirement to enjoy his new status as semi-divine father of the nation ('Horus the Elder'), whilst his virile son fought the battles and governed the land on his behalf ('Horus the Younger').

This rather efficient and more secure form of monarchy required two royal households. The old palace in Memphis was retained as the residence of the senior monarch whilst a new royal residence was built at ITJ-TAWY in Middle Egypt. There, overlooking the new royal capital (now buried under the modern village of LISHT) the first two rulers of the 12th Dynasty erected their pyramids. Later kings constructed their tombs near Itj-Tawy at the Old Kingdom necropolis of Dashur in the north and along the desert edge overlooking the Faiyum basin to the south.

The political and geographical landscape of the Nile valley had undergone considerable upheaval since the 'monumental' days of the Old Kingdom and its subsequent slide into anarchy. The winds of change had swept across the Black Land. Kings were no longer omnipotent – still semi-divine but somehow more down to earth. Their monuments were in keeping with an age of enlightenment brought on by the experiences of the First-Intermediate-Period collapse. Egypt had grown older and wiser. It had learnt how to exploit its blessings without exhausting them in massive royal building projects. There would be no more Great Pyramids.

Size became less important and perfection everything. An era of fine art, literature and poetry blossomed in the Middle Kingdom. This was the age of the DIDACTIC SCHOLAR – a time to learn from past experience. Some of ancient Egypt's most famous literature was written during the 12th Dynasty – 'The Instructions to King Merikare' from the words of Abraham's pharaoh, Khety IV (1876–1847 BC), was set down in writing at this time, and new works were composed such as 'Sinuhe', 'The Eloquent Peasant' and 'The Shipwrecked Sailor' – all masterpieces in didactic literature. What better era could be found to place the Bible's finest story of a young, arrogant boy who was cast into slavery by his own brothers, maturing through adversity into a man of great wisdom, and so rising to exalted rank simply by means of straightforward ability.

One day Pharaoh Nimaatre Amenemhat III summoned his advisers to tell them of a troubling dream which
he had experienced. He described to them how, in his
dream, seven fat cows had surfaced from the waters of the
Nile and climbed onto the bank where they began to eat
the long tufted grass. But then seven more cows – these
thin and emaciated – came up out of the river and began
to devour the fat cows on the shore. What did all this mean,
asked Pharaoh. His courtiers were baffled and perplexed.
Amongst them was the cup-bearer Meketre, who finally
remembered the young Hebrew slave languishing in the
state prison. This was the person to solve the riddle of
Pharaoh's dream.

Joseph was brought from the Great Prison in Memphis
to the royal palace at Itj-Tawy where he was prepared for
his audience with the king. He shaved off his beard (unlike
many of his kin, Joseph was clean-shaven for most of his
life) and then dressed himself in a new woven multicoloured
coat typical of his people. Joseph was ushered into the
presence of Amenemhat to render his interpretation of
Pharaoh's dream.

The Hebrew slave listened carefully to the king describing the seven fat cows being devoured by the seven
lean cows before confidently giving his diagnosis. The seven
fat cows represented seven years of plenty brought by a
series of high inundations of the Nile. This was the reason
why the seven cows had appeared from out of the waters
of the Nile, just as the flood waters rose out of the river to
inundate the banks. The cows represented the fertility of
Hapi, fecundity-god of the inundation, who brought rich
silt from the mountains of eastern Africa to enrichen the
Nile valley fields. The seven years of high floods had
already begun and, as all had witnessed, Egypt was reaping
the benefits with bumper harvests. However, things were
going to change. The seven lean cows which followed the
seven fat cows out of the Nile represented a period of even
higher Nile inundations which would devastate the land.

These floods would bring many times the usual amount of water from the south and the whole of Egypt would be drowned, killing the livestock and washing away the mud-brick villages. But, worst of all, the flood waters would take much longer to dissipate, so that the coming year's crops could not be sown at the proper time. The fields would still be under water in October and November. No planting meant no harvest and Egypt's granaries would lie empty. Starvation would spread throughout the land.

Seven Years of Plenty

Pharaoh's mood darkened. He instinctively knew that the Hebrew soothsayer was foretelling the truth and asked the young man for his advice as to how the worst consequences of the tragedy might be avoided. Joseph advised Amenemhat to tax the people in the years of plenty and set up a new department of state to administer the collection of one-fifth of all grain grown on the private estates. This grain must be stored in new state granaries to be built on the desert high ground, above the flood plain. Pharaoh must also immediately begin to construct a canal to divert the excess flood waters away from Lower Egypt and into the natural basin of the Faiyum oasis. That way he would protect both royal capitals, Itj-Tawy and Memphis, and save the delta farmlands which had become Egypt's most valuable grazing land.

The king was extremely impressed with the decisiveness of Joseph's words and immediately set him to the task of overseeing the strategy. The Hebrew was appointed as the chief administrator of a new grain taxation body known as the 'Department of the People's Giving' (Egyptian *kha-en-djed-remetj*). He was also made vizier and chief architect of the Faiyum canal project which, from then on, was known as the 'Waterway of Joseph' (Arabic *Bahr Yussef*).

Joseph was reunited with his old master Podipare, who quickly offered his own daughter, YASENAT, in marriage to the servant who had now become *his* master. Yasenat bore Joseph two sons named Manasseh and Ephraim. They set up home in the eastern delta in the district of PA-KES. How different Joseph's new life was to the days spent as a boy wandering the hills of Canaan with his sheep and goats or the time spent languishing in Egypt's state prison.

The next few years saw frantic activity from one end of the Nile valley to the other. Huge political changes were also taking place. The regional chieftains were forced to relinquish their hold on district government and many of their large estates were confiscated. Nothing would be allowed to stand in the way of the push to secure maximum grain reserves.

Seven Years of Famine

Eventually everything was ready ... and just in time. The soldiers at Semna fort, where the Nile forms a deep gorge at the Second Cataract in Wawat (Nubia), were the first to witness the start of the great floods which began in Amenemhat's twentieth year. The soldier-observers marked the high point of the flood on the cliff face at forty cubits (20.8 metres) above the normal river level. This was eight cubits (4.2 metres) higher than the flood levels in the years of plenty and eighteen cubits (9.3 metres) above the average inundation level. The brown water, heavy with silt, swept north, destroying everything in its path, just as Joseph had predicted. Animals which had not been moved to the desert plateau were caught in the fields and drowned. The mud-brick settlements on low mounds were washed away and many villagers died ... but the precious grain remained safe and dry in Joseph's desert granaries.

Syene (Aswan) and Ipetsut (Thebes) were swamped and badly damaged but Itj-Tawy and the rest of the kingdom survived, as half the flood water was diverted along Joseph's canal and on into FAIYUM LAKE. Over the following six months this vast reservoir of excess water was gradually released back into the Nile through sluice gates in the canal, thus preventing excessive flooding further north. In this way Lower Egypt was saved from the worst of the floods for the next seven years. However, the famine was still hard and the Egyptians suffered a great deal.

In the second year of the high floods, and when the famine was at its hardest, the senior co-regent, Senuseret III, died in the thirty-ninth year of his reign (1660 BC). Amenemhat continued to soldier on without the support of his father and so came to rely on his Hebrew vizier for advice even more than before. Pharaoh was greatly concerned for his people and much relieved when the famine finally passed. The Nile flood levels continued to be high for a number of years but the people, with Joseph's firm hand guiding them, adapted to their new circumstances and began to produce food once again.

During the years of plenty, before the famine crisis had begun, Amenemhat had rewarded Joseph with a country estate in the eastern delta. The small town of Rowaty was nearby and so the Hebrew vizier turned this old riverside summer residence of Khety IV into one of the two new administrative centres in Egypt. Both were known as the 'House of the Department' (Egyptian *hat-waret*, pronounced 'Haware'), their purpose being to co-ordinate the collection and storage of the country's grain taxation. They were the administrative headquarters of the Department of the People's Giving.

Thus 'Haware of the Valley' (i.e. Upper Egypt) was constructed alongside the Waterway of Joseph and beside Amenemhat's pyramid in the Faiyum. It subsequently became famous throughout the Classical world as the Egyptian Labyrinth located at modern Hawara (clearly retaining its ancient name). In Lower Egypt the delta town of Rowarty was renamed 'Haware of the Delta' – now more familiar to us in its Greek form of Avaris. This was the infamous city in the district of Goshen (Egyptian *Kesen*) where the story of Israelite enslavement would be played out over the coming two centuries, prior to the departure of Moses and the Israelites on the day of Exodus.

Brothers Reunited

It was in the second year of the famine, and shortly after the death of Senuseret III, that Joseph's brothers came down into the Egyptian delta. The famine was not restricted to the Nile valley. The high floods in Egypt were symptomatic of a major climate shift in the Middle East and East Africa. The tropical climate zone had shifted northwards, causing vast quantities of rainfall in Ethiopia and pushing the hot, arid air of Saharan Africa into the Levant. Egypt was enduring potentially disastrous floods but Canaan was suffering under a blistering sun. There had been no rain in the hill country for two years. Like all the pastoralists in the region, Jacob's followers were desperate. They had only one option open to them: head south across Sinai into the Egyptian delta where the Nile was providing water in abundance to feed their flocks of sheep and herds of cattle.

But the Hebrews of Jacob's tribe could not simply drive their animals across Egypt's border. They first had to negotiate entry at the office of the northern vizier in Avaris. Little did the sons of Jacob know that their fate would be placed in the hands of the young brother whom they had sold into slavery a generation earlier.

The brothers arrived in Joseph's court (today buried under the fields near the village of Ezbet Rushdi) and were brought before the vizier. Twenty long years had passed since they had last seen their teenage sibling and they did not recognise Joseph-the-man dressed in his Egyptian finery … but he recognised them and decided to punish them for their crime against him. He accused the sons of Jacob of being spies sent to discover if Egypt might be successfully invaded by their Asiatic kin from the north. He threw them into prison but released them again after three days. He then sent his brothers back to Canaan with grain supplies for the coming months, knowing full well that they would be forced to return to Egypt when their supplies ran out.

His judgement proved correct as the sons of Jacob arrived back in Goshen the following year. This time they were brought to Joseph's residence, at Middle Kingdom Avaris, one kilometre to the south of the administrative centre. There, surrounded by fields of wheat swaying in a gentle breeze, the brothers were led into a house which would have been very familiar to them. The Asiatic vizier's residence had been built in the style of a north Syrian family home, identical to the dwelling in which Jacob had spent his years in Harran, and where his sons were born and grew up. Joseph's house had a broad central living room which was surrounded on three sides by bedrooms and storage areas. This large building was set in an open compound, surrounded by a low mudbrick wall, within which the domestic animals could roam and where the women of the household baked their bread in clay ovens.

This time Joseph found it very hard to keep his feelings hidden and eventually revealed his true identity. Even though he had been cruelly betrayed by his brothers, Joseph could not allow his own blood-kin to suffer in the terrible years of famine still to come. Amenemhat's vizier ordered his brothers to return to Canaan once more and bring their aged father, Jacob, to Egypt along with the rest of the tribe and all their flocks. He had petitioned Pharaoh on their behalf and they would be permitted to settle there, in the region of Goshen, where Joseph had his own lands and estate.

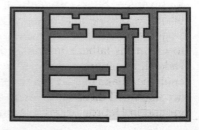

20. Plan of Joseph's first house where his father Jacob resided before his death.

And so Jacob and the Hebrews (seventy males, with their sisters, wives and daughters) came down and settled in Goshen. On a low turtleback mound of sand, to the east of the Pelusiac branch of the Nile and just a short walk from Joseph's residence, they built a small settlement of mudbrick dwellings (today known as Tell ed-Daba – the 'mound of the hyena'). Jacob was given Joseph's old house, built in the Syrian style which he was used to. This was where Jacob spent his remaining years, happy that his 'dead' son had been returned to him alive – but still greatly angered by his other offspring for their wilful and prolonged deceit which had caused their father such pain.

When Amenemhat heard the story from the old man's lips as to how he, Jacob, had believed his son to have been killed by a wild beast but that, all along, he had survived and prospered in Egypt, the king gave Joseph a new Egyptian name. From that day on his vizier would be known as Pa-ankh – 'the one who lives!' The Genesis author Hebraised this into Zaphenath-Paaneah (from Egyptian *djedu-en-ef pa-ankh* – 'he who is called "the one who lives"' – pronounced Zatenaf-Paaneah). This name was soon hypocorised or shortened by the people of Egypt to the familiar name Ankhu.

In the final hours of life Jacob summoned his sons to his bedside to instruct them concerning his burial. He asked Joseph to promise that he would be buried in the cave at Machpelah where Abraham and Isaac had been laid to rest. Jacob then passed away and Joseph covered his father's eyes. The house in which the Hebrew chieftain had lived for seventeen years was demolished, according to custom when the master of a household was no more.

Joseph requested of Pharaoh a small force of soldiers to escort his father's mummified body back to Canaan. Indeed, the entire Hebrew tribe – except for those who could not make the journey through old age or infirmity – accompanied the body of Jacob back to the family burial ground in Hebron. The Egyptian officials under Joseph's command also made the trek, out of respect for their master the vizier. After three weeks the long funeral procession arrived at the field of Machpelah and, in the year 1642 BC, Jacob was laid to rest by Joseph and Benjamin amongst his Hebrew ancestors.

Retirement in Goshen

With the death of Amenemhat III in 1634 BC, Joseph retired from his office of state but continued to retain his title of vizier until his own death eighteen years later. During the previous twenty years he had spent most of his time in Itj-Tawy and Memphis, but now his new pharaoh – Neferusobek (1635–1632 BC), daughter of Amenemhat III – commanded that he be given a small palace or villa which was to be constructed by Egyptian builders over the ruins of Jacob's old Syrian house. With Neferusobek's own death, the 12th Dynasty came to an end, to be followed by King Wegaf (1632–1629 BC), founder of the 13th Dynasty. But even with the change in dynasty, Joseph's splendid new residence continued to expand under royal patronage as the nucleus of his immediate family grew.

At first the villa consisted of a single rectangular building fronted by a colonnaded portico with a pillar for each of Jacob's sons – twelve in all. This led into a large, high-ceilinged hall supported by four slender wooden lotus columns set on stone bases. Here Joseph entertained visitors and lived with his family. On one side of the hall was the vizier's private bedchamber and, on the other, a large storage room. Behind the hall were two rooms – a bathing chamber and a robing room for his collection of multi-coloured, woven coats.

When Joseph's two sons, Manasseh and Ephraim, were old enough to marry and have their own families, their father built two identical apartments in front of his own residence and turned the space between the buildings into an enclosed courtyard. Here the children safely played

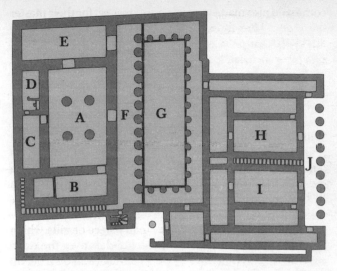

21. Plan of Joseph's palace in Avaris. A – original audience room of the first stage of the residence; B – Joseph's bedroom; C – Joseph's robing room; D – washroom; E – storeroom; F – portico with twelve columns; G – inner courtyard; H – Manasseh's apartment; I – Ephraim's apartment; J – new entrance portico.

whilst the women of the expanded household wove and dyed garments or washed their clothes in the central water basin with its own ceramic-pipe plumbing. Finally, a new building was begun immediately to the east of the old house, but this remained unfinished on the day that the master of the palace passed away.

The Death of Joseph

Joseph lived to a venerable age, witnessing the birth of the third generation of his offspring. In his dotage, the patriarch's favourite pastime was to sit within the shade of an old tamarisk tree growing in the large garden behind his palace. We may imagine him spending many peaceful afternoons, watching his grandchildren and great-grand-

147

children at play, receiving visits from Hebrews and Egyptians alike. Both regarded him as the father of their nation.

With his time drawing to an end, the Hebrew patriarch gathered his large family around him. Joseph knew that, one day, the descendants of his father Israel (Jacob) would leave Egypt and return to Canaan. He commanded his family to make a solemn promise that, when the time of their departure came, his mummified body would be taken out of Egypt with them. Although Joseph had grown to respect and admire the people of Egypt, his tribal roots remained in the hills of Canaan and that was where his bones must eventually find rest. In the meantime, a tomb must be prepared for him in the garden which he loved so much, as a temporary resting place for his mummy.

A week later Joseph died quietly and peacefully in his chair beneath the old tamarisk. His body was sent for mummification and returned to Avaris seventy days later for burial. During that period of embalming, a team of Egyptian builders prepared Joseph's tomb at the bottom of the palace garden. First they excavated a large and deep pit in the ground, within which a small square mudbrick chamber was constructed. The roof of the vault was left open to the sky to receive the body of the deceased. The rest of the pit around the burial chamber was then backfilled with earth. Outside this subterranean vault, a square podium was built, above which a brick pyramid would rise once the interment had taken place.

At the same time the best carpenter in Avaris was busily assembling a fine coffin of Lebanese cedar, whilst a team of sculptors set to the task of carving a magnificent funerary statue in the purest limestone brought from the quarries of Tura near Memphis. All this was a gift of the new pharaoh, Sekhemkare, in gratitude for what Joseph had done for his country during the Hebrew's long and illustrious career as Egypt's northern vizier.

The patriarch's body, wrapped in the finest of his multicoloured robes, was carried to the tomb and placed in the waiting coffin. A domed roof was then added to seal the chamber, more earth packed in to level the platform and, over the following fortnight, a mudbrick pyramid erected above Joseph's mummified body. Finally the whole structure was coated in a fine white plaster which gleamed in the bright delta sunlight. In front of the pyramid a small chapel was added to house the seated cult-statue of Egypt's saviour – it too painted to represent the Asiatic vizier in his

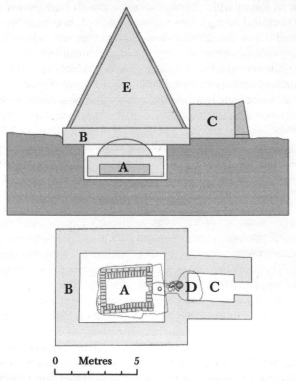

22. Cross-section and plan of the pyramid tomb of Joseph. A – mudbrick, domed burial chamber sunk into the ground; B – rectangular plinth foundation for the pyramid; C – mortuary chapel containing the cult-statue of Joseph; D – 'robber's tunnel' connecting the rear of the mortuary chapel to the burial chamber; E – pyramid superstructure.

famous coat-of-many-colours. This was no ordinary statue. It was nearly three metres high. It depicted Joseph in his prime, with flame-red hair, a pale yellow skin tone (to indicate his northern origins), and a throw-stick held across the right shoulder as his symbol of high office … but also clearly marking him out as an Asiatic (and not Egyptian) servant of Pharaoh. The body of the statue was painted as if wrapped in the full-length robe of the vizier. But it was a vizier's cloak of a very different kind – decorated in an elaborate pattern of reds, blues, blacks and whites to represent the woven 'coat-of-many-colours' of a Middle Bronze Age Asiatic chieftain.

This was an extraordinary burial for a commoner, the like of which had never been seen before in Egypt for someone not directly connected with the royal family. Only the pharaonic élite had previously been buried in pyramids. Only the greatest of Egypt's great were granted colossal cult-statues by the king. All this was tangible proof of the high esteem and love which Pharaoh Amenemhat's right-hand-man had earned from the people of the country he had served for so many years.

Joseph's sons, and those of his brothers who were still alive, brought bricks to the patriarch's palace and sealed up the entrance doorways and windows. The house of the master was closed and the people returned to their homes.

The Patriarchal Age had come to a close with the death of the last of the great patriarchs and the Hebrews' saviour from the famine. So ends the Book of Genesis, which tells the story of the Children of Yahweh's early history – a history which had brought them from the mountains of Eden to the Mesopotamian plain and on to Canaan and Egypt – three thousand seven hundred and twenty-seven years of wandering which were now to end in ignominious slavery and the birth of a nation through adversity.

Part Three

Journey to the Promised Land

Chapter Nine

MOSES PRINCE OF EGYPT

(Exodus 1:1 to Exodus 4:18)

The Bondage Years – Slaughter of the Innocents –
Prince of Egypt – The Kushite War – Escape into Sinai
– Sojourn with the Midianites – The Hidden Name of
God Revealed

oon after Joseph's death in 1617 BC, Egypt's
political stability, established by the Israelite vizier
during the famine years, disintegrated. Joseph
passed away in the twelfth regnal year of Sekhemkare
Amenemhat-senebef (2nd ruler of the 13th Dynasty, 1629–
1617 BC). This king was assassinated in that very same
year and the country was immediately plunged into
anarchy. For six years political infighting prevented the
establishment of a successor. The Black Land fragmented
into small fiefdoms with no one ruler singled out for
recognition as Pharaoh by the powerful Karnak priesthood.
Eventually in 1611 BC, after a protracted civil war, a local
ruler from the eastern delta seized control and was crowned
in Thebes as Sekhemkare Amenemhat V.

During these troubled times, and for the remaining
years of the 13th Dynasty, the royal residence continued

to be based at Itj-Tawy. However, with the coronation of Amenemhat, the summer residence of the royal household was re-established at Avaris (Egyptian *Haware*). Just as in the distant days of Abraham's visit to Egypt, a pharaoh now ruled for part of the year in the eastern delta at the old 'Mouth of the Two Ways' (Egyptian *Rowaty*), amidst the Asiatics who had flooded into north-east Egypt during the Joseph era. As a result, Pharaoh's court began to be dominated by officials and counsellors from the Semitic-speaking population. The exceptional appointment of Joseph the Asiatic vizier had set a precedent which was eventually to bring instability and further internal conflict into the Nile valley.

King Amenemhat V was not directly of the 12th-Dynasty bloodline which had died out with the demise of Sekhemkare Amenemhat-senebef. Although the new king had been given a good Egyptian name at birth, he was of mixed descent – his mother being a member of Joseph's now greatly extended family. It was the common practice in Egypt for newborn males to be named after the reigning monarch, and this child of Egyptian and Israelite descent had come into the world towards the end of the long reign of Amenemhat III.

At his coronation Amenemhat V was in his early twenties, but his reign was to be cut short by further political intrigue. After just three years on the throne the young king was overthrown by the very officials who had promoted his candidature for the twin crowns of Upper and Lower Egypt. The royal diadem then passed into the hands of a series of ephemeral kings, some of whom bore very unroyal names such as Iufni ('he is mine'), Renseneb ('healthy name'), Khendjer ('go to the end') and Mermeshau ('troop commander'). A number of them were also of Asiatic origin.

Whilst the ruling class fought and bickered over the succession, the Israelite descendants of Jacob and Joseph were quietly prospering in the wide, flat farming lands of

Goshen. Many families had migrated south to exploit the rich soil of the Nile valley itself. Israelites were multiplying and spreading throughout the Black Land. The Nile had returned to its regular cycle and the great famine was at an end.

However, even though the natural crisis was passed, a serious political crisis had been left in its wake. Within the native Egyptian population a deep mistrust was beginning to build up against the dominant foreign element now at the centre of government. The generation which took Joseph to its heart for rescuing the people from famine had all but died out. A new generation of Egyptians could only see their position being steadily eroded by Semitic-speaking northerners and their puppet rulers. Resentment festered beneath the surface in the Egyptian population. A backlash was inevitable.

Oppression

The storm broke with the sudden rise to power of a new sub-dynasty of pharaohs who 'did not know Joseph'. This new line of kings was of Upper Egyptian origin, with its seat at the old Middle Kingdom capital of Itj-Tawy. In seizing power throughout the Nile valley from Aswan to Memphis, these southern rulers once again forced a division of the Black Land. The Asiatic pharaohs, who had dominated Egypt's political landscape for the past sixty-six years, were forced to retreat to their summer residence at Avaris. Here they set up a short-lived independent kingdom of some influence, exploiting trading links with Canaan and the northern empires of Mesopotamia and Anatolia. The main Pelusiac branch of the Nile, which connected Upper Egypt with the Mediterranean, flowed through their delta kingdom and the pharaohs of Avaris were thus able to exert considerable control over the affairs of the native Egyptian pharaohs in the southern kingdom of Itj-Tawy.

The founder of the new Egyptian dynasty was Sekhemre-sewadjtawy Sobekhotep III (*c.* 1545–1543 BC). It was during his short three-year reign that the Israelites and their Asiatic cousins living in the Nile valley were first enslaved in large numbers. The Egyptians had finally had enough. Property was seized and livestock confiscated by royal decree. Those Asiatic officials living at the royal court in Itj-Tawy who swore absolute allegiance to Pharaoh and the Upper Egyptian state were permitted to retain their offices – but only under the close scrutiny of their native Egyptian masters.

Suddenly, in a devastating coup, Egypt had taken back control of its destiny and found itself awash with slaves to do its bidding. According to surviving documents such as the Brooklyn Papyrus, as many as fifty per cent of the domestic servant population in the Nile valley at this time bore Semitic names, including Israelite appellations such as Menahem, Issachar, Asher and Shiphrah. Two of these are tribal eponyms derived from sons of Jacob, whilst the last is specifically given as the name of one of the Israelite midwives in the Moses story [Exodus 1:15–21].

The bitter days of Sobekhotep's reign were followed by even more desperate times for the Israelites settled in Upper Egypt. The first oppressor of the Hebrews was succeeded by two brothers whom Egyptologists recognise as the most powerful rulers of the 13th Dynasty – Khasekhemre Neferhotep and Khaneferre Sobekhotep IV. Their parents, the priest Khaankhef and his wife Kemy, were of non-royal lineage but of pure native Egyptian stock.

The first to ascend the throne was the elder brother – Neferhotep (*c.* 1543–1533 BC). Archaeological evidence from the Levant shows that he was a contemporary of Yantin-ammu of Byblos, Zimrilim of Mari and Hammurabi of Babylon, whose reign began in 1565 BC – as determined by astronomical retro-calculation based on the data supplied in the Ammisaduga tablets (Venus Solution 1419 BC).

During Neferhotep's eleven-year reign he reopened trade with the chiefdoms of north-east Africa – particularly the kingdom of Kush – in order to reduce the Nile valley's dependence on the delta rulers with their stranglehold on Levantine trade. Rock inscriptions on Sehel Island, amidst the First Cataract, indicate that Neferhotep despatched at least one expedition from Aswan upstream into Kushite territory – the first to do so since Amenemhat III – no doubt bringing back ivory, exotic woods such as *hebny* (ebony), *antyu* (incense), animal skins and, above all, gold. This initiative forced a degree of co-operation from the king of Avaris, who wanted African produce just as much as Neferhotep needed the produce of Asia.

Over the next decade the political influence of the delta pharaoh gradually waned as that of the Upper Egyptian pharaoh waxed. By the end of Neferhotep's reign the king of Avaris had become little more than a vassal of his more powerful Upper Egyptian neighbour. The Phoenician rulers of the eastern Mediterranean sea ports now dealt directly with the Upper Egyptian state and a large stela found at Byblos confirms that Yantin, the ruler of this crucial trading port, acknowledged Neferhotep as his sovereign lord. Under Khasekhemre Neferhotep the Egyptian state had fully recovered from the decades of weakness which followed the long reign of Amenemhat III.

Neferhotep was briefly succeeded by his son, Sihathor – but the boy's reign lasted just three months. The suspicion amongst the courtiers was that the 'unfortunate accident' which brought his reign to an abrupt end was no accident at all. Sihathor's uncle, Sobekhotep, seized the reins of power, taking the coronation name of Khaneferre ('the perfection of Re shines in the horizon'). The Alexandrian scholar, Artapanus, who wrote a history of the Jewish nation in the third century BC, identified this King Khaneferre (he calls him 'Khenophres') as the pharaoh who raised Moses as a member of the royal household. Neferhotep's younger brother was the dynasty's fourth Sobekhotep ('Sobek is at peace') but, even though his name suggests the trials and tribulations brought upon Egypt by its sacred

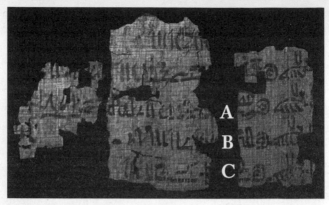

23. The Turin Canon fragment bearing the names (A) Neferhotep, (B) Sihathor and (C) Sobekhotep.

river were over, his rule was no less brutal than that of his sibling predecessor.

Slavery in Goshen

During the years of Asiatic rule prior to the accession of Sobekhotep III the white and red crowns had passed to a king named Hetepibre Amu-sa-Harnedj-heritef, whose nomen or birth-name – 'the Asiatic, son of Harnedjheritef ("Horus who hails his father")' – clearly betrays his non-Egyptian pedigree. At the succession of Khaneferre Sobek-hotep IV (*c.* 1532–1508 BC) in Itj-Tawy, Hetepibre's grand-son, Sekhemre-khutawy Paentjenu (Artapanus gave him the Greek name-form 'Palmonothes'), was now the ruler of the delta kingdom. Seeing an opportunity to expand his influence, Khaneferre made overtures to the ageing ruler in the north and an alliance was sealed between the two royal houses through the marriage of Khaneferre to Meryt (Artapanus' Merris), the eldest daughter of Paentjenu. In effect this union completed the takeover of the kingdom of Avaris by the Upper Egyptian state. Khaneferre had peacefully unified the Black Land once more and gained sovereignty over the eastern delta, with its large population of Asiatics – including the people of Goshen, the original homeland of the Israelites.

It was not long before the state-organised oppression of the Asiatics living in Upper Egypt was extended to encompass the foreign residents of the newly acquired regions. During the twenty-five-year reign of the Asiatic pharaoh, Paentjenu, many of the rights of Jacob's descendants had been gradually eroded, but the Israelites of Goshen now suddenly found themselves in truly dire circumstances – bonded to their Egyptian neighbours as domestic servants with many of the young men sent into forced labour on behalf of Pharaoh Khaneferre's building projects.

In Avaris, the largest of the dwellings (in Tell ed-Daba Area F) – those once occupied by the Israelite tribal chieftains – were handed over to Egyptian overseers. The original Hebrew owners were rehoused in much smaller lean-to huts built within the compounds and set to work as domestic servants for their new masters. The rest of the expanding Asiatic population was housed in overcrowded squalor to the east of the palace settlement (in Tell ed-Daba Area A on the main tell). Here the mudbrick houses, now of Egyptian design, were woven together in a tight network of compounds separated by narrow lanes. The population was so densely packed into the available space that burials had to be located within the compounds and even under the floors of the dwellings.

Anthropological studies of the skeletal remains from Avaris show that the Asiatic population developed serious health problems associated with poverty and malnourishment. Parasitic diseases such as anaemia were observed to have affected at least one third of the population. Harris lines in the long-bones indicated stunted growth. Life expectancy was around thirty-two years (29.7 years for women and 34.4 years for men). The evidence for an oppression of the Asiatic population of Egypt during the

13th Dynasty is clearly there to be seen in the archaeological record.

Khaneferre strengthened his grip on power by building up a large military force loyal to the throne. It was during his long reign that the Egyptian army commanders established, for the first time, a chariot force stationed at Avaris. Horse-drawn chariots had been used in Egypt during the late Middle Kingdom but only as transport for the king and his high officials. However, new developments in warfare amongst the Hurrian nations to the north had demonstrated the effectiveness of chariotry in set-piece battles. The speed with which a well-trained chariot force could reach flash-points and decimate infantry had transformed military tactics. The Egyptians did not hesitate to adopt this new way of warfare, refining it to suit their own circumstances. They developed a much lighter, faster, two-man vehicle with four-spoked wheels. Over the centuries this Egyptian rapid response force would grow to several thousand units, each consisting of the vehicle, two teams of horses, a driver and archer/spearman.

Egypt's main chariotry force remained stationed at Avaris throughout the late New Kingdom. In the early 1990s German archaeologists, under the directorship of Edgar Pusch, found the remains of chariot stables which formed a major part of the later city of Pi-Ramesse. This royal estate of Ramesses II was established on the same spot as Asiatic Avaris, some four centuries after the events being described here. The Ramesside rapid reaction force was there to respond to troubles in the northern lands, long under the wing of the Horus kings of the New Kingdom. However, the initial objective of the newly invented 13th Dynasty mobile force was to control the local Asiatic population within the eastern delta whilst, at the same time, protecting Egypt's northern border from invasion by sympathetic kinfolk wishing to relieve the oppression of their enslaved cousins. The chariot was ideally suited to the wide, flat terrain of northern Sinai.

The Birth of Moses

It was early in Khaneferre Sobekhotep IV's reign that the infamous decree went out to cull all the male infants of the expanding Asiatic community. The king's advisers had determined that the newly acquired slave population posed a potential threat to the security of the state. The Asiatics might rise in revolt if their already large numbers were permitted to grow any further. Given the Hebrews' warrior background and tribal structure, it was prudent to reduce the adult male population to the minimum required for Pharaoh's building programme, whilst keeping the female population higher to maintain domestic work levels on the large Egyptian agricultural estates. In Avaris at the heart of Israelite Goshen, and throughout the land, newborn boys were wrenched from their mothers' arms and smothered or drowned in the Nile.

All over the sprawling city of Avaris the tiny graves of the massacre victims have been unearthed by the Austrian excavators. The normal infant grave population in ancient settlements is around twenty-five per cent – but here in Avaris the figure reaches an astonishing sixty-five per cent. Further direct archaeological evidence of the tragedy comes from the statistics for the remaining adult population of the excavated Israelite graves. For every five female adult burials the archaeologists have unearthed only three male burials. The picture is clear: fewer males survived into adulthood. Once again the archaeological evidence seems to confirm the biblical tradition.

It was in this atmosphere of Egyptian retribution for years of Asiatic dominance that a baby boy was born to Amram and Jochebed – two Israelite residents of Avaris. The Moses genealogy [Exodus 6:16–20] states that he was descended from Levi, Jacob's third son. The Levite family residence, now occupied by Egyptians, stood at the heart of the original village built by Jacob's sons which surrounded Joseph's abandoned palace and pyramid tomb.

Amram's small family lived in abject poverty within the grounds of their former home. They continued to work the fields and tend the flocks – but these now belonged to their Egyptian master. Little of what they produced went to feed Israelite mouths.

The newborn's sister, a precocious ten-year-old named Miriam, had often played in the overgrown garden and crumbling ruins of the vizier's once thriving residence. She, like all the Israelite children, had been told the story of her great-great-uncle Joseph and had often found herself drawn to his magnificent cult-image, still standing in the chapel before his Egyptian tomb. Miriam was proud of her family history. Even though she herself had not been alive to witness the prosperous days of the twelve tribal chieftains, her imagination was fired by the wondrous coat-of-many-colours decorating Joseph's colossal funerary statue. Perhaps it was on one of those visits to her ancestor's tomb that Miriam had decided she was not about to see her then-unborn brother given up to the Egyptian soldiers.

Travelling merchants often came to Avaris from the northlands, bringing tales of the great deeds of kings and heroes. The Babylonians were currently the masters of Mesopotamia and their renowned ruler, the lawgiver Hammurabi (1565–1523 BC), was at the height of his powers. Having conquered many of the surrounding city-states and carved out a great empire for himself, Hammurabi had wished to commemorate his own achievements by associating his deeds with those of the 'mighty men' from the past. He therefore commissioned the writing down of the great oral epics of his Sumerian and Agadaean ancestors, to be stored in a royal library for the benefit of generations of future kings. So it was that the heroic deeds of Gilgamesh were canonised in Old Babylonian cuneiform and subsequently widely dispersed throughout the Akkadian-speaking world. But it was not just the Gilgamesh epic which received such treatment. The stories of Etana, Enmerkar, Lugalbanda, Dumuzi and Sargon the Great were also written down and disseminated across the northern lands – from Hittite Anatolia in the west to the marshlands of Sumer in the east, and even down into Canaan bordering upon Egypt.

Visiting merchants were the mechanism by which the stories were further transmitted to the general population – in this case primarily in oral form. The merchants entertained their customers with recitations of the great epics, as villagers gathered around blazing fires during the long, dark evenings. Needless to say, these stories were very popular with the local children. Such travelling poets had often visited Avaris, their colourful tales holding young audiences in wide-eyed rapture.

Miriam herself had been fascinated by the tale of Sargon the Great (*c.* 2117–2062 BC), founder of the Dynasty of Agade, who had reigned more than five hundred years earlier – in the time of her ancestor Nahor, grandfather of Abraham. Sargon was still remembered as the most powerful ruler the ancient world had ever seen. Miriam was most struck by his humble beginnings – how as a baby he had been set afloat by his mother upon the Euphrates in a reed basket and rescued by the royal gardener, Akki, eventually rising through the ranks of court officials in the palace of King Ur-Zababa of Kish (*c.* 2157–2118 BC) to reach the very throne of Agade itself.

> Sargon, the mighty king, king of Akkad, am I. …
> My mother, the high priestess, conceived me. In secret she bore me. She placed me in a basket of rushes. With bitumen she sealed my lid. She cast me into the river which rose not over me. The river bore me up and carried me to Akki, the drawer of water. Akki, the drawer of water, lifted me out of the river as he dipped his ewer. Akki, the drawer of water, adopted me as his son and reared me. Akki, the drawer of water, appointed me as his gardener. While I was a gardener, Ishtar (Inanna) granted me

her love, and for four and [fifty] years I exercised
kingship. [*Legend of Sargon of Agade*]

It may well be that this story prompted Jochebed's clever
daughter to devise a plan, which she put to her mother as
a way to save the life of her baby brother. Together mother
and daughter made an ark (Hebrew *teba*, Egyptian *tjeba*)
basket in preparation for the impending birth. It was constructed of papyrus, coated in bitumen to keep it watertight.
After the birth of the child, Miriam's plan was put into
effect. The infant was laid inside the ark and carried down
to the river along a sandy track through swampy ground
to the south of the settlement. The basket was then set
afloat on the Pelusiac branch of the Nile at a point a short
distance upstream from Pharaoh's summer residence. Like
Noah in his ark (Hebrew *teba*) the Israelite child drifted
northwards upon the gentle currents whilst Miriam watched
anxiously from the east bank of the river. She was soon
relieved to see the ark slip into the still waters of the royal
bathing area where Meryt, Great Royal Wife of King
Khaneferre and eldest daughter of King Paentjenu, was
relaxing with the ladies of the court. The basket, with its
precious cargo, was drawn out of the water and presented
to the delighted queen.

Even though she knew full well that the baby boy was
of Hebrew stock, Meryt – who was, after all, of Asiatic
descent herself – decided to adopt the child as her own,
giving him the name Hapimose ('offspring of the inundation'). This long form of his name soon gave way to the
simple hypocoristicon 'Mose' by which the Hebrew prince
of Egypt was known for the rest of his long life. Once again,
the biblical author/redactor chose to take this purely
Egyptian name and adopt it into the Hebrew language as
Moshe with the meaning 'drawn out (of the water)'.

The boy grew up in the two great royal residences of
the 13th Dynasty, where he was taught the skills of reading
and writing. He not only learnt the hieroglyphic signs and

their hieratic (cursive) equivalents but also became fluent in the *lingua franca* of the ancient world – Akkadian – written in the wedge-shaped script we now call cuneiform.

Moses was a studious child and shone at all he set out to accomplish. He was soon reading the beautiful didactic literature of the Middle Kingdom – stories such as 'The Shipwrecked Sailor', 'Sinuhe' and 'The Eloquent Peasant', all of which made a deep impression upon him. But Moses also took a great interest in the recently available cuneiform tablets of the Mesopotamian epics, copies of which had been despatched to the Egyptian court as diplomatic gifts from Hammurabi, king of Babylon. The young Egyptian prince even found time to study the great Hammurabi Law Code which was to set the standard in lawgiving for centuries to come. This document would greatly influence Moses 'the Lawgiver' during the wilderness years when he set to the task of formulating the laws and morality codes of Yahweh's people.

The other important aspect of a prince's life in Pharaoh's court was training in the skills of warfare and hunting. Here again Prince Moses excelled, not only in his ability to handle weapons but also in his natural talent for leadership. His childhood friends who had gone with him into the military academy grew to look upon Moses as their natural commander. This loyalty was soon to be tested to the full during the protracted war which descended upon the Black Land towards the end of the second decade of the young prince's life.

War with Kush

The clouds on Egypt's southern border had been gathering for some years. Beyond the fortresses of Semna and Kumma, guarding the second cataract frontier, lay the powerful African kingdom of Kush. The distant days of the 'sons of Ham' were a thousand years in the past and only the eponym of Noah's eldest grandson remained to remind the Egyptian élite of a common ancestry with their southern neighbour. The chieftains of Kush now ruled over a brutal militaristic society. When these warrior-kings died they were buried in huge tumuli – circular mounds of sand and rubble – within the Kushite capital at Kerma just north of the great Dongola bend of the Nile in Sudan. But they did not go to their graves alone. Hundreds of servants were herded into long pits which bisected the funeral mounds. These unfortunate victims were then buried alive beside the bodies of their royal masters.

Such barbaric ceremonies had once been practised by the predynastic and early dynastic rulers of Egypt – as witnessed in the early royal cemetery at Abydos where numerous graves of sacrificial victims have been unearthed by archaeologists. And, once again, the link with Mesopotamia is clear. The surviving epic literature informs us that Gilgamesh went into the underworld accompanied by his wives, officials and servants. Macabre physical evidence for such mass killings was discovered by Sir Leonard Woolley at the city of Ur where he famously came upon the burial pits of the early rulers of this powerful Sumerian city. There, buried deep beneath the modern surface of Tell el-Mukayyar, Woolley and his team unearthed the entombed remains of Sumerian kings and queens, their residences of the underworld replete with ranks of soldiers, chariots pulled by oxen, musicians and servant girls. All had apparently willingly descended into the death-pit to join their rulers in the afterlife. This gruesome Mesopotamian practice had migrated to the African continent with the 'sons of Ham' – but only in the land of Kush had this ritual slaughter continued down into the second millennium.

During the early part of Neferhotep's reign the Egyptians had been forced to look south for their trade because of the delta kingdom's monopoly on Levantine produce. So it was that the Kushites were reintroduced to their powerful northern neighbour. This relationship prospered

Yahweh said to Abram, 'Leave your country, your kindred and your father's house for a country which I shall show you. And I shall make you a great nation. I shall bless you and make your name famous, for you are to be a blessing.' [Genesis 12:1–2]

Plate 11: Statuette of an Amorite cultural type from Mesopotamia (Louvre Museum).

So Pharaoh said to Joseph, 'Since God has given you knowledge of all this, there can be no-one as intelligent and as wise as you. You shall be my chancellor, and all my people shall respect your orders. Only this throne shall set me above you.' [Genesis 41:39–40]

Plate 12: Statue of King Nimaatre Amenemhat III – the pharaoh who appointed Joseph as vizier of Egypt to counter the great floods and famine of the late 12th Dynasty (Luxor Museum).

Plate 13: Joseph's cult-statue found in the chapel of Tomb F/1=p/19:1 at Tell ed-Daba (Avaris), restored by computer technology.

Then there came to power in Egypt a new king who did not know Joseph. 'Look,' he said to his people, 'the Israelites are now more numerous and stronger than we are. We must take action to stop them from multiplying or, if war should break out, they might join the forces of our enemies. They might take arms against us and then escape from the country.' Accordingly they put taskmasters over the Israelites to wear them down by forced labour. [Exodus 1:8–11]

Plate 14: Granite statue of the pharaoh who raised Moses – Khaneferre Sobekhotep IV (Karnak).

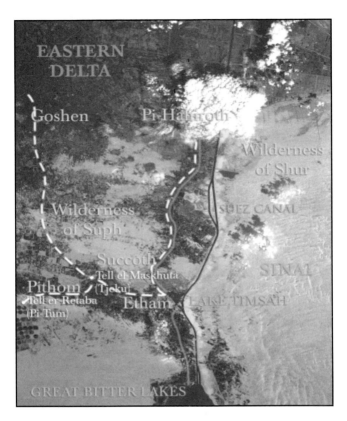

Plate 15: Satellite image showing the landscape of Exodus. The Israelites were forced to follow the border canal which has been traced to the west of (and roughly parallel to) the Suez Canal.

Plate 16: Seal image from the 'early Israelite' period at Avaris, depicting Baal standing on twin peaks, El as a bull and Yam as a serpent. The seal was found in the 'Joseph Palace' of Tell ed-Daba Area F (Austrian Institute for Egyptology).

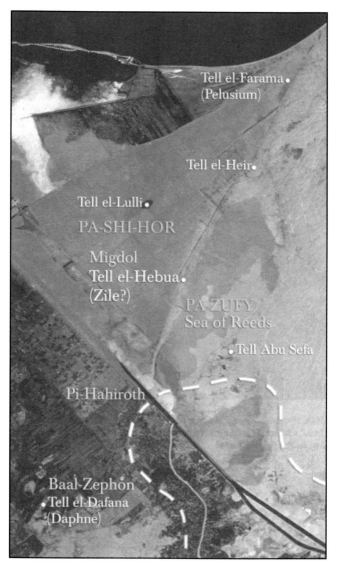

Plate 17: Satellite image showing the now dried up Sea of Reeds (Egyptian pa-zufy) and the proposed Exodus crossing point at Pi-Hahiroth.

Plate 18: Satellite image of Egypt's eastern border, showing the Exodus route from Pi-Hahiroth to Elim.

Plate 19: One of several wells scattered amongst the palm trees of Ain Musa/Elim in western Sinai.

The glory of Yahweh rested on Mount Sinai and the cloud covered it for six days. On the seventh day Yahweh called to Moses from inside the cloud. To the watching Israelites, the glory of Yahweh looked like a devouring fire on the mountain top. Moses went right into the cloud and went on up the mountain. Moses stayed on the mountain for forty days and forty nights. [Exodus 24:16–18]

Plate 20: Mount Horeb – 'Mountain of the Law' – at the heart of southern Sinai.

whilst the Egyptians were denied access to the northern sphere but, as soon as the political tide was turned and control of the Levantine trade routes fell into the hands of Khaneferre Sobekhotep IV, the southern trading network slipped into decline. By Khaneferre's eighteenth regnal year, Egypt's relationship with the Kushite kingdom had sunk to an all-time low. The ruler of Kush decided that, if Egypt was no longer prepared to trade the produce of the pharaonic state for his African treasures, he would take what Egypt had by force of arms.

That year, riding on the crest of the summer Nile flood, the ships of Kush sailed downstream and across the border into Wawat (Nubia). They easily overthrew the frontier posts at Semna and Kumma before besieging the great Egyptian military base at Buhen. After three months the beleaguered garrison fell. Many inside were slaughtered and parts of the defensive ramparts put to the torch. Those Egyptians who survived were either enslaved or, having sworn a loyalty oath to their new Kushite master, remained at their posts. Inscriptions have been found which demonstrate this switch of allegiance by the fortress commander of Buhen.

A similar fate befell a whole string of Nubian fortresses as the invading army moved relentlessly towards Syene (Aswan). Khaneferre despatched a large force from Thebes which met the Kushites south of the First Cataract. Disastrously for Egypt the pharaonic army was poorly led and was no match for their battle-hardened enemy. The Egyptians were routed and the Black Land's southern gateway lay open to the plunderers.

Within six months the sacred city of Thebes had fallen. The beautiful temple of Karnak was stripped of its treasures and the priests sent south into slavery. Still the Kushites continued their relentless march north. Middle Egypt succumbed with little resistance before the invaders were temporarily halted south of Itj-Tawy. Khaneferre Sobekhotep IV and his royal entourage retreated to Avaris for safety. This proved to be a wise move as, before the year was out, the Kushites executed a brilliant flanking manoeuvre which cut the old pharaonic capital off from its northern lifeline. A large force of Kushite infantry struck out to the western desert oases, travelled north parallel to the Nile and fell upon the city of Memphis, taking it completely by surprise. The whole of the Nile valley now lay in Kushite hands.

This was as far as the invasion reached. The long thin strip of fertile land which is the Nile valley has always been a relatively straightforward target for conquest – an army could take settlement after settlement in linear fashion with little concern for the width of the military front. However, things were entirely different in the delta. There the battle terrain was fragmented into slivers of land between branches of the Nile. Crossing from west to east or vice versa was a nightmare, with swamps and waterways at every turn. An army could easily be ambushed and its retreat cut off. The Kushite chieftain and his commanders decided that they had reached the limit of their conquest and, having reinforced their position at the junction of the delta and valley, they began a concerted effort to plunder and ransack the cities and temples of Upper Egypt.

In the meantime Pharaoh Sobekhotep and his generals skulked in Avaris, frightened to take on the Kushites in Memphis. There seemed to be no-one left who could command the confidence of the demoralised Egyptian troops.

With the pharaonic state in crisis, there was dire need of a saviour to redeem Egypt from its oppressors. This was the first of the two great callings in the life of Moses. His second calling was, as yet, far off but the young prince of Egypt leapt to his first challenge with courage and conviction. Appointing his loyal companions from the military training school to the heart of his command structure, Moses set about building a new Egyptian army. The old guard had disgraced themselves, retreating from the Kushites at every step. Now, with a new leader at the helm, the tide of war began to turn. First Memphis was recaptured, then holy Thebes. The Kushite forces were finally turned at Syene, fleeing in the ships back to their homeland. But Prince Moses was not satisfied at the recovery of Egypt to its traditional southern border. With the golden URAEUS serpent standard carried aloft before the army – the symbol of Egypt's other-worldly power – Moses pursued the enemy upstream. Before the Kushites had time to regroup, the Egyptian forces had surrounded their capital of Saba at Kerma.

The siege lasted several weeks, with the Kushite ruler refusing to commit his depleted forces to battle in the open plain against the rampant Egyptian army. Finally, a delegation was sent to the Egyptian camp, offering Kush's surrender and the hand of the king's daughter in marriage to Prince Moses if he would spare the lives of the rest of the royal family. Moses accepted the offer and duly married Princess Tjarbit (Artapanus' 'Tharbis') before returning with the army to Egypt, the fleet heavy in the water with the recovered treasures of Egypt.

The Egyptian fortresses at the Second Cataract were reoccupied and a small military force remained at Kerma to protect the new Egyptian ambassador established there by Moses. The impressive mudbrick platform, upon which the ambassador's residence once stood, is still to be seen today, dominating the landscape and known locally as the Western Deffufa. A large stela (a fragment of which is now in the British Museum) was set up to record the great victory fought on behalf of Pharaoh Sobekhotep IV and a life-size statue of the king erected on the island of Argo, in the middle of the Nile just upstream from Kerma. This was the traditional way of establishing a new pharaonic boundary: the Egyptian forces were expected to protect the image of their royal master as if it were the king of Egypt himself.

Thanks to the bravery and determination of Moses and his generals, Egypt had not only expelled the savage

Kushite plunderers from its soil but had extended the borders of the 13th-Dynasty pharaonic state from the Second to the Third Cataract, a full two hundred kilometres further south.

Upon his return to Egypt, Moses' popularity amongst the ordinary Egyptians soared to new heights. At every town which the victorious army commander and his new wife passed on their return journey down the Nile from Wawat, Prince Moses was lauded for his great victory. This was not so in the palace of Pharaoh Khaneferre, however. There Moses' acclaim by the people was seen as a direct threat to the throne. The adopted Asiatic prince of Egypt was not of the royal bloodline and not the heir apparent.

Sobekhotep IV had been conspicuous by his absence during the bloody fight to purge Egypt from the savage Kushite oppression. Whilst Prince Moses had taken the fight to the invading enemy, Pharaoh himself, along with Crown Prince Sobekhotep and the rest of the royal household, chose to remain safely protected within the confines of the palace at Avaris. Moses had now defeated the Kushites and the victory was duly recorded in the name of his stepfather Khaneferre. But the king remained suspicious of his adopted son's intentions. Had Moses' triumphant procession through Egypt been an exercise in self-aggrandisement and part of a move amongst his army followers to have the prince elevated to the kingship, bypassing the rightful succession? Khaneferre and his advisers waited for the moment to seize back the political initiative.

Flight from Egypt

One day Prince Moses was on his way to visit his natural mother, his elder brother Aaron and sister Miriam. Riding in his chariot along one of the causeways which joined the island settlements making up the city of Avaris, he came across a Hebrew slave being brutalised by an Egyptian overseer as the poor man tried to repair the collapsed embankment. The young Asiatic prince flew into a rage. Leaping down from his transport, he struck the abuser on the back of the head with his ceremonial mace. The Egyptian fell to the ground, limp and lifeless.

News soon spread of the royal 'crime' in which a native Egyptian had been murdered in protection of an Asiatic slave. Moses realised his predicament. He was aware of the resentment brewing in the palace and knew that this was just the excuse the king had been waiting for to have him arrested and executed. There was only one thing for it: Moses disguised himself as an Asiatic trader and headed east – beyond the borders of Egypt and out of Pharaoh's reach – into the desolate wilderness of Sinai.

For several months Moses wandered from oasis to oasis in search of a place of refuge. Having arrived at the mines of Serabit el-Khadim, he found a gang of Asiatic slaves working the jagged mountain in search of the precious blue stone dedicated to the goddess Hathor, 'Lady of Turquoise'. For a while he laboured alongside his kinfolk, unrecognised by the Egyptian supervisor due to his long, unkempt hair and full beard. Then the exiled prince moved on through the Wadi Maghara, heading towards the southern mountains of the Sinai peninsula.

In spite of being hardened by his military campaigns in Upper Egypt and Kush, as well as the months already spent in the Sinai wilderness, the twenty-year-old refugee from Pharaoh's wrath was near to complete exhaustion when he finally reached the territory of the Midianites. There, nestled in a gorge between high granite peaks, Moses came across an artesian well which he gratefully made use of to quench his thirst before resting beneath the branches of a wizened old tamarisk tree. In the welcoming shade of that ancient resident of the desert, the young prince drifted off to sleep, thinking of the beautiful Kushite wife and Egyptian friends he had left behind, and wondering if he would ever see them again.

Jethro the Midianite

Moses suddenly awoke to the sounds of shouting and screaming. He could see that a group of young girls, in brightly coloured dresses, were being tormented by a gang of male shepherds. The damsels in distress were being prevented from collecting water for their flocks of sheep and goats. With what strength he had left, Moses leapt out at the startled tormentors, gesticulating wildly and shouting at the top of his voice. They retreated in panic.

Moses was escorted to the encampment of Jethro, a Midianite tribal chieftain and the father of seven grateful and admiring daughters. There, on the plain of er-Raaha, he was cared for, dressed and fed. The exiled prince of Egypt had finally found secure refuge amongst the Midianite nomads. Moses remained in the sanctuary of Jethro's tent for more than fifty years, marrying the Midianite chieftain's eldest daughter, Zipporah, who bore him two sons. Moses named them Gershom ('[I am] a foreigner there') and Eliezer ('El is my protector').

The Midianites consisted of wandering nomadic tribal groups, occupying eastern Sinai and the north-west territories of the Arabian peninsula. Their common heritage was a tradition of descent from Abraham's son Midian, born to his second wife Keturah. The descendants of Midian had migrated east into the Arabian desert where, unlike their Israelite cousins, they had remained free of enslavement by the Egyptians. The self-imposed isolation of the Midianites had helped them to preserve their traditional customs and beliefs in a way that was not possible for the Israelite slaves, so heavily influenced by the culture of their Egyptian masters. In this respect, Jethro and his people were much closer to Abraham's way of life than the enslaved descendants of Jacob.

It was through his long stay in the company of Jethro that Moses began to understand the true cultural background of his people. Many evenings were spent listening to his father-in-law telling stories of Abraham and his ten great ancestors back to the flood. The flood story itself, and the legends surrounding those heroes who came before the catastrophe – the antediluvian patriarchs – were devoured by Moses, eager to discover his true identity through the Abrahamic ancestral heritage.

The Name of God Revealed

During the early months of spring it was the practice of Jethro's clan to move their flocks into southern Sinai, where new vegetation provided limited sustenance for the short period before the summer heat baked the land. Moses, now in his seventies but still in vigorous health, had found a favourite spot to graze his flocks at the foot of Mount Horeb (near the well where he first encountered the Midianites). He regularly returned here when there had been a reasonably wet winter season. He knew that the desert around Horeb bloomed and the springs were strong following the February rains.

Moses enjoyed the solitude of his desert sojourns at the foot of the mountain, with just his wife and two sons to tend the flocks and look after their solitary tent. Desert existence had changed him. He had grown wise. So it was that the event which was to change his life, and alter the history of the region forever, occurred nearby in the spring of 1452 BC.

Moses had left Zipporah, Gershom and Eliezer with the main flock as he went in search of strays. He heard the bleating of a young goat coming from a craggy outcrop at the centre of a narrow valley leading to the lower slopes of Mount Horeb. He looked up to see a strange glow coming from a cavelike overhang in the rocky hill. Moses climbed to the hollow which protected a small bush (*Rubus sanctus*, Arabic *allayg*) from the burning heat of the midday sun. The story of what followed in this tiny cave was passed down through the generations – the moment when the god of the Israelites revealed his ancient name for the first time to the man about to become Israel's redeemer.

In Moses' vision he saw the bush alight, yet the leaves did not burn; and then a voice spoke to him from within the bush. The voice told him that he was about to fulfil his destiny – that he was to lead his people out of bondage in Egypt and on to a land of milk and honey where Abraham, Isaac and Jacob had once lived. Moses asked 'If I am to go to the descendants of Israel and say to them "The God of your ancestors has sent me to you", what if they ask me your name, what shall I tell them?' The voice from the burning bush replied 'I am he who is called Eya (Hebrew *eyah asher Eyah*). You must tell the descendants of Israel that Eya has sent you. To Abraham, Isaac and Jacob I appeared as El-shaddai; I did not make myself known to them by my name Yahweh.'

A terrified Moses fled the cave and rushed back to his family. Together they returned to Jethro's camp so that Moses could tell his father-in-law of his vision. The old man listened. He then carefully explained that Moses had received a visitation from the great primeval god who had created Adam on his potter's wheel and saved Noah from the flood. The god who had spoken to him in his dream was the god of all things that lived, the god of the life-giving waters, the god of the abyss and the Lord of the Earth. The Sumerians had known him as Enki, the Babylonians as Eya, the people of the desert called him Ya, but the Midianites worshipped him by his full name – Yahweh. During the years of Abraham, the Amorite chieftains had simply referred to their god as El-shaddai – Lord of the Heights, for Eya's original realm lay beyond the high mountains to the north of the two great rivers of Babylonia whence Abraham had come. It seemed that Yahweh, the god of the Midianites, had decided to renew his covenant with Abraham's other lineage – through Isaac – and that the sons of Israel were finally to be rescued from servitude.

Jethro, priest of Midian and tribal leader, now produced a casket which contained an archive of tablets – copies of the Sumerian and Babylonian epics distributed out to the world from the court of Hammurabi in Babylon. Moses immediately recognised the stories from his childhood. His education as a prince of Egypt now came into its own as he spent hundreds of hours rereading the legendary tales, but this time linking them to the oral traditions passed down to him by his father-in-law. In discovering his own roots he was uncovering the origins (Greek *genesis*) of his own people languishing in cultural poverty back in Egypt. The information gathered here in the tent of Jethro would later form the basis of the Bible's greatest epic – the Book of Genesis – originally written by Moses during the forty years spent in the wilderness after the Israelite Exodus from the land of the pharaohs.

Moses studied Jethro's cuneiform tablets to learn what he could about Enki/Eya and asked Jethro to educate him in the rituals of Yahweh worship. Months passed as the reluctant ordained saviour fought with his conscience. Finally, Moses took up his calling and headed west, back to the rich land of Egypt which had first nurtured the young Israelite but then rejected him because of his foreign roots.

Chapter Ten

MOSES
AND THE EXODUS

(Exodus 4:18 to Deuteronomy 34:12)

*Pharaoh of the Exodus – The Ten Plagues – Departure
from Egypt – The Route to the Mountain of the Tablets
– The Wilderness Years – Invasion of Transjordan –
The Death of Moses*

Moses went back to his father-in-law, Jethro, and
said to him, 'Give me leave to return to my kinsmen
in Egypt and see if they are still alive.' And Jethro
said to Moses, 'Go in peace.' [Exodus 4:18]

eanwhile, back in Egypt the burdens upon the
Asiatic slaves had grown even heavier. Khaneferre
Sobekhotep IV had died not long after Moses'
flight into Sinai. After two short reigns, the throne then
passed to Khahotepre Sobekhotep V who reigned for five
years (1504–1500 BC) before being succeeded by Iayib,
who reigned for a further eleven years (1500–1490 BC).
Then came the long-reigned pharaoh Merneferre Ay for
twenty-four years (1490–1467 BC). By the time he was

buried in his mudbrick pyramid in Avaris, Moses had been living with Jethro and the Midianites for forty years. The Israelite's two sons, Gershom and Eliezer, had grown to manhood as their father turned sixty, with flowing white beard. But the self-imposed exile of the prince of Egypt still had some years to run. Nine more 13th-Dynasty pharaohs quickly succeeded, one after the other, before the infamous Pharaoh of the Exodus sat on the throne of Egypt. In 1450 BC Djedneferre Dudimose was crowned in the temple of Amun at Karnak.

In the very first regnal year of Dudimose, Moses and his family set out from Mount Horeb in southern Sinai and headed north, through the oasis of Rephidim in the Wadi Feiran and along the eastern shore of the Sinai peninsula, on their way to the Egyptian frontier at Migdol ('tower' or 'fortress'). At the oasis of Elim they were met by Aaron, who had received a message from Midianite traders that his brother was finally returning to Egypt.

The Land of the Pharaohs was not the place it had been when Moses lived there as a royal prince. The power of the king had waned since the days of Neferhotep and Sobekhotep IV. The population of Egypt is estimated to have been around three million at this time, with a bonded servant population of perhaps six hundred thousand. The vast majority of these Asiatic agricultural workers and those employed in full-time state building projects represented well over fifty per cent of the country's entire labour force. Most lived in the eastern delta within the province the Bible calls Goshen, where Canaanite and Amorite Middle Bronze Age cultural practices predominated. Here, even for the Egyptians, life was more Asiatic than Egyptian. The people of the Black Land had become utterly dependent on their slave population to tend the fields and build the physical infrastructure of the pharaonic state. The very bricks which supported the grain-stores, palaces and villas of the pharaonic élite were being moulded by the impoverished Hebrews, whilst the Egyptians themselves forgot the art of honest work. They must have known how reliant they were on their domestic servants. Moses understood that the challenge to rescue his people from their Egyptian bondage was going to be difficult.

The Ten Plagues

Dudimose spent the summer months in the old palace at Avaris which, during the inundation, stood on an island where the village of Ezbet Rushdi is now located. On its western and northern sides flowed the Pelusiac arm of the Nile and, to the south and east, glistening lakes fringed with tall reeds and stands of papyri. The royal apartments were on the north side of the island, with the audience hall looking out over the Nile. It was here that Dudimose first came face to face with his nemesis – an Israelite chieftain named Moses.

Every year (as had happened in the time of Abraham and Pharaoh Khety) the Egyptian king traditionally received petitions and gifts from the city rulers and tribal chieftains of the north. At the first audience of the summer, Moses and Aaron were brought before Pharaoh and the contest of wills between the two leaders began. Moses asked the king to allow his people – the Israelites – to journey into Sinai for a few days so that they might worship their god, Yahweh, in his wilderness abode. No pharaoh could have granted such a request. To leave the Egyptians without bonded servants to do their bidding would have brought the Nile valley to a standstill. And there was no guarantee that these Asiatic slaves would obediently return to such a lowly existence once they had ventured beyond the boundaries of their enslavement.

Dudimose decided that the Israelites must be subjected to even greater hardship thanks to the brazenness of their foolish leader. The madman with long flowing beard was dismissed from the court. As he was being manhandled out by the palace guards, Moses cried out a dark warning to Pharaoh – the wrath of Yahweh would befall him and the Egyptians if he did not acquiesce to the demands of God's messenger.

> That very day Pharaoh gave the order to the People's taskmasters and their scribes: 'Do not continue to provide the people with any straw for brick-making as before. Let them go and gather straw for themselves. But you will exact the same quantity of bricks from them as before …' [Exodus 5:6–8]

A month passed and then, in late July, the flood waters of the inundation reached the delta. However, this was no ordinary flood. Instead of being a rich dark brown colour, the Nile was a violent blood-red. The polluted river, full of microscopic organisms (flagellates such as *Euglena sanguinea* or *Haematoccus pluvialis*), flowed into the canals and irrigation ditches. The surface of the water rapidly became choked with dead fish, literally suffocated by the algae which had absorbed all the oxygen. A week later river frogs, unable to survive amongst the rotting fish, moved landward and into the villages. Mosquitoes (biblical *kinnim*) and dog flies (biblical *arob*) feasted on the dead fish by day and bit humans and cattle alike by night. At first the livestock were allowed to drink of the polluted waters and died in their thousands. The Egyptians were forced to drink only from the artesian wells cut into the desert shelf above the valley. In the delta, drinking water had to be ferried by donkey caravan from the south. The corpses of the dead animals attracted swarms of flies which flourished on the rotting carcasses and multiplied in the oppressive heat of summer. The pollution was on a massive scale. The flies (*Stomoxys calcitrans*) carried the deadly virus anthrax, which manifested itself in the form of boils or lesions before overcoming its victims. Thousands died an agonising death as the 'pestilence' endured throughout the winter months.

The sophisticated world of the Egyptians was collapsing

into chaos. Order (Egyptian *maat*) had broken down throughout the land. The gods of Egypt appeared to have abandoned their people. Pharaoh and his courtiers now remembered the curse sworn by the chieftain Moses when he had come before Dudimose in the early summer. Could this all be the work of the strange foreign god of the Israelite slaves? Moses was summoned to the court for interrogation. Once more the Israelite leader demanded that his people should be allowed to journey into the desert to worship Yahweh … and once more Pharaoh refused. Moses warned that far greater disasters were yet to come and that a great tragedy would soon befall the Egyptian people.

Within days a vicious hail storm swept across the delta. Large golf-ball-sized lumps of ice crashed down upon the fields and houses, killing much of the livestock which had survived the anthrax. In early spring a vast swarm of locusts swept up the Nile valley from the south, consuming all before it. The nascent crops of Thebes and the Faiyum basin were wiped out in a matter of days. The air was heavy with foreboding. Animals were agitated and distressed. The people sensed that something even more terrible was about to happen.

Towards the end of February, dark clouds suddenly appeared on the western desert horizon. A great dust-cloud was moving in from the Sahara. The sandstorm hit the Nile valley at dusk and filled the air with fine particles of choking grit. The next day saw no dawn. The land remained dark. People struggled to make their way from house to house, village to village. The darkness prevailed for several days as both Egyptians and Israelite slaves huddled in their homes, frightened to venture out into the cold twilight world around them. But, eventually, the wind died down and the sun-god Re broke through. Men and animals tentatively began to appear from their hiding places. The world seemed calm once more – but for how long? What might the Hebrew god Yahweh yet have in store for Egypt and its unfortunate people?

Pharaoh could stand no more of these terrible plagues upon his land and summoned Moses for what would be the final time. Dudimose offered the Israelite leader wealth and high office if only he would placate the wrath of his god. He would even reduce the burden of the Hebrew slaves. But Moses was in no mood to listen. He sensed Egypt's nemesis was near and his god was about to deliver the final and most horrific blow against the Hebrews' oppressors. The Asiatic chieftain returned to his people, crowded together in the eastern slums of Avaris. Many of the slaves had abandoned their lords and masters to be with Moses. The Egyptians were in no position to hold them in servitude any longer. The best of the young Israelite men were sent out to the surrounding Hebrew villages with messages to prepare for a terrible punishment which was about to befall the land. The people should stay within their communities, welcome fellow slaves in search of refuge, but deny the local Egyptians sanctuary. When the wrath of Yahweh had passed Moses would gather them together for a mass Exodus from Egypt. The moment which would mark the beginning of their long-awaited journey to the Promised Land and their nationhood was at hand.

That night the whole earth shook in a cataclysmic convulsion. A great tidal wave swept in from the Mediterranean and engulfed the delta shoreline. The tsunami reached to the very walls of Avaris, drowning hundreds and smashing the mudbrick houses on the northern periphery of the city. The Israelites living on the far, eastern side of Avaris survived.

As dawn broke the Egyptians began to bury their dead. Within the town they dug shallow pits into which the bodies were cast, one on top of the other. There was no time or will to give these unfortunates proper burial. There were many more dead than alive. Abject misery overwhelmed the slave-masters who had been destroyed by the god of the slaves.

The Israelites and their Hebrew kin slowly came out of

their houses to survey the massacre. They walked through the streets of Avaris to find horrific scenes at every turn. The Egyptians, on their own doorsteps, had resorted to truly barbaric practices in a vain attempt to save themselves from the anger of a god they did not know or understand. Lying in the streets were the bodies of the firstborn males – their throats cut. For centuries it had been the custom amongst many in the Asiatic world to deliver the sacrifice of firstborn sons, at a time of crisis, in order to placate angry gods. The Egyptians of earlier times had not been party to this practice but, during the 13th Dynasty, much of the native population in the Nile valley had interbred with the incoming Asiatics and had inevitably adopted many of their traditions. This influx of Canaanite and Mesopotamian ideas had penetrated into the highest echelons of society – even into the royal household itself. As we have seen, many of the pharaohs of this period bore Asiatic names and were therefore of second-generation Canaanite stock. Dudimose was no exception. Filled with terror and superstition, Pharaoh had taken the lead in the barbarism and sacrificed his own firstborn in the temple of Seth (Canaanite Baal) as the initial tremors shook the ground. But Pharaoh's firstborn was no young boy. His eldest was a fully grown man in his late twenties – the heir to the throne of Egypt. The prince struggled to save himself as the palace guards attempted to do their master's bidding. With this dreadful act, Egypt – ruled by a dynasty of Canaanite pharaohs – had reached the very depths of despair and moral degeneration. This collapse of civilisation in the Nile valley is vividly portrayed in the lamentations of a native Egyptian eyewitness to the disaster named Ipuwer, who recorded his distress on a papyrus now known as 'The Admonitions of an Egyptian Sage'.

> Foreigners have become people (not slaves) every-
> where. … The servant takes what he finds. … Poor
> men have become men of wealth. He who could

not afford sandals now owns riches. Men's slaves – their hearts are greedy … their hearts are violent. Storm sweeps the land. There is blood everywhere and no shortage of dead. The shroud calls out to you from afar. Many corpses are floating in the river.

The river is blood. As you drink of it you shrink from people and thirst for water.

Merriment has ceased and is made no more. Groaning is throughout the land, mingled with laments. Every 'have-not' is one who has. … Children of the nobility are dashed against walls.

See how he who lacked shelter now has shelter, whilst those who had shelter are in the dark of the storm. … The whole delta cannot be seen as Lower Egypt puts trust in trodden roads. What can we do?

See how the land is deprived of kingship by a few people who ignore custom. See how men rebel against the Uraeas Serpent. Stolen is the crown of Re – he who pacifies the Two Lands. … If the palace is stripped, it will collapse in a moment.

There is fire in their (the Asiatics') hearts! If only he (God) had perceived their nature in the first generation! Then he would have smitten the evil, stretched out his arm against it, and would have destroyed their seed and heirs! [*Ipuwer Papyrus*, Leiden 344]

Thousands of Egyptians had been killed by the forces of nature, but hundreds more young men and children had succumbed at the hands of their own fathers – and all to no avail. Moses believed a messenger (an angel) of his god had been the agent of destruction ('The Destroyer' as the

MOSES AND THE EXODUS

Bible puts it) and that the might of Yahweh had thus been demonstrated far beyond anyone's imaginings. The Egyptians were in total shock. They pleaded with the Israelites to take themselves and their devastating god as far away from Egypt as they could go. The citizens of Avaris forced their golden possessions upon those who had once been their servants and sent them on their way to the place where Moses was gathering his people together.

> Gold, lapis-lazuli, silver, and turquoise, carnelian, amethyst, *ibehet*-stone are strung on the necks of female slaves. … See how the poor of the land have become rich and the man of property is now a pauper. … What belongs to the palace has been stripped. [*Ipuwer Papyrus*]

Exodus

The Israelite leader knew that time was of the essence. It would not be long before Egypt's terror turned to rage and revenge. Remembering Joseph's dying words, he gave orders for the mummified body of the patriarch to be removed from his tomb in the overgrown gardens of the old, ruined palace.

> Joseph said to his brothers, 'I am about to die; but God will be sure to remember you kindly and take you out of this country to the country which he promised on oath to Abraham, Isaac and Jacob.' And Joseph put Israel's sons on oath, saying, 'When God remembers you with kindness, be sure to take my bones away from here.' [Genesis 50:24–25]

A team of Israelite men began to dig behind the colossal cult statue of their ancestor until a tunnel had been cut into the underground burial chamber – accessed for the first time in nearly two centuries. Joseph's mummiform coffin

185

was carefully removed and all his grave goods collected together for transportation to the patriarch's new burial place in the Promised Land. Nothing was left in the chamber. However, the great limestone cult statue was simply too heavy to take with them and had to be left guarding the now empty tomb. In fulfilment of his dying wish, Joseph – the leader who had brought the Israelites into Egypt – joined Moses – Israel's new messiah (Hebrew *moshiah*) – on the long return journey to their ancestral homeland.

On the fifteenth day of ABIB in the year 1447 BC, five hundred and ninety-eight clan leaders (Hebrew *aluphim*, i.e. armed warriors), supported by five thousand, five hundred and fifty male followers, their families and children, and a 'mixed multitude' of Hebrew slaves (some thirty thousand souls in all) set out with Moses, heading south-east across the barren wastes of the wilderness of *pa-tjufy* (pronounced Pa-Zufy – 'the reeds') in the direction of *Tjeku* (pronounced Zuko – biblical Succoth, Tell el-Maskhuta in the Wadi Tumilat).

> And they departed from Ramesses (i.e. Avaris) in the first month. It was the fifteenth day of the first month – the day after Passover when the children of Israel went proudly out, in the sight of all Egypt, and whilst the Egyptians were burying those whom Yahweh had struck down and all the firstborn. [Numbers 33:3–4]

At Zuko they met up with their kin who had departed from Pi-Tum (biblical Pithom, modern Tell er-Retabah, a few kilometres further west in the Wadi Tumilat), and those Hebrew slaves who had managed to travel to the delta in the days leading up to the final cataclysm. The throng, now swollen to nearly forty thousand, moved off eastwards and pitched camp on the second night of Exodus at *shi-en-ta-mesa* ('waters of the crocodiles' – biblical Etham, modern Lake Timsah), on the eastern edge of Pa-Zufy wasteland.

As dawn broke, the people could see that they were beside the north-west shore of the lake where the town of Ismailiya stands today. Immediately to their east, a wide man-made channel flowed northwards from Etham. This crocodile-infested waterway linked several swampy, reed-lined lakes extending from the Gulf of Suez in the south to the Mediterranean Sea in the north. The whole complex of pools, lakes and water channels acted as a part natural, part man-made eastern border of the pharaonic state.

The canal, known as *ta-denit* ('the dividing [waters]'), had originally been excavated by King Merikare upon the instructions of his father Nebkaure Khety IV (1876–1847 BC) of the 10th Dynasty, in order to prevent any further Asiatic refugee incursions into Egypt, following the unfortunate episode with the Hebrew chieftain, Abraham, when Egypt's hospitality had been so dishonoured.

> 'Dig a canal to its [limits]. Flood it as far as *kem-wer* ('great black', i.e. the Bitter Lakes). Look, it is the umbilical chord for the foreigners. Its walls are fortified, its army numerous. The farmers in it have been trained to take up arms, in addition to the citizens within (its walls). … Look it is the doorway into the delta.' [*Instructions of Merikare*]

This watery border was then repaired and extended by Amenemhat I and Senuseret I of the 12th Dynasty and, as a result, had become a formidable barrier to anyone trying to cross into Egypt or, in the Israelites' case, leave. This eastern frontier, made up of water barriers and a line of forts, became known as the 'Walls of the Ruler', continuing in use right down into the New Kingdom and beyond.

Whilst the Israelites had been gathering at Zuko on the previous day, Moses had sent scouts ahead to reconnoitre a southerly route across the water barrier. That night they had returned to the camp at Etham with the news that there was no obvious passage out of Egypt if the Israelites were to head south. The only way such a large mass of humanity could cross safely into Sinai would be via the recognised border post at the fortress (Egyptian *mktl*, pronounced 'miktol', biblical Migdol) of Zile (Egyptian *Djlw*, biblical Sile). And so Moses bade the people 'turn back' and head north along the western side of the canal towards the frontier post at Migdol.

By nightfall they reached the 'mouth of the canal' (biblical Pi-Hahiroth) where Merikare's water channel flowed out of the northern shore of the Waters of Re (Lake Ballah). A few kilometres due west was the settlement of Zafane(t) (Greek *Daphne*, modern Tell el-Dafana) where a temple dedicated to 'Baal of the Northlands' (biblical Baal-Zephon) stood. Directly ahead was the narrow ridge of sand leading to Migdol Zile (the twin fortresses of Tell el-Hebua) where the highway to Canaan, known as the Way of Horus began. The sand causeway leading to Migdol was bounded on its northern side by the Waters of Horus (Egyptian *shi-hor*) and to the south by the shallow swamp known as The Reeds (Egyptian *pa-zufy*, biblical *yam suph* = Sea of Reeds).

The sandy causeway which the Egyptians had constructed through the crocodile-infested swamp was very narrow and only capable of taking a few people in line abreast. Moses had crossed back into Egypt from Sinai along this road but the huge following he was now leading would only be able to traverse the marshlands at a snail's pace. And, if this was not enough, the fortresses of Zile stood in their way, garrisoned with a platoon of Egyptian border guards. The way ahead seemed hopeless. Moses had led his followers into a deadly trap with no escape.

On the third night in their bid for freedom, the Israelites pitched their tents on a sandy hill beside the Sea of Reeds. Everyone knew that the forces of vengeance might appear on the western horizon at any moment. It was obvious that the Israelites were vulnerable to attack, trapped against the swamps with only a narrow bottleneck of land leading north-eastwards to the relative safety of the Sinai wilderness. But on that bridge to safety stood the turreted walls of Migdol. They did not have to wait long for their worst fears to come true. That night, just before dawn, the lights from a thousand torches glowed on the western desert ridge in the direction of Zafane. The Egyptian army was upon them.

Miracle of the Sea

In Avaris Pharaoh Dudimose had regained his stubborn heart. He mounted his chariot and drove out into the city to survey the destruction. All around him he witnessed mobs of vigilantes roaming the streets, searching for ways to vent their anger on the abandoned homes of former slaves. The graves of Joseph's brothers – the eponymous ancestors of the twelve tribes – were opened and ransacked. At the nearby pyramid of Joseph there was no longer any body to desecrate – but the magnificent cult statue, adorned in its painted 'coat-of-many-colours', was savagely attacked with copper axes. The head was smashed from the body and rolled down into the tunnel leading to the burial chamber dug by the Israelites just twenty-four hours earlier. It was to be found there, where it had lain for over three thousand years, by an Austrian excavation team led by Professor Manfred Bietak, in 1987.

The Egyptian people were now baying for blood and, as Pharaoh, it was Dudimose's destiny to be the instrument of their revenge. The army was assembled and six hundred chariots set off towards Zafane.

The skies above the eastern Delta were still dark and foreboding, thick with heavy storm-clouds and dust. The sun-god Re struggled to break the stranglehold of the long night beside the Sea of Reeds. In the grey light of dawn the Egyptian army prepared for the final assault on the Israelite multitude backed up against the swamp. The slaughter would be on a massive scale.

At that moment a violent wind blew up from the northeast, creating an impenetrable sandstorm. The Egyptian army disappeared from view. The Israelites turned towards the Reed Sea to witness an incredible scene – the shallow waters of the marshes were being pushed back, exposing the sandy floor to the south of the causeway. A way across to Sinai, one hundred metres wide, lay open before the multitude. The people scurried across the two-kilometre land-bridge to safety, driving their flocks before them.

By midday the wind began to ease and the sandstorm abated. Pharaoh, seeing his enemies making their dash for freedom, gave the order to pursue. His second and now eldest son, Khonsuemwaset, Army Commander of the king's chariotry, led the swoop down into the bed of Pa-Zufy. At first the Egyptian forces sped towards the last few stragglers making their hasty escape on the far side – but then the wheels of the chariots began to sink in the soft, wet alluvium. With the wind subsiding, the water of the marshes quickly returned. The ground beneath the Egyptians held them like quicksand. Horses floundered and sank deeper into the mud; soldiers struggled desperately to extricate themselves from their dire predicament; and then the remaining waters which had been held back by the wind came upon them in a terrible onslaught.

24. A relief survives of Prince Khonsuemwaset, son of Pharaoh Dudimose. He sits beside his wife with objects reflecting their lives below the twin seat. Beneath the woman is a mirror and jewellery box; below the man a pair of leather gloves. Such gloves were specifically used by charioteers to prevent chafing from the reins. Khonsuemwaset may well have been the unfortunate commander of Pharaoh Dudimose's chariot force who perished, along with his men and horses, in the Sea of Reeds.

In seconds Khonsuemwaset and his men found themselves up to their chests in a deadly mix of sand and water. The flood kept coming as men and horses, heavily clad in the trappings of warfare, were swept beneath the onrushing tide. From the safety of the shore, Pharaoh Dudimose watched in horror as Egypt's military pride was decimated in the Sea of Reeds. Moses watched from the opposite shore, knowing that Pharaoh would pursue him and his people no more.

The Israelite women, led by Moses' sister Miriam, rejoiced at the victory of their supernatural redeemer.

> Sing to Yahweh, for he has covered himself in glory.
> Horse and rider he has thrown into the sea.
> Yah is my strength and my song.
> To him we owe our deliverance. [Exodus 15:1–2]

Journey to Mount Horeb

The Israelite tribes and the mixed multitude of fellow slaves who had joined their Exodus headed south – the marsh-lands and lakes of the northern tip of the Red Sea to their right and the vast expanse of the desert of Shur to their left. Progress for such a large mass of humanity and their animals was painfully slow, averaging just fifteen kilometres per day. Three days came and went as they passed by the waters of Marah (the modern Bitter Lakes north of Suez) but the water was salty and bitter to the taste. Moses knew that he had to get his followers to the wells of Elim (modern Ain Musa – the 'spring of Moses') before the water supply they had carried with them ran out. Two more days of forced march brought the refugees to the haven of Elim with its seventy palm trees protecting twelve artesian wells. Here the Israelites stayed for a week, gathering their strength and organising resources for the long journey which lay ahead.

Moses knew where he was heading – into the safety of

familiar Midianite territory in southern Sinai – but he had never envisioned having to make the trek through such inhospitable terrain with so many people, all counting on him for their very lives. As the people set off once more, heading along the shore of the Red Sea, Moses despatched Hoshea (later renamed Joshua), son of Nun, with a troop of one hundred tribal warriors to the mines at Mofka(t) (the Egyptian word for turquoise corrupted to Dophkah in Numbers 33:12 – the pharaonic turquoise mines of Serabit el-Khadim). There they were to rescue Israelite and Hebrew mine-workers and rejoin the twelve tribes as they headed south through the Wadi Maghara at the western boundary of the wilderness of Sin. Exactly one month after departing from Egypt, Moses pitched camp in a semi-fertile valley called ALUSH, scattered with tamarisk trees and scrub.

By now the supplies brought out of Egypt were drastically depleted. Food was in short supply and the people began to complain about their lot. 'Why did Moses bring us out of Egypt with its abundant food merely to have us all die of starvation and thirst in this barren wilderness?' Once more, miraculous timing and Moses' own intimate knowledge of Sinai saved the desperate multitude. As evening drew near, the skies above Alush were filled with tiny, chattering quail birds, coming in to land after a long day's flight from Africa. The huge flock was on its spring migration, taking the same route they followed every year into central Europe. The Midianites of Sinai knew of this annual miracle and took full advantage of the banquet which landed so regularly and conveniently in their laps. This phenomenon continues to be observed by the modern Bedouin and western travellers to Sinai of more recent times.

> At twilight you will eat meat and in the morning you will have bread to your heart's content. Then you will know that I am Yahweh your god. [Exodus 16:12]

Moses had always planned on exploiting the natural resources of Sinai to sustain his people and ordered the men to collect their harvest of fresh meat. Thousands of birds were killed as throw sticks struck their exhausted targets, too weak to escape the slaughter. And Moses had another surprise awaiting his flock. The Wadi Mukkatab (biblical Alush) is scattered with hundreds of tamarisk trees which exude a white, sticky dew in the pre-dawn damp of the sandstone desert. Actually, the manufacturers of this miraculous substance are small insects (*Trabutina mannipara* and *Najacoccus serpentinus*) which infest the trees, sucking out sap and depositing the residue like 'glistening pearls' on the branches – some of which falls to the ground to form a carpet of edible crystals. With the warmth of the morning sunlight this 'manna' is devoured by swarms of ants but, if collected at dawn – before the sun draws the ants to the surface – it provides a delicious breakfast. For all their remaining years spent in the wilderness the Israelites enjoyed the miracle of the 'manna from heaven'.

The place of the miracles of the quails and manna – the Wadi Mukkatab ('valley of writing') – passed into folklore amongst the desert tribes of Midian. Over the two thousand years which followed, nomads journeying through the region would stop to carve their names in the strange Sinaitic/Nabatean script of the desert to commemorate the place where Yahweh performed his miracles through the wisdom of his prophet, Moses.

For a whole week the quails kept coming and the manna continued to form on the trees. The people feasted 'to their heart's content', but then it was time to move on. The tribes packed up their tents and gathered their belongings, heading south once more. Slowly but surely the great throng were getting nearer to the next major place of refuge – the lush and abundantly watered oasis of Rephidim nestled in the steep-sided gorge of the Wadi Feiran. But, just as the head of the column reached the plain before Rephidim and with the mouth of the Wadi Feiran in sight, scouts came rushing to Moses with worrying news. They were not alone in the vastness of the rock desert. The oasis of Rephidim was already occupied.

The Israelites were quite unaware of what had been happening in the world around them as they made their way through the deserts and mountains. Their month-long isolation was about to come to an abrupt end in dramatic circumstances. Amalekite tribesmen from the southern Negeb and northern Arabia had been moving through Sinai in their thousands, heading in the opposite direction to the Israelites. The nomadic hordes were on their way to the Nile valley – refugees from famine and disaster themselves – but not simply looking for a land of refuge. They were set upon the conquest of Egypt's riches, knowing full well that the Land of the Pharaohs had been brought to its knees by the disastrous plagues. News of the military catastrophe at the Sea of Reeds had reached far and wide. The north-eastern delta border was now wide open and undefended. What was left of the decimated Egyptian army was incapable of protecting its homeland. Asiatic hordes from the north and east were pouring across Sinai into the fertile delta like scavengers preparing to feast on an unburied corpse. The disaster, long remembered by the people of the Nile, was painfully recalled in the writings of the Egyptian priest, Manetho, as quoted by the Jewish historian, Josephus.

> Tutimaeus (i.e. Pharaoh Dudimose). In his reign, for what cause I know not, a blast of God (i.e. the plagues) smote us (i.e. the Egyptians). And unexpectedly, from the regions of the east (i.e. Arabia and the Negeb), invaders of obscure race (i.e. the biblical Amalekites) marched in confidence of victory against our land. By main force they easily seized it without striking a blow (i.e. because the army had already been annihilated in the Sea of Reeds); and having overpowered the rulers of the

land (i.e. the pharaohs of the 13th and parallel 14th Dynasties), they then ruthlessly burned our cities, razed to the ground the temples of the gods, and treated all the natives with a cruel hostility, massacring some and leading into slavery the wives and children of others.

Finally (i.e. after some considerable time), they appointed as king one of their number whose name was Salitis (i.e. Shalek, founder of the Greater Hyksos dynasty). He had his seat at Memphis, levying tribute from Upper and Lower Egypt, and always leaving garrisons behind in the most advantageous positions. ...

In the Saite [Sethroite] nome (i.e. biblical Goshen) he founded a city very favourably situated on the east (bank) of the Bubastite (i.e. Pelusiac) branch of the Nile, and called it Auaris after an ancient religious tradition (i.e. Vizier Joseph's Hatwaret/Haware/Avaris – the 'Estate of the Administrative District'). [Josephus, *Contra Apionem*]

I have added (in brackets) the elements from our own story of the Children of Yahweh to provide a new insight as to the events and people being described in this famous quotation from Manetho's original account. We will return to the ongoing Egyptian tragedy in a later chapter when I deal with the Israelite Judges and their struggle against Philistine oppression. But, for now, we have a more pressing drama about to be played out in the wilderness of Sin.

There, in southern Sinai, the twelve tribes of Israel were caught up in the Asiatic invasion of Egypt. Confronted by a large band of Amalekite warriors heading for the eastern delta to join in the plunder, there was no way to turn. Moses had to get his people to the water supply at Rephidim and the Amalekites ensconced there just had to be removed. The two nomadic armies clashed in the sandy plain of Rephidim and skirmished, on and off, for most of the day.

By sunset the Israelite tribal warriors, led once more by Hoshea, had prevailed and the Amalekites were forced to retreat from their base in Rephidim Oasis. The next day, with the water supply secured, the twelve tribes and their followers moved into the Wadi Feiran and rested within the shade of a thousand welcoming palm trees.

The Ten Commandments

Once again the Israelites took respite from their journey so that they could water their flocks and gather strength for what still lay ahead. To the south rose the spectacular jagged peaks of Gebel Serbal, touching the heavens. The people of Israel had finally reached the mountain homeland of their god and would soon be in Yahweh's presence. After a few days, Moses and Aaron went ahead on the direct but steep and narrow path known as the Pass of the Wind (Arabic *Nagub el-Haawa*) which leads to Mount Horeb, leaving Hoshea and the tribal leaders to bring the multitude on the longer but easier route around the central mountain massif and through the Watiya Pass.

After his mission to Egypt Moses had returned to the place of the burning bush. Jethro was waiting to greet his son-in-law and there was much rejoicing at his safe return. The Midianite high priest of Yahweh offered up a kid-goat to the god of Sinai in gratitude for the safe and successful completion of Moses' mission. Preparations were then made for the arrival of the mass of refugees from Egyptian oppression and the Giving of the Law which would establish the identity of Moses' multitudinous flock as the chosen of Yahweh.

A week later the people had arrived and pitched their huge camp in the wide open plain of er-Raaha ('the resting place'), facing the dark red mountains of Sinai. Before them stretched a long narrow valley guarded by giant pinnacles of granite (Ras Safsaafa), their wind-smoothed faces glistening in the sharp desert light. Hidden from sight, beyond the valley where Moses had been drawn to the burning bush, rose precipitous Mount Horeb (Gebel Musa – 'Mountain of Moses'), looking out northwards to Gebel Serbal, Rephidim and, beyond, the whole expanse of the Sinai wilderness.

Few places in the world come close to matching the majesty and sense of awe the visitor discovers upon approaching the foot of the legendary Mountain of the Ten Commandments.

In the first week following their arrival at the holy mountain, the tribes set about the task of establishing a permanent camp near the springs of Sinai. Moses appointed tribal lieutenants to give advice and settle disputes whilst he departed from the people to prepare for his encounter with Yahweh. He spent several days alone at the top of the jagged mountain beyond the valley of the burning bush before returning to the camp. The people of Israel were then assembled around a large, dome-shaped rock at the entrance to the valley, there to await the commandments of the god of Sinai. From his rock pulpit, Moses informed the throng that he would now ascend once more to the summit of Mount Horeb, in the distance behind him, this time to meet Yahweh, their redeemer. The people were to await his return in er-Raaha, from where they could safely witness God's power from afar. Moses would then bring Yahweh's message down from the mountain.

The Golden Calf

Moses began the long climb to the summit of Mount Horeb in the company of his loyal adjutant, Hoshea. Just a few hundred metres from the pinnacle they reached a natural hollow in the mountain, scattered with acacia trees. Moses asked Hoshea to remain there while he went on up to the top of the mountain alone. That night a pall of dark clouds descended from the north and enveloped the mountains of Sinai. Thunder crashed around the jagged peaks,

bouncing from the walls of the valleys in an almost conti-
nuous roar – yet there was no rain. A hard wind howled
through the cracks in the rocks around the summit of Mount
Horeb as Hoshea crouched in the shelter of the hollow.
Down in the valley the whole congregation watched in
uneasy wonderment as lightning danced from peak to peak
in a majestic ballet of light.

By morning all was calm. The dark clouds had moved
on south towards the Arabian peninsula. The air was still
but cold. A damp mist had settled in the valleys of Sinai,
its black peaks rising up through a sea of grey. Then the
sun burst upon the horizon, flooding the tops of the mist
clouds in its golden light. Slowly the grey sea was burnt
away as the mountain shadows slid back into the earth.
The people encamped in Raaha, at the foot of the mountain,
came out of their tents and waited for their leader's return
... but Moses did not come down from the Mountain of
God. The elders gathered for several days at the rock where
Moses had bade them wait for him ... but God's messenger
did not return to them. Hoshea remained in the hollow,
waiting to assist his master down the mountain ... but there
was no sign of Moses.

> Mount Sinai was entirely wrapped in smoke,
> because Yahweh had descended on it in the form
> of fire. The smoke rose like smoke from a furnace
> and the whole mountain shook violently. [Exodus
> 19:18]

Days passed, then weeks. Moses still did not appear. The
people were gripped with fear. Perhaps the charismatic
leader who had brought them out of Egypt and guided
them through the wilderness was dead? Perhaps Yahweh
had been defeated by the powerful gods of Egypt in a great
cosmic battle over Sinai?

The slaves from the mines at Mofkat, rescued by
Hoshea, had been devotees of the goddess Hathor, patron

deity of Sinai. The turquoise mines were located around a high plateau upon which the temple of Hathor 'Lady of Turquoise' had been built by their ancestors in the time of Amenemhat III and the vizier Joseph. These men had not been witness to the miracles of Yahweh in Goshen or at the Reed Sea. They began to stir the people, saying that Hathor must be appeased for Israel's entry into her realm without the proper ritual oblations. Soon a large agitated throng had gathered at the tent of Aaron, demanding that he make a statue of Hathor at which the people could make libations in praise of the goddesses of fertility and mother-hood. Aaron was unable to resist the demands of the people without his strong-willed brother by his side. He ordered the collection of a great part of the gold taken from the Egyptians on the day of Exodus and handed it over to the miners for smelting.

Ten days later, a great golden calf – the image of the cow-goddess Hathor – stood on the rock where Moses had departed from the multitude five weeks earlier. Hathor's statue had been skilfully crafted by the metalworkers of Mofkat. Between her horns a large sun-disc supported two tall plumes gleaming in the sunlight. Around her neck she wore a golden chain on which hung the Egyptian symbol of life. All this was familiar to the Hebrew slaves. What they saw before them was tangible, touchable, comforting – not like the nebulous, invisible, angry god of Moses whom they so feared. The people rejoiced at their return to the worship of the benevolent Egyptian goddess of love and fertility. The celebrations continued throughout the night.

Meanwhile, that very evening, Moses had descended from his retreat on the peak of Horeb and spent the night with Hoshea in the hollow. At dawn the two men descended from the mountain, the old man supported by the young as he carried a pair of large stone tablets bearing the 'Ten Words' commanded by Yahweh.

Those words – which we know as the Ten Command-ments – were carved in the world's most ancient alphabet.

Scholars call the script Proto-Sinaitic because it was first discovered scratched on the rocks of the Mofkat mines at Serabit el-Khadim and around the copper mines of Wadi Maghara in central west Sinai. The signs which represent the letters of this alphabet are Egyptian hieroglyphs – but they cannot be read as Egyptian words, for they are Semitic letters. The ox head represents *aleph*, the eye *aiyn*, the house sign the letter *bet*, and so on. This new invention, which would eventually evolve into the Greek and (subsequently) modern alphabets, was the creation of Hebrew slaves. They had taken the Egyptian symbols and adapted them for writing their names and a few simple phrases in their own language. But it took the multilingual skills of an educated Hebrew prince of Egypt to turn these simple first scratchings into a functional script, capable of transmitting complex ideas and a flowing narrative. The Ten Commandments and the Laws of Moses were written in Proto-Sinaitic. The prophet of Yahweh – master of both the Egyptian and Mesopotamian epic literature – was not only the founding father of Judaism, Christianity and, through the Koranic traditions, Islam, but also the progenitor of the Hebrew, Canaanite, Phoenician, Greek and therefore modern western alphabetic scripts.

As Moses and Hoshea reached the valley of the burning bush they saw, ahead of them, the golden idol perched on top of the rock. No-one was to be seen – the exhausted people had all retired to their tents. Hoshea roused the men of Levi and ordered his kin to arm themselves. His élite troops swept through the camp slaughtering three thousand victims amongst the slumbering mass of humanity. The clatter of arms awoke the people who scattered in every direction. The Levites completed their bloody orders. They were then instructed to round up the survivors and bring them to the place where Moses stood on the crest of the rock beside the golden idol. He smashed the tablets of the Ten Words – the slabs shattering into a dozen fragments. He then ordered Hoshea to overthrow the golden calf and have it utterly destroyed. The message was clear – there would be no wavering from the path of Yahweh. There would be no other god but Yahweh.

Ark of the Covenant

Once again Moses went up the Mountain of God and, after several days, returned carrying a fresh pair of tablets. This time the people remained faithful to Yahweh, receiving the commandments through the voice of their prophet.

Many months were spent preparing a portable shrine to house Yahweh's testimony. A golden ark was crafted by Bezalel, son of Uri, to contain the tablets of the law. It was designed in the form of an Egyptian robing box, countless numbers of which the carpenter Bezalel had made during his time as a slave in the royal workshops of Avaris. The one difference was that this box was portable, supported on carrying poles so that it could move at the head of Yahweh's army as it marched into the Promised Land. When the Ark of the Covenant rested it was protected within a tented pavilion, which itself stood in an open court surrounded by a screen of fabric suspended between acacia-wood posts. This design would eventually form the basis of the great Solomonic temple in Jerusalem in which the Ark of the Covenant was placed four hundred and eighty-seven years later.

The Israelites spent a bitter cold winter in the plain of er-Raaha as the craftsmen laboured over the tabernacle shrine. In that time Moses selected the men of the tribe of Levi as the priests of Yahweh and trained them in the cultic rituals. Aaron was appointed the first Israelite high priest of Yahweh and given fine robes befitting his office. When the work on Yahweh's portable shrine was finally complete, the sacred compound was erected outside the camp at Raaha and Moses entered the 'Tent of Meeting' to receive further instructions from his god before the Ark of the Tablets. Now that this potent symbol of Yahweh's power was finished, the Israelites were ready to take on anything that lay before them. The Ark of the Covenant would be their secret weapon – the standard before which all their enemies would succumb – the sole symbol by which future generations would know the god of Sinai who had rescued the Israelite slaves from Egyptian oppression.

The Wilderness Years

With the building of the tabernacle complete, it was time to leave the Mountain of God. And so, 'on the first day of the second month, in the second year after they had come out of the land of Egypt', the Israelites headed north towards the Promised Land [Numbers 1:1]. Jethro had departed with Moses' wife and sons for his tribal homelands in the southern Negeb soon after the meeting with his son-in-law. He went ahead to prepare for the arrival of the Israelite tribes and to make sure that the vital wells needed for such a large migrating population were secured. However, Jethro's other son, Hobab, remained with Moses to guide him through the oases of eastern Sinai. It took the multitude three days to reach Kibroth-ha-Taavah and then several more days before they arrived at the spring of Hazeroth (Arabic *Ain Hudera*), where they rested.

Progress was painfully slow as Moses led his people down towards the eastern shore of Sinai before turning north along the Wadi Nasb, parallel to the Gulf of Akaba, and on into the wilderness of Paran in north-east Sinai. The itinerary of camps on the long march is listed in Numbers 33:15–37: setting out from Mount Sinai the Israelites stopped at Kibroth-ha-Taavah – Hazeroth (Ain Hudera) – Rithmah – Rimmon-Perez – Libnah – Rissah – Kehelathah – Mount Shepher – Haradah (Gebel Arada) – Makheloth – Tahath – Terah – Mithkah – Hashmonah – Moseroth – Bene Jaakan – Hor-Gidgad – Jotbathah (Taba) and Abronah before they reached Ezion-Geber near the modern resort of Eilat on the Gulf of Akaba's northern tip.

They then entered the great stony wilderness of Zin (the south-eastern Negeb desert), heading for Jethro's ancestral land – the place to which Hagar, the Egyptian concubine of Abraham, brought her son Ishmael and where the Midianites – sons of Abraham's other concubine, Keturah – had also settled.

On the boundary between the deserts of Paran and Zin was an ancient holy mountain where these nomadic descendants of Abraham had worshipped El-shaddai, but whom they now identified with Yahweh. The broad flat-topped summit and sandy plain below were scattered with stone altars and blackened standing stones from that bygone age of the sons of Abraham's concubines (EB/MB to Middle Bronze I). Bedouin tradition calls the place Jebel Ideid, which Arabic scholars believe means either 'Mountain of the Multitude of the Preparation' or 'Mountain of Commemoration'. The modern Israelis have dubbed it Har-Karkom ('Saffron Mountain').

The archaeologist who has been overseeing an archaeological survey of the site, Professor Emmanuel Anati, believes it to have been the mountain of the Ten Commandments (i.e. Mount Horeb). He is wrong in this assumption, but he has indeed found one of the most important places in the Exodus story, for this is the true site of Kadesh-Barneah – the holy gathering place where the multitude of Israel prepared to enter the Promised Land and where they commemorated their covenant with Yahweh for the first time on top of the sacred mountain.

For twelve months of the desert wanderings, the Israelite tribes sojourned in the wildernesses of Paran and Zin, scratching out an existence in the inhospitable terrain – thanks to the few Midianite wells and springs which dot the landscape around Kadesh. Moses camped at Bir-Ideid (Israeli *Beer-Karkom*), a short distance to the north-west of the holy mountain where the tabernacle stood, guarded by the Levites. Bir-Ideid is the place the book of Genesis calls Beer-Lahai-Roi, between Kadesh and Bered, where

Hagar and her son Ishmael sought refuge following their expulsion from Abraham's camp at Beer-Sheba four hundred years earlier [Genesis 16:7–14].

All around Mount Paran (Kadesh) Anati has discovered rocks carved with figures of animals (ibexes, wild goats, asses, etc) and hunters (with bows, staffs, maces and lassoes), typical of early rock art throughout the deserts of the region (including the Sinai and Egypt's Eastern Desert). But there is also religious iconography here of unknown date, including symbols such as a staff standing before a serpent (the staff of Moses?) and what appears to be a horned altar or stone tablet divided into ten panels (the Ten Commandments?). Numerous carved human figures are shown with arms raised in prayer. All over the desert floor small stone circles, altars and pillars (biblical *masseboth*) have been erected. A number of the grouped standing stones consist of twelve masseboth (the twelve tribes?). Many of the man-made structures are the monuments of earlier times, but a good number were erected by the Israelite tribes in dedication to Yahweh at this second major holy resting place on their journey to salvation.

Whilst the Israelites rested at Kadesh, Moses sent spies into the country north of the Negeb desert to scout out the terrain and bring news back about the land and its people. After a month they returned carrying the fruits of the region with them. But they also reported that this land 'overflowing with milk and honey' was inhabited by powerful kings living in strong-walled cities. The scouts convinced the tribal elders that any attempt to occupy the Promised Land would end in rout and disaster. As if to make the point, a force of Israelite warriors went on a scavenging raid into the hill country around Arad but they were quickly repelled and then slaughtered at Hormah as they fled back into the Negeb. Moses decided that the Israelites were not yet ready for the task that Yahweh had set them. Many years would be needed to build a large army of young, brave warriors capable of taking the walled towns of Canaan. The invasion would have to wait for a new generation, hardened by desert life and thirsty for the milk and honey which awaited them beyond the horizon.

Journey to Mount Hor

In the eleventh month of the long sojourn in the Paran desert Moses' sister, Miriam, died. She was buried on the summit of Gebel Ideid. The twelve tribes, having gathered together for the thirty-day mourning period, then set off on their journey to the third great holy site of the wandering years. They headed eastwards, via the wells at Ada, Ashalim and Menuffa, entering the Arabah basin at the point where the Wadi Paran drainage system disgorges into the great rift valley. From here it was just one more day's march due east across the Arabah to the mountains of Seir and the majestic canyons surrounding Mount Hor.

In his years of exile spent with the Midianites, Moses had been told of a hidden valley within the sandstone mountains of Transjordan on the opposite side of the rift valley. This was the place where Esau, Jacob's twin brother, had settled and where his offspring had grown into the tribes the Bible refers to as the Edomites (in the north) and Midianites (in the south and west). These nomadic peoples were the Israelites' distant cousins and therefore unlikely to wage war on the stateless refugees from Egypt.

The natural stronghold of Esau's old domain was amply supplied with water and easily protected from attack. It lay on the southern borders of Edom, at the edge of the Jordanian plateau and close to the King's Highway which led north through Edom and the Amorite lands of Moab and Ammon. The place was called Moserah [Deuteronomy 10:6] but we know it today by its Classical Greek name of Petra – the Rose-Red City of the Nabateans, carved out of the rocks of Mount Seir a thousand years after the Israelites had arrived at Moserah. Even so, the local descendants of the Midianites continue to call the place Wadi Musa (the 'valley of Moses') in memory of the prophet's stay there. Close by is another 'Ain Musa' – spring of Moses – where, tradition holds, Yahweh's messenger struck the rock to bring forth the waters which still feed the valley of Moses.

It was here in the multicoloured canyons of Moserah/ Petra that the twelve tribes remained for thirty-seven long summers and winters. Soon after they arrived, the Israelites set up an altar of piled stones facing the Promised Land on the summit of a rocky pinnacle overlooking their camp. Here at this 'high place' the tribal elders met in council and offered sacrifice to Yahweh. And here too Moses spent the remaining years of his life compiling the sacred history of the Children of Yahweh – what we know as the books of Genesis and Exodus. In the writing of Genesis on leather scrolls, he would have drawn upon the rich literature of Middle Kingdom Egypt, as well as the numerous oral traditions told to him by his father-in-law, Jethro, and the archive of cuneiform tablets obtained from Hammurabi's Babylon by Midianite caravaneers. Remember that, as an educated Egyptian prince, he had learnt how to read Akkadian cuneiform and was therefore familiar with much of the epic literature of the ancient world, widely dispersed at this time thanks to the influential Amorite dynasty of Babylon I (1667–1362 BC).

So it was that the stories of Eden, Enoch, the Great Flood, Nimrod and the Tower of Babel came to be included in the history of Israel. The dramatic events of the Exodus from Egypt were, of course, part of Moses' own direct experience. Indeed, he had been at the centre of the story. The three remaining books of the Pentateuch – Leviticus, Numbers and Deuteronomy – were formulated by later redactors, but they too were based on the governances and ritual practices laid down by Moses and Aaron in Kadesh and Moserah. All these ancestral stories and religious laws became the foundation covenant of this new nation forged by Yahweh in the mountain wildernesses of Sinai, Paran and Seir. Moses' great work, long recited in oral tradition, would be much edited, amended and added to in later years, but the major part of this impressive enterprise (which, as we saw in the Introduction, biblical exegetes call J – the Yahwistic element) was originally collated and fashioned by Yahweh's greatest prophet at Petra within the red mountains of Seir.

Near the end of their generation-long sojourn in Wadi Musa, Moses' brother Aaron, the first Israelite high priest of Yahweh, was nearing the end of his life. It was time for him to make his last journey – the ascent of the highest rocky peak in the Petra region where the god of Israel was awaiting his priestly servant. Moses and Eleazar, Aaron's eldest son, helped the old man climb up to the 1,396-metre-high summit of Mount Hor whilst the people watched his slow progress from Wadi Thugra below the mountain.

Finally the moment had come for Aaron to depart this world. Stripping to his undergarments, Aaron handed over to his son the robes and symbols worn by the high priest of Yahweh. He then knelt down on a slab of rock facing the Arabah and, beyond on the distant horizon, the hills of Kadesh. There, by Yahweh's command, Moses' brother and spokesman was gently 'gathered to his people'.

Aaron was buried in a small cave atop Mount Hor, overlooking Petra, where a tiny whitewashed Muslim shrine dedicated to the 'Prophet Harun' still stands to this day. At some distant, forgotten time, between then and now, a stone sarcophagus was placed in the cave beneath the shrine within which the prophet's bones were laid to rest.

Invasion of Moab and Ammon

After thirty days of mourning for the high priest, the twelve tribes were on the move once more. The requisite number of years had passed and the time had finally come to make their way to the River Jordan. Aaron's death marked the end of the generation who had set out from Egypt. The great majority of the people who now made up the twelve tribes had not been born into slavery like their parents. They were free men and women who had come into this world as children of the wilderness, untainted by the bondage years. They were young, fit and ready for war.

Moses was four years younger than his brother Aaron and it was clear to those around him that their leader's life was also drawing to a close. Israel's saviour knew he had to fulfil his duty to Yahweh and get the people to the borders of the Promised Land before he breathed his last.

In the spring of 1407 BC, the twelve tribes, now organised into a well-trained and structured fighting force, marched down into the Arabah once more and headed north to Zalmonah (Roman *Calmonah*) and then on to the copper mines of Punon (Arabic *Feinan*). The king of Arad (who had repelled the Israelite raid thirty-eight years earlier when they had tried to enter the Promised Land from Kadesh in the south) came once more to challenge the large force approaching his territory. At Hormah, the place of the original slaughter of the Israelite warriors, Arad's army, to the last man, was put to the sword. The new army of Yahweh, the Ark of the Covenant carried before them, was blooded and ready for what lay before them.

At the furnaces of Punon Moses cast a bronze image of a serpent to protect his people from snake bites. The standard of the protective serpent was carried before the army, alongside the Ark, just as Pharaoh's uraeus serpent went before the Egyptian army during Moses' victorious campaign against Kush all those years before. The aged nomadic chieftain who had once been a youthful prince of Egypt had not forgotten the impact of symbols of power.

Destruction of the Amorite Kingdoms in Jordan

Moses certainly would have preferred to take the Israelites through Edom along the King's Highway but King Rekem of Edom, descendant of Esau, refused permission to allow his distant kin access to Moab and Ammon through his own territory for fear of reprisal from his northern neighbours. Besides, the Israelites had already demonstrated their military prowess and were perceived, therefore, as a dangerous people who might well turn on their hosts. Rekem relied on tribal kinship oaths to protect Edom from a full-blown invasion by the Israelites. His judgement proved well founded. Moses reluctantly took the more inhospitable route, skirting Edom on its western side and heading north through the Arabah basin.

The Israelite army headed past Aboth and crossed the brook of Zered (Wadi el-Hesa) into Moabite territory. Continuing along the eastern shore of the Dead Sea to the ruins of Zoar – the place to which Lot had escaped following the destruction of Sodom – they reached the gorge of the River Karak, up which they climbed to the southern boundary of the kingdom of Ammon. And now, in the fortieth year after the Exodus from Egypt, the slaughter which characterised the Israelite conquest of the Promised Land began.

King Rekem of Edom had been right to fear the Children of Yahweh. Over the coming years, the Israelite warrior lord Hoshea – whom Moses had renamed Joshua ('Yah has saved') – would lead a bloody campaign across the nomadic kingdoms of Transjordan. No-one was spared. Sihon, king of Ammon, and Og, king of Bashan, were put to the sword. Joshua's forces 'utterly annihilated' their civilian Amorite kinfolk 'destroying every town, man, woman and child', their cattle and goods taken as booty [Deuteronomy 3:6–7]. They even eventually turned on the Midianites who had sheltered them. No-one, friend or foe, was saved from the wrath of Yahweh's army.

The progress of the Israelite horde eventually saw them camped down on the plains of Moab for the winter. The great tented city was situated at Abel-ha-Shittim, to the east of the Jordan river, just north of the Dead Sea.

News of the slaughter had quickly reached the people across the Jordan and they were gripped with panic. For centuries the region had seen relative peace, but now a great calamity was about to descend upon the hills and valleys of Canaan from the east. The book of Joshua records how peace and security died in this majestic landscape with the Israelite crossing of the River Jordan. The legacy of that traumatic time still lies behind the deep and abiding mistrust which exists between the 'sons of Abraham'.

Death on Mount Nebo

At the ordained moment when the Israelites were ready to enter the land promised to them by Yahweh's prophet, Moses addressed his people for the last time. His life was to end here on the east side of the Jordan. The winter of 1407/1406 BC – forty years on from the departure out of Egypt – was nearing its end and a new age was about to dawn with the coming of spring.

There, before the assembled tribes, Moses handed the leadership of Israel to his army commander, Joshua. The two men then climbed to the summit of Mount Nebo where Moses, 'his eye undimmed', beheld the entire land which Yahweh had given to his children. He was quietly gathered to his ancestors 'according to the Lord's command'.

Moses was buried in a cave, hidden within a valley near Beth-Peor, where his bones lie undisturbed to this day. The secret hiding place was entered only once in the centuries which followed. In the days before the fall of Jerusalem, Yahweh's prophet Jeremiah brought the Ark of the Covenant from the Temple of Solomon and placed it in Moses' tomb. As Jerusalem and its holy temple smouldered in ruin, and as the Children of Yahweh were led off to Babylon – into slavery once more – the tablets from Mount Horeb lay safe in their golden box beside the bones of the man who had freed the people of Israel from their original bondage and forged them into a nation.

Chapter Eleven

JOSHUA
AND THE CONQUEST

(Joshua 1:1 to Joshua 24:33)

*Jericho – Ai – Gibeon – The First Southern Campaign
– Hazor and the Northern Campaign – The Second
Southern Campaign – The Shechem Covenant – Sheshi
and the Amalekites*

The year is 1406 BC. The Israelite army is encamped at Shittim in the plain of Moab, opposite Jericho. It is late spring and Jericho's harvest is safely secured within the city walls. The farmers of the Jordan valley have fled their villages, seeking refuge within the ramparts of their 'City of the Palms'. The king of Jericho is confident that the walls of his stronghold will withstand an attack from the Israelite horde – after all, two generations of his predecessors had been responsible for building and reinforcing the defences of this impressive Middle Bronze Age fortress-city. Jericho – the front line in the fight against the invaders – was impregnable.

Its defences had been well thought out. Any attacking army would have to cross a deadly killing zone before even reaching the walls. Encircling the city was a four-metre-high stone revetment wall supporting the base of a steeply sloping glacis. The thirty-five-degree angle of the glacis slope was covered in a gleaming white lime-plaster coating, its slippery surface almost impossible to scale. And on top of this mighty earthen rampart stood a seven-metre-high mudbrick wall, three metres thick at its base. From top to bottom, the height of Jericho's perimeter rampart and wall was twenty-two metres (72 ft) and its overall thickness more than twenty-four metres (79 ft).

A frontal assault on such defences could only result in mass slaughter as arrows, sling-stones and fire rained down on any assailant attempting to scale the slippery slope. The spears of the attacking troops would hardly reach the top of the fortress wall and no battering ram could get anywhere near that wall to undermine it. The ruler of Jericho was confident that the Israelites were not going to get the better of his city in a full-frontal attack and, if siege was the alternative, then, with storage jars in the city overflowing with grain and the Jericho spring secure within the city walls, the people could hold out almost indefinitely. But, in spite of the king's assurances, the ordinary citizens of Jericho were afraid. They had heard what the Israelites had done to the nomads of Transjordan and the story of Yahweh's destruction of the Egyptian army at the Sea of Reeds was known to everyone. The psychological war had already been won. Terror had become Israel's most powerful weapon.

All this was reported back to Joshua by two spies who had been sent into Jericho to reconnoitre the city's defences. They had stayed in the house of the prostitute, Rahab, located in the northern part of the city. There a lower terrace, between the upper city wall and a secondary wall at the bottom of the slope above the outer revetment, contained tightly packed houses of Jericho's lower-class citizens. This was the city's red-light district. As in other parts of the city (especially on the east side of the hill) the dwellings were built above street-level shops and storage rooms. Just as the book of Joshua states, Rahab's house was built against the inner face of the outer wall immediately above the stone revetment. The spies escaped from the city by being let down from a window which looked out over this outer northern wall.

> She (Rahab) let them down from the window on a rope, as her house was against the city wall and she lived within the wall. [Joshua 2:15]

And the Walls Came Tumbling Down

The Israelite tribes assembled on the eastern bank of the Jordan, ready to cross over into the Promised Land. Once again, at this auspicious moment, Yahweh performed the 'miracle' of the parting of the waters. Upstream, in the vicinity of Adamah, there was a minor earthquake, so typical of the Jordan rift valley. The high mud cliffs on the western side of the river collapsed and dammed the waters so that the bed of the Jordan was exposed and the people of Israel, downstream, were able to cross on dry land. The miracle of the Reed Sea which heralded the departure from Egypt was repeated, on a lesser scale, as this new chapter in the story of the Children of Yahweh begins.

In the exposed riverbed, Joshua ordered the erection of twelve standing stones and twelve more river stones were taken from the Jordan and erected in the Israelite camp at Gilgal ('circle' or 'pile of stones'). Within hours of their crossing, the temporary dam at Adamah collapsed and the River Jordan once more continued on its course down to the Dead Sea.

The Israelites had entered the Promised Land on the tenth day of Abib (the first month of the Canaanite calendar year). They celebrated Passover at Gilgal. All the men who had been born in the wilderness years were circumcised with flint knives in preparation for their holy war. The flints used in the ritual were collected from a flint outcrop just a couple of kilometres north-east of Jericho where the holy site of Gilgal was located.

After several days of painful recuperation the army was ready to march on Jericho. Joshua and the elders sensed things were about to happen. As in the days of Exodus and the time spent at Mount Horeb, strange signs and portents were present. The earthquake at Adamah was the first of numerous rumblings of the earth beneath their feet. The great rift valley was awakening from its long slumber, following centuries of passivity since the overwhelming of Sodom and Gomorrah.

For six days the Israelite warriors marched in silence – save for the trumpeting of the priests' *shofar* ram's horns – around the walls of Jericho. The people of the city stared out from their high ramparts, fear gripping hearts as they saw the golden ark of Yahweh leading the huge, silent army. On the seventh day the earth shuddered and groaned; the ground convulsed and roared; and the mighty walls of Jericho cracked and crumbled, tumbling down the glacis slope and plunging down the steep revetment into the ditch below. A choking dust cloud enveloped the plain, blotting out the sun.

Eventually, after what seemed an eternity, the shaking stopped as suddenly as it had begun. The Israelites dusted themselves down and turned their eyes towards the city as its silhouette slowly began to reappear through the settling dust cloud. The sun's rays once more shone down upon Jericho and Joshua's warriors found themselves staring in silent awe at the mighty work of their adopted god. Yahweh had torn down their enemies' defences, leaving the city wide open to attack.

With a deafening war cry, eight thousand warriors rushed up the slope of fallen bricks and through the breaches into the city. Those within the fortress who were still alive following the collapse of walls and houses were slaughtered in the streets. The blood of two thousand men, women and children choked the city drains as Jericho burnt.

Storage jars full of grain were charred black, the grain carbonised. Nothing was left untouched – save for the house of Rahab who had protected the Israelite spies. The prostitute and her family were safely escorted from the destruction to join the conquerors. She married an Israelite from the tribe of Judah and, through her son Boaz, was long remembered as an ancestor of King David and therefore, ultimately, Jesus the Nazarene [Matthew 1:5].

Jericho was left a smouldering ruin, cursed and abandoned for forty-five years (and then only temporarily occupied) – a salutary message to all who would oppose the will of Yahweh and his chosen people.

> Accursed before Yahweh be any man who rises up to rebuild this city! On (the corpses of) his first-born he will lay its foundations, on his youngest son he will establish its gates! [Joshua 6:26]

The Archaeology of Jericho

The story of Joshua's destruction of Jericho remains one of the most powerful biblical legends. Yet archaeological investigations of the ruin-mound of Tell es-Sultan (the modern name of Jericho) have produced no evidence to confirm that a city existed there at the end of the Late Bronze Age. The orthodox chronology had placed the arrival of the Israelites in Canaan at the beginning of the Iron Age (on the basis of identifying Ramesses II as the Pharaoh of the Exodus) and the expectation was that the destructions of the Israelite Conquest would be revealed when sites such as Jericho were excavated. Unfortunately, as the various digs progressed, it became apparent that none of the cities which the Bible claims were captured and burnt by Joshua were destroyed at this time – either they were already abandoned ruins during the Late Bronze Age, or they continued to flourish without interruption, or, if a destruction had taken place, it was stratigraphically dated to either before or after the proposed archaeological horizon of the Israelite Conquest. As a result, Joshua's Conquest became another biblical myth. If there was no Jericho for Joshua to destroy, then perhaps there was no Joshua either. Perhaps the whole story was made up and the Israelites never seized the region in a military campaign? Perhaps they were always part of the indigenous population and simply evolved over time to become the nation of Israel? The biblical narrative, which contradicts this 'evolutionary' model, is now simply ignored.

In the New Chronology, however, the Conquest took place during the last phase of the Middle Bronze Age (MB II-B, c. 1440–1353 BC).* At this time all the cities conquered by Joshua and the Israelites were indeed destroyed according to the archaeological record. Joshua's invasion of the Promised Land did not take place at the end of the Late Bronze Age as scholars have believed for decades. The archaeological evidence is unambiguous. The momentous events of the Israelites' Conquest of Canaan occurred during the last phase of the Middle Bronze Age.

Into the Hills

The way into the central hill country was now open. Before the Israelite invaders, north-west of Jericho, was the mouth of the Wadi Mukkuk, which sweeps upwards to the high central ridge and the road which Abraham had trodden on his descent from Mesopotamia to Egypt in 1854 BC. At the head of the wadi, close to Abraham's highway, stood the town of Ai (KHIRBET EL-MUKKATIR), next in line to succumb to the brutal onslaught. Its citizens marched out from the single-chambered gate-house in the northern wall of the little fortified town of just three acres to meet the Israelite vanguard. With such complete victory at Jericho, the twelve

---

* The last phase of the Middle Bronze Age (otherwise known as the MB II-C or MB III) extends into and therefore overlaps with LB I-A (which starts within the Greater Hyksos Dynasty in Egypt).

tribes had become complacent and, at first, only sent a token force of three thousand to take Ai. The soldiers of Ai repulsed the Israelite warriors and pursued them down the Wadi el-Gayeh as far as the *shebarim* ('broken rocks') – a jagged cliff of white limestone three kilometres east of Khirbet el-Mukkatir. There they killed thirty-two of Joshua's leading fighters before retreating safely within the three-metre-thick walls of their town (in some parts built of large, almost Cyclopean boulders). Joshua, dismayed at the failure, now planned a subterfuge to draw the defenders of Ai away from their well-built stronghold, leaving it vulnerable to an attack from the rear.

During the hours of darkness, the major part of the Israelite army was ordered to take position in the deep Wadi Sheban to the west and out of view of the town. At dawn another assault force approached up the Wadi el-Gayeh to the north-east, in full view of Ai's defenders. Joshua himself stood with his commanders on top of the Jebel Abu Ammar – a ridge overlooking Ai from the north.

Once more the brave men of Ai marched out from the northern city gate and clashed with their attackers in the Wadi el-Gayeh. Once more they pushed the Israelites back, driving them down towards the Jordan valley. But then they looked back to find a great black pall rising from the town. Ai was burning. The men of Ai disengaged from the fight and rushed back to save their kin only to find themselves trapped between two Israelite armies. The large force hidden in Wadi Sheban had attacked an undefended Ai from the west and were in the act of ransacking the town. The Israelites in the Wadi el-Gayeh regrouped and pushed up to the city gate. There was no escape for the brave defenders of Ai. The pattern had been set in Ammon and Moab, brutally reinforced at Jericho, and would be continued throughout the Promised Land campaign. Ai was burnt to the ground. No-one was left alive. The town was never rebuilt and the curse of Yahweh still hangs over its crumbling walls.

Bryant Wood and his American team of volunteers partly excavated the site of Khirbet el-Mukkatir in the late 1990s.* They found a heavily burnt fortified town which had lain unoccupied until Hasmonean times, when a fortress was built on the long-abandoned ruins. In those ruins they have unearthed scores of sling-stones (lying in a layer of burnt debris) which may well have belonged to the Israelite attackers. Dr Wood has also found documents attesting to a different name for the site of Khirbet el-Mukkatir. At the turn of the last century, when archaeological research in the Holy Land was still in its infancy, the locals knew the hill at the end of the Wadi el-Gayeh as Khirbet Ai – the 'ruins of Ai'.

Joshua's Eclipse

The population of the hill country of Canaan was panic-stricken at the news of the fall of Jericho and Ai. Who would be next? The elders of the town of Gibeon met in counsel and decided that they were very much at risk – unless they could peacefully surrender themselves to the new military power. A delegation was despatched to Joshua to plead with him to spare Gibeon and accept their city as an ally. Joshua agreed to the petition and swore to leave the city of the Gibeonites unharmed. However, the rulers of Jerusalem, Hebron, Jarmuth, Lachish and Eglon formed a coalition and marched upon Gibeon, laying siege to the town. On 13th July 1406 BC, Joshua, now obligated by oath to defend his new Gibeonite allies, marched up from the base camp at Gilgal to meet the southern confederation. The battle lasted all of the following morning and well into the afternoon. At 3.15 pm the sky suddenly darkened as the moon passed before the face of the sun. The clash of weapons fell silent for a moment as the combatants looked

* The topographical details of the Ai campaign are taken from Bryant Wood's research of the landscape surrounding the site of Khirbet el-Mukkatir, which closely matches the biblical narrative.

up at the celestial omen. The Canaanites took it as a sign of their own gods' anger – the Israelites as another demonstration of Yahweh's awesome power. In those two twilight minutes of totality the tide of battle was turned. The Israelites surged forward and struck hard at the stunned enemy, their determination fortified by Yahweh's presence in the skies above them. By nightfall the twelve tribes had roundly defeated the Canaanite confederation outside the walls of Gibeon.

The next morning Joshua pursued the survivors down the pass known as the descent of Beth-Horon as far as Makkedah. There he captured the five defeated kings and executed them with his own sword in front of the commanders of Israel's army. The royal corpses were then hung on the branches of trees for all to see their humiliation, before being taken down at sunset and thrown into a nearby cave.

The town of Makkedah was seized and all its people killed. The Israelites then marched on to Libnah and Lachish, both of which were destroyed and their populations eradicated. Horam, king of Gezer, came out to do battle with the Israelites, but he too was defeated and his city taken. Joshua marched on south to Eglon, which also fell under Yahweh's 'curse of destruction'. The Israelite army then turned north-east and headed back into the hill country to seize Hebron and Debir, which were razed to the ground, the people wiped out. As winter drew near, Joshua finally took his forces back to Gilgal and the oasis of Jericho, leaving in his wake nothing but smouldering ruin.

The Head of All Those Kingdoms

In the spring of the following year (1405 BC) the warriors of the twelve tribes were mustered once more beside the ruins of Jericho. Joshua marched them up the Wadi el-Gayeh once more, past the ruins of Ai, and onto the high-road which runs along the spine of the central hills. This time he turned the army to face north – the direction of that year's campaign of conquest.

The towns of the Shechemite kingdom, with their ancient ties to Abraham and Jacob, were quickly absorbed. Shechem itself was taken. The Israelites then crossed the Jezreel valley to attack the settlements of the northern hill country of Galilee. Joshua and his warriors were gradually working their way towards the most powerful city in the region – a prize of riches and plunder equal to all Israel's other conquests put together.

JABIN, king of HAZOR, held sway over all the cities of the north. Joshua 11:10 describes Hazor as 'the head of all those kingdoms' and archaeology has confirmed its pre-eminence during the Middle Bronze Age. Surrounded by a massive earthen rampart, the lower city covered an immense one hundred and seventy-three acres. On its southern side, the upper royal city (25 acres) contained Jabin's palace (mostly still to be excavated beneath the Late Bronze Age palace) and the main temple, consisting of a large rectangular chamber.

The two city compounds (upper and lower) were joined by a broad stone staircase which descended from the royal quarter. Here the people listened in silence as King Jabin stood before them to inform his subjects of the grave news emanating from the south. Their very existence was threatened by a new kind of warfare. The whole population would be asked to defend the kingdom – every able-bodied man should take his farewells of his family, collect his weapons and join the standing army mustering outside the main city gate. Hazor's allies in the northern confederation – Canaanites, Amorites, and their Indo-European-speaking city-lords – were already marching to join the national defence force.

An army of forty thousand 'as numerous as the sands of the sea' assembled on the plain beside the waters of Merom to await the Israelite invaders. Joshua's force was outnumbered three to one – but by now they were hardened, ruthless fighters. Much of Jabin's army was made up of ordinary citizens. The Israelites smashed through the static ranks of the northern alliance, targeting the city rulers standing to the rear in their golden chariots and dressed in their royal finery. The suddenness of the attack and the narrow concentration of the assault took the defenders by surprise. Jabin and his fellow lords soon found themselves within javelin-range of Joshua's vanguard troops. Panic gripped the mighty Canaanite king. He turned his chariot and fled back to Hazor.

With its leaders retreating from the battle, the morale of the northern alliance crumbled. Those who could escape fled to their cities; the rest met their end beside the Merom spring. The rout was total as the Israelites pursued the defeated conscripts back to their homes. City after city capitulated – from the borders of Phoenicia in the west to the vale of Mizpah below the desert plateau in the east. For once these towns were not destroyed but later became the centres of the Israelite tribes whose lot it was to occupy the northern sector of the Promised Land. With the north secured, Joshua then turned back and marched his victorious army up to the walls of mighty Hazor.

The great battle of Merom marked the end of any concerted resistance from the indigenous population of Canaan. Nothing, it seemed, could stand before the wrath of Joshua's army.

A short siege of Hazor was followed by a vicious assault. The lower city (Stratum 3) was razed to the ground by fire, the population put to the sword. The upper city held out for a while but, eventually, it too fell. When Joshua's commanders entered the palace, they found King Jabin seated upon his ivory throne, his children beside him. Hazor's illustrious family awaited their fate in dignified calm. The royal wives, sons and daughters were cut down before Jabin's eyes. Joshua then personally thrust his sword into the old king's chest and Canaan's most powerful dynasty of Middle Bronze Age rulers was extinguished. The royal palace was torched and the ruins 'sown with salt'.

The Covenant Stone

The third campaign (following the Transjordanian wars and the central hill country conquests) had lasted eight months. As the winter of 1405 BC began to set in, Joshua summoned all the people to Shechem. A great assembly was held in the courtyard of the sacred compound where Abraham had rested beneath the oak tree and where Isaac had built a shrine to El-shaddai. There Joshua erected a large white limestone slab of rock, around which the tribal elders were gathered, the people watching from the surrounding hills. The whole congregation of Israel swore an oath to follow Yahweh in all his 'statutes and ordinances' which Joshua had written in the Book of the Law of God. With the covenant ceremony complete, Joshua ordered the reburial of Joseph's bones, brought out of Egypt, in the plot of land acquired from Hamor by Jacob in 1691 BC. The tomb of the patriarch is still there today in the heart of modern Nablus. Sadly it was ransacked and seriously damaged during the recent *intifada* because it had become a traditional place of Jewish pilgrimage.

With the ritual at Shechem complete, Joshua dismissed his troops to their encampments scattered throughout the hill country. Those tribes which had been allocated the northern territories – Issachar, Asher and Naphtali – went back to that region to maintain control over the newly conquered lands. The tribes of Reuben, Gad and Manasseh crossed the Jordan to settle the lands of Gilead and Bashan, seized from the Amorite kings Sihon and Og during the Transjordanian wars. Those still awaiting territory in the far south – the tribes of Judah and Simeon – prepared themselves for a fourth campaign in the following spring.

Joshua selected a small piece of land as his own at Timnath-Serah in the highlands of Ephraim and settled down there with his clan followers. Joshua's days of military action were over. The conquest of the remaining cities of the Promised Land would be left to the tribal leaders who had fought with him at Jericho, Ai, Merom and Hazor.

The winter was cold and long that year. As the spring thaw began to reveal the wild mountain flowers, Joshua son of Nun passed away and was buried in a rock-cut tomb along with the flint knives used to perform the mass circumcision at Gilgal in the days before the fall of Jericho.

Pharaoh Sheshi

At the third Passover spent in the Promised Land the remaining as-yet-unsettled tribes were ready to set out on the military campaign for that year (1404 BC). Caleb, chieftain and commander of the tribe of Judah, preparing to seize his allotted territory, conscripted the support of the tribe of Simeon and marched south. It was time to take on the old enemy who had clashed with the Israelites during the wandering years – first at Rephidim and then when the people had been encamped at Kadesh. The Amalekites of southern Canaan were ruled over by powerful Indo-European warlords known as the Anakim. They were Anatolian migrants described in the 'King of Battle' text (found amongst the tablets at Tell el-Amarna) as the people of Anaku ('Tin Land'). In the days of Sargon I (2117–2062 BC) they dwelt along the southern coast of Anatolia (modern Turkey).

In the centuries following the Early Bronze Age city-state collapse, many Indo-European-speaking Anatolian groups had moved into the Levant, where they established themselves as rulers over the local pastoralist populations. The Bible refers to them as Anakim, Avvim, Jebusites and Hittites. At the time of the Israelites' arrival in Canaan, three Anakim lords dominated the lands south of Jerusalem centred on Kiriath-Arba (later known as Hebron) where Abraham had lived four hundred and fifty years earlier. A tribal chieftain named Arba had been the Anakim's great ancestor and founder of the town which Joshua had destroyed in the previous year's campaign. But the three ruling descendants of Arba were still powerfully entrenched in their fortified cities scattered throughout the southern desert and coastal plain of southern Canaan.

Whilst the Israelites had been wandering for forty years in the wilderness, the Amalekite clans and their Anakim masters had taken advantage of the political and military collapse in Egypt, resulting from the disaster at the Reed Sea, and had invaded the Nile delta. They had plundered the land and treated the Egyptians with great cruelty. Let me remind you of what the Egyptian priest Manetho (speaking through the writings of Josephus) has to say about this tragic episode in Egyptian history.

> ... unexpectedly, from the regions of the east, invaders of obscure race (i.e. Amalekites and Anakim) marched in confidence of victory against our land. By main force they easily seized it without striking a blow; and having overpowered the rulers of the land (i.e. the remnant 13th Dynasty), they then ruthlessly burned our cities, razed to the ground the temples of the gods, and treated all the natives with a cruel hostility, massacring some and leading into slavery the wives and children of others.

This all began in the reign of Dudimose, Pharaoh of the Exodus, who had been forced to retreat to Memphis, leaving the Amalekite tribes from the Negeb and Transjordan free to establish themselves in the eastern delta and, in particular, occupy the fertile land of Goshen recently vacated by the Israelites. At first, the invaders made temporary use of the ruined houses of Avaris (Stratum G), constructing bivouacs against the mudbrick walls still standing after the Exodus earthquake. Eventually the town was rebuilt (Stratum F) and a large sacred precinct founded at

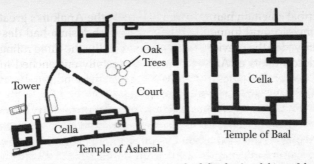

25. Plan of the MB II-B temenos at Avaris built by the Amalekites of the Lesser Hyksos dynasty. This is the temple of Seth/Baal, the foundation of which was celebrated in the Year 400 Stela of Ramesses II (the fourth-centenary event is dated to the reign of Haremheb when Ramesses' father, Seti I, was vizier).

the heart of the Israelite district, consisting of several temples and shrines.

The main compound, fronted by two temples, was dedicated to the worship of Baal – storm-god and warrior deity. The larger of the two temples ('one of the largest sanctuaries known from the Middle Bronze Age world') was the House of Baal, whilst the second, smaller temple was dedicated to his consort, Astarte/Asherah, in the form of a sacred tree. A stone altar was set up in the precinct within the shade of oak trees, planted at the foundation of the temple complex, the evidence for which came in the form of acorns discovered by the Austrian archaeologists who excavated the site in the 1960s. Within this cultic temenos the Amalekite warrior chieftains were buried, along with Egyptian slave girls sacrificed as part of their master's funeral rite. The burials of these warriors were richly adorned with gold plundered from Egypt's tombs and palaces. Four hundred years later (968 BC), in the reign of Pharaoh Haremheb, the vizier Seti (later Seti I) commemorated the foundation of this temple dedicated to Seth (the Egyptian Baal), the ceremony of which was recorded on the 'Year 400 Stela' of Ramesses II.

Whilst the Amalekites – the Egyptian texts refer to them as Aamu – settled in the delta so as to raid their Egyptian neighbours to the south, the invaders' Indo-European rulers remained in southern Canaan, based around the old tribal heartlands. There they had built several strongholds as military staging-posts between Egypt and the hill country towns, the most important of which was SHARUHEN, from where the Anakim oversaw the plunder and exploitation of the Nile delta. Here, in the spring of 1405 BC, the fortress became a refuge from the Israelite conquerors of the north.

The territory of the Amalekites was divided up into the fiefdoms of three great Anakim rulers – Sheshi, Ahiman and Talmi. Sheshi (biblical Sheshai, Numbers 13:22) was the most powerful. As the leader of the Nile delta Asiatic invaders – and therefore usurper of the Red Crown of Lower Egypt – he had even been given pharaonic titles, including the coronation name Maibre. Numerous mixed-race Asiatic and Indo-European rulers – all bearing Egyptian throne names – would succeed Sheshi until a new dynasty of foreign kings from the far north arrived on the scene. The Anakim pharaonic dynasts were referred to by the native Egyptians as *hekau-khasut* ('rulers of the hill country') because they hailed from the southern hill country of Canaan. Manetho calls them 'Hyksos' because they were rulers (Egyptian *hekau* or *hykau*) of the shepherds (Egyptian *shosu*), in other words the Amalekite nomads of the Negeb and southern uplands. The foreign dynasty from the far north, which was to appear on the scene a century later, were later referred to as *shemau* ('migrants' or 'aliens') but also included in their titulary the epithet heka-khasut. As a result, Egyptologists have lumped all these southern (Aamu) and northern (Shemau) together under the collective designation 'Hyksos' and misleadingly dubbed the whole era 'the Hyksos Age'. However, as we shall see in the next chapter, the northern 'Greater Hyksos' dynasty was not of the same descent or ethnicity as the 'Lesser Hyksos' of southern Canaan who preceded them.

The first of these Lesser Hyksos was the Anakim chieftain Sheshi. Prior to the Israelite invasion of Canaan, his influence had stretched far and wide. Scarabs bearing Maibre Sheshi's name have been found all over southern Palestine and were even recovered from the very last burials of the Middle Bronze Age cemetery at Jericho. These crucial finds suggest that Jericho fell to Joshua just a few years after Sheshi and the Amalekites had conquered Egypt. At Tell el-Ajjul, Sheshi scarabs were dug up from the earliest levels of City II whilst the latest levels of this city contained scarabs of King Apopi – the penultimate Hyksos ruler before Pharaoh Ahmose expelled the foreigners from Egypt in 1192 BC. So Sheshi was one of the earliest foreign kings, ruling prior to the Greater Hyksos dynasty, and Jericho was therefore destroyed some time before that dynasty seized power in 1298 BC.

Despite their fearsome reputation, Caleb and his army successfully drove the Amalekites out of their fortified encampments in the highlands surrounding Kiriath-Arba (Hebron) and Kiriath-Sepher (Debir), confining their enemy to the coastal plain around Sharuhen and Gaza (the region later defined as the land of the Philistines or Philistia). The Israelites secured the whole of the Negeb as far south as Kadesh-Barneah, bordering on the old Edomite territory of Esau. Sheshi and the leaders of the Amalekites put up little resistance. They, after all, still occupied the richest and most fertile area of the Anakim domain – and they had the whole of Lower Egypt at their mercy.

The scarabs of Maibre Sheshi/Sheshai were not the only tantalising archaeological clues from the era of the southern conquest by the tribes of Judah and Simeon. A potsherd from the MB II-B stratum at Gezer (conquered by the Israelites) bears three Proto-Sinaitic signs scratched into its surface. The letters k-l-b spell out the name Caleb ('dog') and, as we have seen, this was the name of the Israelite chieftain who led the war against the cities of the south.

The Tribal Territories

And so it was that the Hebrews – now a united confederacy of tribes called Israel – returned to live in the land once occupied by their great ancestors Abraham, Isaac and Jacob. Judah and Simeon dwelt in the south and in the hills of the Shephelah, facing the Canaanite coastal plain; Benjamin and Ephraim dwelt in the central hill country, north of Jerusalem; Issachar, Zebulun, Naphtali and Asher lived to the north of the Jezreel valley; whilst Reuben, Gad and Manasseh settled across the Jordan; Manasseh also held land on the west side of the Jordan south of the Jezreel valley. Only the tribes of Dan and Levi were left without a territory. Dan was never able to conquer the coastal plain which was their allotment because the cities there were very powerful and protected by the Hyksos pharaohs. The most important trading route in Canaan – the Via Maris ('way of the sea') – ran north through the coastal lowlands and was strategically crucial to Egypt. The Danites could not have taken this part of Canaan without incurring the wrath of the Hyksos or their successors, the native Egyptian rulers of the New Kingdom. However, the tribesfolk of Dan would soon find a home in the far north where they captured the town of Laish and renamed it Dan after their eponymous ancestor.

As the tribes of Israel set down roots in the hills, their neighbours in the surrounding lowlands and in Transjordan took every opportunity to attack and harass the Children of Yahweh in revenge for the slaughter of their kin. Over nearly four hundred long years the Israelites suffered attacks by one regional power after another. The Bible records the events of this bleak dark age in the Book of Judges to which we shall now turn.

Chapter Twelve

JUDGES
A KINGDOM IN WAITING

(Judges 3:7 to 1 Samuel 7:17)

*Shechem and Shiloh – The Early Judges – The Capture
of Laish – Slaughter of the Benjaminites – Arrival of
the Philistines – Deborah and Barak Against Hazor –
Gideon Against Midian – Identifying the Philistines –
Abimelech and Migdol Shechem – Samson – Samuel
and the Philistine War*

ollowing the death of Joshua and the end of the
war of conquest, the twelve tribes were loosely held
together by men (and one woman) of renown who
exercised spiritual and military authority over the tribal
confederacy for twenty generations. In archaeological
terms, their era – known to Bible scholars as the Judges
period – spanned the second half of the MB II-B down to
the end of the LB I (*c.* 1400–1000 BC). These leaders bore
the title *shopet* (loosely translated 'judge', Akkadian *shapitum*)
and rose to both govern and administer the laws of Yahweh,
as well as direct the resistance to Israel's oppressors amongst
its Canaanite and Amorite neighbours. The Israelites of
the Judges period were essentially nomadic pastoralists

26. The two phases of the MB/LB temple at Shechem (left original MB and right secondary LB). The second temple was destroyed by Abimelech in 1169 BC.

living in semi-permanent communities. The political structure of the tribal confederacy was a fairly haphazard affair, based on the covenant to Yahweh and an undertaking to defend each tribal territory from outside aggression. The Judges were the thread which held this loose weave together. Their roles varied with the circumstances of their times. Some were consulted as people of renown within the community for both political and religious matters; others were war-leaders who came to the fore in order to save Israel from military threats. All were heroes – and that is perhaps the best way to understand the *shopetim* (plural of *shopet*) of the Judges era.

The Israelite Cult Centres

For four hundred years the tribes lived in tented settlements within their allotted areas, separated from each other by the complex geography of the region and only rarely brought together *en masse* in times of national crisis. However, in spite of the disparate nature of Israelite tribal society, the ritual of the Shechem covenant was re-enacted every year on the anniversary of the erection of Joshua's great white covenant stone. This place, at the heart of Tell Balatah, had been sacred to the Hebrews for centuries because it was the spot where the patriarch Jacob had earlier erected his altar and shrine (Hebrew *makom*) dedicated to El-shaddai (MB II-A, Shechem Temenos 1) and where his ancestor Abraham had rested beside the oak of Moreh.

During the early years of the Judges period, the tribal elders, escorted by their élite clansmen, arrived from all parts of the Promised Land – the entire assembly acting as CORVÉE labour to erect a great mudbrick temple built on thick stone foundations. They called this first sanctuary dedicated to Yahweh the Temple of Baal-Berith ('Lord of the Covenant') and, less formally, Migdol Shechem ('Tower of Shechem') because it was fronted by two tall towers (seven metres wide by five metres deep). It also had a third name – the House of the Millo ('filling'), because its foundations had been constructed on a large platform of rubble covering Jacob's original courtyard shrine. In front of the huge temple (measuring fifty by forty sacred cubits = twenty-six by twenty-one metres) the covenant stone was re-erected in an open court, three metres above its original position, and a new altar placed before it for ritual sacrifice.

Around the whole complex, and much of the inner city, the Israelite workforce laboured to build an impregnable Cyclopean defensive wall, over ten metres high and four metres wide at its base, with two impressive gateways constructed in massive masonry. It took over twenty years for the whole enterprise to come to fruition. Each year the men of Israel would arrive at Shechem for the covenant ceremony. And each year, for the duration of a lunar month, they worked as one to build the temple and encircling wall. At the appearance of the next new crescent moon they ceased work and gathered to renew their oath of allegiance to Yahweh before the covenant stone. The men of Israel then returned to their families in the tribal homelands. This heavily fortified Middle Bronze Age city of Shechem (MB II-B, Temenos 6) became the ceremonial capital of the Israelite tribal confederacy and a place of annual pilgrimage until the capture of Jerusalem by David in 1005 BC.

But Shechem was not the place where the Ark of the Covenant was kept. The Levite priests (descended from Aaron and the men of the tribe of Levi) built their own fortified sanctuary at Shiloh (modern Seilun), within the central highlands south of Shechem. A small rocky mound, nestled in a deep valley surrounded by forested hills, was enclosed in a stone casemate wall, protected on its outer side by a plastered glacis similar to that at Jericho and other Middle Bronze Age town sites. The casemate wall, made up of an outer and inner wall joined at regular intervals by cross-member walls, provided storage rooms accessed from the inner court. Here the priests kept the ritual vessels and supplies for the sanctuary itself, located on the summit of the hill. The tiny holy of holies was also made of stone and consisted of a single chamber in which the Ark rested. Outside the fortified enclosure, on a rectangular area of flat ground to the north, the Tent of Meeting, which had been constructed at the foot of Mount Horeb, was permanently erected. Tribal council meetings were occasionally held there and it served as a hostel for pilgrims visiting the shrine of the Ark (though, of course, none but the high priest could enter and stand before the casket containing Yahweh's commandments).

The heartland of Israelite territory was thus centred on the two fortified sacred strongholds at Shechem and Shiloh. The outer territories, north of the Jezreel valley, east of the Jordan and in the Negeb to the south of Hebron, were much more vulnerable to attack from their angry and resentful neighbours whose land they had conquered. And it was immediately after Joshua's death that the first of the foreign 'oppressions' of the Israelite tribes began.

Othniel and Ehud

In 1404 BC the Edomites – who had been attacked by their Israelite brothers during the Transjordanian campaign

– began to raid the tribes living in the Negeb bordering on Edomite territory. Under their king, Kushan-Rishathaim, the Edomites oppressed and harried the southern clans of Judah and Simeon for eight long years. Then OTHNIEL, younger brother of Caleb, 'rose up' to lead the people against their Edomite oppressors. After a series of skirmishes and minor battles during the spring and summer of 1397, the Israelites finally succeeded in pushing Kushan-Rishathaim and his marauders back into their own territory and Judah's boundaries were made secure.

The tribal territories saw peace for thirty-seven years before the Moabites, under King Eglon, waged war on the tribes settled beyond the Jordan. After eighteen years (1361–1344 BC) EHUD, son of Gera of the tribe of Benjamin, decided to take matters into his own hands. He went to the court of Eglon in Jericho, bearing tribute from his tribe. Once in the royal residence he tricked the king into being alone with him by announcing that he had important information which was only for the ears of Moab's ruler. Then, drawing a dagger from the folds of his cloak, Ehud assassinated the obese Eglon, thrusting the blade deep into his belly, before fleeing back to Israelite territory. Ehud roused the tribal warriors with the proclamation that their oppressor was dead. The Moabite army came in pursuit of the assassin but was met by a large force of Israelite soldiers. Once more the seasoned fighters of Israel defeated their enemy, and once again the land was free from foreign incursions – this time for nigh on eight decades (1344–1268 BC).

Massacre and Mayhem

Even so, there was no real peace for the Israelite settlers because they continued to quarrel amongst themselves. The barbaric nature of early Israelite history in the Promised Land is reflected in two stories which complete the book of Judges but which actually took place fairly early in the era: the taking of Laish by the tribe of Dan and the massacre of the tribe of Benjamin.

The Danites had not succeeded in seizing the land on the coastal plain allocated to them by lot because the cities there were too large and well defended. As a result, they looked for easier pickings further afield, beyond the Galilean hills in the far north. There Danite spies, purporting to be traders, found a town called Laish, occupied by Phoenicians from the coastal city of Sidon. These people were peaceful and welcomed strangers. They had not taken the precaution of heavily fortifying their settlement. The Danite spies, having been generously treated by their unwary hosts, returned to Israelite territory, gathered an army of six hundred men, their families in train, and marched north to attack Laish. They easily took the town, slaughtering everyone and burning all the houses to the ground. The site was then rebuilt and renamed Dan after its conquerors.

We know that this episode occurred within fifty years of the initial invasion of Canaan because Judges 18:30 states that the first priest of Dan was Jonathan, son of Gershom (born some years before the Exodus), son of Moses, and that the descendants of Jonathan continued to serve as priests of Dan until the population was carried off into exile by the Assyrians in the eighth century BC.

The story surrounding the fate of Benjamin also comes from this time and is even more brutal. The concubine of a Levite was gang-raped until half dead by a bunch of Benjaminite louts from the town of Gibeah.

They had intercourse with her and ill-treated her all night until morning. When dawn was breaking they let her go. At daybreak the girl came and fell on the threshold of her husband's host and she stayed there until it was light. In the morning her husband got up and, opening the door of the house, was going out to continue his journey when he saw

> the woman, his concubine, lying at the door of the
> house with her hands on the threshold. 'Get up,' he
> said, 'we must leave!' There was no answer. He then
> loaded her on his donkey and began the journey
> home. [Judges 19:25–28]

The unfortunate woman was then butchered into twelve
pieces and despatched by her husband to the tribal territories by way of a call for revenge. A war of retribution
was called by the remaining tribes to punish all of Benjamin
for the crime of a tiny minority. Thousands were killed in
the ensuing conflict. Gibeah was put to the flames and the
townsfolk massacred. Virtually the whole tribe of Benjamin
was wiped out, save for six hundred men who escaped
down the Wadi Suwenit to the rock of Rimmon where
they remained as outcasts for four months. Having almost
annihilated one of the original tribes of Jacob, the rest of
Israel then, somewhat late in the day, realised that the
punishment had far outweighed the crime. Their remedy
was to compound the injustice even further.

The people consulted Yahweh through the high priest
Phinehas, son of Eleazar, son of Aaron, who was based at
Bethel. It was decided to send an army across the Jordan
to Jabesh-Gilead because the Gileadites had failed to send
a contingent to fight against Benjamin. In the attack upon
the town, all the men, women and children of Jabesh were
killed – with the exception of the virgins who were brought
back to the central highlands and offered as wives to the
surviving warriors of Benjamin holed up at Rimmon. Even
then the Benjaminites were not satisfied with their 'compensation' because there were not enough Gileadite virgins
to go round. They demanded more for their blood-price.
So the elders of the other tribes arranged for the surviving
warriors of Benjamin to go to the annual festival of Yahweh
held at Shiloh. The Benjaminites were then permitted to
forcefully carry off the local girls who had gathered to dance
during the festivities. The Benjaminites returned to their

allotted territory, rebuilt their villages and re-established the tribal seat at Gibeah where, centuries after the massacre, the first true king of all Israel would be born to the family of Kish.

The Arrival of the Philistines

During the judgeship of Ehud (1344–1268 BC) only one minor *external* conflict occurred in this long period of internal squabbling amongst the tribes. Shamgar, son of Anath, came up against a raiding party of Philistines (Hebrew *Pelishtim*) in the Shephelah hills which border the coastal plain. As had happened with the Edomites and Moabites, here too the Israelites managed to push this new enemy back from their territory. But behind this apparently insignificant biblical story – which occupies just one line in the book of Judges [Judges 3:31] – is a momentous event in the history of the ancient Near East. This first mention of Philistine soldiers heralds the arrival of a new Indo-European-speaking political force in the region.

The year of Shamgar's run-in with these strange foreigners from a far-off land was 1300 BC. In Egyptian terms, this places the Philistine 'arrival' on the biblical stage right in the middle of the Hyksos period – a little over a century after the invasion of the eastern delta by King Sheshi (in *c.* 1409 BC) and the subsequent demise of the remnant native 13th Dynasty. But who were these Philistines and where did they come from?

Of course, in the conventional chronological scheme, the Philistines appear in Philistia not during the Middle Bronze Age but at the beginning of the Iron Age (OC – *c.* 1200 BC). They are identified with a group called the Peleset who attack Egypt by land and sea in the 8th year of Pharaoh Ramesses III (OC – 1177 BC, NC – 856 BC). These Iron Age invaders are indeed Philistines – but they are not the first 'Sea Peoples' to arrive in the region. In the New Chronology the original incursion of Indo-European peoples from the Aegean occurs towards the end of the Middle Bronze Age (NC – *c.* 1350 BC). The Peleset of Ramesses III's time are a secondary wave of migrants moving into the Levant (to dwell alongside their ancestral Philistine kin) during the period of collapse of the Mycenaean Bronze Age city states of Greece. This collapse was triggered by the long and debilitating campaign of the Trojan war (NC – *c.* 872–863 BC) and the subsequent Dorian invasion (NC – *c.* 820 BC) which pushed the Mycenaean élites onto the islands of the eastern Mediterranean and into the Levant itself. But these events are hundreds of years in the future as the original Philistine migrants arrive on the Canaanite coast during the Hyksos period.

Towards the end of the Middle Bronze II-B era a new kind of pottery begins to appear in the Levant – particularly on the coastal plain and at Tell ed-Daba (ancient Avaris) in Egypt. This 'bichrome ware' is finely decorated pottery with designs painted in black and red on a beige slip (background). The designs include metopes (rectangular boxes) running around the shoulder of the vessel, within which stylised birds and geometric designs are placed. The basic principles of such decoration are witnessed once more,

27. A comparison between the Late Bronze Age I pottery of the Levant known as bichrome ware (NC – *c.* 1250 BC) and the Early Iron I pottery known as Philistine ware (NC – *c.* 880 BC). In the New Chronology, the two bichrome vessels on the left belong to the first phase of Philistine migrations into southern Canaan, whereas the two bichrome vessels on the right belong to a second wave of migrations of Sea Peoples (including Philistines) following the Trojan war. Note the backwards-looking bird motif common to both types of ceramic decoration, four hundred years apart.

three hundred years later, when the so-called 'Philistine ware' proper appears in the archaeological record at the beginning of the Iron Age (around the time of Ramesses III). This later pottery is Aegean in origin and is regarded as being a rather degraded development from Mycenaean Bronze Age ceramics. Given that the earlier bichrome ware of the late MB II-B/LB I is very similar in terms of its decoration to the Iron Age 'Philistine ware', you should not be surprised to learn that the clay from which many of the earliest bichrome pots were made comes from Cyprus, thus confirming a Mediterranean connection to the culture which introduced it into the Levant and Egypt. It seems that the first generation of bichrome ceramics was made in Cyprus and brought by newcomers to the southern Levant who then began to produce these distinctive vessels from local clays found in their newly adopted lands.

At about the same time as the sudden appearance of the distinctive bichrome ware, a new and impressive form of grandiose dwelling shows up in the archaeological record of the coastal plain cities. Archaeologists have dubbed these residences 'patrician houses' because they seem to have belonged to wealthy élite merchant-rulers. We might describe them as villas or small palaces, and they are clearly connected with the bichrome ware newcomers. In fact, in the New Chronology historical model, they are the residences of the early Philistine lords of the Greater Hyksos age – known to the biblical author as the *Caphtorim* from the land of Caphtor (the *Keftiu* of the later Egyptian New Kingdom records).

Mizraim (i.e. the founder of Egypt) fathered the people of Lud, of Anam, Lehab, Naphtuh, Pathros, Casluh and **Caphtor, from which the Philistines came**. [Genesis 10:13–14]

As Dr John Bimson has brilliantly argued, the Philistines who fought against Shamgar were from Cyprus, the southern coast of Anatolia and the other islands of the Aegean.*

These foreign settlers were Indo-Europeans – in other words speakers of an Indo-European language rather than Semites. They came from the north, landing near the city of Ugarit before setting off on their march south towards Egypt, their fleet moving down the coast in support of the land army. During the first stage of this military migration, the largest tribal group of the Caphtorim confederacy – the Pelasts (known in the later Greek literature as Pelasgoi from an original Pelastoi) – had allied themselves with another group of migrants from the Zagros mountains known as the Hurrians.

In later years the Egyptians would refer to Syria as Hurri-land (or Kharu) after the new settlers in the region, whereas the Bible calls the allies of the Philistines 'Horites'. In the Classical period, the Greeks knew them as the Kares (Carians). Together the two allies from the north virtually took over the territories which the Israelites (who were still contained within the hill country) had failed to occupy. They massacred the indigenous ethnic population known in the biblical text as the Avvim and even came to rule over the Aamu/Amalekites of the Egyptian delta. These élite Indo-European rulers founded both the 'Greater Hyksos' Dynasty at Avaris and the kingdom of Mitanni beyond the Euphrates river. The latter would be a powerful political and military force in the region during the Late Bronze I period when they at first became the principal enemy and then subsequently (during LB II-A) the main political ally of the Egyptian 18th-Dynasty pharaohs.

Deborah and Barak

Whilst Egypt was being stripped of its past glory by the merchant lords of Avaris, the Israelite tribes were continuing to do battle with their vengeful neighbours. The Judge Ehud

---

* J. J. Bimson: 'The Philistines: Their Origins and Chronology Reassessed' in *Journal of the Ancient Chronology Forum* IV (1990), pp. 58–76.

had died and once more conflict had broken out – this time between the northern tribes beyond the Jezreel valley and a new Canaanite King Jabin of Hazor, who bore the same dynastic name as the ruler slain by Joshua.*

Deborah was an Israelite prophetess living in the hills near Bethel in Ephraimite territory, where she dispensed justice from beneath an old palm tree. For twenty years Hazor had been oppressing the Israelites, raiding their northern settlements and striking south across the Jezreel valley into the central hills. The traders who interlinked the tribal settlements and pastoralist encampments became too frightened to use the regular roads for fear of attack from Hazor's patrols. They took to travelling at night and by difficult tracks.

The commander of Jabin's army was named Sisera and he had at his disposal a large force of nine hundred chariots. The Israelites had nothing to match this fairly new military technology which had been perfected by the Hurrian *marianu* horse-breeding warriors from the north. Sisera was himself a marianu who had been commissioned by Jabin to train and equip his chariotry. Many of Hazor's charioteers were themselves of Hurrian stock, hired for their expertise at handling horses. The chariot had proved itself to be a devastating weapon against infantry ... and foot-soldiers, of course, made up one hundred per cent of the Israelite

---

* This Jabin (Canaanite *Ibni*) was ruler of the rebuilt city (Upper City Stratum XV; Lower City Stratum 2) which had once again become a centre of Canaanite power in the region – though not on the same scale as before. Israel's northern tribes were somewhat separated from the strong heartland of the tribal network at Shechem and Shiloh in the territory of Manasseh and Ephraim. Many of the Middle Bronze Age towns in the north had not been destroyed during the original Conquest campaign of 1405 BC and there was still a considerable Canaanite population in the Galilean hills and further north. The tribes of Issachar, Asher and Naphtali had been powerless to prevent the reoccupation and rebuilding of Late Bronze Age Hazor. Now in 1268 BC – one hundred and thirty-seven years after the city's destruction by Joshua – Hazor had risen once again to threaten Israel's security.

army. However, the tribes had one great advantage – chariots were useless in the rocky mountain terrain of central Canaan. They may have been a deadly force on the relatively flat coastal plain and in the Jezreel valley, but they could not operate in Israel's mountainous heartland.

Deborah was no longer prepared to see her fellow tribesmen in the north subjugated under Hazor's yoke. She summoned one of the northern tribes' most respected elders – Barak, son of Abinoam of the tribe of Naphtali – and asked him to lead the revolt against Canaanite oppression. Barak accepted his role as military commander but insisted that the prophetess Deborah accompany the army to dispense her spiritual counsel. Deborah's presence also ensured the participation of the central hill country tribes of Ephraim, Benjamin and Manasseh (the latter represented by the clan of Machir).*

Barak was able to muster a total of ten thousand troops from the tribes of Naphtali and Zebulun, including contingents from the neighbouring clans of Issachar. The rest of the army amounted to another twenty thousand men from the central highlands.

Deborah and Barak devised a clever stratagem to take maximum advantage of their resources and to neutralise the Canaanite chariotry. Barak's ten thousand marched to Mount Tabor in the southern hills of Galilee and positioned themselves atop the great domed hill, where they waited for Sisera to appear. The rest of the army waited on the ridge of Gilboa north of Shechem, overlooking the Jezreel valley. Deborah then persuaded Heber the Kenite (who was a member of the Midianite clan of Moses' father-in-law) to go to Hazor, pretending to be an informant. He should tell the Canaanites that the Israelites of Galilee had assembled an army under the leadership of Barak.

---

* However, the southern tribes of Judah and Simeon, the western tribes of Dan and Asher, and the Transjordanian tribes of Gad (Gilead) and Reuben, did not offer their fighters for the coming war.

Heber delivered the news to King Jabin and commander Sisera was summoned. Within hours the army of Hazor was ready to march south to Tabor. The Canaanite force duly arrived for the set-piece battle, Hazor's chariots lined up in front of the massed ranks of infantry. However, the Israelites did not immediately engage the enemy. Instead they remained stationed on the heights of Tabor where the chariots could not reach. Deborah had chosen the timing of the campaign carefully. She had planned to confront the Canaanites in the month of Tebet (December/January) when the region's weather pattern tended to produce sudden heavy rain showers. As the Israelite army had marched up to Tabor, the skies had gradually darkened, heavy with precipitation. On the day that Sisera and his army arrived at the battlefield the rains held off – but that night the storm broke and the ground of the valley floor became drenched. Deborah knew that the time had come to strike. She immediately sent messengers across the Jezreel to order her southern troops to advance upon the city of Taanach in the valley. The central hill country tribal warriors engaged the defenders of Taanach by the 'waters of Megiddo' and, as anticipated, the Canaanite king of the city sent messengers to plead for Sisera's intervention. The commander of Hazor's forces took the bait and sped headlong into the Jezreel in order to join battle with the attacking Israelites. This was a classic military blunder and the men of Hazor paid dearly for their general's mistake.

The ten thousand infantry troops under Barak's command rushed down Tabor's slopes and attacked their enemy from the rear. Sisera's chariots advancing at the head of the army were blocked from retaliation by their own ranks of infantry. But things were about to get a lot worse. As the marianu mercenaries reached the valley floor by the torrent of Kishon, they found themselves trapped in a quagmire of mud from the previous night's thunderstorm. Once more chariots had succumbed, just as they had done in the marshy waters of the Sea of Reeds. Horses floundered as wheels sank deeper into the soft ground. Barak's warriors broke through Hazor's infantry ranks and headed for the trapped chariots. They dragged the foreign charioteers from their vehicles and slew them in the mud. The remnants of the Canaanite infantry witnessed the bloody slaughter, turned and ran. Sisera himself leapt from his stranded chariot and fled eastwards on foot through the mountains in an attempt to reach safety within the territory of Hazor.

Now the rest of Israel's army, skirmishing with the defenders of Taanach, broke off their engagement and joined in the pursuit of the Canaanites fleeing from the real battle across the valley, cutting down thousands. Sisera managed to escape as far as the western shore of Lake Galilee (also known as Kinneret), where he sought refuge in the camp of his supposed ally, Heber the Kenite. Whilst the captain of King Jabin's roundly defeated army slept, exhausted, Heber's wife, Jael, crept into his supposed place of refuge and drove a wooden tent-peg through Sisera's skull, killing him instantly.

And so Israel was delivered from Canaanite oppression and lived in peace for another thirty-seven years (1250–1214 BC). Jabin and his successors continued to rule in the city of Hazor, but the northern tribes were never to suffer again under the yoke of the Canaanite kings from the north.

Gideon and the Midianites

The next revenge-seekers were the Midianites, aided by their neighbours the Amalekites. For seven years (1214–1208 BC) they raided the southern territory of the tribes of Judah and Simeon, sometimes reaching as far as the coastal plain near Gaza. Even though the Israelites had lived in the Promised Land for over two centuries, they were still leading a semi-nomadic way of life in tents, struggling to cultivate small stands of wheat and grazing their animals on the barren hills. Midianite strategy was to attack just before harvest, burning the crops and carrying off the newly

CHAPTER TWELVE

born livestock. As a result there was great distress and
famine amongst the southern tribes. A saviour was sorely
needed.

The hero of this chapter in the Judges period was a
little-known warrior from the tribe of Manasseh named
GIDEON, son of Joash of the clan Abiezer. Following their
settlement in the Promised Land, many of the Israelites
had gradually resorted to the worship of local Canaanite
deities – especially the weather-god, BAAL. The pious
Gideon saw this adoration of false gods as the root cause
of Israel's woes and decided to cut out the cancer of pagan
worship amongst his people. As his first act of defiance
against the Canaanisation of the twelve tribes, Gideon overthrew the altar of Baal in his own home village of Ophrah,
along with its Asherah pole (representing the sacred tree
of Astarte/Ishtar), thus rejecting the false Canaanite deities
and re-establishing Yahweh as the true god.

The Midianites were expanding their military ambitions
and beginning to seek out richer plunder in the northern
territories where Gideon lived. In 1208 BC a large force
marched up the Jordan valley and into the plain of Jezreel,
bringing with them a contingent of Amalekite warriors.
Gideon called the tribes to arms. He came to meet the
invaders with the support of several thousand fighters from
the tribes of Manasseh, Asher, Zebulun and Naphtali. The
Israelites camped at the spring of Harod, beneath the high
ridge of Mount Gilboa, with the Midianites stationed on
the opposite side of the Jezreel valley on the lower slopes
of the hill of Moreh.

Gideon employed a now well-practised and successful
Hebrew military strategy. The tribes could not hope to
succeed in full-frontal, formal battle. Instead, their guerrilla-
style tactic was to fall upon the enemy whilst they were
still preparing for the set-piece battle. Gideon ordered his
main force to remain stationed on Gilboa (just as Deborah
had done) whilst he personally led his best commandos
on a night raid into the enemy camp. Burning tents and

blasting their ram's horns, the Israelites succeeded in causing maximum confusion amongst the Midianites and their allies who, thinking they were being attacked by a much larger force, fled back to the Jordan in disarray. As dawn broke, the fresh Israelite reserves on Gilboa surged down into the plain to spearhead the rout, chasing the exhausted invaders all the way to Zarethan and killing many before they reached the safety of their own territory.

However, Gideon did not pause at the northern border of Midian in his pursuit of the enemy. He chased the rump of the Midianite army – fifteen thousand men – into the heart of their kingdom on the heights of Transjordan and captured Midian's two kings – Zebah and Zalmunna.

On his way back to the central hill country, Judge Gideon took bloody revenge on the Israelite tribes to the east of the Jordan who had refused to join the attack on Midian or provide food and supplies to Gideon's army when they were in hot pursuit. As a punishment for their lack of enthusiasm for Israel's cause, Gideon had the elders of the town of Succoth executed and the people of Penuel slaughtered, destroying their fortified stronghold. Having made an example of those who were not prepared whole-heartedly to support the tribal confederacy, Israel's new judge sealed his victory by personally putting the two kings of Midian to the sword – just as Joshua had done when he killed Jabin of Hazor – as a clear and uncompromising message to all who would oppose the Children of Yahweh.

This message was heard far afield and Israel remained secure for a further thirty-nine years (1208–1170 BC), during which time Gideon judged the tribes from his home village of Ophrah.

The Expulsion of the Hyksos

Much had happened in the world outside the tribal territories during the previous decades. In Egypt, the Greater Hyksos Dynasty had fallen, perhaps amidst a great natural calamity. The consequences for the ancient world were dramatic and far-reaching. In the second month of Shemu (spring) of his eleventh regnal year (1192 BC), the young Theban pharaoh Ahmose had entered Heliopolis (Egyptian Iona/*Iwnw*, biblical On, now part of modern Cairo) at the head of a large Egyptian army and prepared to challenge the Hyksos ruler, Asherre Khamudy, ensconced in his fortified citadel at Avaris.

> Year 11, second month of Shemu: His majesty entered Heliopolis. [*Rhind Mathematical Papyrus*, recto note, line 1]

Ahmose then moved north to besiege Avaris and blockade the Pelusiac branch of the Nile in order to prevent supplies getting into the city by ship. Just three months later, on day 23 of the first month of Akhet (inundation, August), Pharaoh's army was recorded as 'pushing' the Hyksos occupiers of the delta towards the frontier town of Zile beside the Sea of Reeds.

> First month of Akhet, day 23: The king pushed the one (leader) of the Shemau (aliens) towards Zile. [*Rhind Mathematical Papyrus*, recto]

In that short period the Shemau had sued for peace and successfully negotiated their unmolested departure from Egypt. Josephus, quoting Manetho (and despite some confusion over the names of people and places), gives an account of this remarkable event:

> Thummosis (Ahmose), the son (really brother) of Misphragmuthosis (Kamose), attempted by siege to force them (i.e. the Hyksos) to surrender, blockading the fortress (of Avaris) with an army of 480,000 men. Finally, giving up the siege in despair, he concluded a treaty by which they should all depart from Egypt

and go unmolested where they pleased. On these terms the shepherds (Amalekites), with their possessions and households complete – no fewer than 240,000 persons – left Egypt and journeyed over the desert into Syria (i.e. the Levant).

We should perhaps be asking why they were forced into so sudden a capitulation and ignominious retreat. The answer may perhaps be found in the aftermath of the catastrophic eruption of the Aegean volcanic island of Thera (Santorini).* According to Professor Hans Goedicke, a brief record of just three lines, scribbled on papyrus, appears to describe something very unusual which took place at this time.

Year 11, first month of Akhet, (on) the birthday of Seth, the majesty of this god caused his voice to be heard; (then on) the birthday of Isis the sky rained.
[*Rhind Mathematical Papyrus*, recto note, line 3]

This was no ordinary thunder, nor any sort of ordinary rain, for these events occurred in the dry Egyptian summer and on different days (twenty-four hours or so apart), ruling out a regular thunderstorm. If this brief text is an Egyptian record of the Theran eruption, then we are presented with a highly plausible explanation for the Hyksos retreat from the Egyptian delta.

---

* The New Chronology currently has the fall of Avaris in 1192 BC, but the major tree-ring frost signature in the Irish bog oaks falls in 1159 BC. If this climatic marker is evidence of the Theran eruption (rather than the usually favoured 1628 BC frost signature), then we would have a 33-year chronological discrepancy. In the NC the eruption would have taken place in the reign of Amenhotep I and not Ahmose. However, given the assumptions upon which the Late Bronze Age dendrochronology has been formulated and the fact that the frost-signature only occurs in the Irish tree-ring chronology, it may be that this problem will be resolved by later research or the conclusion reached that the eruption did not leave its mark on the tree-ring Bronze Age sequence.

Archaeological evidence from the Aegean islands and Crete has given historians every reason to believe that the cataclysmic eruption of Thera wreaked havoc in the eastern Mediterranean, especially amongst Khamudy's principal trading partners – the Cretans. A tidal wave, generated by the collapse of the volcano's caldera, must undoubtedly have destroyed Crete's fleet moored in the ports on the island's north shore. And so much of the sea transport for the Hyksos exchange network would have been decimated.

A second Egyptian document (Papyrus Hearst), also dated to this time, suggests that the tsunami even attacked the Nile delta, sweeping across the marshes of Lake Manzela and up to the walls of Avaris before exhausting itself forty kilometres from the coast. According to Goedicke, the Egyptians believed that the storm-god Seth of Avaris had prevented the destruction of the Hyksos city. Goedicke interprets the crucial line as referring to Seth 'banishing' the waters as they approached Avaris.

The gods had turned against Egypt's seafaring oppressors and delivered them into Pharaoh's hands. But the Egyptian army was simply not strong enough to take Avaris by force-of-arms. Ahmose knew that the foreigners were still strong and secure behind their mighty defensive wall, built by the dynasty founder Shalek (Manetho's Salitis) and strengthened by Khamudy's predecessor, Auserre Apopi (Manetho's Aphophis). Terms were agreed to avoid further bloodshed, allowing the Shemau and their Amalekite followers to leave Egypt unmolested. Ahmose's troops 'drove' the fleeing Shemau and their Asiatic horde beyond the frontier post at Zile and out onto the 'Way of the Philistines' which led across northern Sinai to the Canaanite coastal plain. So it was that the expulsion of the Hyksos from the eastern delta inaugurated the prosperous era of Egypt's New Kingdom.

Some of the Hyksos departed from the delta in those of their sleek ships which had survived the tidal wave, to resettle in the Aegean islands and in the Argolid plain of the Peloponnese on mainland Greece. There they founded a new dynasty which was destined to ignite the heroic era of Bronze Age Greece. The deeds and exploits of the Danoi (the descendants of Danaus and the Danuna of the later Egyptian texts) would be extolled throughout the ages, culminating in the renowned corpus of 'Homeric' poems which sing of their ultimate triumph over Troy and subsequent ignominious fall at the hands of Dorian invaders. But that is another story.

The rest of the Shemau/Pelast nobility, including King Khamudy, joined the Aamu in their flight across northern Sinai and on into the southern coastal plain of Palestine where they sought refuge in the old Hyksos cities – in particular the heavily fortified stronghold of Sharuhen, from where Maibre Sheshi had ruled more than a century earlier.

Pharaoh Ahmose entered the abandoned city of Avaris and proceeded to strip the Hyksos palace of its decadent fresco-paintings of bull-leaping and red-lipped ladies of the court in their flounced skirts. The shattered fragments were ignominiously tossed over the edge of the palace terrace where they were discovered, three thousand years later, face down in the dirt, by Professor Manfred Bietak's team of Austrian excavators However, Ahmose did not tear down the building, nor the fortification walls of Avaris, because the Egyptians, practical as ever, knew that they would need this ready-built garrison town to aid them in a new military adventure.

The Theban kings had endured decades of suppression, hemmed into their tiny kingdom whilst the rest of Egypt suffered at the hands of foreigners. The trauma of these bitter years ran deep, and the early rulers of the New Kingdom were determined that the Black Land would never be vulnerable to foreign invasion again. In spite of the fact that he had sworn an oath permitting the Asiatics a safe retreat out of Egypt, Ahmose knew that he could not stand by and allow the enemy to remain entrenched on his northern border. Once the Aamu and their Shemau leaders were across the Brook of Egypt – the wadi bed which was traditionally the border of Pharaoh's kingdom – Ahmose (his treaty-oath now fulfilled) gave orders for their hot pursuit and annihilation. The Egyptian army surrounded Sharuhen and besieged the city for three long years. This time there was no negotiated peace. Eventually, the Hyksos stronghold fell and Egypt's long-time abusers were put to the sword.

It was not normal pharaonic policy to indulge in mass slaughter – but, in the aftermath of such brutality and humiliation heaped upon the Egyptian people, the northerners needed to be taught a lesson. Egypt was no longer going to be a soft touch for invasion and an easy source of plunder. The destruction of Sharuhen (possibly MB II-B Tell el-Ajjul, City II) marked the birth of the Egyptian empire period during which time pharaonic interests – both north and south of its heartland – would be secured by military power. The age of the New Kingdom warrior pharaohs had begun.

The rest of the Hyksos élite waited in their cities along the coastal plain for the expected Egyptian retribution ... but it did not come. Revenge was sated with the bloodbath at Sharuhen and pharaonic interests began to focus on securing the trading network left by the Hyksos merchant princes. There was no time to indulge in year after year of siege just to take a few Philistine cities in the southern coastal plain. There were bigger fish to catch further north.

Once access to the sea had been recovered with the taking of Avaris, the Egyptians were quickly able to renew contact with Phoenician Byblos in order to secure supplies of valuable Lebanese cedar. In effect, the Palestinian coastal plain was bypassed by sea. The Egyptian military also chose to wage their wars in the far north, first attacking the Indo-European satellite states in Syria and then later reaching into the heartland of the Mitannian kingdom beyond the Euphrates in Naharina, from where the Hurrian allies of the Hyksos had come. All this was achieved by sailing up the coast to Byblos and Simyra from where the Egyptian army launched its northern campaigns.

It did not take many decades before the remnant Hyksos/Pelastoi in Palestine made peace overtures to Egypt, offering their loyalty to the new rising power in the region. The VIA MARIS was thus secured – not by military conquest but rather by political treaty. The cities of the coastal plain and Jezreel valley fell under the hegemony of the pharaohs of the 18th Dynasty whilst the highlands to the east – a political backwater with few resources to interest the Egyptians – were left pretty much alone for two centuries. These were the centuries of the late Judges period (from the time of Gideon onwards) when the Israelite tribes, still living in their tents, continued to fight off the ever-mounting 'oppression' of their western neighbours – the Philistines – in an attempt to hold onto land 'promised' to them by their god, Yahweh.

Historically speaking, it is simply a matter of perspective – biblical or pharaonic. The Israelites perceived the barren hill country where their great ancestor Abraham had lived as a land overflowing with milk and honey. To them it was the centre of their universe. But the Egyptians had no interest in the region occupied by their former slaves. Pharaoh's interests lay in the lucrative trade routes to and from the great powers of the Mesopotamian north. There was no strategic value in occupying the Israelite territories – so long as the nomadic tribes kept to themselves and did not try to disrupt the Late Bronze Age commercial network. To ensure that the Israelites did not terrorise the main highways and the vassal towns along those vital trading arteries, the Egyptians made Israel's neighbours strong enough to continuously threaten the tribal confederacy in the hills. In effect, the Philistines living along the Via Maris and the Amorites living along the King's Highway in Transjordan were Egypt's police force in the northern empire. So, from a biblical perspective, we should understand that the Egyptians of the 18th Dynasty were the real, unnamed power behind the oppressions of the Judges period. It would take the coronation of a weak pharaoh and the simultaneous rise of a strong-willed Israelite leader from the tribe of Benjamin to break Egypt's hold on the southern Levant, heralding the birth of Israel's United Monarchy – but that day was still a long way off as a would-be king of Israel now made his move to seize power in the highlands of Ephraim.

Abimelech and Migdol Shechem

Gideon had numerous wives and concubines who bore him many sons, one of whom was called Abimelech – a man of driving ambition who would allow nothing to stand in the way of his destiny.

After Gideon died in 1170 BC the people immediately began to worship the image of Baal once more and took to celebrating Canaanite festivals in the great Migdol Temple at Shechem. Abimelech, the son of Gideon's concubine who had lived in Shechem, incited the elders of his mother's clan to raise a small army of HABIRU mercenaries which he led on a brutal raid into his father's territory. Abimelech assaulted the village of Ophrah, captured all of Gideon's other sons and put each and every one of his half-brothers to death upon the large altar stone where his father had made offerings to Yahweh. Only Jotham, Gideon's youngest son, managed to escape and flee into the hills. Upon his return to Shechem, Abimelech was proclaimed king before Joshua's great covenant stone. So began three years of brutal oppression by Israel's first elected monarch (1170–1168 BC).

The elders of Shechem soon began to see their error in raising a megalomaniac as king over the central tribes. In the third year of Abimelech's reign they plotted to murder him on the highway, hiring Gaal son of Obed as the leader of the assassins. But Zebul, Abimelech's governor in Shechem, got wind of the plot and sent messengers to his master who was dwelling at Tirzah (Tell el-Farah North). The king summoned his Habiru mercenaries and laid an ambush of his own outside the gates of Shechem. When Gaal and his men came out to undertake their mission, the royal body-guard fell upon them. Most of the rebels were killed but Gaal escaped back within the Cyclopean walls of the city. Abimelech withdrew to nearby Aruma.

That evening the elders of Shechem were persuaded by Zebul to expel Gaal and his brothers for fear of the King's wrath. But Abimelech was not the sort of man prepared to forgive so easily at such a gesture. The next day, as the people of the town came out to tend their fields, they were massacred by the King's soldiers who then forced their way inside the city, slashing and burning. The remaining citizens fled into the Migdol Temple and barricaded themselves behind the great cedar doors. They were not to be spared. Abimelech ordered the cutting down of trees on the slopes of Mount Zalmon and the timber was piled high around the temple. The pyre was set alight and the whole building incinerated with one thousand men, women and children inside.

In 1926 German archaeologist Ernst Sellin excavated the huge Temple of Baal-Berith at Shechem (Fortress Temple 1-b, Temenos 7), exposing a layer of burnt debris which marked the destruction of the Middle Bronze II-B to Late Bronze I sanctuary. The rest of the city had also been burnt to the ground and part of the defensive wall toppled. Unlike the cities of the coastal plain and Jezreel valley, no Aegean-style bichrome ware was found at Shechem, indicating that the Indo-European foreigners (whom we have identified with the biblical Philistines) had no influence in this most Israelite of cities (as one might expect). It was clear from the excavations that the MB II-B/LB I destruction by fire was followed by a gap in occupation of nearly one hundred years before a more modest structure (datable to the LB II-A Amarna period or thereabouts) was erected over the surviving foundations of the old structure (but with a five-degree shift in its axis).*

Having exacted his revenge upon the Shechemites, Abimelech left the smouldering ruins of the city and marched upon Thebez (modern Tubas, 16 km north of Shechem). As had happened at Shechem, the citizens retreated inside a fortress tower in the centre of the town and bolted the door. Abimelech first indulged his men in the ransacking of the houses of Thebez before organising the burning down of the tower with everyone inside. This tactic had worked to his satisfaction at Shechem and there was every reason to believe that it would succeed here as well ... but fate had a different outcome in store. As Abimelech approached the bolted door, a woman on the roof of the building toppled a heavy millstone down from the battlements, crushing the king's skull and leaving him mortally wounded. Abimelech died by the sword of his armour-bearer to prevent a lingering death and to avoid the humiliation of being slain by a lowly female.

The men of Tirzah and those Habiru mercenaries who had fought for their rampageous paymaster quickly realised that the game was up and dispersed back to their homes. Israel's first abortive experiment with kingship was at an end. It would be another one hundred and fifty-seven years before the Israelites once again asked for a king to rule over them.

Two Judges ruled in the half-century which followed Abimelech's death. First came Tola, son of Puah, of the tribe of Issachar. He judged Israel for twenty-three years (1168–1146 BC), giving counsel from his home town of Shamir in the highlands of Ephraim. Next came Jair of

---

* All this fits perfectly with the biblical story of the great Migdol Temple of Baal-Berith, first mentioned during the final phase of the Conquest campaign (MB II-B, 1405 BC), then destroyed by Abimelech during the first part of the Late Bronze Age (LB I, 1168 BC), contemporary with the reign of Amenhotep I in Egypt (1178–1158 BC), and rebuilt on a more modest scale during the early years of the United Monarchy period (LB II-A, c. 1011 BC).

Gad, who judged Israel for twenty-two years (1146–1125 BC) from the town of Kamon in Gilead, across the Jordan.

Jephthah

> The Israelites again began doing what is evil in Yahweh's eyes. They served Baal and Astarte, and the gods of Aram and Sidon, the gods of Moab and those of the Ammonites and Philistines. They deserted Yahweh and served him no more. Yahweh's anger then burned against Israel and he gave them over into the power of the Philistines and the power of the Ammonites who, from that year onwards, crushed and oppressed the Israelites for eighteen years – all those Israelites living on the other side of the Jordan in Amorite territory, in Gilead. Furthermore, the Ammonites would cross the Jordan and also make war on Judah, Benjamin and the House of Ephraim, so that Israel was in distress. [Judges 10:6–9]

And so, once again, the Israelite tribes were at war with their neighbours – a war of attrition which lasted eighteen years. Finally, in 1108 BC a large invasion force of AMORITES crossed the River Jabbok and marched into Gilead – the territory allocated to the tribe of Gad. The Israelites of Transjordan massed at Mizpah, where a council of war was held to decide who should lead them. The elders chose a warlord named Jephthah as commander of the army because of his many years of experience leading a band of adventurers on raids into Amorite territory.

Jephthah sent messengers to the king of Ammon in an attempt to avoid the impending conflict, reminding the Ammonites that they had come off very badly last time they had fought against Yahweh's host when Moses led his people through their territory. That had been three hundred years ago (1408 BC) [Judges 11:26] but Yahweh was still strong and would protect his children against those who would challenge their right to exist in the land. But the Ammonite ruler ignored the threat and battle ensued. Jephthah's warriors pushed the Amorite army back across the Jabbok as far as the region of Minnith and the town of Abel-Keranim, inflicting a humiliating defeat on Ammon. In gratitude to his god for guiding him to victory, Jephthah sacrificed his own daughter on Yahweh's altar and burnt her lifeless body in the offering flames.

In these bloody times the tribes of Israel were rarely united and often at each other's throats. There had been long-standing animosity between the Transjordanian tribes and the clans of Ephraim on the west side of the Jordan river (as exemplified by the slaughter at Jabesh-Gilead in the time of the Judge Othniel). With the crushing victory over Ammon behind them, Jephthah's Gadite army marched against Ephraimite territory. On the west bank of the Jordan the two tribes clashed and Ephraim was roundly defeated. From that day on, until the unification of the tribal confederacy under King Saul, the Gadites controlled the Jordan crossing points and prevented traders from Ephraim entering the lands to the east of the river.

After six years of rule over the Transjordanian tribes, Jephthah died. The next three *shopetim* ('judges') were Ibzan of Bethlehem (who judged Israel for seven years), Elon of Zebulun (who judged Israel for ten years) and Abdon of Ephraim (who judged Israel for eight years). Then, in 1081 BC, after nearly thirty years of relative peace, the final and most devastating oppression emerged from the west in the form of early Israel's greatest foe – the Philistines.

The Philistine Oppression

The Philistines, who had departed from Avaris a little over a century earlier in 1192 BC, were growing rich and powerful in their city states along the coastal plain. They had capitulated to the 18th-Dynasty pharaohs and, by swearing loyalty oaths to Egypt, had received both the patronage and protection of their New Kingdom masters.*

The vast trading network which came out of the 18th-Dynasty military conquests in the north brought untold riches into the Nile valley along the Via Maris – and therefore directly through Philistia. The Philistine lords (*seranim*) had grown prosperous from their role as middlemen for Canaanite goods flowing into the Nile valley and Egyptian goods heading north into Mesopotamia and Anatolia. The five seranim of Gath, Ashdod, Ashkelon, Ekron and Gaza realised that they were onto a good thing and had to ensure continuing safe passage of this trade throughout the region. They therefore formed a coalition and took it upon themselves (with Pharaoh's blessing) to act as international policeman, with the special brief of keeping the unruly tribes in the highlands under control.

For years they raided, threatened and harassed the Israelites, eventually stationing garrisons at strategic locations in the hill country and within the Shephelah foothills bordering the coastal plain. So began the seventy-year Philistine oppression which lasted from 1081 to 1012 BC. During the first twenty years of Philistine dominance, a Danite warrior, renowned for his strength and prowess, did much to antagonise Israel's powerful neighbour and bring about severe retribution in the following decades.

Samson

Samson was the son of Manoah, chieftain in the village of Zorah, who raised his son as a *nazir* – a chosen of Yahweh. A nazir was supposed to be a man of god – one who refused

---

* Between 1112 and 1095 BC, Pharaoh Thutmose III – the Napoleon of ancient Egypt – had fought fourteen military campaigns to forge a mighty northern empire. In 1112 BC he had defeated a strong coalition of Syrian kings at the battle of Megiddo and had subsequently made all the Canaanite states, as far north as Kadesh-on-the-Orontes in Syria, vassals of Egypt. Kadesh was conquered in the king's thirtieth regnal year (1105 BC).

to cut his hair and chose never to indulge in wine, women and song. Samson only managed to conform to the first of the attributes – he did not cut his hair. As for the rest, the truth is that he was a wild, womanising drunkard. He married into a Philistine family living in Timnah and was very much a part of both Israelite and Philistine societies.

Samson was hot-headed and violent. He often brawled with his Philistine neighbours and managed to kill several in one incident in the city of Ashkelon. On another occasion he burnt the cornfields of Timnah and, in retaliation, the citizens of the town killed his wife and parents-in-law. Samson fled into Israelite territory but was handed over to the Philistines by his own people. He soon escaped, slaying his captives with the jawbone of an ass. His deeds transformed him into a local folk-hero and young men flocked to his side in the guerrilla war against Israel's oppressors.

Years later, and ever the womanising drunkard, Samson became infatuated with another Philistine girl named Delilah who was sent to trap the Israelite warrior by means of her sexual guiles. Having succeeded in her task, Delilah quickly betrayed her lover, who was captured and taken to the seran of Gaza. Once again Samson was in Philistine hands but, this time, he was not allowed to escape so easily. The Israelite wild man from the hills was shorn of his long flowing locks, blinded, shackled, and forced to grind corn like oxen. His one-man revolt against Philistine oppression was still, however, unfinished. Chained to the columns which supported the entrance to the temple of Dagon as an 'entertainment' for the crowds attending a religious festival, Samson summoned all his remaining strength to force the pillars apart and bring the façade of the shrine down upon his captors. Legendary hero that he was, Samson son of Manoah was still unable to bring down Philistine overlordship over the Israelite tribes. The lords of Philistia continued to dominate the highways from their garrison forts and exact dues from the poor farmers and shepherds of the central hill country.

Samuel

Living in those hills at the time of Elon's judgeship over Israel (1097–1088 BC) was a devout follower of Yahweh from the clan of Zuph of the priestly tribe of Levi. His name was Elkanah, son of Jeroham, and he lived in the village of Ramah (modern Ramah near Ramalah), though his clan seat was at Ephrath (the ancient name of Bethlehem). Every year he made the short journey northward along the Shechem highway to make sacrifice to his god before the 'temple of Yahweh at Shiloh' [1 Samuel 24] – the stone shrine built to house the Ark of the Covenant. Elkanah had two wives, Hannah and Peninnah, but the former was apparently barren. In the year 1095 BC she accompanied her husband to Shiloh and prayed to Yahweh that he might bless her with a son. Hannah soon conceived and gave birth to a healthy boy, whom she named SAMUEL. Elkanah and Hannah were so taken with their little 'miracle' that they promised their new offspring into the service of Yahweh at Shiloh.

As soon as Samuel was weaned, the infant was delivered into the hands of the high priest, Eli, who had the child raised within the walls of the sanctuary. Over the years Eli grew old, blind and infirm, as Samuel grew up 'in the presence of Yahweh' and was recognised by all the tribes of Israel as a 'prophet' (Hebrew *nabi*).

The full force of the Philistine oppression began in 1062 BC, following the death of Samson (when Samuel was thirty-two) and climaxed with the battle of Ebenezer in 1024 BC, when the Ark of the Covenant was captured by the Philistines. Israel's prophet was then in his seventies.

Capture of the Ark of the Covenant

The story of Israel's loss of the casket containing the tablets of the Ten Commandments is told in chapters four to six of the first book of Samuel. The Philistine *seranim* had

259

mustered their troops to wage war against the Israelites. The tribal warriors of the coalition marched down from the hills to meet them on the coastal plain due east of Aphek at a place called EBENEZER. The first clash of arms ended in stalemate, with many men on both sides falling in the fray. That night the tribal chieftains slipped back to Shiloh whilst the Israelites held their lines through the hours of darkness. The elders returned at dawn carrying the Ark of the Covenant before them, to be greeted by a mighty roar from the camp. The Israelites were filled with renewed confidence as their war talisman was paraded at the head of the army. And so they marched out to confront the enemy once more.

This second round of battle was even more fierce, prolonged and bloody than the first. Many thousands died that day as Israel suffered its first great defeat at the hands of a bordering state. For once, the power of the Ark did not protect the Children of Yahweh and guide them to victory. The Philistines were too powerful, with their heavy chariots and cavalry, whilst Israel's strength did not lie in fighting big, set-piece battles on open ground. They had forgotten how the earlier judges had employed both the terrain and surprise guerrilla tactics to defeat Israel's strongest enemies. Now the tribal warriors had paid a heavy price for their overconfidence. The Tablets of the Law, housed in their golden box, fell into Philistine hands and were taken off to the city of Ashdod as war booty.

A messenger from the tribe of Benjamin fled the battlefield to bring news of the military disaster to Eli at Shiloh. The high priest and judge was sitting at the gate of the fortified shrine when the exhausted messenger reached him. The old, blind man was so shocked to hear of the loss of the Ark that he had a heart attack, fell backwards off the stone bench he was sitting on, struck his head against the gateway to the cult centre and broke his neck. And so, with the death of Eli, Samuel became judge over Israel in a time of great crisis.

Meanwhile, the Philistines were celebrating their victory

throughout the lowland towns. The Ark of the Covenant was put on display in the temple of Dagon for several months before it went on a tour of the other Philistine capitals at Gath and Ekron. But the celebrations were not to last long. At this time the 'Asiatic Plague' – what we today call the bubonic plague – was spreading like wildfire amongst the northern empires of the Middle East where it had already decimated the populations of southern Anatolia and northern Syria. Now it was beginning to take hold in the densely populated cities of Egypt's northern empire trading network. In Egypt itself, Pharaoh Amenhotep III (1048–1012 BC), monitoring the situation with some concern, ordered the carving of seven hundred and thirty statues of the pestilence-goddess Sekhmet – two for each day of the year – in an attempt to placate her wrath and prevent the deadly disease from reaching the Nile valley.

The plague quickly began to ravage the Philistine cities, carried by rats on board trading ships from the north. The superstitious citizens of Ashdod, Gath and Ekron perceived the onset of the pestilence as a sign of Yahweh's anger against them for taking the Israelite god away from his people. They therefore resolved immediately to return the Ark of the Covenant to Israel.

And so in the winter of 1024 BC, after having been seven months in the possession of the Philistines, the Ark was placed on a cart pulled by oxen and brought to the village of Beth-Shemesh, in the valley of Sorek, where it was abandoned within sight of Israelite territory. From there local tribesmen took Israel's most sacred symbol up into the hills and to the settlement of Baalah (later known as Kiriath-Jearim), where it remained for twenty years under the protection of Eleazar, son of Abinadab.

Part Four

Legendary Kings

Chapter Thirteen

SAUL AND THE HEBREW REVOLT

(1 Samuel 8:1 to 2 Samuel 1:27)

The Choosing of a King – Labaya of Benjamin –
The Hebrews – Uprising Against the Philistines –
Akhenaten and the Amarna Letters – The Rise of the
Habiru – Elhanan and Goliath – The Hebrew Fugitive
– Elhanan and Achish of Gath – The Battle of Gilboa

our hundred and thirty-five years had passed since
the days of Exodus, and the loose confederation
of tribes were finally ready to become a nation –
the United Kingdom of Israel. The clan elders came
together at MIZPAH, where they convened a great council.
The Philistines were still oppressing the Israelites and the
people had become impoverished under the yoke of their
oppression. By contrast, the Canaanite populations of the
coastal plain and Jezreel valley were prospering as they
took full advantage of the Middle East's burgeoning trading
network. The hill country continued to be a political
backwater.

It was obvious to many why Israel was failing to participate in the Late Bronze Age trading revolution: they

265

were not regarded by Egypt or their neighbours as a king-dom or unified country with a recognised head of state. In other words, they did not have a king. How could the Israelites join with all the other city-states surrounding them and reap the benefits of association with Egypt's New King-dom empire if they were politically invisible? Only if Israel were to become a kingdom, with a monarch at its head, would it be recognised by Pharaoh and his vassals.

And so the clan chieftains unanimously decided to ask their prophet for a king. Samuel, now eighty-four years old, received Israel's petitioners at his home town of Ramah.

> The elders of Israel all assembled, went back to Samuel at Ramah and said, 'Look, you are old, and your sons are not following your example. So give us a king to judge us, like the other nations.'
> [1 Samuel 8:4–5]

The seer was, at first, reluctant to agree to the demand, for he recalled the disastrous short rule of Abimelech which had led to the destruction and abandonment of Shechem eight generations earlier. But the clan elders were insistent that they needed a king, and so their prophet began his search for a natural leader to become the first sovereign over all Israel.

Now amongst the tribe of Benjamin was a high-ranking chieftain – Kish, son of Abiel of the clan Matri. He had a son named Labaya ('great lion [of Yah]') who, at forty-one years of age, was handsome, tall and strong – as strong as a great lion.

In the spring of 1012 BC, Labaya and his servants made their way from his home town of Gibeah ('hill' – modern Geba, east of Ramalah) towards Ramah in search of asses which had strayed from his father's land. The men of Gibeah met Samuel at the gate of Ramah just as the prophet was heading up to the high place of the town to conduct a sacrifice. Samuel immediately recognised Labaya to be the one chosen by Yahweh as Israel's first king and redeemer from the Philistine oppression. The Benjaminite warrior was taken aback by the seer's prediction of his elevation to power, protesting that he, of all people, should be the last person to be anointed ruler of all Israel, simply because of his lowly status.

> 'Am I not a Benjaminite from the smallest of the tribes of Israel? And is not my family the least of all the families of the tribe of Benjamin? Why are you saying such a thing to me?' [1 Samuel 9:21]

Labaya attended the meal of sacrifice as Samuel's guest and then stayed the night in the prophet's house. The next day, at a secret ceremony, sacred oils were poured over the head of Kish's eldest son, making him Yahweh's anointed – a prince-in-waiting. He was then sent on his way back to Gibeah, to his father's house. Soon after, Samuel despatched messengers throughout the tribal territories, summoning the clan leaders to Mizpah once more. There, at the behest of Israel's great prophet, Labaya son of Kish was proclaimed king and war-leader.

You may be wondering who this Labaya is – after all he does not appear anywhere in the Bible. In fact, Labaya, king of the hill country, was indeed a major player in the history of Israel's United Monarchy period. But he is remembered by his traditional name – Saul – which means 'asked for' because the people asked for 'a king to judge us, like the other nations' [1 Samuel 8:5]. A later writer/ redactor of the Old Testament (probably the editor known to scholars as the Deuteronomist) knew the early kings of Israel by their traditional names which tended to characterise the reigns of the United Monarchy kings. And so Saul (Hebrew *Shaul*) was 'asked for' by the people; David (Hebrew *Dud/Dwd*) was the 'beloved' of Yahweh; and Solomon (Hebrew *Shelomo*) reigned in relative 'peace' throughout his long reign. We will learn David and Solomon's real Late Bronze Age names when we come to deal in turn with their stories but, for now, we must continue to follow the career of Yahweh's 'Great Lion' – King Labaya of the hill country – scourge of the Philistines.

Labaya the Warrior King

Many of the clansmen from distant parts were openly contemptuous of Samuel's choice of a lowly Benjaminite as national ruler. However, Labaya was soon to prove himself a strong military commander and thus unite all the tribes in their war of liberation. One month after his proclamation as king, Labaya was returning from the fields in Gibeah when he heard news of an incursion into the territories of Reuben and Gad by Nahash, ruler of the Ammonites. The men of Israel's tribes across the Jordan were being rounded up and mutilated. Nahash had ordered that each should have his right eye gouged out in retribution for Moses' slaughter of the Ammonite king's ancestors in 1407 BC. The wounds of that terrible episode still ran deep.

Israel's first king knew that he had to act quickly if he was to unite the tribes behind him. He slew the oxen with which he had been ploughing, cut up their carcasses and sent the pieces to all corners of the kingdom. Just as with the Levite who butchered his concubine and despatched her parts to the clans as a call to arms [Judges 19:29–30], so Labaya's message was equally effective, though for different reasons. The implicit threat was that, if the clan warriors failed to heed the call-to-arms, then the king would cut their oxen up just as he had done his own.

Labaya gathered the warriors of Benjamin and their men-at-arms and headed north to Bezek where the Israelite army was assembling. A large force of three hundred and thirty tribal warriors and their foot soldiers (totalling nearly three thousand) crossed the Jordan overnight and, in a surprise attack, routed the Ammonite army encamped outside Jabesh-Gilead. The victorious Israelite army then returned across the Jordan and gathered at Gilgal where Joshua had erected the twelve standing-stones. Before the assembly, Labaya was confirmed as king by acclamation and Samuel formally relinquished his judgeship over Israel. A new era in the history of the Children of Yahweh had finally dawned – the era known to scholars as the United Monarchy.

The Israelite Revolt

Whilst the vast majority of the army retired to their own homes, Labaya retained the services of three hundred men-at-arms as a standing army which he stationed in the central highlands. These were mainly soldiers of fortune or mercenaries hired by the king from the local stateless nomads. These people were known as 'Habiru' – the Apiru of Egyptian texts and the Hebrews of the Bible. But the Israelites and Hebrews were not one and the same people. The Israelites regarded themselves as different – because they were the chosen of Yahweh. It was true that they had once been Habiru (Hebrew *Ibrim*, the descendants of Abraham's ancestor Eber), but the forging of their nationhood under Moses as the Children of Yahweh and now their unification under the national banner of Labaya/Saul's Israel differentiated them from the rest of the Habiru peoples scattered about the Levant – at least in their own eyes. The Philistines and Egyptians, on the other hand, still regarded the Israelite tribes as Habiru, even if they had chosen a king for themselves and had pretensions to nationhood. The term Habiru had become a pejorative – an expression of abuse used to describe any miscreant or reprobate who challenged authority or stood outside Egypt's beneficent hegemony. The Habiru/Hebrews were the ancient world's gypsies and brigands.

So, in the time of Labaya, two groups of people lived side by side in the hills of Canaan – the Israelites and the

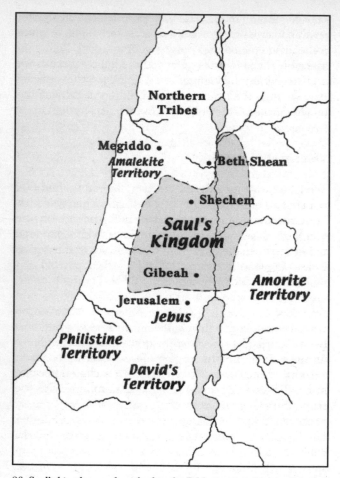

28. Saul's kingdom as described in the Bible is precisely the area ruled over by Labaya according to the el-Amarna letters, including the territory in Transjordan.

Hebrews. The latter were not averse to hiring themselves out to anyone who would pay them to fight on their behalf. Bands of Habiru mercenaries were to be found amongst the troops of many city-states in the region. The hirelings

were excellent fighters but, like the Mujahidin of Afghanistan's tribal network, switched sides as political fortunes
in the region ebbed and flowed.

Labaya, the new king of Israel, simply behaved exactly
as his neighbours had done. He did not hesitate in acquiring
his own force of Habiru to act as his personal bodyguard
and the professional army for Israel's nascent kingdom.
Two hundred were housed at Michmash (modern Muk-
kmas) on the north side of the Wadi Suwenit and in the
hills around Beth-El, under the command of the king, whilst
the remaining hundred were garrisoned at Gibeah (modern
Geba) on the south side of the wadi, under the command
of Labaya's eldest son JONATHAN. With victory over the
Ammonites and his professional army in place around the
heartland of the highland kingdom, Labaya knew the time
had come to challenge Philistine authority in the region
and set Israel on its course towards independence.

Jonathan went to the high place at Gibeath-Elohim ('hill
of the gods') next to the village of Gibeah where, amongst
the Israelite standing stones, the Philistines had set up a
large freestanding pillar (Hebrew *netsib*) – the physical
symbol of their control of the region. Modern Bibles have
chosen to translate this word *netsib* as 'governor' – a later
meaning of the original word specifically chosen because
such officials were 'pillars of the community'. But the
primary meaning of *netsib* was simply 'pillar' and should
be translated as such where it occurs in the books of Samuel.
The king's son, Jonathan, did not overthrow (or kill) the
Philistine governor at Gibeath-Elohim – he simply overthrew the Philistine monolith which crashed to the ground,
splitting into large fragments. Ram's-horn trumpets were
sounded throughout the highlands to let the people know
that the revolt against Philistine rule had begun.

The seranim in the cities of the coastal plain soon heard
about the toppling of the netsib and sent a large force into
the hills to suppress the uprising. The Philistine army
quickly re-established control, pushing Labaya, Jonathan

and their Habiru back down into the Jordan valley. Many of the mercenaries fled into Transjordan, but Labaya's most loyal fighters were able to regroup at the standing stones of Gilgal. The Israelite peasants living in the hills abandoned their villages and tents for fear of massacre and hid in caves. Believing that the revolt was at an end, the overconfident Philistines returned to the coastal plain, leaving only a brigade of troops garrisoned at Michmash to monitor the situation in the aftermath of their easy victory.

For seven days Labaya waited at Gilgal. He then marched his men back up the Wadi Kilt and into the Wadi Suwenit before reoccupying Gibeah (Geba). From there his brave son Jonathan led a small force against the Philistine garrison at Michmash and retook the town – helped by another (this time minor) earth tremor. Those Habiru mercenaries who were in the pay of the Philistines, and who made up half the garrison at Michmash, saw that the tide had turned in favour of the Israelite king and effortlessly switched sides, whilst the Israelite farmers returned home from their hiding places and took up arms against the fleeing enemy. Scores of Philistine soldiers and their commanders were taken captive and the rest fled back to the cities of the coastal plain in disarray.

> Those Hebrews (Habiru mercenaries, as distinct from Israelites) who had earlier taken service with the Philistines and had accompanied them into camp (at Michmash) now defected to the Israelites who were with Saul and Jonathan. Similarly, all those Israelites (as distinct from Hebrews) who had been hiding in the highlands of Ephraim, hearing that the Philistines were on the run, chased after them and joined in the fight. [1 Samuel 14:21–22]

And so the geopolitical situation was pretty much back to square one, the only difference being that nominal Philistine control of the highlands had been weakened. The seranim had clearly triumphed in the initial battle – but Labaya had won the military campaign with his strategic retreat and subsequent reoccupation of the ground initially lost to his enemy. He knew that the Philistines could not afford to keep their huge army stationed permanently in the highlands. All the Israelite king had to do was give ground and then retake it once the Philistines had made their withdrawal back to the coastal plain. This cat-and-mouse game between the Philistines and Israel soon came to the attention of the Egyptians who, after fifty years of peace and stability, were not at all amused by what was happening in their backyard.

The Amarna Age

Since the days of Thutmose III's spectacular military campaigns, Egypt had become astonishingly wealthy. Thutmose's son and successor, Amenhotep II (1087–1057 BC), attempted to continue his father's wars in the north but, in spite of his obvious sporting and military prowess, things did not go as well for the new king. Although the Egyptian records are silent on the matter, it seems likely that Amenhotep suffered a military reverse during his Year 7 campaign into Syria (1081 BC). He attempted to camouflage the failure by transforming his military adventure into an elephant hunt in the country of Niy. Nonetheless, something had gone drastically wrong which, soon after, led to a cessation of hostilities on Egypt's part. Almost certainly as a direct consequence of this military setback, we witness the adoption of a new foreign policy in the next generation of the 18th-Dynasty royal line.

With the coronation of Thutmose IV (1057–1048 BC) begins the era of political marriage alliance. Somewhat ironically, the old enemy – the Indo-European kingdom of Mitanni which had been the target of so many of Thutmose III's campaigns – became Egypt's closest ally through a series of marriages between the pharaohs and the royal daughters of NAHARINA. First Thutmose IV, then his son Amenhotep III, married foreign princesses, turning the royal palaces of Egypt into truly cosmopolitan courts. The policy was so successful that foreign rulers from far and wide clamoured to send their daughters to Egypt in exchange for peace with the great power (and a not insubstantial dowry of Egyptian gold). Within a few decades, some of the world's most powerful kingdoms, including Mitanni, Babylonia, Hatti and Arzawa, had sealed peace and trading treaties with the land of the pharaohs in this way. Each bride was inevitably escorted to Egypt by a large entourage of servants and officials, turning Pharaoh's royal residences into vast international complexes of harems and ambassadorial offices. Peace had broken out all over the ancient Near East – except, that is, for those irritating Hebrews holed up in their highland strongholds of southern Palestine. How could the Egyptians have known that these insignificant tribesmen from the hills were about to change the political landscape of the region forever?

Things came to a head towards the end of the long reign of Thutmose IV's son, Amenhotep III (1048–1012 BC), often regarded as the wealthiest of Egypt's pharaohs. Throughout his time on the throne, Amenhotep had felt it unnecessary to exercise Egyptian military power. There was no major enemy to concern the empire and the tribal brigands from the hills were being controlled by the troops of Egypt's vassal city-states on the coastal plain of Canaan. This policy of 'peace and police' had been successfully followed for over half a century. But this happy state of affairs came to a sudden end with the appearance onto the historical stage of three very different personalities. In Egypt we have reached the Amarna age and the reign of the notorious heretic pharaoh, Akhenaten (1023–1007 BC). In the hill country of Canaan the Israelites have a new king and war leader in Labaya/Saul, whilst a young man named Elhanan, from the tribe of Judah, is about to make his play for power.

A window of opportunity was about to open which would produce the circumstances for major political disturbance in the southern Levant. Egypt was soon to lose interest in its empire because of the failings of a self-indulgent, messianic pharaoh, whilst Israel would seize the moment to establish itself as the dominant military and political force in the region. Distracted by a damaging internal religious revolution, Egypt was caught napping as it turned in on itself and left the northern empire to disintegrate.

Pharaoh Akhenaten instigated a monotheistic cult in the Nile valley based on the worship of light and warmth. The generator of these life-giving forces was the solar disc, which the Egyptians named 'Aten'. However, behind this simple and dramatic symbol lay a complex theology and mythology of the god of creation – Atum – the original sun-god, made manifest in Re-Harakhty, the dawn solar disc. The rejection of Amunism in favour of Atenism was no doubt partly instigated to wrest political control away from the Karnak priesthood which had become far too powerful during the middle years of the 18th Dynasty. But the Atenist revolution was much more than political manoeuvrings – it was a fundamental reawakening of primeval belief systems. In effect King Akhenaten ('glorious spirit of the sun-disc') was attempting a reformation – a return to the old way of worship with its focus on a purist form of sun worship. It is difficult to know to what degree the young pharaoh was also influenced by all those foreign ideas permeating the court of his father which brought about the strange mix of old and new typifying the Aten cult.

The two pharaohs Amenhotep III (the father) and Akhenaten (the son) were co-regents for twelve years (1023–1012 BC) – a time of stupendous change in Egypt with Amenhotep III elevated to godlike status (as the human embodiment of Aten) and Akhenaten driving the religious and philosophical revolution forward at breakneck speed. The latter's queen, NEFERTITI, was herself daughter of the

Arzawan king, whilst Akhenaten's second wife, Queen Kiya, was the sister of King Tushratta of Mitanni. Did one of these foreign princesses spark the new faith by introducing her own religious ideas into the melting pot of international syncretism? In other words, was Akhenaten the mover and shaker, or simply a convert – albeit a remarkable one – to a wave of personal monotheism spreading through the royal dynasties at this time? Akhenaten had been educated by famous wise men of the era, including the scribe, architect and philosopher, Amenhotep son of Hapu, and the vizier and royal tutor, ABD-EL. The first was a native Egyptian but, as his name implies, Abd-El (also known in the modern Egyptological literature as Apir-El) was a foreigner – a man who worshipped the Israelite god in his patriarchal name-form, so typical also of this time.* The implications for our understanding of the Amarna religious heresy take on a whole new perspective once it is realised that one of the closest advisers of the young prince Amenhotep (later to be called Akhenaten) was a worshipper of El.

And, of course, in the New Chronology, Akhenaten is no longer to be regarded as history's first great monotheist. That title rightfully returns to a prince of Egypt from an earlier era who met his god on a mountain top in the wilderness of Sinai.

Letters to Pharaoh

The news of Labaya's revolt was brought to the attention of Egypt's commissioner, Addaya, stationed in the southern coastal port of Gaza, and he, in turn, reported the highland skirmish between the Philistines and Israelites to Akhenaten at Amarna. Pharaoh sent a letter to Labaya warning him that such activities would not be tolerated. The Israelite king's remarkable reply has survived amongst the archive

---

* Samu-El – 'offspring of El'; El-kanah – 'El has created'; El-hanan – 'El shows favour'; Abi-El – 'El is my father'; El-eazar – 'El has helped', etc.

of tablets found in the ruins of the 'House of Pharaoh's Correspondence' at Amarna and makes interesting reading.

Far from being the usual grovelling response, so typical of Egypt's vassals, Labaya gives as good as he gets. Whatever the city rulers of the plain may have said to Addaya, all he was doing was recovering his own towns (Gibeah and Michmash) from invaders who had taken them by force. Moreover, when they had captured his home town, the Philistines had seized his family's high place (Gibeath-Elohim) where the standing stones and altar of Yahweh/El stood. He, after all, was only exercising his legitimate rights as ruler over the hill country tribes. In the middle of this robust defence, Labaya issues a not too subtle threat to Akhenaten in the form of a good old, biblical-style proverb which basically warns that, however small and insignificant his people might be, they can still be an irritant to mighty Egypt and its allies – if provoked.

> It was in war that the town (of Gibeah) was seized. After I had sworn my oath to keep the peace – and when I swore the (Egyptian regional) governor swore with me – the town, along with my god, was seized. And now I am slandered before the king, my lord! Moreover, if an ant is struck, does it not fight back and bite the hand of the man that struck it? How could I hold back this day when two of my towns (Gibeah and Michmash) had been seized? … I will keep imprisoned the men who seized the town [and] my god. They are the despoilers of my father, and so I will keep them (as hostages). [EA 252]

We do not know how Akhenaten reacted at receiving such a response. Whatever his reaction was, the subsequent reprimand did not apparently extend to military action and Labaya continued his policy of expansion to secure the whole territory of the tribal homelands as his kingdom.

Israel's new king was playing a clever political game, professing his loyalty to Pharaoh and paying tribute to Egypt's commissioner in Gaza in order to smooth relations whilst, at the same time, allocating the old town of Shechem and its surrounding lands to the Habiru mercenaries who had fought with him to repulse the Philistines. This greatly worried the Philistine seranim who saw this move as a military threat against the cities of the Jezreel valley just to the north of Shechemite territory. In correspondence from a few years later, Abdi-Heba, king of Jerusalem, wrote to Akhenaten warning of the ever-increasing threat posed by the Habiru in the highlands. In this letter EA 289, the Jebusite ruler of Jerusalem refers back to the time when Labaya ceded territory to his Habiru mercenaries which, in effect, was the start of all Pharaoh's troubles.

> Are we to act like Labaya did when he gave the land of Shechem to the Habiru? [EA 289]

Egypt's control over the region, through its surrogate Philistine police force, was beginning to unravel and Akhenaten's failure to act decisively soon led to complete chaos in the northern empire.

Labaya quickly seized the moment and attacked the Amalekites living on the Carmel ridge and in the hills of Samaria to the west of Shechem. The campaign against this northern Amalekite enclave was particularly bloody. At the behest of Samuel, the Israelite king ravaged the tented villages of Israel's old enemy, slaughtering everyone and everything – except, that is, the Amalekite ruler Agag, whom he took captive along with his prize livestock. This greatly displeased Yahweh's prophet who, in spite of his great age, grabbed Labaya's sword and cut Agag to pieces. For his 'sin' in sparing the Amalekite's life, Samuel cursed Labaya and pronounced that his descendants would forever be denied the kingship over Israel. Samuel then left Labaya's presence. He never saw him again.

The Pretender

Towards the end of Labaya's first year as king of Israel (1012 BC), a young man from the family of Yishuya (Hebrew *Yishay*, biblical Jesse) of Ephrath (Bethlehem) appeared in the king's court at Gibeah. The youngest son of Yishuya was called ELHANAN and, although a simple shepherd, was skilled in the playing of the lyre. Elhanan's gentle music did much to soothe the troubled mind of Labaya, who was prone to dark depressions. The young musician soon became one of the king's favourites in the new court. We know Elhanan as the biblical David – the title given to him by Achish, the Philistine ruler of Gath, and his Hurrian bodyguard when the young Israelite warrior was made ruler of Hebron following the death of Saul.

The Philistines now took action on behalf of Pharaoh to curb Israelite territorial ambitions. A large army of coalition forces assembled at Socoh in the tribal territory of Judah. They then pressed on to Azekah and the vale of Terebinth. Labaya gathered his troops and marched down to meet them. Both armies took up positions on high ground, with the valley between them, and a challenge was issued for the champions of each side to meet in single combat. This was very much the custom in Bronze Age Indo-European warfare and, of course, the Philistines were from that part of the world which gave us the Iliad with its mortal combats between heroic champions.

Out of the ranks of Philistine infantry appeared a mighty bronze-clad warrior, huge in stature and brimming with confidence. This champion of the city-state rulers was a warrior from Sardis in western Anatolia named Gulatu (biblical Goliath) who had proved himself on countless occasions, fighting in the service of Shuwardata (biblical Achish), seran of Gath.

On his head was a bronze helmet and he wore a breastplate of scale-armour, the latter weighing five

> thousand shekels of bronze. He had bronze greaves
> on his legs and a bronze scimitar slung across his
> shoulders. The shaft of his spear was like a weaver's
> beam and the spearhead weighed six hundred
> shekels of iron. [1 Samuel 17:5–7]

This was, as I say, a warrior in the Homeric mould – from
the Late Bronze Age world of golden Mycenae and windy
Troy. The Philistine champion strutted up and down in
front of the Israelite lines issuing his challenge to anyone
who dared meet him in mortal combat. To the victor would
go the war and the loser's nation would become subjugated
to the king whose champion won the day.

None of the Israelite warriors were prepared to take on
such a formidable foe and the battle lines remained rooted
to the slopes for several days. Each morning Gulatu would
issue his challenge and receive no response. Each day
Labaya's humiliation grew more acute. Finally, the scrawny
teenager Elhanan,* from the tribe of Judah, sallied forth
armed only with a leather sling and a collection of round
pebbles selected from the nearby stream. Gulatu laughed
in contempt as he stepped forward to smite the boy with a
single blow of his sword. But before he even had time to
draw the weapon, the giant crashed headlong to the ground,
struck between the eyes by a deadly accurate sling-shot.
Elhanan rushed to the prostrate and dazed Philistine, drew
Gulatu's sword and cut off his head. The ease by which
the Israelite youth had vanquished Gath's mightiest warrior
filled the Philistine soldiers with shock and horror. They
turned and fled, the Israelite army in hot pursuit right to
the gates of Gath and Ekron. The abandoned Philistine
camp was plundered as Labaya's victory against Israel's
greatest persecutors was celebrated long into the night. The
king appointed Elhanan as a captain of the army, and the
youngest son of Yishuya soon became very close to Laba-

---

* See 2 Samuel 21:19 where the true name of the slayer of Goliath is
recorded – not David but Elhanan.

ya's own son and crown-prince, Jonathan. In addition
Elhanan was given Labaya's second daughter, Michal, as
his wife, thus making him a son-in-law of Israel's king. The
bride-price was two hundred foreskins of slain Philistines
which Elhanan and his troops duly provided from raids
down onto the coastal plain.

In the months which followed, Elhanan gave Israel
victory after victory as he raided Philistine territory and
harassed their settlements with his band of Habiru mercenaries. As a result, the people hailed him as their champion.
Labaya now grew jealous of his protégé. A clash between
the two was inevitable and it soon came, with Elhanan
and his band of guerrillas escaping the king's wrath and
heading into the barren hills of Judah. In effect Israel had
fallen into civil war within a year of becoming united under
its first king.

In spite of the enmity between the king and his mercenary army commander, Jonathan's friendship with Elhanan
continued in secret. Rumours were rife that their relationship was more than platonic. Crown-prince Jonathan was
playing a dangerous game associating with a potential rival
to the throne and enemy of his father the king. Labaya
eventually found out that his eldest son was consorting
with the rebels through a letter of warning sent to him by
the Egyptian governor at Gaza. His embarrassment is
obvious from the reply he subsequently sent to Pharaoh in
Egypt in which he protests that he was completely unaware
that his son had been mixed up with Elhanan's Habiru
rebels.

> Moreover, the king wrote concerning my son. I did
> not know that my son was consorting with the
> Habiru. I herewith hand him over to Addaya (the
> Egyptian commissioner). [EA 254]

As soon as Jonathan returned from one of his clandestine
meetings with Elhanan, the king confronted him.

> 'Son of a rebellious slut! Do I not know that you side
> with the son of Jesse (i.e. Elhanan/David) to your
> own shame and your mother's dishonour? As long
> as the son of Jesse lives on Earth, neither you nor
> your royal rights are secure.' [1 Samuel 20:30–31]

Jonathan was then sent to Addaya to receive his reprimand
from Egypt's representative in southern Canaan.

Labaya now turned his attention to the city of Gezer
which protected the western pass leading up from the
lowlands to the mountain kingdom. The Amorite rulers of
Gezer had been allies of the Israelite tribes since the time
of Eli and Samuel, but Labaya wanted to guarantee their
participation in securing Israel's western boundary from
Philistine incursion whilst he devoted his limited resources
to the pursuit and eradication of Elhanan and his Habiru
rebels. The Israelite king therefore marched into Gezer
and seized the city from the Amorite ruler, Milkilu. There
he stationed a garrison of his own Habiru soldiers to secure
the road up into the hills, making Milkilu Israel's vassal.
This, of course, did not play well with the Philistines or
their Egyptian masters. Labaya was now perceived as
Egypt's foremost enemy in southern Canaan and the king
of Israel became the most notorious 'Habiru' of all. He
protested his innocence, professing loyalty to Pharaoh, but
the political die had been cast and, although he did not
know it, time was running out for Israel's first monarch.

> To the king, my lord and my Sun: Thus I Labaya,
> your servant and the dirt upon which you tread,
> seven times and seven do fall at the feet of the king,
> my lord. I have obeyed the orders that the king, my
> lord, wrote to me on a tablet. I am a servant of the
> king like my father and my grandfather (a servant of
> the king from long ago). I am not a rebel or
> delinquent in my duty. Here is my act of rebellion
> and here is my delinquency: when I entered Gezer,

> I spoke as follows: 'The king treats us kindly.' Now
> there is indeed no other purpose for me except the
> service of the king, and whatever the king orders, I
> obey. [EA 253]

Labaya's flannel did not wash with Pharaoh and he gave
orders for the Israelite king to be captured. The seranim of
the five major Philistine cities began to organise a grand
coalition of forces from all over the region to put an end to
the terrorists in the mountains. Months passed as the Philistines and their allies prepared for war. In the meantime,
King Labaya was preoccupied in hunting down his own
internal terrorists – the Habiru forces led by Elhanan, holed
up in the wadis and caves of Judah.

The Labaim

Throughout the winter months of Labaya's first regnal year,
the king personally led the posse to ferret out the Judahite
troublemakers from their mountain hideaways. The king
was accompanied by his bodyguard known as the Labaim
('Great lions') – so named after their lord and master.

The most famous incident in the hunt for Elhanan took
place in the deep gorge of En-Gedi which drops down
from the highlands of Hebron to the western shore of the
Dead Sea near the drowned city of Sodom. Elhanan and a
small band of his men were trapped there in a deep cave
as Labaya unwittingly chose to 'cover his feet' (i.e. defecate)
out of sight of his troops within the mouth of the cave.
Elhanan crept up behind the crouching king and cut off a
piece of his cloak with his dagger. Later the fugitive caught
up with Labaya and, calling down from a ridge, let the
humiliated king know that he could have easily killed him.

A similar occasion took place at Hachilah in the desert
of Ziph. This time Labaya was asleep in his camp, surrounded by his élite Labaim bodyguard. Elhanan – ever
the reckless extrovert – tiptoed through the slumbering

mass of bodyguards, each armed to the teeth, and stole Labaya's spear and drinking flask from the king's side. And so Israel's first monarch was humiliated once more by his impudent rival. A later song, now known as Psalm 57, composed by King David, appears to recall these two incidents in splendid metaphor.

> Take pity on me, O El take pity on me! For in you I take refuge. In the shadow of your wings I take refuge until the calamities are past. I call to El-elyon, El who has done everything for me. May he send down from heaven to save me from those who harry me. May El send his faithful love and everlasting truth. For I lie surrounded by great lions (Hebrew *labaim*), greedy for human prey. Their teeth are spears and arrows, their tongue a sharp sword. [Psalm 57:1–4]

These not very subtle pieces of Davidic propaganda are just two examples of Elhanan/David's daring-do which were composed to reflect badly on Labaya/Saul's short reign and legitimise the rise of the Judahite dynasty of David. By staying his sword and, at the same time, humiliating Labaya, the youthful David of legend was painted as a Robin Hood figure unreasonably pursued by a mad king playing the part of the Sheriff of Nottingham. The later official version of David's rise to the kingship portrays him as the innocent victim of his own successes and popularity in defeating the Philistines, but even this sanitised version of history, as we shall see in the next chapter, fails to entirely suppress the flawed character of Saul's messianic successor who steals wives from other men (including the king!) and has rivals murdered.

Elhanan and Akish

The last nine months of Labaya's second (and final) regnal year were fraught with tension. Everyone realised that the armies of Canaan and Israel were heading for all-out war. A flurry of letters was sent to Egypt by the city-state rulers of the lowlands, warning of the Habiru menace ... but Akhenaten refused to commit Egyptian troops to sort out the mess. The Amalekite territory in the Carmel hills had been seized by Labaya and now the city of Gezer had fallen into the hands of the Habiru chieftain. He had garrisoned his Habiru mercenaries in Shechem and it was all too clear that Labaya's ambitions lay in the direction of the rich Jezreel valley. Something had to be done to stop him.

At one point Egypt almost had the troublemaker in its grasp. Labaya was captured, whilst on his way to meet with the northern tribes in Galilee, and taken to Megiddo in the western Jezreel. However, as Israel's king was being escorted to the coast for transportation by ship to Egypt, his gaoler, the ruler of Akko, accepted a handsome bribe and allowed Labaya to escape. Biridiya, the furious king of Megiddo, reports directly to Akhenaten of the betrayal.

> It was Surata (of Akko) who took Labaya from Magidda (Megiddo), saying to me 'I will send him to the king (in Egypt) by ship.' Surata then took him but, instead, sent him from the region of Hinnatuna (Hannathon) back to his homeland – for Surata accepted from him a ransom payment. [EA 245]

The political machinations in Amarna Canaan were tortuously complex and not dissimilar to the faction-ridden Afghanistan of modern times. No-one trusted his neighbour and the Israelite king, with his Habiru mercenaries, had been exploiting this chaos to gain maximum territorial advantage. The Philistines were told by the Egyptian governor in Gaza that the disorder could not be tolerated for very much longer.

The Philistine king of Gath took charge of the situation and began to organise a coalition of cities to confront the highlanders and destroy the new Israelite kingdom once

and for all. And that meant getting Labaya and his sons –
snuffing out Israel's royal line in a single blow. To this end,
Shuwardata sent messengers to the rebel leader Elhanan,
offering him and his mercenaries service in the army of
Gath. That way the Philistines would not only cock a snook
at Labaya by protecting his principal political adversary
but the seranim might also learn a great deal about Israel's
monarch from someone who had actually spent time in
Labaya's company as his personal musician. Shuwardata
also saw an opportunity to split the loyalties of the tribes
by supporting a popular rival to the throne from within
the tribe of Judah.

The first book of Samuel calls the ruler of Gath 'Achish',
which derives from the Philistine king's Hurrian name –
Aki-Shimige. It is important at this point to understand
that Hurrians and their Indo-European rulers still formed
a major stratum in Canaanite society in the Late Bronze
Age. As we have seen, when the Hyksos fled Egypt, many
settled in southern Canaan within the cities of the coastal
plain. These large colonies, with their mixed Hurrian and
Indo-European populations, are the 'Philistine' cities of the
Bible. So the ruler of Gath carried two names: his Indo-
European name 'Shuwardata' ('the sun-god has given') and
his Hurrian popular name 'Akish' – a hypocoristicon or
shortened form of AKI-SHimige ('the sun-god has given').
The general population knew him by the latter name, which
was then passed down into the biblical tradition as Achish.

When Elhanan's Habiru were hired by Shuwardata/
Akish as Gath's mercenary contingent, Hurrian warriors
were assigned to the six hundred Habiru troops to act as
military advisers. These Hurrian commanders were to
remain loyal to their new Israelite leader throughout the
ensuing years, eventually to the detriment of their original
Philistine overlord. In effect they switched sides. Thus, as
Peter van der Veen has pointed out to me, we find Hurrian
military men in the ranks of King David's most trusted
followers throughout the second book of Samuel: the army

captain Ittai of Gath (2 Samuel 15:22, Septuagint Ethei, Hurrian *Eteia* – the same name as Yidiya of Ashkelon in the Amarna letters); David's royal scribe Shawsha (1 Chronicles 18:16, Hurrian *Shawshka*); and the warrior Naharai (2 Samuel 23:37, Hurrian *Nihria*).

How did Elhanan become known as David? The answer lies in understanding the influence which Hurrians had within the early Israelite military élite. Hurrian officers under Elhanan's command began to refer to the Habiru chieftain by the Hurrian equivalent of biblical 'David' – Tadua – the name which appears in the el-Amarna correspondence for Israel's second king.*

And so the name David (Hebrew *Dud/Dwd*) is actually a Hurrian title or coronation name ('beloved [of deity N]') which was given to Elhanan when he became king of Hebron in 1011 BC. It was then later Hebraised as Dadua and, later, Dud/Dwd ('beloved [of Yah]'). Solomon too carried this title or coronation name in its fuller form – JEDIDIAH.

From now on, for the sake's of familiarity, we shall refer to Elhanan, the son of Yishay of the tribe of Judah, by his biblical name – David – the rebel Hebrew chieftain soon destined to become Israel's greatest monarch.

The Battle of Gilboa

The forces of the Philistine confederation had been massing at Aphek in the Sharon plain ('flat country') for several weeks – an army of ten thousand made up of contingents from Gath (led by Shuwardata/Akish), Ashkelon (led by Yidiya), Ashdod (led by Shubanda), Ekron (ruler not known) and Gaza (led by Yahtiru). In the autumn of 1011 BC the huge army moved north, through the Carmel hills via the Aruna pass, and came out into the plain of Jezreel

---

* This nomen is also familiar to us from Amarna Egypt, where it was borne by the Mitannian princess Tadu-Hepa ('beloved of the goddess Hepa'), sent as a young child to marry Amenhotep III but who eventually became Akhenaten's second queen, known affectionately as Kiya.

beside Megiddo. There they were joined by the troops of that city (led by Biridiya) and neighbouring Taanach (led by Yashdata). By nightfall of the following day the Philistine army was encamped at Shunem on the north side of the Jezreel opposite the slopes of the Gilboa ridge.

David, with his mercenary force of six hundred Habiru, offered to fight on behalf of Akish but the rest of the Philistine seranim were very disturbed by such a large presence of potential enemies amongst their ranks. After all, David was an Israelite and had once been loyal to Labaya. What if, in the heat of battle, the hireling suddenly switched sides? What if he was an enemy from within sent by his former lord to turn on his new masters at a crucial point in the campaign and kill all the Philistine leaders with a single strike? Akish, still convinced of David's loyalty, reluctantly sent his mercenary contingent back south from Aphek to their fortified settlement of Ziklag in southern Judah. And so David was prevented from taking up arms against his own people through the fears of Israel's enemies.

Meanwhile, Labaya's spies had observed the Philistine manoeuvres at Aphek and scurried into the highlands to inform their king. Labaya did not hesitate to send out the call-to-arms and, by the time the Philistines were passing by Megiddo, the Israelites were assembled at Shechem, along with the king's Habiru army, ready to march north to confront the enemy in the Jezreel. By the morning of the Philistines' first day at Shunem, Labaya's army of four thousand foot-soldiers had crossed the vale of Gina and arrived at the 'fountain' of Jezreel (modern En-Harod), located at the foot of Gilboa ridge. Scouts sent up the ridge returned with disturbing news – the confederation forces encamped across the valley had swollen to over fifteen thousand with hundreds of chariots; they practically filled the floor of the Jezreel flood plain. The Israelites were out-numbered four to one and, of course, they had no chariots.

Labaya decided that his only recourse was to take his infantry up onto Mount Gilboa where the Philistine chariots could not reach and, at the same time, force the enemy infantry to climb the steep northern slope of the Gilboa ridge before they were in position to engage the Israelite front line. This was a well-tried tactic in Israelite warfare and had been successfully employed by Barak in the defeat of Sisera. The advantages of the Israelite position would be some compensation for the imbalance in numbers between the two armies. And so the Israelites redeployed on Gilboa, looking down on the Jezreel valley floor glinting with bronze armour and weaponry.

The vassal Amalekite allies of Labaya (led by Tagu of Gath-Carmel), living in the Carmel hills and in the vale of Gina, were positioned north of the village of Gina (modern Jenin) to secure the Israelite rear from a western, outflanking attack. These northern Amalekites had been defeated by Labaya just six months earlier and were now the reluctant subjects of Israel. Battle lines were drawn and the climax of the war between Israel and the Philistines was ready to be played out.

The Philistine infantry approached the foot of Gilboa's northern scarp and began the steep ascent through a forest of pines. The Israelites braced themselves for the assault, hoping that the enemy would be exhausted by their efforts to reach the summit. But the wily Shuwardata/Akish of Gath, leader of the coalition, had a trick up his sleeve which he hoped would wipe out Israel's strategic advantage and lead to a quick victory. He had secretly been in contact with Tagu of Gath-Carmel and had done a deal with the Amalekite chieftain to persuade him to switch sides.

Before dawn on the morning of battle the chariots of Gath, Taanach and Megiddo had slipped out of the Philistine camp and headed west to the opening in the mountains which led to the vale of Gina. The Amalekites stationed there to protect Labaya's western flank had silently slipped away during the night. There was nothing to stop the Philistine chariots from skirting the Gilboa ridge and approaching the Israelite army from the rear.

Transported in the chariots were a platoon of Gath's best archers. They were quickly carried up the gentle southern slopes of the ridge to within a kilometre of the Israelite rear, positioned on the summit and facing north. Labaya, Jonathan and the Israelite commanders were completely taken by surprise. A hail of arrows struck the Israelite strategic command centre, killing many of the key personnel and mortally wounding Labaya himself. Jonathan and his brothers also fell as the Philistine archers rained their arrows down upon the ranks of foot-soldiers just as the Philistine infantry were about to reach the summit of the ridge from the steep northern slopes. In a panic the Israelites ran straight into them as they tried to escape the deadly salvo of arrows. The battle was over within two hours of bloody hand-to-hand fighting.

Labaya did not live to witness Israel's ignominious defeat. The arrow which had struck him between the shoulder-blades had caused great loss of blood. Rather than being taken alive and sent in shackles to Pharaoh, Israel's first king chose a warrior's death, falling upon his sword.

Akhenaten had given instructions to his Philistine vassals that the rebel leader of the Habiru should be captured alive and brought to Egypt for ritual execution. Labaya's suicide had prevented this outcome and the king of Megiddo wrote to Pharaoh with his own excuses as to why he personally had not been able to deliver on the promise.

> Moreover, I (Biridiya, ruler of Megiddo) urged my brothers (the Philistine lords), 'If the god of the king, our lord, brings it about that we overcome Labaya, then we must bring him alive to the king, our lord.' But, with my mare having been felled, I rode with Yashdata (of Taanach) and positioned myself behind him (i.e. to the rear of Labaya's forces). However, before my arrival they (the Philistine archers) had killed him (i.e. Labaya). [EA 245]

The body of the Israelite king and those of his sons, Jonathan, Melchishua and Abinadab were collected by the victorious Philistines and taken down from the heights of Gilboa to the fortress of Beth-Shean at the eastern end of the Jezreel valley. There the heads of Israel's royal family were severed from their bodies to be carried aloft on spears as the army of Gath returned to Philistia in triumph. The corpses were hung on the walls of Beth-Shean as a warning to all those who might in future dare to challenge Pharaoh's authority or the rule of Egypt's vassal city-states. Three thousand years later, the excavator of Beth-Shean, Amihai Mazar, would come across a tiny cylinder seal inscribed in cuneiform with the following tantalising message:

> To Labaya, my Lord, speak. Message from Tagu:
> 'To the king my Lord. I have listened carefully to
> your message to me …' [the rest damaged]

This fortuitous archaeological discovery is an extraordinary personal witness to the tragic and dramatic fall of Israel's first monarch. King Labaya had received this message from the very ally who had betrayed him on the day of battle, pretending that he was loyally following the Israelite king's battle deployment instructions. Such short messages were regularly transported in cylinder-seal form, strung on cord around the neck of the messenger. Labaya, already stationed at his Gilboa command post, had slipped Tagu's message around his own neck for safe keeping. The tiny cylinder had then been transported to Beth-Shean, still attached to the king's corpse, before falling to the ground from Labaya's suspended remains to await miraculous retrieval on 14th October 1993.

How are the Mighty Fallen!

News of Labaya's defeat and death reached David in Ziklag, brought by an Amalekite from the same tribe of Gina which had betrayed the Israelite king. David, the Habiru chieftain, had hardly been a loyal friend and devotee of his father-in-law the king, but he was genuinely devastated by the news that Israel had been so heavily defeated at the hands of the Philistine lords. After all, he himself was an Israelite from the southern tribe of Judah and was married to Labaya's daughter. David was also grief-stricken over the death of Jonathan. He tore his clothes in mourning for the death of Yahweh's anointed and the loss of Israel's bravest sons. The Amalekite was summarily executed for being the unfortunate bearer of such bad tidings.

During the days which followed, and as the tribes went into deep mourning over the tragedy, more details of the battle on Mount Gilboa began to emerge. David learned of the deal struck between his paymaster Shuwardata/Akish and the men of Gina which had led to the successful Philistine assault up the gentle southern slopes of Gilboa and how the king had died through an act of betrayal by his own supposed allies. The young man who had once played his lyre and sung to soothe the troubled mind of Israel's first monarch now picked up that lyre once more, this time to compose a lament over Labaya's tragic and dishonourable death.

> (O Gilboa!) Does the splendour of Israel lie dead on your heights? How are the mighty fallen! Do not speak of it in Gath, nor broadcast it in the streets of Ashkelon, for fear that the daughters of the Philistines rejoice, for fear that the daughters of the uncircumcised gloat. You mountains of Gilboa, no dew, no rain fall upon you, O treacherous fields where the hero's shield lies dishonoured! [2 Samuel 1:19–21]

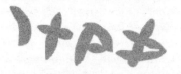

DAVID THE WARRIOR KING

(2 Samuel 2:1 to 1 Kings 2:11)

*Mutbaal and David – The Death of Abner – Mutbaal's
Assassination – The Capture of Jerusalem – Defeat of the
Philistines – David's Building Works – The Davidic Wars –
Hadadezer – Egypt's Empire Crumbles – Bathsheba –
Absalom's Revolt – The Plague – Adonijah and the Succession*

Let the king, my lord, be informed that the Habiru
(singular) who was raised up against the lands; the
god of the king, my lord, delivered him to me, and
I have smitten him. [EA 366]

his was the brief message sent to Akhenaten from
the seran of Gath to report on the death of Labaya/
Saul in battle. It is Akhenaten's thirteenth year on
the throne (1011 BC). His father and co-regent, Amenhotep
III, has been dead for less than a year and Egypt's beautiful
queen, Neferneferuaten Nefertiti, occupies the old king's
place as Pharaoh's co-regent. The name Nefertiti disappears
from history as this daughter of a foreign ruler receives the
red and white crowns and assumes a new pharaonic identity

– Ankhkheperure Neferneferuaten. At the same time El-hanan – the biblical David – seizes the moment, whilst Israel reels from the death of King Labaya and Crown-Prince Jonathan. The pretender to his father-in-law's throne is anointed King of Judah, where he rules from the old patriarchal seat of Hebron. However, David is not the sole claimant to kingship in the land of Israel.

Not all of Labaya's sons died on Mount Gilboa. Before he could be captured or killed, MUTBAAL was escorted away from the battlefield by Labaya's army commander, ABNER, and taken across the Jordan to safety in Gilead. There the king's second eldest son was proclaimed Labaya's successor and established his royal residences in exile at MAHANAIM and at Pella a few kilometres further north on the east side of the Jordan valley opposite Beth-Shean (EA 256).

The men of Jabesh-Gilead went on a daring nighttime raid across the Jordan to Beth-Shean where they removed the bodies of Labaya, Jonathan, Melchishua and Abinadab from the city wall and spirited them back to Mahanaim for token cremation and burial. Unfortunately a full and proper laying to rest was not possible with Labaya's head being paraded around the Philistine cities to suffer ritual abuse.

With the Jezreel valley firmly in the hands of Israel's enemies and a Philistine garrison stationed at Beth-Shean (EA 289), there was little that Mutbaal could do to unite the tribes in the north with those in the central hills and Transjordan. At the same time, his father's old enemy, David, had succeeded in driving a wedge between the royal house of Benjamin and the leading Judahite family of Yishuya (Jesse). By offering his forces to the Philistine king of Gath to fight against Labaya, David had effectively severed his tribe from the confederacy. The kingdom of Israel had been divided in two, with Mutbaal ruling over the majority of the tribes in the north and east, and David commanding the loyalty of the large tribe of Judah based in the highlands south of Jerusalem.

At first this arrangement seems to have been tacitly accepted by both parties, the principal concern at that stage being to counter Philistine gains and secure what remained of the kingdom in the aftermath of Gilboa. David, still playing the dual role of Israelite tribal leader and Habiru mercenary to the king of Gath, moved his base from Ziklag in the Negeb up to the old Anakite town of Hebron where the Hebrew patriarchs had been buried in Machpelah cave. Within weeks of Labaya's death the youngest son of Yishu-ya, given the name Elhanan at birth, was crowned as King Tadua/Dadua by his Hurrian and Judahite followers. So began the seven-and-a-half-year reign of David in Hebron.

David, of course, had his own somewhat tenuous claim to the Israelite throne through his marriage to Labaya's daughter Michal. This made him a 'son' (-in-law) of the king and, in spite of their falling out, Labaya had continued to acknowledge David as such (see for example 1 Samuel 24:17). Even Akish of Gath saw the advantage in recognising his junior ally as king in the southern hills. The Philistine seran had his own ambitions to recover control of the town of Kiltu (biblical Keilah), which had recently switched its allegiance to Abdi-Heba, ruler of the Jebusite enclave at Jerusalem. With David stationed at Hebron, on Abdi-Heba's southern border, and Akish pressing from the west, it would be hard for the Jebusites to hold on to Kiltu. And indeed, it soon returned to Gath. In a letter written to Pharaoh, Shuwardata/Akish, just like his old enemy Labaya, claims that he was only recovering a town which had gone over to the ruler of Jerusalem as a result of financial inducements.

> Say to the king, my lord, my god, my Sun: Message of Suwardata, your servant, the dirt at your feet. … The king, my lord, permitted me to wage war against Kiltu (Keilah) and I waged war. It is now at peace with me. My town is restored to me. Why did Abdi-Heba write to the men of Kiltu saying 'Accept silver

and follow me'? ... Moreover, Labaya, who used to take our towns, is dead, but now Abdi-Heba is another Labaya and he seizes our town! [EA 280]

And so, for a while at least, David continued to act as a vassal of Gath – simply because he needed his Philistine neighbour as an ally whilst making his own secret preparations to seize the Jebusite enclave and capture Jerusalem. By acting in consort with Akish against Abdi-Heba, he was able to camouflage his own ambitions to control the whole highland region, after which he would turn on his Philistine masters in the western lowlands. Whilst he bided his time David had other matters to attend to.

Seeking Revenge

Following the battle of Gilboa, the immediate thought in the minds of both Mutbaal and David was revenge – revenge against the Amalekites of Gina who had betrayed Israel's first king. The two Israelite kings began to put pressure on the local city rulers of the northern Sharon plain to wipe out Labaya's betrayers – something they could not do directly themselves because of the strong Philistine presence in the lowlands. Political coercion was the only weapon available to them. A letter from BALU-MEHIR reports to Akhenaten that the two surviving 'sons' of Labaya were pressing him to take action against the men of Gina for their 'crime'.

Say to the king, my lord: the message of Balu-mehir, your servant. May the king my lord be aware that the two sons of the rebel against the king my lord – the two sons of Labaya – have made the loss of the land of the king my lord their purpose, over and above the loss that their father had caused. May the king my lord know that for days the two sons of Labaya have been calling me to account saying

'Why have you handed Gath-Padalla to the king,
your lord – a city which Labaya, our father, had
captured?' And the two sons of Labaya keep talking
to me like this saying 'Wage war against the people
of Gina for having killed our father. And if you do
not wage war, then we will become your enemies.'
I have answered the two of them thus: 'The god of
the king my lord prevents me from waging war
against the people of Gina, for they are servants of
the king my lord.' [EA 250]

So, for a while at least, the two 'sons' of Labaya co-ordinated
their efforts to strike back at their common enemy, at a
time when Israel's morale was at its lowest ebb. But the
rivalry between the two successors of Labaya soon came
to a head when forces from each side met at the pool of
Gibeon to the north-west of Jerusalem. In a sketch worthy
of 'The Life of Brian' twelve warriors from each camp
paired off, drew their swords and thrust them into their
opponent's midriff. Twenty-four men dropped to the
ground dead in this bizarre prelude to the ensuing skirmish
between the Benjaminite soldiers of Mutbaal, led by Abner,
and the Judahite soldiers of David, led by Ayab/Joab. In
the end, having suffered three hundred and sixty casualties,
Abner's men took to their heels with Mutbaal's commander
himself being chased by Ayab's fleet-footed, younger
brother Asahel. Abner turned on his pursuer and killed
him before escaping across the Jordan to Mahanaim – a
deed for which his rival Ayab would soon seek retribution.

Murder and More Revenge

It soon became clear that Mutbaal was no Labaya. The
king's 'son of his loins' was not as strong-willed as Labaya's
'son by marriage'. In a written reply to a now-lost reprimand
from the Egyptian governor in Canaan, Mutbaal passes
the buck for all the current political disturbances onto his

co-ruler in the south, professing that he had no idea where David's military commander Ayab (biblical Joab) – the principal agent of the unrest – was hiding. If Pharaoh's commissioner wanted to arrest the wayward captain of David/Tadua's army, he should interrogate the king of Judah and his father in Hebron rather than accuse the innocent king of Israel ruling peaceably in Transjordan.

> Say to Yanhamu (the new Egyptian governor) my lord: message of Mutbaal (Ishbaal), your servant. I fall at the feet of my lord. How can it be said in your presence 'Mutbaal has fled. He has hidden Ayab (Joab)'? How can the king of Pella flee from the commissioner, agent of the king his lord? As the king my lord lives! As the king my lord lives! I swear that Ayab is not in Pella. In fact, he has [been in the] field (i.e. on campaign) for two months. Just ask Benenima. Just ask Dadua. Just ask Yishuya. [EA 256]

In this remarkable document, discovered in the ruins of the House of Pharaoh's Correspondence at Amarna, we find several names associated with the early Israelite monarchy period:

(a) Mutbaal (biblical Ishbaal, 'man of Baal') – Labaya/Saul's son and successor;

(b) Tadua (biblical Dud/David, 'beloved [of Yah]') – king of Judah;

(c) Ayab (biblical Yaab/Joab, 'Yah is the father') – David's general;

(d) Yishuya (biblical Yishay/Jesse, 'man of Yah') – David's father;

(e) Benenima – a variant writing of Baanah/Ben-Ana ('son of Ana'), with majestic-plural ending – a local Israelite warlord soon to participate in the assassination of Mutbaal.

Things were not going well for Mutbaal. His control over the tribes of Israel was weakening with every month that passed as the influence of David, king of Judah, gained the ascendancy. It did not take long for Mutbaal's powerful military commander, Abner, to see that he had chosen to support the wrong side in the schism following the Gilboa disaster. The Israelite warlord began to make clandestine overtures to David which led to a secret meeting of the two in Hebron. At the time (as Mutbaal indicates in his letter to Yanhamu) Ayab was away campaigning. David's general arrived back in Hebron on the day that Abner set out to return home to Mahanaim. Seething with anger that David had not consulted him over the secret negotiations with his sworn enemy, Abner sent messengers after Mutbaal's general. They caught up with him at Sirah. The reluctant warlord was brought back to Hebron under the pretence that David needed to confer with him further. But as Abner and his escort reached the gates of the town, Mutbaal's general was taken to one side to find Ayab waiting for him. David's general then ran his rival through in revenge for the death of his younger brother, Asahel. Of course, King David shed public tears of anguish at the murder of such a brave Israelite warrior, rending his clothes as he had done upon hearing the news of the death of Labaya. But, tellingly, Ayab was not arrested for his crime and continued to serve as David's army commander. This would be just the first in a series of unfortunate deaths and assassinations during the early years of David's reign as he proceeded to secure his political and sexual ambitions.

Next in line for eradication was Mutbaal himself. The second-born son of Labaya had moved up from Pella in the Jordan valley to the summer palace at Mahanaim where he was resting in his chamber one afternoon in the ninth month of his second regnal year. Two Benjaminite chieftains – Benenima (biblical Baanah) and Rechab – arrived at Mahanaim, entered the royal apartments and murdered the king whilst he was asleep in his bed. The assassins cut off Mutbaal's head and brought it to David thinking that he would reward them for their act of loyalty to the king of Judah. But, as with the messenger who brought the news of Labaya's death, David executed Mutbaal's murderers and bemoaned the loss of another monarch from the royal line of Benjamin. We will never know if David knew in advance of the plan to assassinate his rival. What we can say is that the removal of King Mutbaal opened the final door to David's succession as ruler over all Israel. In the space of two years all the obstacles to David's rise had been removed: King Saul was dead; all his true sons – Jonathan, Mutbaal, Melchishua and Abinadab – were dead; the powerful warlord Abner was dead.

Mutbaal's head was placed in the grave where Abner had been buried in Hebron and, with this act, the short-lived royal dynasty of Benjamin was brought to an end. David was proclaimed king of Israel and the royal dynasty of Judah was ushered in – a dynasty from which, a thousand years later, Jesus of Nazareth himself would claim descent through his father Joseph, the Bethlehemite.

The Taking of Jerusalem

The Jebusites living in Jerusalem were increasingly under threat. An unlikely alliance of neighbouring city-states had formed in the aftermath of the battle of Gilboa and King Abdi-Heba of the Jebus was feeling the pressure. He does not mince his words in a series of frantic letters to Akhenaten. Egypt's northern empire was disintegrating under the strain of Habiru aggressions and the connivance of their ambitious allies. Milkilu of Gezer and Shuwardata/Akish of Gath were instrumental in supporting the Habiru for their own personal territorial gains.

> Here is the deed against the land which Milkilu and Shuwardata did: against the land of the king my lord they ordered troops from Gezer, troops from

Gath and troops from Keilah. They seized Rubuti.
The land of the king has deserted to the Habiru!
[EA 290]

But the real movers and shakers behind the troubles were
David and his co-ruler, Mutbaal.

This is the deed of Milkilu and the deed of the sons
of Labaya who have given the land of the king to
the Habiru! [EA 287]

The political and military manoeuvrings were complex.
Everyone was jockeying for position in the chaotic world
of a Canaan ruled over by an indecisive pharaoh far off to
the south. Even the Egyptian governor in Gaza was playing
his part in destabilising the region by removing Pharaoh's
troops from their protectorates. Jerusalem had been left
vulnerable. Abdi-Heba reports the grim tidings to Egypt.

Gath-Carmel now belongs to Tagu (the ruler of the
Amalekite enclave in the north) and the (Philistine)
men of Gath are garrisoned in Beth-Shean (following
the battle of Gilboa). Are we to act like Labaya (Saul)
when he gave the land of Shechem to the Habiru
(Hebrew mercenaries following the battle of Michmash)? Milkilu (the Amorite king of Gezer) has
written to Tagu and the sons of Labaya (Mutbaal
and David) saying 'The both of you be on your
guard. Grant to the men of Kiltu (Keilah) all their
demands and let us isolate Jerusalem.' Addaya (the
Egyptian commissioner) has taken the garrison that
you sent under the command of Haya (Amenhotep)
the son of Miyare (Meryre). However, he (Addaya)
has stationed it (the garrison) at his own residence
in Hazzatu (Gaza) and has sent twenty men back to
Egypt. May the king, my lord, know that no garrison
of the king is with me (in Jerusalem). ... The entire

> land of the king has deserted (given over to the
> rebels)! [EA 289]

Here we see, in vivid detail, how the city which was soon to become Israel's capital came under severe pressure from the west and south, as a direct result of the Philistine success in defeating Labaya. The vacuum left by the death of Israel's first king had completely destabilised the region. The forces of Gath were now stationed in the Jezreel valley, whilst Gezer and (as we have seen from other letters) Gath were allying themselves with Labaya's surviving sons and conspiring against Jerusalem. Even the Egyptians had withdrawn their military support from the beleaguered Abdi-Heba. This first batch of letters from the king of Jerusalem had all been written in the two-year period when Mutbaal was ruling from Mahanaim and Pella, whilst David was enthroned in Hebron as a vassal of Gath. After Mutbaal had been assassinated, Jerusalem found itself under even greater threat as David's ambitions to seize the city were finally exposed.

> May the king give thought to his land! The land of
> the king is lost! All of it has attacked me. I am at
> war as far as the land of Seru (Seir) and as far as
> Gath-Carmel. All the rulers are at peace (with each
> other) but I am at war. I (myself) am treated like a
> Habiru and I do not visit the king my lord because
> I am at war. I am (alone) like a ship in the midst of
> the sea. The strong arm of the king took the land of
> Naharim (Mitanni) and the land of Kashi (Kush),
> but now the Habiru have taken the very cities of
> the king. Not a single ruler remains (loyal) to the
> king my lord – all are lost! … Behold, Turbazu was
> slain at the gate of Sile (Zile on the border of Egypt).
> The king did nothing! Behold, servants who were
> connected with the Habiru smote Zimredda of
> Lachish, whilst Yapti-Hadda was (also) slain at the

gate of Sile. (Again) the king did nothing! ... may
the king send a commissioner to fetch me, along
with my brothers, and then we will die near the
king our lord. [EA 288]

Things had become so desperate that Abdi-Heba was ready
to give up his rule over Jerusalem and flee (under the protection of Egyptian soldiers) to Pharaoh's court where he could
at least die in old age. The region had become so unsafe
that city rulers who had tried to reach safety without an
escort had been murdered at Egypt's very frontier post.

This is the last we hear of Abdi-Heba, king of Jebusite
Jerusalem, in the Amarna letters. His desperate pleas for
rescue fall silent. In a brief sentence the second book of
Samuel tells us why.

And David conquered the stronghold of Zion (Heb.
Tsiyon = Jerusalem) which is (now called) the City
of David. [2 Samuel 5:7]

The Bible gives the name Araunah to the Jebusite ruler of
Jerusalem defeated by David but *arwana* is simply the
Hurrian word for 'ruler'. The el-Amarna letters furnish us
with his real name, which is what is called a *Mischname* or
'mixed-name' made up of Canaanite *Abdi* (meaning 'servant of') and Hurrian *Heba* (the name of a goddess).

Few details survive about the taking of Jerusalem by
David and his army. However, it appears that the heavily
fortified Jebusite stronghold was penetrated by a small force
of commandos who managed to open the gates of the city
from within. In this case, the Trojan horse was the water
spring located on the eastern flank of the ridge on which
the citadel of Zion stood.

The thick stone wall of Late Bronze Age Jerusalem (built
in the MB II-B) followed a contour roughly halfway down
the slope of the hill. Just outside the fortifications was the
source of the town's water supply – the spring of Gihon

(named after one of the rivers of Eden). The Middle Bronze Age builders of the fortress wall had also constructed a massive tower (now called the 'Spring Tower'), with four-metre-thick walls, over the water source to prevent it from being cut off by besieging forces. A deep horizontal channel (Hebrew *tsinnor*) ran from the spring southwards along the hillside to supply irrigation water for the fields in the Kidron valley below. This channel was covered in slabs of stone and then earth to conceal its existence. Some seven metres from the source of the spring, a second underground chan-nel diverted half of the water westwards into a huge rock-cut basin which acted as the citadel's reservoir. This was, in turn, flanked by two more towers (now known as the 'Pool Towers') which isolated the water tank from the outside world. The reservoir was accessed from within the walls of the town via a downward-sloping tunnel which enabled the water carriers to fill their containers in safety, protected by the large pool towers, and return into the town without having to set foot into the open air beyond Zion's encircling wall. David realised that this was the potential weak point in Jerusalem's otherwise impressive defences.

General Ayab volunteered to take a small troop of men into the water system under the cover of darkness. Some way along the irrigation channel they uncovered a stone slab and levered it from its setting to gain access to the aqueduct. The men then waded northwards along the channel until they reached the junction where the second channel turned westwards to feed the reservoir. Within a few metres they were in the great tank and scaling the rock sides to gain access to the water-carriers' tunnel leading beyond the outer defensive wall into the stronghold. Whilst Jerusalem slept Ayab reached the main gate, overpowered the guards and opened the town to David's army which had silently gathered below in the Kidron valley. The Israelites, their Habiru mercenaries and Hurrian military commanders rushed into Zion, killed hundreds in their beds and seized Abdi-Heba and his kin. No more letters were sent to Egypt by the Jebusite ruler of Jerusalem.

The Final Philistine Conflict

When Shuwardata/Akish of Gath received news that Tadua/David had seized Jerusalem from the Jebusites he knew that he had been betrayed and that he would now face an even greater challenge to his control over the region. The Philistine king's only recourse was to attack his former ally before David had a chance to establish himself and gain more territory. The army of Gath marched up into the hill and deployed in the vale of Rephaim just to the south-west of Jerusalem.

> When the Philistines heard that David had been anointed king over all Israel, they all marched up to seek him out. On hearing this, David went down to the stronghold (of ADULLAM). When the Philistines arrived they deployed in the vale of Rephaim. [2 Samuel 5:17–18]

The two armies clashed in the summer of 1004 BC and the Philistines were pushed back into the lowlands. The site of the battle was later named Baal-Perazim ('lord of the breaches') because the enemy battle lines were easily breached by David's mercenary army.

Once more Akish sent his troops up into the hills and once more they were defeated, being chased all the way back to the pass of Gezer. And so David's new capital was at last secure as the threat from the Philistines subsided. Shuwardata/Akish had been humiliated by his former vassal and this defeat was a signal to all the Habiru in the service of their Philistine lords to revolt. Milkilu of Gezer writes to Egypt that he and the king of Gath were now under severe pressure from the Habiru of the hill country (i.e. David and his forces) and even from their own Habiru servants. No-one was safe in the new world order which came into being following the Battle of Gilboa.

> May the king my lord know that the war against me and against Shuwardata is severe. So may the king my lord save his land from the power of the Habiru. Otherwise, may the king my lord send chariots to fetch us lest our servants kill us. [EA 271]

Again, like Abdi-Heba of Jerusalem, the letters from Milkilu abruptly stop and a new ruler of Gezer now writes to Pharaoh. His name is ADDA-DANU and he, with the support of Egypt, makes new moves to contain Israelite expansion down from the highlands onto the lowlands. He immediately stations troops at Manhatu (biblical Manahath) on the boundary between Gezer's territory and the new kingdom of the Israelites.

> I have heard the orders which the king my lord wrote to his servant: 'Protect your (Egyptian) commissioner and protect the cities of the king your lord'. ... May the king my lord be informed about his servant. There being war against me from the mountains, I have built a fortress – its name is Manhatu – to make preparations before the arrival of the (Egyptian) archers of the king my lord. [EA 292]

The Egyptians had obviously become extremely nervous of the rising power in the hill country and, as is clear from Adda-danu's reply, had sent further instructions ordering the king of Gezer to protect the trade routes in the coastal plain at all costs.

> I have heard the order that the king my lord wrote to his servant: 'Guard the place of the king where you are (i.e. Gezer).' I am indeed guarding it day and night! [EA 293]

It appears that this show of force, backed up by Egyptian troops, was sufficient to stop the Israelites from a full-scale invasion of the coastal plain. The old Philistine heartlands and the Sharon plain remained outside David's conquered territories and firmly in the hands of Egypt's allies. Gezer itself was never forcibly taken by Israel but came into its possession peaceably – given as a dowry by Pharaoh Haremheb when Solomon married the Egyptian king's second-eldest daughter.

The story in the book of Samuel which covers the painful birth of Israel's early monarchy – Saul's revolt against the Philistine oppression, his brief but action-packed rule over a united Israel, the tragic death of the king and his sons on the heights of Gilboa, the subsequent political struggle between his two surviving 'sons', the assassination of Mutbaal and, finally, the rise of David to rule over all Israel with his seizure of Jerusalem – is a truly wonderful tale, regarded by many as one of the Bible's finest historical and literary passages. But how much more fascinating and rich the era has become now that we have the contemporary records of the Amarna letters to fill in all the missing detail – the political intrigues, the murders of rulers, the secret pacts and deadly treachery.

The New Chronology's realignment of the Amarna period with Israel's Early Monarchy period (c. 1012–1000 BC) has had major consequences for our understanding of both eras. Akhenaten is cast in a new light, his religious reforms now set in an era of biblical Psalms when Yahweh himself was associated with solar imagery. The window of opportunity which opened up for the Children of Yahweh during the introspective years of the Amarna heresy period allowed the new kingdom of Israel to arise out of the chaos of weak Egyptian rule in southern Canaan. In the final analysis, it was Akhenaten's Atenist revolution which led directly to the chaotic political events within Egypt's northern empire which eventually brought King David and his warriors to the gates of Jerusalem.

CHAPTER FOURTEEN

Building a Royal City

It is 1004 BC – the eighth year in David's reign and his
first as king of Jerusalem. Akhenaten is dead and a young
boy named Tutankhamun sits on the throne of the pharaohs
in Memphis. The city of Amarna remains occupied by
Smenkhkare and her court – but Egypt's experiment with
monotheism is coming to an end as the light begins to fade
on the place of Akhenaten's magnificent obsession.

Having conquered the Jebusite stronghold, David's first
priority was to build a palace fit for a king in the new
Israelite capital city. He made overtures to Ahiram, the
Phoenician ruler of Tyre on the coast of Lebanon. The
Phoenicians were skilled sailors who had for many centuries
been trading partners with Egypt. As a result they possessed
great artistic skills acquired in providing the pharaohs with
luxury hand-crafted products from the north. They also
built in stone and had an unlimited quality timber resource
in the mountains rising behind the narrow coastal plain.
Lebanon was the 'land of cedar'. It was therefore almost a
prerequisite that royal residences should be built by the
very best craftsmen in the region – and that meant the
Phoenicians.

David and Ahiram (biblical Hiram of Tyre) sealed an
accord which provided the new king of Israel with a team
of Phoenician masons, carpenters and ivory carvers to
construct and adorn David's palace in Jerusalem. The
edifice was erected on a large platform at the highest point
on the hill which formed the old Jebusite town. In addition
to the great wall which encircled the hill and the towers of
the water system, the Jebusites had built a series of terraces
extending down the eastern slope. These terraces were
constructed out of fieldstone walls which were backfilled
with rubble to form shelves or giant steps upon which
houses could be built. As a result of all this engineering
work, the overall space within the city walls had been
increased to provide additional living areas for the expand-

ing population. This terrace structure was known as the *Millo* – a word which simply means 'filling'. David would later continue the building of the Millo by adding new sections and repairing the old Jebusite terraces. But his immediate priority was to enlarge the area of the palace platform and reinforce that part of the site which was closest to the steep eastern slope of the town. His Phoenician masons therefore constructed a massive stone revetment wall (today known as the 'stepped stone structure') which covered the upper terraces of the Millo and prevented any possible subsidence which might be brought on by the weight of the new palace above.

The new 'City of David', also known as ZION, was a hive of noisy activity for several years as the palace rose from its foundations. Three lower courses of stone were capped by a layer of cedar beams, on top of which came two more courses of stone. This was a traditional building technique of the Phoenicians, with the cedar layer designed to absorb any movement during the regular earth tremors which affected the whole region of the Levant. On top of the fifth course of stones stood the cedar walls and roof of the royal residence with the throne room looking out over the Kidron valley.

Immediately to the north of the palace was a courtyard within which a new tabernacle tent was erected to house the Ark of the Covenant. The casket containing the Tablets of the Law was finally brought up from its temporary lodgings in the house of Abinadab in Baalah (later known as Kiriath-Jearim) where it had remained for nineteen years, since the Philistines had returned the prize of war to Israel following its capture at the battle of Ebenezer in 1024 BC. The sacred casket was carried into the city of Jerusalem twenty years after it had been removed from the shrine at Shiloh in the days of the high priest Eli. The Ark procession was met by David who, throwing off his royal robes, danced before Yahweh's potent symbol of power as the golden box was carried up to its new resting place in the royal

309

compound. It was intended that, eventually, the tablets of
Moses would be placed in a new temple on Mount Moriah
– the rocky summit looking down onto the City of David
from the north – near the spot where Abraham had laid
his son Isaac on the sacrificial altar. However, the building
of Yahweh's temple was to remain beyond the means and
will of King David as he concentrated all his efforts on
expanding the kingdom and defeating Israel's enemies far
and wide. The task of erecting the Temple of Jerusalem
was to fall to David's famous son and successor – Solomon
the 'merchant prince'.

The Davidic Wars

With the Philistines of the coastal plain subdued (at least
for the moment), David next turned east to extend his
influence across the Jordan into the lands of Moab. The
Moabites were quickly subsumed and made into vassals,
with much tribute paid into Israel's royal coffers. The
borders of David's kingdom were secure in the west and
east, but now a new enemy threatened from the north –
HADAD-AZIRU ('Hadad is (my) helper', the biblical Hadadezer), king of the Aramaeans of Zobah. His sprawling
kingdom centred on the Syrian plain east of the Lebanese
mountains and to the north-west of Damascus – the region
the Egyptians called Amurru (the 'Amorite lands'). In the
Amarna letters this Hadad-aziru is identified by his simple
hypocoristic name – Aziru.

During Labaya's days (1012–1011 BC), the king of
Zobah had been Abdi-Ashirta but, by the time David had
conquered Jerusalem, Aziru was the new power in the
Aramaean lands. Abdi-Ashirta and Aziru – just like Labaya
and David – proved to be thorns in the side of Egyptian
authority in the region. Both nascent kingdoms – Israel
and Zobah – seized windows of opportunity to rebel against
Egypt's northern empire, made moribund by the weak
pharaohs of the late 18th Dynasty. And both employed

Moses did as Yahweh ordered. With the whole community watching, they went up Mount Hor. Moses took Aaron's robe off him and dressed his son Eleazar in them, and there Aaron died, on the mountain-top. Moses and Eleazar then came back down the mountain. The whole community saw that Aaron had died, and for thirty days the whole House of Israel mourned for Aaron. [Numbers 20:27–29]

Plate 21: The little white mosque/shrine on top of Mount Hor which marks the spot where Aaron died and was buried. A stone sarcophagus lies in a cave beneath the chapel.

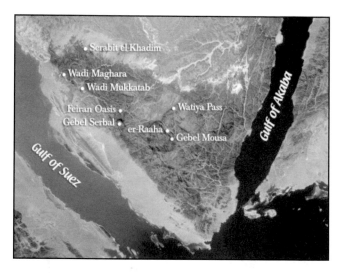

Plate 22: Satellite image of southern Sinai and the granite mountain massif surrounding Mount Horeb. The route from the coast of west Sinai to Mount Horeb follows the network of wadis through Maghara and Mukkatab to the oasis of Feiran; then on to the plain of er-Raaha via the Watiya Pass.

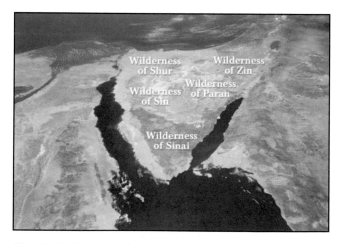

Plate 23: Satellite image of the Sinai peninsula, showing the five wilderness areas mentioned in the book of Exodus.

In the second year, in the second month, on the twentieth day of the month, the cloud rose from where the dwelling of the testimony was, and the Israelites set out, in marching order, from the desert of Sinai. [Numbers 10:11–12]

Plate 24: Bedouin camel riders in the wilderness beneath Mount Sinai.

X

Plate 25: The two stone-cut altars (of Nabatean or Edomite date) on top of the 'High Place' at Petra. The altars are directly aligned towards Mount Hor and the tomb of Aaron (marked by an X).

Plate 26: Kenyon's Trench I at Jericho with remains of the glacis (A) and upper city wall (B).

Plate 27: Hazor's Upper City with the corner of the MB II palace (A) and MB II temple (B) still partially buried under the Late Bronze Age remains (C) and Iron Age gate (D).

Plate 28: A fragment of an MB II-B cuneiform tablet found at Hazor. The tablet was discovered in the dump material of the excavators who originally uncovered the corner of the Middle Bronze palace on the Upper City tell. The text is a letter to a King Ibni-Addu who was clearly ruling at Hazor prior to its destruction in the MB II-B. Scholars (including the current excavator of Hazor, Professor Amnor Ben-Tor) have recognised that the Canaanite name Ibni corresponds to the biblical name Jabin (Hebrew Yabin) – carried by the king of Hazor who was killed by Joshua when the city was destroyed by the invading Israelites. This is further confirmation that the biblical Conquest should be dated to the second half of the Middle Bronze Age and not the end of the Late Bronze Age as conventionally assumed.

Plate 29: The fortified sanctuary of Shechem (now located within the city of Nablus). A = the Cyclopean circuit wall; B = the northern gateway; C = the stone foundations of the migdol temple known as the Temple of Baal-Berith; D = Joshua's gleaming white covenant stone erected before the temple entrance; E = the original courtyard sanctuary of Jacob at a lower level, the excavators having cleared the millo filling within which it was sealed by the Israelites of the early Judges period.

Plate 30: The Cyclopean wall surrounding the sanctuary of Shechem built by the Israelites of the early Judges period (MB II-B/LB I).

Plate 31: Joshua's Covenant Stone still standing before the MB II/LB I temple at Shechem.

That day Joshua made a covenant for the people. He laid down a statue and ordinance for them at Shechem. Joshua wrote these words in the Book of the Law of God. He then took a large stone and set it up there, under the oak tree in Yahweh's sanctuary. Joshua then said to all the people, 'Look, this stone will be a witness to us, since it has heard all the words that Yahweh has spoken to us. It will be a witness against you in case you should deny your God.' Joshua then dismissed the people, everyone to his own heritage. [Joshua 24:25–28]

Plate 32: Joshua's Covenant Stone in Shechem (modern Nablus).

Habiru mercenary forces to great effect as their agents of destruction against neighbouring lands loyal to Egypt.

The collapse of Egyptian control in northern Canaan, as a result of the activities of the two Aramaean warlords, is painfully documented in the letters of Rib-Hadda of Byblos (Canaanite *Gubla,* Arabic *Gebeil*), sent in their scores to insular, inward-looking Amarna. Egypt's loyal Phoenician vassal pleaded for military assistance to counter constant attacks from Amurru – but Pharaoh simply failed to heed his warnings of impending disaster. This is quite astonishing, given the importance of Byblos to Egyptian sea trade and for supplies of high-quality timber. It is even more astonishing when Rib-Hadda's desperate letters make it clear that the key strategic town of Sumur (Egyptian Simyra), at the western end of the Homs-Tripoli gap, was the principal target of Aramaean military aggression. This was an Egyptian stronghold, previously used as a staging post for the campaigns against Mitanni by Thutmose III, and which in future days would once more become a key military outpost of Ramesses II (known then as 'Simyra of Sysa'). But here, in the dark days of Egypt's heresy period, the garrison of Sumur was left to its own fate by an Egyptian pharaoh consumed by religious reforms and vainglory. I will quote Rib-Hadda's own (much-abridged) words as witness to Egypt's shocking abdication of responsibility towards its long-loyal northern ally. At first Rib-Hadda's reports are reasonably confident but, at the same time, make the developing situation very clear.

> Rib-Hadda says to his lord, king of all countries, great king: may Baalat Gubla ('Lady of Byblos' = Hathor) grant power to the king my lord. Seven times and seven times I fall at the feet of my lord my sun. May the king my lord know that Gubla, the loyal maidservant of the king, is safe and secure. However, the war of the Habiru forces against me is extremely severe. And so may the king my lord

not neglect Sumur lest everyone becomes allied to the Habiru forces. [EA 68]

Who is this Abdi-Ashirta (slave and dog!) that he seizes the land of the king for himself? Why are his auxiliaries so strong? It is because of the Habiru (mercenaries) that his auxiliaries are strong! [EA 71]

These letters were written during the early years of the Amarna court (Akhenaten's Year 6 to 11 = 1018–1013 BC) and concern Abdi-Ashirta's activities. For the last six years of Akhenaten's reign (1012–1007 BC) it was Aziru, the son of Abdi-Ashirta, who delivered the final blows which tore northern Canaan away from Egypt. This new ruler of Amurru was even more dangerous than Abdi-Ashirta, having murdered his own father to gain the throne. Whilst David was establishing himself as king in Hebron and preparing to seize Jerusalem, Aziru/Hadadezer was busy threatening Egyptian interests on the northern coast of the Levant, having secretly switched allegiances to a growing power from the north – the Hittites of Anatolia. Meanwhile, back in Egypt, major changes were taking place within the Amarna royal dynasty.

Shortly after the great DURBAR celebrations of Akhenaten's twelfth year (1012 BC, following the death of his father and co-regent Amenhotep III earlier in the year), Queen Neferneferuaten Nefertiti had been made her husband's co-regent. She had taken the coronation name Ankhkheperure to become the pharaoh Ankhkheperure Neferneferuaten (1011–1000 BC). With this act of supreme affection on the part of Akhenaten, the name Nefertiti disappears from history.

For many years Egyptologists believed that Akhenaten's beloved queen had died or been disgraced in some way, but now we know that she simply transmuted into an entirely new historical character. Following the death of Akhenaten in 1007 BC, Ankhkheperure Neferneferuaten took on a new nomen to become Ankhkheperure Smenkh-kare (1007–1000 BC). At the same time she adopted the boy-king Nebkheperure Tutankhaten as her co-regent. Four years later, the now twelve-year-old pharaoh was renamed Tutankhamun and established his own court at Memphis whilst Smenkhkare remained senior co-regent in Akhet-aten. This arrangement of dual-kingship – with Tutankh-amun governing Lower Egypt and taking charge of the army whilst Smenkhkare concerned herself principally with religious (i.e. Atenist) affairs – continued until the death of the latter in 1000 BC. During the five-year era of the twin palaces at Mennefer (Memphis) and Akhetaten (Amarna), letters continued to be sent (or copied) to both courts from the city-state vassals in the north. And it was at this time that Aziru was called to account – summoned to Egypt to explain his actions.

The king of Zobah had been under suspicion of dis-loyalty to Egypt from the day he seized the throne by murdering his own father in 1011 BC. Following in Abdi-Ashirta's footsteps, he continued to harass Rib-Hadda (as the last thirty-six letters from the king of Byblos attest). But Pharaoh Akhenaten had done nothing to stop him. Only when Tutankhamun left Amarna and set up his adminis-tration in Memphis in 1004 BC did the Egyptians take action to trim their wayward vassal's ambitions. In 1003 BC Aziru was ordered to Memphis for 'consultations'. After a year of prevarication he eventually turned up at the northern capital where he remained under house arrest for twelve months. Amarna letter EA 169 informs us that the king of Zobah was in Egypt as the 'guest' of an official named Tutu (Egyptian *Dudu* – 'beloved') who was the diplo-mat tasked with interrogating the Aramaean warlord. In an example of remarkable political flannel, Aziru appears to have persuaded the Egyptians that he continued to be a loyal vassal and, as a demonstration of his loyalty, would volunteer to act as Pharaoh's policeman in southern Canaan where the Philistines of Gath had pointedly failed to quell the Habiru uprising. Aziru offered his 'services' to put down what was still perceived to be the greatest threat against Egypt's control over Canaan – David's Israelites. The Aramaean's price for a full military onslaught against Israel was that Egypt should turn a blind eye to Zobah's territorial gains in northern Canaan. This political deal would have made good sense to the Egyptians at that time, since they were in no position to take military action themselves on account of Akhenaten's neglect of the army.

Having regained his freedom in the winter of 1002 BC, Aziru returned to Amurru and made the call to arms. But he did not immediately campaign against Israel. With Egypt's blank cheque in hand, the king of Zobah occupied his time with more productive matters, such as seizing control of Damascus and undermining his old enemy, Rib-Hadda of Byblos. Piece by piece Aziru carved out his own little empire in the north with the assistance of his Habiru mercenaries and troops from Hatti. By 1001 BC he had captured the Egyptian garrison town of Sumur (Simyra), killing the military governor, Pawura (Egyptian *Paweru* – 'great one'). As a result, Aziru had gained control of the landward access route to the coastal plain of Phoenicia. Rib-Hadda continued to send his letters to Egypt, but now they had become even more desperate.

> May the king my lord know that the war against us is very severe. You may have been reassured that 'Sumur (still) belongs to the king', but may the king know that there was an attack on our garrison (there), and (Aziru) the son of Abdi-Ashirta seized it. … Moreover, all my towns have gone over to the Habiru, and all of them are (now) extremely hostile to me … Look, Aziru and Yapah-Hadda have made an alliance against me … Accordingly, my situation is extremely grave. … Who are they, these sons of Abdi-Ashirta, that they have taken the lands of the king for themselves? [EA 116]

After months of constant raids by the Aramaeans of Zobah, Rib-Hadda abandoned Byblos and fled to Beirut, from where he wrote his final letters to the royal court at Amarna.

> Previously I wrote to the king but he did not heed my words. Now I am living in Beirut like a dog and my word is still unheeded. If the king would listen to his servant and (Egyptian) troops were given to me, the city (of Byblos) [would return] to the king. … When I am dead, my surviving sons, servants of the king, will continue to write to the king, asking 'Please restore us to our city.' Why has my lord abandoned me? [EA 138]

These were the last words from the faithful Rib-Hadda. Byblos and Sumer had been lost to Aziru and his allies. Egypt's last vestige of influence in the region had died with the demise of its most loyal vassal. The strategically important city of Kinza (Kadesh-on-the-Orontes) fell in 999 BC. Syria and Phoenicia had gone over to the Hittite sphere and the Aramaean king of Zobah was playing a dangerous game in an attempt to keep his former masters in the south misinformed of the true position whilst sucking up to his new masters from the north who now held the real power.

With his ambitions in the west fulfilled and an alliance with the Hittites sealed, Aziru finally turned his attention to the south. David, now resident in Jerusalem, watched with growing concern and made hasty preparations for war. The clash came in the spring of the following year by a rather strange turn of events. King Nahash of Ammon died and was succeeded by his son Hanun. David sent ambassadors across the Jordan to offer Israel's condolences over the death of their longstanding ally. However, having seen what David's Israelites had done to their neighbours in Moab, the Ammonites were convinced that these ambassadors were really spies sent to determine Ammon's military strength in anticipation of invasion. David's emissaries were humiliated by having their hair shorn and their beards shaved off in front of jeering crowds. They were then unceremoniously escorted back across the Jordan.

> When David was told (what had happened to his ambassadors) he sent someone to meet them since the men were overcome with shame. 'Stay in Jericho', the king said, 'until your beards have grown again, and come back then.' [2 Samuel 10:5]

The ambassadorial mission remained 'in exile' at the old abandoned city of Jericho until their embarrassment was lessened by a couple of years of hair growth.

This was only the second time that Jericho had been occupied since the curse of destruction placed upon the smouldering ruins in Joshua's day. As we saw in Chapter Eleven, Middle Bronze Age Jericho was destroyed through violent earthquake and conflagration in 1406 BC. Following this destruction, the site lay abandoned for decades until the Late Bronze I period when a single residence/building was constructed atop the ruins of the MB II-B city. This 'Middle Building' was associated with both LB I and LB II-A pottery, making its two occupation phases contemporary (in the New Chronology) with King Eglon of Moab (early Judges period *c.* 1360 BC) and then the reign of David (1011–971 BC). Thus the LB II-A phase may well be linked to the residence of the ambassadors, exiled from Jerusalem until their beards had grown back. It is remarkable to find that the archaeological record coincides so precisely with a biblical tradition spanning a period of four hundred years – but this, of course, is only the case in the New Chronology historical model.

According to 2 Samuel 10:6–7, Hanun, the new king of Ammon, realised that his humiliation of the Israelite diplomatic mission would not go unpunished, and so he sent agents to Aziru/Hadadezer, offering the Aramaeans of Zobah payment to fight on their behalf against Israel.

Whatever the reality behind the strange tale of the shaven-headed ambassadors, it seems clear that Ammon and Zobah allied together in order to challenge the rising power of the Davidic kingdom – now in its second decade and growing stronger with every year that passed. No doubt the move was also supported from behind the scenes by Egypt.

In David's thirteenth year (999 BC) a large Aramaean army marched down from the Golan Heights, heading south into Ammon where the tribes of Manasseh and Gad had settled. In order to protect his Israelite kin, David sent his army, under the command of Ayab/Joab, to meet the threat. General Ayab, his brother Abishai and all the tribal warriors crossed the Jordan at Gilgal with a force of thirty thousand men-at-arms. From there the Israelite army marched up onto the Jordanian plateau and positioned itself outside the town of Madeba (east of Mount Nebo). The soldiers of Ammon marched out of their city to confront the Israelite army. At the same time, the Aramaean hirelings were massing a couple of kilometres to the north. Ayab quickly realised that he had to fight on two fronts. He left Abishai in command of the main infantry (ordered to hold their position against the Ammonites at all costs) whilst he himself sallied forth with twelve thousand of Israel's best warriors to meet the huge force of thirty-three thousand soldiers conscripted from the Syrian states of Beth-Rehob, Zobah, Maacah and Tob.

At first the close-quarters fighting was ferocious but within an hour the outcome was decided. The Aramaean conscripts, in spite of their superiority in numbers, proved to be no match for Ayab's battle-hardened warriors. The hirelings turned and fled.

Meanwhile the soldiers of Ammon had remained rooted in front of their strong city gates, thinking that the Aramaeans would overwhelm the opposition and leave them to 'clean up' any Israelite survivors. Instead, to their horror, they witnessed the retreat of Hanun's allies and realised that they would be next in line. With Ayab's crushing victory, Abishai ordered the advance against the Ammonite lines. However, the Israelite reserve did not need to fight – the soldiers of Ammon turned and ran in panic within the strong walls of their city. Ayab and the victorious Israelites broke off the military campaign and returned across the Jordan to Israel.

Eleven months passed before the Aramaean challenge resurfaced. Aziru, furious at the defeat of his mercenaries before Madeba, mobilised Amurru's forces once more – this time reinforced by a huge contingent of fifteen thousand infantry from Damascus. But Aziru did not personally lead his troops in the war because of failing health.

Man of Pakku

In his absence, the Aramaean army was led by Shupak – Aziru's experienced Hittite military commander. During the year that Aziru had been a 'guest' in Egypt, General Shupak had captured the kingdom of Amuk (Amka) and then seized Kinza (Kadesh) on behalf of the Hittite alliance in 999 BC. A letter written to Aziru in Egypt by his officials during his year of detention has survived which reports on Shupak's activities at that time.

> To the king our lord: message from Baaluya and Betili. ... All goes well here in the lands of our lord. ... As soon as you can, meet with them (i.e. the officials of Pharaoh) so that they will not delay you there (in Egypt any longer). Moreover, the troops of Hatti under Lupakku have captured the cities of Amuk ... and we have also heard that Zitana has come with ninety thousand infantrymen! [EA 170]

The Bible calls the Aramaean army commander 'Shupak', which means 'he (who is of) Pak(ku)'; the el-Amarna letters name him Lupakku, which means 'man (of) Pakku'. The

Aramaean army commander also appears in the annals of the Hittite emperor Shuppiluliuma I (1030–993 BC) to whom Aziru had secretly sworn allegiance in an act of betrayal against his Egyptian overlord. Zitana also appears in the Hittite records as Zita, the younger brother of Shuppiluliuma and commander of the Anatolian forces. Now, in the spring of 998 BC, Shupak was given the task of eliminating the Israelites at the behest of his master Aziru and his master's master – the Egyptian pharaoh.

Shupak brought his huge army south and, once more, the Israelites sallied forth to meet them – this time led by King David himself. The battle took place at HELAN and, once more, the Israelites were victorious. Shupak was killed. All told, the Israelites slew twenty-two thousand of the enemy troops, captured one thousand seven hundred chariots and took a further twenty thousand foot soldiers prisoner to work as slave labour on David's extensive building projects. The remnants of Aziru's shattered army retreated back to Amurru. In the Israelite David and his commander Ayab, Aziru the Aramaean warmonger and his Hittite army commander had finally met their match.

The Israelites kept just one hundred of the enemy chariots along with their horse teams, hamstringing the rest simply because, as a mountain kingdom, they had little use for, nor the resources to maintain, such a large chariot force (which was really only suited to plain-based warfare). It was with David's successor, Solomon, that Israel first built up a significant chariotry division for the standing army – mainly because, by that time, the cities of the Jezreel valley (such as Megiddo and Taanach) had been encompassed within the Solomonic kingdom.

The spoils of the Aramaean war were brought back to Jerusalem and stored in the royal coffers, including the golden shields belonging to Aziru's élite brigade killed trying to protect their famous military commander, Shupak of Hatti.

David now received an emissary from the northern

city of Hamath (modern Hama in Syria) led by Hadoram, son of King Tou. The crown-prince brought gifts of silver, gold and bronze to congratulate David on his victory over their common enemy, Aziru and the Aramaeans of Zobah. King Tou of Hamath is also attested in the Amarna archive through a single letter (EA 58) which he wrote to Akhenaten, complaining about the earlier maraudings of Abdi-Ashirta and his sons. There he calls himself Tehu-Teshub – a name of uncertain meaning associated with the Hurrian weather-god Teshub.*

With the crushing defeat of his army, Aziru's health further deteriorated. In 997 BC the King of Zobah and Damascus died and was succeeded by his son Du-Teshub. This name is formed from an abbreviation of the Sumerian logogram *dumu* (meaning 'son') and the Hurrian weather-god Teshub, giving us 'son of Teshub'. He is the biblical Bar-Hadad/Ben-Hadad ('son of (the Syrian weather-god) Hadad') whom the Bible records as the successor to Hadadezer.

So we can now add a new list of biblical identities sourced from the Amarna letters – this time from northern Canaan.

(f)   Aziru (biblical [Hadad]-ezer, 'Hadad is helper') – the ruler of Zobah;

(g)   Du-Teshub (biblical Ben-Hadad, 'son of Hadad') – successor of Aziru;

(h)   Lupakku (biblical Shupak, 'man of Pakku') – King Hadadezer's Hittite general;

(i)   Tehu-Teshub (biblical Tou, '[unknown]-Teshub') – the Hurrian ruler of Hamath.

---

* Scholars McCarter and Mercer have both suggested that the biblical name Tou is a variant writing of Hurrian Tehu. They are indeed right: Tehu-Teshub of EA 58 is one and the same as Tou of Hamath [2 Samuel 8:9]. This is another example of a hypocoristicon taken from a longer formal name linked to a personal god where the theophoric element has been omitted.

Expanding the 'Empire'

In the year following his decisive and historical victory over the Aramaeans, David despatched Ayab and the army back to Ammon to finish off Hanun and his people. With their Aramaean protectors vanquished, the Ammonites of Rabbath (modern Amman) were at Israel's mercy ... however they received none. In the long, hot summer of 997 BC, Ayab besieged the town until its citizens were starved into surrender. The Israelites then marched through the gates and massacred the population.

Whilst the army was away from Jerusalem, King David had an affair with Bathsheba – the wife of one of Israel's prominent foreign mercenary soldiers. As a result of this clandestine relationship, the woman had become pregnant whilst her husband was fighting on behalf of his king. Although Uriah the Hittite was not of Israelite blood, he was one of David's most loyal army captains. Yet, in spite of this, the king of Israel plotted to have Uriah 'killed in action' so that Bathsheba could become a royal concubine. David secretly ordered Ayab to place Uriah in the front line at the siege of Rabbath where he was likely to fall victim to a hail of arrows raining down from the city walls. It was a sentence of death. Uriah the Hittite did not return from Ammon.

David then took Bathsheba as his own. She bore him a daughter, but the infant died within a week of the birth. However, Bathsheba was soon pregnant again and provided the king with a healthy son whom the prophet Nathan named Daduya (biblical Jedidiah, 'beloved of Yah'). History would know him by his traditional name, reflecting a glorious reign of nearly forty years in which peace prevailed in the land of Israel. Solomon (Hebrew *Shelomoh*) simply means 'peaceable' (from Hebrew *shalom*, Arabic *salam* – 'peace').

With the Aramaean army destroyed, the Israelites undertook a number of successful raids into Syria, bringing back rich plunder and erecting standing stones or pillars to mark their triumphs over the conquered territories. Most Bibles translate 2 Samuel 8:6 as 'David then imposed governors on Aram (Syria) and Damascus, and the Aramaeans became David's subjects and paid him tribute'. However, the Hebrew word here translated 'governors' (*netsibim*) is the same as that used for the overthrowing of the 'pillar' (*netsib*) by Saul's son Jonathan during the initial Israelite uprising against Philistine oppression in 1012 BC. It has been difficult for most scholars to accept the proposition that King David controlled a vast empire, extending northwards to the river Euphrates, through the establishment of regional governors on the Egyptian political model. But, if we rather interpret the 'establishment of governors (*netsibim*)' as the 'setting up of pillars (*netsibim*)', then a quite different and more believable picture emerges.

David and his large force of Israelite warriors and foreign mercenaries were able to make these raids into the north because of the disintegration of Egyptian and Mitannian control in the region. The vast tracts of conquered lands described in the Bible did not constitute a formal kingdom as such. The Davidic 'empire' was more akin to a tribute-paying hegemony based on quick sorties to collect dues and seize plunder from those who refused to pay up. David's territorial conquests were therefore opportunistic. They were allowed to take place precisely because there was a political vacuum in the Levant during the Amarna and immediate post-Amarna era (the reigns of Tutankhamun and Ay – 1007–987 BC) – a vacuum quickly filled by the Hittites under Shuppiluliuma I (1030–993 BC) and his son Murshili II (991–967 BC).

Changes in the Political Landscape

The northern empire had collapsed and Egypt's old ally, Mitanni, had fallen. The former powerful Indo-European kingdom, with its Hurrian population living in the rich grazing lands between the Euphrates and Khabur rivers, had been divided up by its conquerors. The rising power of Assyria had swallowed up the eastern provinces, whilst the expanding empire of the Hittites seized the west around Carchemish and controlled the Syrian dependencies in the south. The Hebrew/Israelite revolt, initiated by Labaya/ Saul but brought to a successful conclusion by Tadua/ David, was the major factor in breaking up the Egyptian hegemony in southern Canaan. However, Abdi-Ashirta and Aziru/Hadadezer were equally responsible for destabilising northern Canaan. When the latter was then defeated by David, the whole region as far as Damascus fell under Israelite sway for a couple of decades whilst Egypt slowly awoke from its Atenist nightmare. A letter sent to Amarna by the citizens of Tunip in Syria shows that it was not just Rib-Hadda of Byblos who had been abandoned by Akhenaten and the other Amarna pharaohs.

> To the king of Egypt, our lord: Message of the citizens of Tunip, your servant. … When Aziru entered Sumur (Simyra), he did to them as he pleased, in the house of the king, our lord. But our lord did nothing about these things. And now, Tunip, your city, weeps, and its tears flow, and there is no grasping of our hand. We have gone on writing to the king, our lord, the king of Egypt, for twenty years, and not a single word of our lord has reached us! [EA 59]

This twenty-year silence, which began with the coronation of Akhenaten, ended with Tutankhamun's move from Akhetaten to Memphis in 1004 BC where he took up residence in the old palace of his ancestor Thutmose I. The delusory veil of Atenism was lifted from Egypt's eyes and Pharaoh could finally see the calamity which had befallen Egypt as a result of his elder brother's disastrous reign.

Now when his majesty (Tutankhamun) appeared (i.e. was crowned) as king, the temples of the gods and goddesses from Elephantine (Aswan) [down] to the marshes of the delta [had been neglected and] fallen into ruin. Their shrines had become desolate and had become mounds overgrown with [weeds]. Their sanctuaries were as if they had never been. Their halls were a footpath. The land was in chaos and the gods turned their backs upon this land. If [soldiers were] sent to Djahi (the Levant) to extend the frontiers of Egypt, no success whatsoever came to them. … Now when his majesty was (established) in his palace, which is in the House of Akheperkare (Thutmose I) (in Memphis), like Re in the heavens, then his majesty was conducting the affairs of this land and the daily needs of the Two Banks. … The hearts of the gods and goddesses who are in this land are (now) in joy. The possessors of shrines are rejoicing (once more). The regions are in jubilee and exultation is throughout the [entire] land. The good [times] have returned! [*Tutankhamun Restoration Stela* from Karnak]

But it was all too late for the empire. Under the Amarna heresy, the Egyptian military had been neglected along with the state temples. For nine years (1012–1004 BC) bubonic plague, introduced into Egypt at Akhenaten's Year 12 durbar, had ravaged the land and decimated the population. Egypt was in no fit state to launch a major offensive to recover its foreign interests.

Tutankhamun did despatch his general, Haremheb, along with what troops were available, in an attempt to clean up some of the mess left in the wake of Akhenaten's neglect. In 1001 BC (Tutankhamun's seventh year), the Egyptian army commander (soon to become Pharaoh himself) managed to re-establish partial control along the southern coastal plain, capturing the city of Gezer in the process. But the rest of the wild country – in the hills of Canaan, the tableland across the Jordan and the rolling Syrian plain – remained outside Egypt's influence for nearly half a century. Only when the prolonged military campaigns of Seti I and Ramesses II of the 19th Dynasty got under way did Egypt re-establish its grip on the southern Levant. However, it was actually a clever piece of political manoeuvring on the part of their predecessor Haremheb which laid the foundations for the recovery. But more on that later.

Now, at the turn of the millennium, as Tutankhamun, Ay and Haremheb devoted Egypt's resources to rebuilding the internal political, judicial and religious structure in the Nile valley, King David of Israel was allowed to expand his control of the region unchecked. Having halted Philistine aggression from the west, crushed the Aramaeans to the north (establishing political pacts with Ahiram of Tyre and Tehu-Teshub of Hamath) and subjugating the Ammonites and Moabites in the east, David now turned south. In the valley of salt (i.e. the southern part of the Dead Sea basin) the Israelite army clashed with the Edomites, killing eighteen thousand. Once more David set up stone pillars to mark his victory as Edom was subsumed into the Davidic 'empire'.

Israel was now a fully fledged state and a recognised part of the political landscape of Canaan. Egypt would have to find new ways of dealing with the 'Habiru' troublemakers from the hills. They were now a nation ruled by a powerful warlord and sovereign. The kingdom of Israel had, within two decades of political chaos, become Egypt's most powerful neighbour.

Absalom's Revolt

In Jerusalem, palace intrigue – so typical of Israelite rule – continued to undermine the nascent monarchy. Prince Amnon (David's eldest son by Ahinoam of Jezreel) raped the beautiful Tamar (David's daughter by Maacah, princess of Geshur). Tamar's brother, Absalom (the king's third eldest son), murdered Amnon in revenge for his sister's disgrace and fled the court. For three years (993–991 BC) Absalom was exiled to his maternal grandfather's home in Geshur. He was then permitted to return to Jerusalem but did not meet his father the king for another two years. Finally, in 988 BC (David's twenty-fourth regnal year), king and crown-prince were reconciled ... but Absalom was already plotting to overthrow his father and seize the kingdom. He departed for David's old capital of Hebron where he gathered his allies. Four years later, with many of the tribal leaders having gone over to him, Absalom was ready to strike. In 985 BC he declared himself king of Hebron and marched to Jerusalem. David, realising that all the tribes of the central hill country were against him, abandoned his own capital and fled across the Jordan to Mutbaal's old palace at Mahanaim, accompanied by his most loyal forces – mostly made up of foreign warriors including Gittites (Hurrians from Gath), Hittites, Cherethites (Cretans) and even Pelethites (Philistines). Meanwhile Absalom and the Israelite rebels entered Jerusalem unopposed.

Safely across the Jordan, David called the tribes of Manasseh and Gad to arms. They had remained loyal to the king because he had saved them from the Ammonite and Aramaean oppression. The civil war came to its climax in 984 BC when Absalom and the remaining Israelite tribes marched into Transjordan to crush the last vestige of resistance to the king of Hebron's takeover. The two sides met in the forest of Ephraim and once more there was terrible slaughter. This time twenty thousand Israelites lay dead beneath the trees as David's military élite pulled off yet another remarkable victory. The news was brought to the king in Mahanaim that his son Absalom had been cut down whilst trying to escape. David mourned the loss of another son for several weeks before preparing to return to Jerusalem. It took a full twelve months before the tribal leaders were ready to accept David as their king once more and an uneasy peace was restored to the kingdom.

Plague and Pestilence

In the following year (982 BC) the bubonic plague, which had been raging through the cities of the lowlands and had decimated the Egyptian and Hittite royal families, finally penetrated the highlands. Seventy thousand Israelites and Habiru perished in three years of desperate existence. David called upon Yahweh for redemption from the terrible pestilence. In an act of reconciliation following Absalom's revolt and to emphasise the need for stability in the tribal kingdom, the king made the first practical step towards establishing a state temple in the capital for Israel's national god. If the kingdom was truly at peace with itself and attention was directed away from war towards the worship of Israel's saviour, then this terrible curse might be removed from the land.

David purchased a threshing-floor belonging to the old Jebusite ruler of Jerusalem, Abdi-Heba. Having wisely acknowledged David as his sovereign when Jerusalem was captured in 1005 BC, the arwana (ruler) of the Jebus had continued to live in his estate outside the city and farm the land. Abdi-Heba's threshing-floor was located on a flat area of exposed limestone at the summit of Mount Moriah, north of and overlooking the City of David. Immediately to the south of the threshing floor, at the highest point on Moriah (where the Dome of the Rock now stands), was the knoll of rock where Abraham had prepared to sacrifice his son Isaac to Yahweh. And so this place had great sanctity in Israelite eyes. The arwana's threshing-floor was acquired for fifty shekels of silver and an altar to Yahweh set up on the place where Solomon's temple would later stand. The plague gradually subsided and peace slowly began to reside in the hearts of the Children of Yahweh.

But, as David was growing old and thoughts of the

succession began to loom, this relative calm endured for less than a decade. During these years of respite there were a number of skirmishes with their old enemy, the Philistines, in the Shephelah hills bordering the plain, but David left these clashes in the safe hands of his vastly experienced generals and 'champions'. Now in his seventies, it was time to make preparations to meet his god and ensure that the kingdom of Israel was left in safe hands.

Intrigues Over the Succession

As death drew near, in the fortieth year of David's reign (972 BC), the succession was on everybody's mind. The king's first-, second- and third-born sons – Chileab, Amnon and Absalom – were all dead, leaving ADONIJAH, younger brother of Absalom, as crown-prince. The heir-apparent, believing that he was on the verge of kingship, invited his supporters and city-officials to a sacrificial feast at EN-ROGEL in the Kidron valley. Like any modern political campaign, it was who was seen to support your candidacy that really mattered, and Adonijah, as the eldest surviving son of the king, had some big names in tow, including the old army commander Ayab and the Israelite high priest ABIATHAR. There, at En-Rogel, Adonijah was proclaimed king by acclamation, even though his father was not yet in his grave. Back in the palace, the prophet NATHAN, the Jebusite high priest ZADOK and BENAIAH, commander of David's élite bodyguard, quickly moved to block Adonijah's claim to the throne. They were supporters of Daduya/Solomon, son of Bathsheba, whom they knew to be the old king's favourite son. As David lay on his deathbed, he was approached both by Bathsheba and Nathan, asking him to proclaim Solomon as his successor, and informing him that Adonijah had already assumed the kingship without his father's blessing. King David immediately ordered that his fourteenth-eldest son should be anointed to rule over Israel so that the arrogant and presumptuous Adonijah could be stopped in his tracks.

The king's mule was prepared to carry Solomon down from the palace in royal procession to the Gihon spring where the anointing ritual was to take place. Just as Christ would do on Palm Sunday a thousand years later in imitation of this ancient Israelite succession ceremony, Solomon rode his white mule down the winding street which led to the city gate beside the Spring Tower, escorted by David's personal bodyguard of Cretans and Philistines under the command of Benaiah. The prophet Nathan and Zadok the high priest led the procession, so all the people of Jerusalem could see that both the king and Yahweh were giving their blessing to Solomon's anointing.

With the sacred oils having been poured over Solomon's head, Zadok ordered the sounding of the SHOFARS so that Adonijah and his followers would hear the rival celebrations from their own feast just a kilometre away down the valley at En-Rogel. Adonijah's supporters soon learned of what had occurred and that Solomon now sat upon Israel's throne. They took fright and melted away, leaving David's eldest alone and in mortal fear for his life. Adonijah's concerns were certainly justified in a time when brothers of kings often met sticky ends – but not in his case for the moment. King Solomon swore an oath that his elder brother would not be harmed if he prostrated himself before his new king and swore allegiance to David's chosen. And so Adonijah's survival was assured for a few months – at least whilst David was still alive. The bloodletting would wait until the old king had 'fallen asleep with his ancestors' and was buried in the tomb prepared for him within the walls of the City of David.

Eight months later, after a prolonged illness, King Tadua/David – the 'beloved of Yah' – was dead. The son of Yishuya (Jesse) had reigned for just over forty years, in which time he had not only secured Israel's borders but had extended Israelite control over a vast area in all directions. Whilst Egypt faltered under a misguided religious reformer, Israel blossomed in the firm hands of its ambitious and charismatic Habiru leader – the deadly scourge of the Philistines, Moabites, Aramaeans, Ammonites and Edomites. But now the age of the 'warrior king' was at an end and the bountiful era of the 'merchant prince' was about to begin.

Chapter Fifteen

SOLOMON

(1 Kings 2:12 to 1 Kings 11:43)

*The Deaths of Adonijah and Ayab – Solomon's
Egyptian Queen – The Temple of Jerusalem – Solomon
the Builder King – The Queen of Sheba – Israel at the
Battle of Kadesh – Jeroboam's Revolt*

With his father laid to rest, Solomon immediately set about eliminating any threat to his kingship from the leading figures of the previous reign. He ordered the killing of his elder brother Prince Adonijah at the hands of the royal bodyguards. The high priest Abiathar was stripped of his office and exiled to his country estate at Anathoth. The priest's life was only spared because he had carried the Ark during David's reign and had been a loyal servant of the king. Ayab, Israel's greatest general, knew his time was up and fled to the sanctuary of the Tent of Yahweh, where the Ark resided. Solomon had ordered his execution for the murders of Abner and Amasa a generation earlier when the new king was not yet born. Benaiah, captain of the guard, found Ayab in the tented shrine and cut him down in front of the Ark of the Ten Commandments. As a reward for his loyalty, Benaiah was appointed commander of the whole army and Zadok became high priest of Yahweh in place of the disgraced Abiathar.

Pharaoh's Daughter

Back in Egypt, the army commander Haremheb now sat on the throne of the pharaohs. Following the death of Tutankhamun under suspicious circumstances in 998 BC, his uncle, the vizier and chariot commander Ay, had reigned as Pharaoh for twelve years (998–987 BC).* He was already in his sixties and had not been expected to enjoy a long tenure. To ensure that Egypt would succeed in extracting itself from the disaster of the Amarna heresy, Ay accepted his colleague, General Haremheb, as co-regent in 990 BC.

So, when Solomon was anointed king of Israel in 971 BC, Haremheb had been ruling Egypt for twenty years. During that time this assiduous 'commoner' had applied his not inconsiderable administrative skills to the task of re-establishing order in the Nile valley. New laws had been drafted, the restoration of the temples (begun by Tutankhamun) completed, and the neglected army resupplied – its morale boosted by the appointment of new, able commanders such as Seti, son of Haremheb's old friend and colleague, Pramesse (the later Ramesses I). Even so, Egypt was still in no fit state to mount any concerted military effort to recover the empire – not yet at least. However, this was not going to prevent the astute Haremheb from re-establishing Egyptian influence in the region. He knew it was essential that trade continued to flow into Egypt if Pharaoh's kingdom was to sustain its recovery.

Haremheb was married to Mutnodjmet, daughter of Ay and therefore, through the latter's sister – Queen Tiye – cousin to the brothers Akhenaten and Tutankhamun. Haremheb and Mutnodjmet had been man and wife for

---

* Ay is identified in the New Chronology with Manetho's Acherres II (given 12 years in the Africanus redaction and 8 years in the Eusebius redaction because of his co-regency with Haremheb).

thirty-five years, but the queen had been unable to provide a male heir for the king. Instead Haremheb had been blessed with five daughters, now all of marriageable age. Unlike previous 'blue-blood' pharaohs of the 18th Dynasty who had refused to entertain the idea of an Egyptian royal princess marrying a foreign king, Haremheb was a practical man and quite prepared to make use of his 'assets'. One of his daughters – the lady Sharelli – became the bride of King Nikmaddu of Ugarit in order to secure the allegiance of the most prosperous and influential port on the Levantine coast. But there was a bigger prize for Egypt's ruler to aspire to – renewed peace and stability in southern Canaan.

Ambassadors were despatched to Solomon's recently established court with an offer of the hand of Haremheb's second-eldest daughter in marriage to the Israelite king. In addition Pharaoh proposed, as dowry, the hand-over of the city of Gezer which he had seized whilst campaigning on Tutankhamun's behalf thirty years earlier. The remark-able deal was struck and Solomon accepted the daughter of Haremheb as his principal queen in exchange for politi-cal and military co-operation with Egypt. Pharaoh now had a surrogate to control and secure all the trade routes on his behalf. Political expediency had triumphed over noisy breast-beating and hugely expensive military effort. Egypt had married back into power without having to throw a single spear or discharge a bow.

Solomon too gained from the relationship. Marriage treaties of the time included certain guarantees for both parties of the alliance, including military assistance if either was threatened by external forces. Solomon's father, David, had fought endless wars to secure and extend his kingdom. However, the Bible is almost silent about Solomon's mili-tary exploits – he appears not to have been a warrior-king in his father's mould. How did he protect his large, inherited domain from attack and incursion for forty years? Solomon certainly built up a large force of chariots and developed the concept of the 'rapid reaction force' in the form of his élite brigade of young commandos known as the Nearim ('young braves'). But Solomon also had Egypt on his side through the Haremheb marriage alliance.

The Israelite monarch wisely handed over the town of Beth-Shean, at the eastern end of the Jezreel valley, to an Egyptian garrison, which was stationed there to police and control the eastern entrance into the heart of the Israelite kingdom. Thus the forces of Egypt protected Solomon's realm from marauding Habiru and Aramaeans for as long as the treaty between Egypt and Israel held – and that was many years.

Solomon's reputation as a wise monarch is famously exemplified by the tale of the baby claimed by two prostitutes [1 Kings 3:16–28] in which the king chose to cut the baby in half to test the true mother's love for her child. But Solomon's most astute decision was to marry Pharaoh's daughter and, by accepting an Egyptian military presence within one city in his kingdom, he enjoyed not only pharaonic protection on his eastern borders but also a virtual monopoly in trade heading in and out of his father-in-law's still wealthy kingdom. The two neighbours – Egypt and Israel – prospered under the new arrangement for the first ten years of the Israelite king's reign – the decade when Solomon gained his reputation as the wealthy 'merchant prince' and builder of Yahweh's great temple in Jerusalem.

Pharaoh's daughter (whose name has not been preserved) did not live with her husband, for this was clearly a political marriage. Instead Solomon built a palace for her beside the road to Shechem (now called the Nablus road) to the north of the City of David and Mount Moriah where the sacred temple was to be erected. A short passage in 2 Chronicles explains why.

> Solomon moved Pharaoh's daughter up from the City of David to the palace which he had built for her. 'A woman', he said, 'must not live because of me in the palace of David, king of Israel, for these

buildings to which the ark of Yahweh has come are sacred.' [2 Chronicles 8:11]

In these politically sensitive times it seems that a foreign princess who worshipped foreign gods was not welcome amongst Israel's almost fanatical Yahwists. Labaya and Jonathan had suffered a terrible downfall for not respecting Yahweh, each naming a son after Baal (Mutbaal/Ishbaal and Meribaal). David, on the other hand (and despite his obvious failings), remained loyal to Yahweh – the one true god – and had been blessed with numerous military victories throughout his long reign. Solomon was strongly advised to walk in the footsteps of his father and keep Jerusalem pure. Haremheb's daughter, replete with her large entourage of retainers, was to be kept well away from Yahweh's holy ground.

The surviving vestiges of the Egyptian compound, with its royal residence and tombs, has been unearthed in the area of St Etienne monastery, the Anglican 'Garden Tomb' and the German convent school, just to the north of the Damascus Gate. Numerous artefacts have been found including a serpentine statuette, alabaster vases (late 18th Dynasty), a limestone funerary stela (depicting the deceased offering flowers to the god Seth), a *hotep*-style offering table; at least two palmiform column capitals, a scarab (bearing the motif of a *khepri*-beetle raising the sun-disc within crescent moon), faience rosettes (probably used to adorn a funeral canopy), and a faience ushabti figurine. All this points to the burial of an Egyptian of high status in the area – and just such a tomb has been identified by Professor Gabriel Barkay of Tel Aviv University. The rock-cut rooms are all scaled to the Egyptian royal cubit and the main, innermost burial chamber contains three rock-cut sarcophagi (as opposed to the table-type burial installations generally found elsewhere in Jerusalem).

The date of the tomb is, needless to say, somewhat difficult to ascertain, given that many such tombs were reused over the succeeding centuries. However, there *are* clues to the date of the Egyptian artefacts found in close proximity to the cliff-cut funerary complex of St Etienne (of which the 'Garden Tomb' forms a part). The alabaster vases are stylistically of the late 18th to early 19th Dynasties; the funeral stela shows the faded remains of a figure of Seth (a very unusual feature which suggests an early 19th Dynasty date); and the scarab motif (of *khepri* and rising-sun-with-crescent-moon) is found on several items in Tutankhamun's jewellery collection. But one further object so far not mentioned – a large heart-scarab found in the German school compound – clinches the date. Unfortunately this most important object is now missing, but Israeli archaeologists did see it and have confirmed that the inscription on the scarab 'bore the cartouche of a King Seti'.* All this leads to the conclusion that a high-ranking Egyptian was buried in Jerusalem at around the time Seti I was ruling in Egypt. Seti became Pharaoh in 961 BC (according to the New Chronology, just ten years after Solomon married Haremheb's daughter) and died in 943 BC. This leaves a window for the burial of Solomon's Egyptian queen between the tenth and twenty-eighth years of her husband, but most likely towards the end of this period in around 946 BC when she would have been aged about fifty.

The Building of the Temple

Construction work began on the Temple of Yahweh in Solomon's fourth year (968 BC) – four hundred and eighty years after the Israelites had departed from Egypt in 1447 BC. David's altar standing at the centre of Abdi-Heba's old threshing-floor was cleared and the northern area of Mount Moriah levelled and prepared for the temple foundations.

---

* Discovered by Professor Gabriel Barkay and seen by an Egyptologist colleague who read the cartouche as Seti.

King Ahiram of Tyre continued his support for the Israelite monarchy by agreeing to supply timber for the construction work and a team of specialist stonecutters and craftsmen. Solomon despatched a large force of a thousand labourers to Phoenicia charged with the task of dragging the felled cedar and juniper logs from the Lebanese mountains down to the coast. These workers were replaced after a month with another thousand, and once more, a month later, a third force of a thousand men were sent from the labour levy organised by Adoram. With the rotation complete, the first team were redespatched, having taken two months of rest.

From the port of Byblos the timbers were towed behind Phoenician ships down the coast to Joppa (modern Jaffa) where they were brought ashore and dragged back up into the hills to the city of Jerusalem. At the same time, another huge gang of fifteen thousand was set to work quarrying the local limestone, cutting it into regular ashlar blocks and transporting the fashioned stones up to the Temple Mount for assembly. The dressing of the stones and timber was completed by the skilled artisans of Byblos, sent by King Ahiram to make Yahweh's house into the finest temple in Bronze Age Canaan.

The first block to be placed in situ was the foundation stone (Hebrew *Even-Shetiyah*) upon which the Ark of the Covenant would stand. This large smooth stone still remains today, fifty metres north-west of the Dome of the Rock (Arabic *Kubbet es-Sakhra*), beneath a small dome (supported by eight slender columns) known as the 'Dome of the Tablets' (Arabic *Kubbet el-Alwa*). The tripartite temple followed the basic form of the old tented tabernacle of the Ark which Moses had built beneath Mount Horeb – but on double the scale. The alignment of Yahweh's sanctuary was east/west, with the *debir* (holy of holies) in the west and the *ulam* (entrance portico) to the *hekal* (cella or hall) facing due east towards the rising sun.

During the United Monarchy era (and later) Yahweh-worship involved a number of solar elements. Yahweh was 'the light'. Sacred sites (such as the high place at Geba/ Gibeah and the Jerusalem temple) faced towards sunrise. The famous Israelite cult stand from Taanach depicts a winged sun-disc over a bull, thus confirming to many scholars' satisfaction Yahweh's solar affinities. In many ways the Yahwism of David and Solomon's time was akin to the Atenism of Akhenaten's Amarna age. Given that the two eras co-existed near the beginning of the tenth century (in the New Chronology revision), this may be no coincidence. The parallels which scholars have noted between Akhenaten's 'Hymn to the Aten' and David's Psalm 104 may thus be explained as a direct borrowing by the young king David from his senior contemporary, the religious reformer and Egypt's first monotheist – Pharaoh Akhenaten.

Many of the furnishings for Yahweh's temple were fashioned of bronze and it has often been wondered where copper ore, in such large quantities, was sourced. Initially it was believed to have come from the copper mines at Timnah in the southern Arabah (not far from the Gulf of Akaba) – which is why the site acquired the name 'King Solomon's Mines'. However, archaeological excavations undertaken by Professor Beno Rothenberg in the 1960s and 70s revealed that the mines were active during the Egyptian New Kingdom – specifically during the 19th and 20th Dynasties (ending soon after Ramesses V) and not later. Of course, in the conventional chronology, Solomon reigned several centuries after the Timna mines fell into disuse. So, according to modern scholarship, 'King Solomon's Mines' were nothing of the kind. However, the New Chronology now places Solomon at the same time as Seti I and Ramesses II of the early 19th Dynasty when mining activity at Timna was at its peak. And so 'King Solomon's Mines' have been reinstated as King Solomon's mines, providing the copper ore for the decoration of the Temple of Yahweh in Jerusalem with the support of Egyptian officials administering the mining operation.

Hymn to the Aten	Psalm 104
(a) You (Aten) appear, beautiful on the horizon of heaven, you living sun-disc, the beginning of life! When you rise on the eastern horizon, you fill every land with your beauty.	(a) ... Yahweh, my God, how great you are! Clothed in majesty and splendour, wearing the light as a robe! [Lines 1–2] (This is a clear reference to Yahweh's solar aspect.)
(b) When you set in the western horizon, the land is in darkness, in the manner of death. ... Every lion comes forth from his den ...	(b) You bring on darkness and night falls, when all the forest beasts roam around. Young lions roar for their prey, ... [Lines 20–21]
(c) At daybreak, when you arise on the horizon, when you shine as the sun-disc by day, ... The (people of the) Two Lands are in festivity every day, awake and standing upon (their) feet, ... Throughout the world they do their work.	(c) The sun rises and away they (the forest beasts) steal, back to their lairs to lie down; and man goes out to work – to labour until evening falls. [Lines 22–23]
(d) The ships are sailing north, and south as well, ... your rays are in the midst of the great green sea.	(d) Then there is the sea with its vast expanses, teeming with its countless creatures, ... there ships pass to and fro, ... [Lines 25–26]
(e) How manifold it is, that which you have made! ... You created the world according to your desire ... all men, cattle and wild beast, whatever is on earth, going upon (its) feet and what is on high, flying with its wings.	(e) How countless are your works, Yahweh, all of them made so wisely! The earth is full of your creatures. [Line 24]
(f) You set every man in his place, you provide their needs. Everyone has his food and his time of life is reckoned.	(f) They all depend upon you, to feed them when they need it. You provide the food they (the people) gather. Your open hand gives them their fill. [Lines 27–28]
(g) For you have established a Nile in heaven, so that it may come down for them and make waves upon the hills.	(g) You fixed the earth on its foundations. For ever and ever it shall not be shaken. You covered it with the (watery) deep like a garment, the waters overtopping the hills. [Lines 5–6]

Solomon's Palace

With the temple complete in Solomon's eleventh year, building efforts turned to a royal palace in the City of David. This too was constructed of fine ashlar blocks and Lebanese timber. Like the temple court and all large public buildings of the time (Late Bronze II-A) the construction technique took cognisance of the earthquakes which were so prevalent in the Middle East. Cut-stone blocks were laid in their foundation trenches to a height of three tiers, at which point cedar beams were laid on top of the third course, flush with the inside and outside faces of the wall. The inner cavity between the narrow beams was then filled with gravel before the fourth course of stones was laid upon the beams. This complex Phoenician building technique, also found at Megiddo (Stratum VIII) and in the Late Bronze Age palace of Nikmaddu at Ugarit, was designed to absorb vibrations and shock waves rising up from the foundations during an earth tremor.

The king's palace and the private residence of Pharaoh's daughter took thirteen years to build, with the royal building programme finally complete in 948 BC. The large labour force was then turned to other tasks. Part was retained in Jerusalem to repair and extend the Millo, whilst other teams were despatched to Gezer, Megiddo and Hazor to build gateways and royal residences for the king's visits to different parts of the realm.

Although the Solomonic buildings in Jerusalem still lie buried beneath modern occupation and under the paving stones of the Temple Mount, we can still inspect a fine example of the king's impressive architecture at Megiddo, where the LB II-A gate of Stratum VIII stands, in some places, to a height of over three metres and preserves the three-course-plus-cedar-beam construction. That this technique was introduced into Israel by the Phoenicians is clearly demonstrated by a famous excavation which took place at Ras Shamra on the coast of Syria, just north of the city of Latakia. In the 1950s, French archaeologist Claude Schaeffer excavated the magnificent Late Bronze Age palace of King Nikmaddu of Ugarit (the ancient name of Tell Ras Shamra) where just such building techniques were copiously employed. According to the Amarna letters, Nikmaddu was a contemporary of Akhenaten and therefore of David. As I have suggested, he also married a daughter of Haremheb. This huge royal residence – with its ashlar and cedar beam construction – is the very palace which had been partially burnt down following the evil omen of the near-sunset solar eclipse in 1012 BC.

A New Power in Egypt

In 946 BC (Solomon's 26th year on the throne) his Egyptian queen died and was buried in her tomb in the grounds of what is now the monastery of ST ETIENNE. Israel's relationship with Egypt continued to be cordial, even though a new dynasty of pharaohs had come to the throne in Memphis in 962 BC.

Haremheb had taken his colleague, the vizier Pramesse, as co-regent. The old army general from Avaris was of King Haremheb's generation, distantly descended from the Hyksos rulers of the 17TH DYNASTY. Both pharaohs were nearing the ends of their lives. The senior regent had ruled Egypt for twenty-nine years but had failed to produce a male heir. Pramesse – now crowned as Menpehtire Ramesses I – was chosen precisely because he had a vigorous son in his mid-thirties to succeed him and therefore strengthen the Egyptian throne. Seti, son of Ramesses I, had been raised at Avaris in the ways of the military. He was the right man to lead the effort to regain the empire by force and push back the southerly advance of the Hittite empire into Canaan.

When Tutankhamun had died, thirty-five years earlier in 998 BC, his widow Queen Ankhesenamun had sought to secure a marriage alliance with the Hittite emperor,

Shuppiluliuma I, ruling in Anatolia. She was desperately seeking to avoid a forced marriage to her hated uncle Ay, already in his fifties and suspected of involvement in the sudden death of her husband in a chariot accident. If Ankhesenamun were to fail to find a suitable husband before the burial of Tutankhamun (following the seventy days of mummification) then Ay would perform the 'Opening of the Mouth' ceremony on the mummy of the outgoing pharaoh and therefore take the throne as the next in line of succession. Ankhesenamun had sent letters to Shuppiluliuma whilst he was in the act of besieging the city of Carchemish on the Euphrates river during his thirty-second regnal year (999 BC). After some hesitation the Hittite king agreed to the Egyptian queen's offer and sent his son Prince Zananza south to Egypt to become Ankhesenamun's husband and the next pharaoh. This would have been an astonishing alliance between the ancient world's two greatest powers of the day, but Ay was not ready to see his ambitions thwarted. Zananza was assassinated as he crossed the Egyptian border at the frontier post of Zile.

When Shuppiluliuma heard of the evil which had befallen his son, he was incandescent with rage. Egypt would not go unpunished for its deceit. From this moment on, as Pharaoh Ay sat upon the throne with his reluctant new bride beside him, the Hittite empire was at total war with Egypt – a war which would last seventy-five years and only end with another, this time successful, marriage between an Egyptian king and a Hittite princess.

King Seti I had been carefully groomed to take on the Hittite menace from the north. He now had a rejuvenated army of two thousand chariots and thirty thousand infantry to command, and a mission to seize back territory lost in the days of the Amarna heresy. Whilst Seti I and Solomon reigned as neighbouring powers, the alliance between Israel and Egypt, established in the time of King David, was maintained.

In Seti's first year he was actively undertaking his treaty

obligations by sending troops to the eastern Jezreel around Beth-Shean and the upper Jordan valley to quell disturbances instigated by the town of Hamath (a local Hamath, not the city of Hamath on the Orontes in Syria). The details of the Egyptian expedition are recorded on two stelae found at Beth-Shean dated to Seti's early reign. Pharaoh's men struck at Habiru rebels in the north around Lake Kinneret (the Sea of Galilee) and around Rehob in the Jordan valley (opposite the city of Pella which was also involved in the troubles). The Egyptian troops, having arrived in the region, quickly seized the rebellious towns 'within a single day'. The armies of Amun (Thebes) and Seth (Avaris) took Hamath and YANOAM respectively, whilst the division of Re (Heliopolis) occupied Beth-Shean. Because of this incident, Solomon consented to an Egyptian garrison remaining stationed at Beth-Shean to police his northern border and protect the lucrative trade routes running through the Jezreel valley.

In Seti's second year the Egyptian army headed up the Via Maris once more, through Solomon's territory in the Jezreel, and on into the Bekaa valley. A second force was despatched to Simyra by sea, from where it marched east through the Homs-Tripoli gap to meet the main force coming up from the south. In a single campaign the Egyptian pharaoh managed to push the Hittites out of southern Syria and seize Kadesh-on-the-Orontes (Kinza), where the fragment of a stela bearing Seti's cartouche has been unearthed. For a while at least Egypt was back in charge of Aziru's old stamping ground.

Solomon, in turn, benefited from the restoration of Egyptian power in the region and the stability which this provided for the trading networks. He had his Phoenician allies in Tyre, Sidon and Byblos; he was also successfully acting as middleman for Egypt in the acquisition of horses from the north and incense from Arabia. And it is to the latter that we shall now turn as a large camel train arrives at the gates of Jerusalem bringing exotic spices, myrrh, frankincense … and its most precious cargo – the beautiful Arabian Queen of Sheba.

Queen of Sheba

With Solomon's wealth growing with every year he was able to look much further afield for exotic produce to adorn his kingdom or trade-on to other states. Phoenician ships had been plying their trade up and down the eastern Mediterranean seaboard and out into the islands of the Aegean and Crete for centuries, but the Red Sea had seen little activity since the days of the sons of Ham on their migration to Africa from Mesopotamia. Yet it was from southern Arabia and the land of Poene (Punt) on the African continent that much of the ancient world's incense and exotic, perfumed woods originated. Egypt occasionally ventured south along the west coast of the Red Sea on trading missions to Poene, but all the produce of these rare trips remained in Egypt and was not exported into the Levant. Solomon's Israel, with access to the Gulf of Akaba, was the only major state in Canaan in a position to exploit this profitable gap in the market.

Representatives of the king of Jerusalem were already active in the southern Arabah, supervising the mining activity at the copper mines of Timnah in co-operation with Egypt. It was therefore only a short step to opening up a new southern trade route. Solomon decided to build a harbour just a short distance away from Timnah at Ezion-Geber (near modern Eilat) at the head of the gulf of Akaba. There he had a fleet of three ships constructed using surplus Lebanese timber from the temple and palace building projects which was transported down into the Arabah from Jerusalem. King Ahiram (now in his thirty-third year on the throne of Tyre) provided skilled navigators for the expedition which set out in 947 BC for the land of Ophir.

For the first two weeks the Israelite fleet hugged the west coast of the Red Sea, heading for the main entrepôt of Poene in what is today's north African state of Eritrea. Having exchanged goods there and collected much-needed information on the currents beyond the Bab el-Mandeb strait, the ships sailed out into the Arabian Sea and continued following the coast around the Horn of Africa before swinging south. A month later they had reached the land of Ophir (modern Mozambique) where the merchants and representatives of the king stayed for a year, overseeing trading negotiations with the local tribes and acquiring gold from the rich deposits of the region. Some of the Israelites married the daughters of tribal chieftains and remained behind as the progenitors of new tribes following in the ways of Yahweh. Recent DNA analysis of the Lemba tribe (scattered throughout Zimbabwe, Mozambique and northeast South Africa) has shown that they are descendants of the Levite priestly line – something that they have always claimed but nobody believed simply because they are black-skinned, typically Negroid people. It is an astonishing thing to witness the Lemba as they still today continue to follow Judaic religious practices in their tribal rituals.

The fleet eventually set off on its long return journey carrying four hundred and twenty talents of gold and a myriad of other products from southern Africa, including hundreds of elephant ivory tusks. As they·sailed up the eastern side of the Red Sea, the trading mission briefly harboured on the coast of Sheba (ancient Saba in Yemen). The land of Sheba had grown prosperous on the Arabian frankincense and myrrh trade, through its cultivation of incense trees growing on man-made terraces clinging to the humid westerly slopes of the Red Sea mountains. The queen of Sheba, having observed the richly cargoed ships of Solomon's trading mission to Ophir, realised that here was a man she might be able to do business with to their mutual benefit. She could send the sweet-smelling produce of her kingdom (so much valued for Canaan's temple rituals) by camel train to Israel, and Solomon could then disperse that produce throughout the Levant via his already extensive and growing trading network. As Solomon's fleet departed on the final leg home to Ezion-Geber, Queen Nikulis of Sheba's female ruling dynasty (the Nikaulis of Josephus, the Bilkis of Arabian tradition and the Ethiopian Makkedah) made plans to visit her potential business partner in his splendid new capital.

In 945 BC (the year following the death of Pharaoh's daughter) the huge camel train, bringing Arabia's beautiful queen and heavily laden with gifts of spices, incense, gold and precious stones from the desert mountains, arrived at the gates of Jerusalem. Nikulis was greatly impressed by her host's civilised court with its high officials, pomp and religious ceremony. She was struck by the magnificent temple with its lavish decoration and mysterious, invisible god. In King Solomon she had found the perfect partner for her trading ambitions but also a partner in other ways as well. The queen stayed in Jerusalem for three years before returning to her desert homeland. Nikulis never saw her friend and ally again but carried something precious back to Sheba which would remind her of Solomon for the rest of her days.

Nikulis gave birth to a baby boy whom she named Menelik. He became the founder of a new royal line which, for millennia, has continued to claim descent from the Solomonic throne. Many cultural contacts with ancient Israel remain to this day, including the Ethiopian Falasha Jews and the tradition that the ancient city of Aksum has the Ark of the Covenant in its possession. The last of Menelik's royal line (or so it is claimed) was Haile Selassie ('mighty of the trinity', 1892–1975), emperor of Ethiopia and patron saint of the Rastafarian faith (his pre-coronation name being Ras ('prince') Tafari).

Solomon's Wealth

Over the first two decades of his forty-year reign, King Solomon of Jerusalem became one of the wealthier rulers in the Levant – on a par with the king of Ugarit or Israel's erstwhile ally the king of Tyre. The outlying cities of the kingdom – places such as Megiddo, Gezer and Hazor – became major trading centres, acting as conduits for exotic goods heading for the royal court in the capital. A toll was levied on Arabian trade coming through Israelite territory; regional governors despatched local goods to the state's tax office. All in all Solomon received over six hundred talents of gold each year – or so 1 Kings 10:14 informs us. With such wealth, the king was able to lavish extravagant gifts upon Yahweh's temple on Mount Moriah and embellish the royal palace in the City of David. Two hundred large shields and three hundred smaller shields of beaten gold were crafted to adorn the 'House of the Forest of Lebanon' (i.e. the palace). An ivory throne was carved for the king's audience hall, elaborately decorated with winged lions (sphinxes) on either side. Just such a throne appears on the famous ivory from the palace of Stratum VIII at Megiddo which, in the New Chronology, is dated to the Solomonic era. The ivory shows a king seated upon a throne, flanked by winged sphinxes, receiving a drinking cup from his queen. The queen wears a flat-topped crown similar to those worn by the royal ladies of the Amarna court and she carries an Egyptian lotus flower in her hand. Behind her a singer of psalms plays his lyre. The king is surrounded by doves – the symbol of peace.

The fleet at Ezion-Geber undertook a mission to Ophir every three years, spending a year and a half away each time. And so Solomon's coffers were replenished with the

29. Line drawing of the Megiddo ivory, showing Solomon and his Egyptian queen (Rockefeller Museum, Jerusalem).

produce of Africa – gold, silver, ivory, scented woods, exotic animal skins, apes and baboons – on a regular basis.

Such wealth enabled the king to build up Israel's military strength from the somewhat rag-bag warrior-based infantry (supplemented by Habiru mercenary fighters) into a professional army with garrisons at the major cities of Gezer, Megiddo and Hazor. These three towns were refortified and provided with stable-yards for a large contingent of chariots and their horse teams. For the first time in Israelite history the chariot played a major part in military tactics and battle strategies. The age of guerrilla warfare – so effective in the Judges period – was over and Israel had become an organised military power just like all the other major states of the region. As we have seen, Solomon had treaty obligations with both Egypt and Phoenicia which required the provision of trained army contingents in any conflict that members of the coalition were involved in.

As we have also seen, Solomon instituted a new military academy for the training of young Israelite warriors. These recruits were assembled into an élite force, somewhat akin to a modern brigade of special forces or commandos. This Solomonic contingent of the tripartite alliance was known as the Nearim – the 'brave ones'.

The Battle of Kadesh

In the thirty-third year of Solomon's reign (939 BC), the new pharaoh in Egypt – Ramesses II – marched through Zile and across Sinai, accompanied by the battalions of Amun (Thebes), Re (Heliopolis), Ptah (Memphis) and Seth (Pi-Ramesse/Avaris). The four huge columns, each with five hundred chariots and five thousand men-at-arms, headed north along the Via Maris – half a day's march apart, with the king and his royal guard at the head of the whole army.

Nothing like this had been seen since the days of Thutmose III. Even Ramesses' father, Seti I, had not been able to muster such a fighting machine when he captured Kadesh-on-the-Orontes back from the Hittites in 960 BC. The youthful Ramesses – just nineteen years of age and only five years on the throne – was determined to rid Egypt of the Hittite threat once and for all. For too long the emperors Shuppiluliuma I (1030–993 BC), Murshili II (991–967 BC) and now Muwatali II (966–939 BC) had occupied territory in Amurru which formerly belonged within the Egyptian sphere. Kadesh had slipped back into the hands of the Hittites and their allies. And so Ramesses was on his way to recapture the city, just as his father had done – but this time he would push the Hittites back out of Syria.

As the Egyptian army was marching past Solomonic Megiddo and into the Jezreel valley, the élite Nearim troops of Israel were boarding the Phoenician fleet at Dor – on their way to Sumur (known at this time as 'Simyra of Sysa' after Ramesses' familiar name), three hundred kilometres up the coast. The old treaty obligations (agreed in Haremheb's day) meant that they were required to join Ramesses at Kadesh, just sixty kilometres east of Sumur, by marching through the Homs-Tripoli gap in the Lebanese mountains.

Two weeks later Ramesses and the army of Amun were at the northern end of the Bekaa valley (ancient Amka) and within a day's march from Kadesh. The brigade of Re was at Baalbek, whilst Ptah had only just reached Kamidi (Kamid el-Loz). And Seth was still passing by Mount Hermon at the southern end of the Bekaa. As Ramesses was crossing the ford of the Orontes river south of Shabtuna, he was informed that two Shosu (Bedouin) spies had been captured who, after interrogation, had divulged that the Hittite army was still far to the north at Aleppo frightened to engage the might of Egypt's forces. Ramesses was delighted with the news and pressed on to Kadesh at speed with the brigade of Amun in tow. By nightfall he had set up camp on the west side of the great hill which is Kadesh-on-the-Orontes, its summit ringed by an impressive mud-brick wall. The army of Re would arrive early the following morning, whilst the battalion of Ptah was not far behind them. These would be all the forces Ramesses needed to secure Kadesh without the protection of the Hittite army and its allies. Little did the young pharaoh realise that things would not turn out quite the way he had envisaged when he retired to his tented pavilion that evening.

As is often the case in the fertile Orontes valley, dawn broke with a heavy mist over the landscape. In the early 1990s, when excavating at Tell Nebi Mend (ancient Kadesh) with the Institute of Archaeology (London) mission, I some-times took a moment to stand on the Late Bronze Age ramparts in the early morning and look out over a sea of mist covering the fields. The mound itself appeared like a great island in some Gothic fantasy. But, three thousand years earlier, on the memorable 'Day 10, 3rd month of Shemu' in Year 5 (939 BC) that fantasy landscape would be all too real and deadly for the Egyptian expeditionary force. Ramesses had been woken in the middle of the night to receive the devastating news that, far from being two hundred kilometres away in Aleppo, the Hittites were just on the other side of the city of Kadesh. During the early hours of darkness enemy scouts had been captured by an Egyptian patrol. The stark truth was quickly beaten out of them. The Egyptian king had been duped by the false reports of the Shosu spies. The cunning Hittite emperor, Muwatali, along with three-and-a-half thousand chariots and thirty-seven thousand infantry, was just three kilometres away from the Egyptian camp. Trumpets were sounded to call the men to arms and a horseback rider sent south to summon the division of Re quickly to the field of battle – but it was too late.

Muwatali's chariots had moved stealthily through the darkness and had crossed the Orontes river south of Kadesh. By dawn they were waiting in the mist ready to cut Ramesses off from the rest of his army. Appearing from the east out of the morning light they crashed into the strung-out column of the army of Re which had been marching since before dawn to meet up with Ramesses. The soldiers of Re were completely taken by surprise. Their ranks immediately disintegrated. The survivors of the first onslaught were scattered to all corners as the Hittite chariots swung northwards to attack the Egyptian camp with the army of Amun still mustering in confusion a kilometre to the north. Disaster was only seconds away … but then Ramesses did a remarkable thing. Instead of retreating to safety, leaving his men to fight a rearguard action in his defence, the brave young son of Seti leapt into his chariot and charged headlong into the Hittite phalanx. Time and again he drove his golden chariot into the mellée, creating havoc and confusion amongst the enemy. Ramesses could have been killed on any one of his reckless sorties but his undoubted courage brought him luck. He later claimed divine intervention from the great god Amun of Karnak who had acted as his protector.

All this foolhardy bravery would have been to no avail if it had not been for the timely arrival of Solomon's Nearim troops. Marching in good order from Simyra overnight, they took the Hittite forces by complete surprise as their chariots too appeared out of the blue – this time from the west.

The tables had been turned. The Israelite Nearim infantry dragged the Hittites and their Amorite allies from their chariots, trapped in the mellée of battle, just as Barak had done to Sisera's charioteers three centuries earlier. The fight had turned decisively in Ramesses' favour. With the Hittite advance checked, the troops of Re regrouped and belatedly advanced to protect their valiant king.

The Hittite charge had ground to a halt and, within three hours, their surprise attack had been turned into their own rout. The king of Aleppo, commander of the Hittite chariots, ordered the retreat. The remnant of Hatti's pride were driven back towards the Orontes, whereupon the situation got even worse for them. Muwatali had kept his huge infantry force in reserve, stationed on the east bank of the river. Instead of committing them to the attack in support of the chariots, they had remained rooted to the spot. Now, as Muwatali's chariots attempted to cross the Orontes back to safety, they found their escape blocked by their own massed ranks of infantry. Men and horses were trapped in the swirling waters as they were picked off by Egyptian archers. The ruler of Aleppo was taken from the water, half dead. Several Amorite chieftains never made it across the river and the best of Hatti's chariot commanders were killed.

By this time the army of Ptah had arrived on the scene. Egypt's troop levels had risen to thirteen thousand, plus the five thousand Nearim from Israel. The two armies held their respective banks of the Orontes as the battle continued into a second day. But eventually it was realised that Hatti and Egypt had fought themselves into a bloody stalemate. Muwatali knew that he had suffered considerable losses and that Ramesses would claim a victory. Yet he also knew that the Egyptians could not remain in Syria forever. They would soon have to retreat back into Canaan, leaving Hatti holding on to its Amorite territories. Ramesses had come to take back Kadesh and push Muwatali out of Syria. He had undoubtedly failed in both ambitions and trouble was bound to surface amongst the Egyptian dependencies once the news was out that Pharaoh had returned to Egypt empty-handed.

Over the next two years a major revolt gradually developed against Egyptian rule in Canaan. Ramesses' perceived military failure left Egypt vulnerable to Hittite and Aramaean pressure from the north. The city-states on the fringes of Egyptian control were the first to break away. But even the cities of Galilee and the Jezreel were soon refusing to pay their dues as a consequence of pressure from the Aramaeans led by King Rezon (992–937 BC) of Damascus. As Egypt's ally and agent, Solomon's position was seriously undermined. Discontent was rife throughout the land.

Internal Revolt

Having spent two decades building the temple and royal palaces in Jerusalem, the wealthy Israelite monarch had not as yet fulfilled his ambitions. Solomon did not reduce the workload placed upon his own people. If anything the forced labour had become worse as new building projects were inaugurated across the kingdom. Gezer, Megiddo and Hazor were adorned with new gates, royal palaces and governors' residences. The Millo in Jerusalem was vastly extended with a major project to link the City of David with the temple mount by means of broad terraces. Years went by, and yet the work did not pause. The people were becoming tired and angered by their heavy burdens.

Jeroboam the son of Nebat, the supervisor of the Millo work-gang, was a man from the tribe of Ephraim. He was a strong, energetic nobleman and the people began to see him as a leader. Within five years he had become a major political figure in Israel and a focus for the general movement against Solomon's autocratic and indulgent rule. The prophet AHIJAH of Shiloh had also taken against Solomon for erecting shrines to Chemosh (the Moabite god) and Milcom (the god of the Ammonites) in honour of his many foreign wives. The king had built these high places for astute political reasons, in order to ensure that his various marriage alliances were secured by good reports from the foreign queens back to their homelands. But the priests of Yahweh were enraged by this officially sanctioned worship of foreign deities on Israelite soil. Led by Ahijah, they began to stir the population to revolt, using Jeroboam as their rallying point.

In the last decade of Solomon's reign the kingdom had begun to fall apart. Two dangerous enemies had risen up on Israel's eastern and northern borders. King Hadad the Edomite incited the people of Transjordan to overthrow Israelite rule in revenge for Israel's invasion of his land. During the Edomite war of 996 BC, David's general, Ayab, had spent six months on a campaign of terror, slaughtering most of Edom's population as he went from settlement to settlement. The royal family managed to flee south into Egypt, where the young Hadad was offered sanctuary by Pharaoh Ay. During the succeeding reign of Haremheb, the Edomite king-in-exile had become a favourite of the Egyptian court and had even married the sister of Queen Mutnodjmet. The Bible calls Pharaoh's wife 'Tahpenes', but this is simply a Hebraising of the Egyptian phrase *ta-pa-nisu* ('the one of the king') – in other words the chief wife of Haremheb. When David had subsequently died and Ayab had been killed by Solomon's men, Hadad begged Pharaoh to allow him to return home to Edom so that he could rebuild his ravaged nation. Thirty years later, the kingdom of Edom was once more strong enough to challenge Israelite domination of its territory. Now, in this time of crisis and uncertainty, Hadad set about destabilising Solomon's eastern border.

Towards the Syrian north, a successor to Aziru had also risen up. In 992 BC Rezon, son of Eliada, had seized Damascus and killed Aziru's son, Du-Teshub (the biblical Ben-Hadad I).* His marauding bands of Aramaean raiders had plundered and pillaged the northern tribal settlements for thirteen years until they were finally taken out by David's forces in 980 BC. But now, four decades later, Rezon returned to the conflict, sensing that Solomon had become weakened by Ramesses' failure at Kadesh. In 938 BC he attacked the Israelite royal city of Hazor, burning the palace to the ground and mutilating the Egyptianised statues which decorated the royal apartments, smashing off their heads and limbs.

The remains of this grand Solomonic edifice were discovered recently by Amnon Ben-Tor, current excavator

---

* Du-Teshub is probably a Mischname or mixed-name formed from the Sumerian logogram *dumu* ('son') and the Hurrian weather-god, *Teshub*; Ben-Hadad is composed of Hebrew *ben* ('son') and the Syrian weather-god, *Hadad*. Both names therefore mean 'son of the weather-god'.

of Hazor. The large mudbrick residence, with its open courts, columned entrances and inner halls, materially illustrates the true status of Israel's greatest builder-king. But Ben-Tor's excavation of this magnificent Late Bronze Age building has also revealed Rezon's wanton destruction of the Stratum XIII royal compound in Area A of the upper tell. The archaeological remains show unambiguous signs of an all-encompassing fire which charred the bricks and cracked the basalt steps leading into the court.

It had once been thought that the burning of Stratum XIII at Hazor was the work of Joshua when he slaughtered the population and burnt Jabin's city in *c.* 1200 BC (conventional dating). But Ben-Tor has realised from the pottery associated with his palace destruction that the date of Hazor's Late Bronze Age fall was somewhat earlier – around the time of the early 19th Dynasty (Seti I or early Ramesses II) at around 1280 BC (again conventional dating). Thus, in the orthodox scheme, which places the Conquest at the end of the thirteenth century (i.e. towards the end of the 19th Dynasty), Hazor had already been destroyed nearly a century before Joshua and the Israelites are supposed to have arrived in the region. Rather like the Jericho situation, there was no flourishing Hazor – 'the head of all those kingdoms' – for Joshua to destroy when the Israelites arrived at the beginning of the Iron Age.

In the New Chronology we are in the closing years of Solomon's reign and the time of Rezon's raids into Galilee (*c.* 938 BC). The archaeological story from Hazor paints a disturbing picture of wanton destruction in the north whilst the old king was caught up in self-aggrandising building projects in the state capital. Solomon was clearly losing his grip on the kingdom carved out by his father, the warrior-king David.

All these troubles were causing considerable tension within the heartland of the Israelite state. The tribal population was being forced to build the trappings of empire whilst the kingdom – still only seventy years in existence – was beginning to disintegrate at the edges. Through ordinary eyes, nothing made sense in Solomon's Israelite Camelot.

Ahijah and the priests stirred up resentment within the forced-labour corvées. They incited the charismatic Jeroboam to lead the challenge against Solomon's authority and the country rose up in fully fledged revolt. The king's Nearim troops were sent into action and quickly snuffed out the uprising – but they failed to capture Jeroboam. The leader of the popular uprising fled to the Mediterranean coast and sailed to Egypt where, like Hadad the Edomite before him, he was given political refuge.

Jeroboam arrived at Ramesses II's court at Pi-Ramesse (Avaris) in the spring of 937 BC just as Pharaoh was preparing to march out of Egypt on a mission to put an end to the general disorder in his northern empire. Ramesses, now in his seventh year, was in no mood to appease his faltering Israelite ally by returning Jeroboam for summary execution. The fact that Solomon's élite troops had saved the young Pharaoh's bacon at Kadesh three years earlier weighed for little in the broader picture of regional instability and revolt currently concerning the Egyptian military strategists. Indeed, Ramesses had come to perceive that Jerusalem and its pretentious king were a part of the problem. The score-settling which was now going on by all those nations massacred and oppressed in David's time lay at the heart of the troubles. Pharaoh therefore saw the arrival of a popular Israelite leader in opposition to Solomon as a potential opportunity to split the Israelite kingdom, leaving Jerusalem isolated. But that would have to await the day when the Israelite king passed away and the battle for the succession could begin.

Part Five

The Two
Kingdoms

ϕWᒐW

Chapter Sixteen

SCHISM

(1 Kings 12:1 to 2 Kings 16:34 and 2 Chronicles 10:1 to
2 Chronicles 16:14)

*Shishak and Jeroboam – The Plundering of Solomon's
Temple – Asa of Judah – The House of Omri and Ahab
– 19th Dynasty Collapse in Egypt – The End of the
Bronze Age*

With the death of Solomon, we now enter a new era
in Israelite history, which scholars have dubbed
the 'Divided Monarchy period', when the unified
state of Israel was suddenly split into two kingdoms at the
'Schism' of 931 BC. For the following two centuries the
Northern Kingdom of Israel (representing ten of the twelve
tribes) was ruled over by kings based at the royal cities of
Tirzah and Samaria, before the latter was captured by the
Assyrians in 722 BC and the people deported to Mesopotamia. The Southern Kingdom of Judah continued to
exist for another one hundred and thirty-five years before
Jerusalem was sacked by Nebuchadrezzar II in 587 BC
and its population exiled to Babylon.

Our story of this complex political era begins with the
Schism and the arrival upon the scene of the first Egyptian
pharaoh to be specifically named in the Bible.

> And so it happened that in the fifth year of King Rehoboam, Shishak king of Egypt advanced on Jerusalem and carried off all the treasures of the Temple of Yahweh and the treasures of the royal palace. He took everything away, including all the golden shields which Solomon had made. [1 Kings 14:25–26]

However, the biblical name given to this Egyptian king has led to a far-reaching misunderstanding amongst scholars of the ancient world which, in my opinion, lies at the heart of all the problems we hear about concerning the historicity of the biblical narrative. The lack of a comprehensive and satisfying synthesis between Levantine archaeology and the Old Testament story – highlighted in so many books and television documentaries – all comes down, in the end, to the misidentification of a single historical character – the Egyptian pharaoh who plundered the treasures from the Temple of Solomon in Jerusalem.

Pharaoh Shishak

For the last one hundred and seventy years the Egyptian king the Bible calls Shishak has been identified with the founder of the 22nd Dynasty – Hedjkheperre Shoshenk I. This has been primarily on the basis of the similarity of name and the fact that Shoshenk did indeed record a campaign into Canaan on the walls of the temple of Karnak in Thebes. However, Dr John Bimson has successfully demonstrated that Shoshenk's military activities in no way match the activities of Shishak as described in 1 Kings 14:25–26 and 2 Chronicles 12:2–9.

It is clear from the Karnak Bubastite Portal inscription that Shoshenk campaigned against the kingdom of Israel in the north whilst the biblical Shishak, as an ally of Israel, attacked the kingdom of Judah in the south. Shoshenk marched north and past Jerusalem whilst Shishak besieged the city and then plundered the Temple of Solomon of its treasures. Shoshenk did not record the name of Jerusalem in the city-list of his campaign – even though he is supposed to have plundered it in the guise of the biblical Shishak in 927 BC according to the biblical chronology.

Moreover, a statue fragment of Pharaoh Shoshenk I was found at Byblos, bearing the name of the Byblite ruler Abibaal alongside the Egyptian royal cartouche. According to the annals of Tiglath-pileser III of Assyria (744–727 BC), Abibaal's third-generation successor – Shipitbaal (Assyrian *Shibitibiili*) – was ruling in Byblos in 737 BC. Three to four generations earlier than this fixed historical date takes us back to 820 BC, at the earliest, for Abibaal and therefore Shoshenk I. Thus Pharaoh Shoshenk, ruling at the end of the ninth century BC, can hardly be one and the same as the biblical king Shishak who plundered the Jerusalem temple in the last quarter of the tenth century BC (not unless he reigned for a hundred years that is!).

There is no getting away from it. Shoshenk I cannot be identified as the Bible's Egyptian 'king Shishak', plunderer of Solomon's temple. According to the New Chronology, the real historical figure behind Shishak is none other than Ramesses II, whose hypocoristicon – Sysa (Semiticised as Shysha) – was common currency both in Egypt amongst the general population and in Canaan where towns such as Sumur (Egyptian *Simyra*) were renamed '(Town/Fortress X) of Sysa' after this most famous of warrior-kings.

Ramesses II was perhaps the greatest of the Egyptian pharaohs – conqueror of many lands and builder of some of Egypt's greatest monuments. In the later Classical world he was regarded as the ancient world's most celebrated king. The Greeks and Romans called him Sesoosis or Sesostris after his popular name, Sysa. Egyptologists often paint him as an arrogant ruler whose sole purpose in life was self-aggrandisement. Biblical historians, too, have given him a bad press as the villain of the Exodus – the stubborn pharaoh 'who would not let the people go'. However,

Pharaoh 'Sysa' must be seen in the context of an ancient world in which great men ruled empires through their ambition and will. In ancient times individual men could really change the world into which they were born. Ramesses the Great was one of those men and he made sure that history would remember his deeds by recording them on every surface of the monuments he erected throughout Egypt. There he labelled his battle-scenes with his formal names and titles – Usermaatre-setepenre Ramesses-meriamun (pronounced something like Washmuaria-shatapnaria Riamashesha-miamana), but the people simply knew him as Sysa, by which he passed into legend as Sesoosis and Sesostris.

Peter van der Veen has proposed that Sysa would have been Semiticised as Shysha, where the Egyptian *s* has been rendered into Hebrew *sh* (*shin*). This was a common practice with Akkadian (where the name Ramesses is written as Riamashesha), but is also attested in Hebrew. For example, the Egyptian hypocoristicon Mose (the traditional name of the hero of the Exodus) becomes Moshe in Hebrew; likewise the coastal city of Ashkelon in Philistia takes its modern name from the Bible – but the Egyptians referred to it as Askelan. So we can reasonably propose that Egyptian Sysa was pronounced Shysha in Semitic-speaking Canaan. Peter van der Veen has also explained the extra *k* (*qoph*) in the biblical name Shishak as the Hebraising of a foreign name (something fairly common in the Bible) to turn the pharaoh's popular hypocoristicon into a Hebrew word originating from the verb *shakak* ('to fall upon [the spoils]', Akkadian *shakaku*). Thus the biblical writer turns the short form of the name Ramesses (Shysha) into the word 'plunderer' (Shyshak) in order to characterise the deed done to Jerusalem by the Egyptian king. When the prophet Jeremiah foretells the capture of Babylon by the Persian king Cyrus II in 539 BC, he refers to the city as 'Sheshak' because Babylon, under its king Nebuchadrezzar II, had plundered and destroyed the capital of Judah in 587 BC.

> What! Has Sheshak (i.e. Babylon) been seized and
> conquered – the pride of the whole world? [Jerem-
> iah 51:41]

Two plunderers of Jerusalem, three hundred and forty years
apart – and both referred to as Shishak/Sheshak? Could
this really just be a coincidence?*

Ramesses – Plunderer of Jerusalem

It is the seventeenth year of Ramesses II's rule in Egypt.
The date is 927 BC and twelve years have passed since the
near disaster at the battle of Kadesh. In that time Egypt's
Asiatic empire had been under severe pressure from the
northern Hittite-Aramaean confederacy. The city-state
rulers of southern Canaan were uneasy, sensing a political
change in the wind. In Ramesses' seventh year (Year 35 of
Solomon) there had been a major revolt in the region
against Egyptian rule. The pharaoh had immediately campaigned to crush the rebellion and put down his wayward
vassals, continuing the fight into his eighth year. He then
inaugurated a programme of foreign policy reform to make
the Egyptian presence in the region more tangible. The
vassal rulers were no longer going to be Egypt's sole eyes
and ears within the northern empire. Ramesses established
military governors in the major strategic cities of Gaza (on
the southern coastal plain), Beth-Shean (in the Jezreel
valley), Zarethan (Tell es-Saidiyeh in the Jordan valley),
Kamidi (Kamid el-Loz in the Bekaa valley) and Simyra

---

* It must be noted that the verb *shakak* (Hebrew *shqq* – 'to plunder') is
written with two qophs whereas the cryptogram Sheshak (based on AT-
BaSH word-play) of Jeremiah 25:26 & 51:41 is written with a kaph and
(as proposed by M. Garsiel) may therefore derive from the verb *shakak*
(Hebrew *shkk* – 'to abate'). On the other hand, F. Clancy (in *JSOT* 86
(1999)) proposes to read the Sheshak of Jeremiah as 'destroyer'. The
names of the two sackers of Jerusalem – Egyptian and Babylonian – are
probably linked simply by paranomasy or extended alliteration.

(Tell Kazel on the Phoenician coastal plain), protected by garrisons. But troubles amongst the vassals continued to haunt the Egyptian king. Not least of his concerns was the situation in Israel, where his previously reliable political agent, Solomon, was getting old and, perhaps more significantly, losing his grip on political power over the Israelite vassal states conquered by David a half century earlier.

For years the Aramaeans of Damascus, under King Rezon (992–937 BC), had been raiding the Galilee region and had even sacked the Israelite royal city of Hazor. The Transjordanian kingdoms had also broken away from Solomon's hegemony, refusing to pay tribute. Nevertheless Solomon continued to expend his country's resources on major royal building programmes rather than military efforts to secure the northern and eastern territories for his Egyptian masters. So, in 937 BC, when the articulate and charismatic Jeroboam turned up at Pharaoh's court as a refugee from Solomon's oppressive regime, Ramesses began to see him as a natural successor to Israel's throne. A vassal who would remain loyal to Egypt and perhaps help stabilise the situation – at least in the north where he retained much of his political support amongst the tribes. Jeroboam quickly convinced the ruler of Israel's most powerful neighbour and ally that he would be the man to restore the confidence of the people and thus strengthen Pharaoh's control over the region.

When Solomon died in 931 BC, Ramesses despatched Jeroboam with Egyptian support to challenge for the succession. A great tribal council was held at Shechem where the forty-one-year-old Rehoboam, son of Solomon by the Ammonite concubine Naamah, was offered the kingship of all Israel if he would only reduce the burdens placed upon the people by his father. The new king of Jerusalem refused, announcing that he would increase the workload rather than become a servant to his father's subjects. Upon hearing this, the vast majority of the Israelite people left the assembly, refusing to swear their loyalty to Solomon's son and heir. And so the Schism which brought about the division of the kingdom of Israel came into being through the foolishness of an arrogant new king who failed to comprehend the legitimate concerns of his people.

Rehoboam returned south to rule over the tribal territories of Judah and Benjamin with his capital at Jerusalem, whilst Jeroboam I was anointed king over all the other tribes, resident at his new capital of TIRZAH in the hill country of Ephraim. The United Monarchy period of Israelite history was over – having lasted a mere eighty-one years – and two tribal kingdoms now divided the Promised Land between them.

Jeroboam realised that, so long as the principal centre of Israelite worship remained focused on the temple in Jerusalem, his position as ruler of the northern tribes would be undermined. And so the new king of Israel fashioned two golden calves, similar to that made by Aaron at the foot of Mount Sinai. In this case the young bovids were manifestations of the old god El, still held in high esteem by the Israelite people.* The two golden bulls were set up in shrines at Bethel ('house of El') and at the northern city of Dan for the people to worship – the clear intent being to stifle pilgrimage to Yahweh's temple in the old capital.

With Egypt's strong political support for his northern rival, Rehoboam feared for his much shrunken kingdom. He could probably hold off any threat from the new state of Israel on his northern borders – but what if the powerful Ramesses or his Philistine allies on the coast were to attack from the south? Jerusalem's king immediately set about fortifying the towns along the western and southern limits of the hill country of Judah in anticipation of a military move from the Egyptian pharaoh. In each citadel he stationed one of his sons to command the home-guard, providing them with weapons and provisions. Rehoboam's concerns proved to be justified.

---

* As exemplified in the numerous names of the period containing the theophoric element -*el*, e.g. Samu-El, Othni-El.

In 927 BC (Rehoboam's fifth year) Ramesses marched across Sinai with a huge army of thirty thousand Egyptians, Kushites and Libyans (the biblical figure of sixty-thousand-plus troops is undoubtedly exaggerated). He first seized the coastal town of Ashkelon before heading inland to retake the city of Gezer – previously given to Solomon as a dowry when he married Pharaoh Haremheb's daughter. One by one the fortified towns of Judah were captured until, two weeks later, Ramesses II stood before the gates of Jerusalem in his golden chariot.

> When Rehoboam had consolidated the kingdom and become strong, he and all Israel with him, abandoned the law of Yahweh. And thus it happened that in the fifth year of King Rehoboam, Shishak king of Egypt marched on Jerusalem – because they had been unfaithful to Yahweh – with twelve hundred chariots and sixty thousand cavalry and countless hordes of Libyans, Sukkiim and Kushites who came from Egypt with him. They captured the fortified towns of Judah and reached Jerusalem. [2 Chronicles 12:1–4]

There was nothing that Rehoboam could do. He had to capitulate. Pleading for mercy, the king of Jerusalem opened the city gate to receive the Egyptian plunderers. Ramesses' soldiers stripped the palace of Solomon's golden shields and removed the elaborate ivory filigree decorating the magnificent throne. They then ascended to Yahweh's holy shrine on the Temple Mount where they removed the treasures of Israel's god. Fortunately, the time devoted to plundering the royal compound in the City of David had allowed the priests of Yahweh to spirit away the Ark of the Covenant – the only treasure not to find its way back to the city of Pi-Ramesse in Egypt's eastern delta.

Ramesses departed from Jerusalem and headed north to capture the rebel city of Yanoam in Galilee whilst a huge, heavily protected baggage train was despatched to Egypt carrying the wealth of Solomon's Jerusalem to its new home in Pi-Ramesse. The golden shields were subsequently melted down and made into thick sheets of gold-foil to cover the floor of the throne-room in Ramesses' lavishly decorated palace. The conquest of Israel was recorded on the wall at Karnak which contains the Hittite treaty text of Ramesses' twenty-first year.

Rehoboam, humbled and in fear for his life, was forced to swear a loyalty oath to the Egyptian pharaoh in order to remain on the throne of Judah. The Southern Kingdom was not only stripped of its gold but also of its power, making the Northern Kingdom of Israel the strong political force in the hill country of Canaan. Supported by 19th-Dynasty Egypt, and in close contact with the trading networks of the coastal plain and Jezreel, Jeroboam I prospered for more than a decade whilst the rump state of Judah, under Rehoboam, became a political backwater.

After reigning for seventeen full years, Rehoboam died in 914 BC and the Judahite throne passed to his son ABIJAH in the eighteenth year of Jeroboam. The new king of Jerusalem immediately marched north to do battle with his rival and the two armies met at Mount Zemaraim near Shechem. Abijah's forces were victorious and pushed Jeroboam back towards his capital at Tirzah. The soldiers of Judah then seized the holy town of Bethel, where they tore down Jeroboam's golden calf. They also took the towns of Jeshanah and Ephron, expanding the tribal territory of Benjamin northwards. Jeroboam I of Israel was much weakened by this surprise military defeat but continued to rule for another three years before he was succeeded by his son Nadab in 911 BC. One year earlier, the short but successful rule of Abijah of Judah had come to an end with the accession of his son Asa (912–872 BC) who, over his long reign, proved to be one of Judah's mightiest kings.

In 910 BC (contemporary with Asa's third year) Nadab of Israel was assassinated by Baasha (the son of Ahijah, prophet of Shiloh), who then seized the throne. He immediately set about butchering all the descendants of Jeroboam I so that the whole house of the Northern Kingdom's first king was wiped out in a matter of days. Baasha (910–887 BC) then ruled at Tirzah for twenty-four years.

Asa, King of Judah

Asa was a devout Yahweh worshipper. He dismantled all the shrines dedicated to other gods which had proliferated in Judah during Rehoboam's reign. The Asherah poles (symbols of sacred trees), representing the female consort of Baal, were torn down. In later years Asherah would be associated with Yahweh in the popular religion of Judah. The ordinary people (as opposed to the élite priesthood) felt it only natural that their god should have a spouse just like all the other male deities in the ancient world. Asherah, however, was synonymous with Astarte/Ashtaroth and hence the Mesopotamian Ishtar – and, as such, was an abomination to the priestly hierarchy of Yahweh's monotheistic cult.

Baal ('Lord') was the most popular god in the ancient Middle East. He was both storm-god and warrior, regarded as a legendary hero-king of the past. Baal was an abomination to the Israelite priests precisely because he was a human elevated to divine status. In my view this universal god known as 'Lord', son of El, was none other than the mighty hunter and warrior, Nimrod, the first potentate on Earth. As we saw in Chapter Four, the celebrated king of the 1st Dynasty of Uruk built the Tower of Babel and founded the cities of Ashur and Nineveh. To the Assyrians he was known as Ninurta; to the Babylonians, Marduk. His divine consort was Inanna, also known as Ishtar, who in Canaan took the name Astarte – the Ashtaroth and Asherah of the Bible.

For ten years (912–903 BC) Asa enjoyed a peaceful reign with no conflicts. In this time he was able to rebuild the fortified towns destroyed by Ramesses/Shysha and build the army of Judah back up to full strength. Ramesses, now in his late fifties and in his forty-second year on the throne, was advised of the new threat. He despatched a large force of Kushite and Libyan mercenaries, under the command of General Zerah (himself a Kushite), to crush Judah's military ambitions. However, once more Judah routed its enemy – this time at Mareshah – and pursued the fleeing Kushites back to the city of Gerar on the coastal plain, plundering towns under the Egyptian protectorate as they went. Ramesses the Great and mighty Egypt had been humbled. Pharaoh would not trouble Jerusalem and its kings again.

King Asa had proved his strength to all his neighbours and, as a result of this single action, gained fifteen more years of peace and security. But then, in 887 BC, Baasha of Israel marched on Judah and fortified nearby Ramah. This was a direct challenge to Asa, who did not meet it with a counterattack but rather chose to bribe King Ben-Hadad I (c. 893–874 BC) of Damascus to break off his alliance with Israel and raid the Galilean towns of Dan, Ijon and Abel-Maim belonging to the Northern Kingdom. The diversion worked. Baasha rushed to meet the Aramaean threat and abandoned his strategic position in Ramah. Asa's men then marched out of Jerusalem and dismantled the fortifications there, using the stones to strengthen Geba (Saul's old home town) and Mizpah.

The fight against Ben-Hadad and the Aramaeans of Damascus quickly led to the demise of Baasha, who died in that same year, to be succeeded by his son Elah (887–886 BC). The new king of Samaria lasted less than two years, assassinated by Zimri the commander of the royal chariotry. The king had been invited to dine at the house of his 'master of the palace' – a Syrian named Arsa – who was almost certainly in on the plot. Once Elah had indulged himself into a drunken stupor, Zimri entered the room and struck the king down. News spread quickly that Elah had been killed and that Zimri had made himself ruler over the Northern Kingdom. At this time the army was besieging the Philistine town of Gibbethon. The Israelite clan-warriors immediately proclaimed their own military commander, Omri, as the rightful king and marched to confront the murderer at Tirzah. When Zimri saw that his position was hopeless, he burned down the royal palace over his own head, having reigned for just seven days.

The Northern Kingdom was in political turmoil. Civil war broke out between two factions supporting rival claimants to the throne – Omri and another nobleman named Tibni. After three years Tibni was killed and Omri assumed the sole rulership of the Northern Kingdom. A couple of years later (in 881 BC) he moved the royal capital of Israel away from Tirzah in the east to the new site of SAMARIA on the western slopes of the central hill country, facing the coastal plain of the Mediterranean Sea.

The House of Omri

> In the thirty-first year of Asa king of Judah, Omri became king of Israel and reigned for twelve years. He reigned for six years at Tirzah. Then, for two talents of silver, he bought the hill of Samaria from Shemer and, on it, built a town which he named Samaria, after Shemer who had owned the hill. Omri did what is displeasing to Yahweh, and was worse than all his predecessors. In every way he copied the example of Jeroboam (I) son of Nebat and the sins into which he had led Israel, provoking the anger of Yahweh, God of Israel, with their worthless idols. [1 Kings 16:23–26]

This is pretty much all we know from the Bible about the founder of the Northern Kingdom's new capital at Samaria. But Omri's name occurs on the famous Moabite Stone (see next chapter), where it states that Omri had regained the lands of Moab for Israel but that, at the end of his reign, Moabite independence was once more established. None of Omri's military achievements are mentioned in the biblical narrative, which seems more concerned with decrying the Israelite kings for their lack of allegiance to Yahweh. In this respect, some of the most powerful rulers of Israel are given scant attention in the books of Kings and Chronicles.

Excavations on the 'hill of Shemer' (Samaria) have revealed pottery from the Early Bronze Age, followed by a gap, before pottery from the Early Iron Age indicates a new occupation of the hill. This Iron Age I-A pottery was discovered in the trenches of a later building complex dated to the Iron Age II-A period when the site was cleared and levelled for the construction of a royal residence. In the New Chronology, this palace is the work of Jeroboam II (782–742 BC) and the Iron Age I-A pottery thus represents the original occupation of the hill under Omri (886–875 BC) during the last six years of his reign. In my view the remains of his residence have not, as yet, been unearthed by the archaeologists and lie under the olive orchards on the eastern part of the hill.

Omri was succeeded by his son Ahab (in the thirty-eighth year of Asa in Judah). The new king of Israel married the Phoenician princess, Yezebul (biblical Jezebel), daughter of King Ittobaal (biblical Ethbaal) of Sidon. Jezebel is one of the Old Testament's most notorious females, character-ised as a harlot and conniving temptress – the exact opposite of what an Israelite woman should be. The biblical polemic against Ahab's Phoenician queen was, of course, written by the later Judaean priests of Yahweh who regarded all foreign influences in the court of the Northern Kingdom as abominations. Jezebel's eventual demise – thrown from a palace window by her own servants – was regarded as just retribution for her corruption of Israel's monarchy. It was Jezebel who introduced Baal worship into the royal court at Samaria. The king even constructed a temple to Baal and erected an Asherah pole for the worship of Baal's consort. Ittobaal of Sidon had recently seized control of the neighbouring city of Tyre to become ruler of the whole of southern Phoenicia, so, through the marriage alliance, he became Omri's powerful ally on Israel's northern border.

Omri also persuaded the next king of Judah – Jehoshaphat son of Asa – to accept his daughter, Athaliah by Jezebel, as a bride for the Judahite crown-prince, Jehoram. Thus peace between Israel and Judah was also secured through matrimonial treaty.

These marriage alliances (between Ahab and Jezebel, and Athaliah and Jehoram) greatly strengthened Ahab's political position. The secure north-western and southern borders of the kingdom provided unhindered access to the Mediterranean sea-trade of Phoenicia and the spice-trade of Arabia. Ahab quickly became the wealthiest and most powerful monarch in the region. As a result, he was able to build a large army (consisting of two thousand chariots and ten thousand infantry) to protect his long north-eastern border with Amurru (Syria). For a while this policy seemed to work but, as we will see, momentous changes were already taking place in the Middle East – changes which would lead to instability on the fringes of Ahab's kingdom and an influx of Israelite refugees from a series of devastating raids by the Aramaean kings of Damascus.

A Curse Fulfilled

It was during the twenty-three-year reign of Ahab (874–852 BC) that the ruin-mound of Jericho was reoccupied on a *permanent* basis by the Israelite clan chieftain, Hiel of Bethel. As had been the custom for centuries in the ancient Levant, Hiel ritually sacrificed his eldest and youngest sons, Abiram and Segub, in order to lay their bodies as foundation deposits beneath the chieftain's new residence and town gate. Thus Joshua's curse, made before the smouldering ruins of Jericho over five centuries earlier, came to be fulfilled.

> Accursed before Yahweh be the man who rises up
> and rebuilds this city (of Jericho)! On his firstborn
> will he lay its foundations! On his youngest son will
> he set up its gates! [Joshua 6:26]

Hiel's new town is represented in the archaeological record
by Iron Age pottery found at Jericho, the succeeding phases
of which continue on down into Byzantine times. Now that
the Holy Land stratigraphical timeline has been resyn-
chronised with the New Chronology historical timeline (and
therefore biblical history), the pattern of archaeological
remains at Tell es-Sultan (the ruin-mound of Jericho) corresponds remarkably with the biblical narrative.

First the well-fortified Middle Bronze II-B city is
destroyed by fire and abandoned for decades, its walls
having tumbled down in an earthquake – this, of course, is
Joshua's Jericho destroyed during the 1406 BC conquest
of the Promised Land. A brief occupation of the site by
Eglon, ruler of Moab, follows (represented by the 'Middle
Building' and LB I pottery). Then, after several centuries,
there is another brief reoccupation by David's ambassadors
in 1000 BC (reuse of the Middle Building and LB II-A
pottery). This too was abandoned and the site left to the
wind and rain for a further one hundred and ninety years
before Hiel's resettlement in 869 BC (Iron Age I remains).

The Jericho of the conventional chronology – a site
which consistently failed to match the biblical story at every
archaeological stage – moves out of the realms of mythology and suddenly fits like a freshly cut key. The New
Chronology has unlocked what was regarded as the Bible's
greatest obstacle to its acceptance as a true history.

The Winds of Change

Meanwhile, back in Egypt, the rule of Ramesses the Great
had finally come to an end in his sixty-seventh regnal year
(877 BC – the tenth year of Omri in Israel and Asa's thirty-

sixth year in Judah). The longest reign in Egyptian history since the ninety-four years of Pepi II (6th Dynasty, 2168–2075 BC) had produced a very unstable situation for the succession. The extended royal family was huge, with dozens of surviving sons and hundreds of grandsons of the deceased 'king of kings' all vying for a slice of the great man's inheritance. Twelve crown-princes had died before their father. The thirteenth in line – Prince Merenptah – had been crowned as Ramesses II's co-regent in the old and ailing king's fifty-sixth regnal year (888 BC).

The last few years of Ramesses' life had seen the mighty warrior humbled by infirmity. Egypt's neighbours sensed a weakness and sought to test Egypt's resolve. King Merenptah (already himself in his fifth decade of life) successfully fought off invasions by Libyans and Aegean/Anatolian seafarers whilst his father was still alive. But the power and influence of the pharaonic state appeared to be on the wane. The ancient world was entering a new era and, this time, the winds of change were blowing from the north.

One of the triggers for that change had occurred several centuries earlier when the island of Thera had exploded in a massive volcanic eruption towards the beginning of the 18th Dynasty (1159 BC or later). This had led to the overthrow of the Minoan civilisation during the reign of the Egyptian pharaoh, Thutmose III (c. 1100 BC). Mycenaean warlords from Greece and the Peloponnese had seized a weakened Crete (whose fleet had been destroyed by the great Theran tsunami) and, ever since, a dynasty of ACHAEAN kings had sat upon the throne at Knossos.

The Hittite emperors were constantly concerned over Ahhiyawan raiders from overseas who had been busy plundering the cities of the western Anatolian coast following the demise of the Minoan fleet. These are Homer's Achaeans (Greek *Achaioi*). In the correspondence of the Hittite emperor Tudhaliya IV (c. 890 BC), one of the leading Ahhiyawan protagonists is given the name Atarisiyas. He is Homer's Atreus, founder of a new dynasty at Mycenae and the father of Agamemnon and Menelaus. Some of these Mycenaeans had even settled on the Anatolian coast (later known as Ionia) in cities such as Miletus (Hittite *Milawanda*) and were in direct contact with the kingdoms of Wilusa and Arzawa which lay between the Mediterranean and the Hittite homeland in the central interior of Anatolia. Wilusa is Homer's Ilios – the kingdom whose capital was at 'windy Troy'.

In the east, the Assyrians had risen to challenge Hittite hegemony over the territory of Hanigalbat following the overthrow of the kingdom of Mitanni by Shuppiluliuma I and his son Murshili II during the first half of the tenth century BC. The Hittites, by defeating their fellow Indo-European dynasts, had created a political vacuum which later Assyrian warrior-kings such as Ashurnasirpal II (883–859 BC) and Shalmaneser III (858–824 BC) readily exploited.

The outer reaches of Egypt's northern empire were also in flux. The Aramaeans had switched their loyalties from Egypt to Hatti during the Amarna catastrophe but, with Hittite fortunes in sharp decline, they now found themselves under threat from expansionist Assyria. The 'domino effect' was at work in a most dramatic way.

Pressures from the distant north, with the Mycenaean Greeks and Kaskan tribes of north-east Anatolia destabilising the Hittite empire, had loosened the latter's control over their south-eastern vassal states and allowed the Assyrians to fill the gap left by the fall of Mitanni. Assyrian military activity had destabilised Amurru/Syria, which had itself caused the Aramaean tribal kingdoms (especially Damascus) to raid and plunder their southern neighbours – in particular the tribal territories of Israel. With two aged co-regents ruling in the Nile valley, that other great power in the region – Egypt – was in no real position to do anything about the disturbances amongst its northern vassals. Merenptah was too preoccupied with fending off Libyan incursions from the west to despatch an army to counter Aramaean raids into northern Canaan. King Ahab and his successors were on their own.

Arsa – The King-Maker

With the death of Ramesses II in 877 BC things now got decidedly worse. Egypt plunged headlong into civil war – one faction supporting the legitimate king, Merenptah, another backing a royal usurper called Amenmesse. Manetho tells us (through Josephus*) that Amenmesse – here called by his hypocoristicon Mose – was a priest of Heliopolis who had previously borne the name Osarsiph. Mose seized Avaris and requested support from Jerusalem in his bid to overthrow Merenptah – here called Amenophis son of Rampses (i.e. Ramesses II) by Josephus but Amenophthis in all the other redactions of Manetho.** Mose reminded the people of Jerusalem that they had once lived at Avaris (a direct reference to the Israelite sojourn in the eastern delta during the seventeenth to fifteenth centuries BC). And so, according to Manetho, the Jerusalemites (i.e. Judahites) sent troops to fight on behalf of Mose who, as a result, was able to overthrow Amenophis. The old king fled into exile, heading south into Kush where he found

---

* Josephus' legend of Amenophis/Amenophthis seems to be a conflation of two separate characters and eras. The story surrounding Akhenaten (Amenhotep IV) and his religious revolution is certainly one element – especially the part of the story dealing with the polluted people settled in the quarries on the east bank of the Nile (i.e. el-Amarna) and the role played by Amenophis son of Paapis (i.e. Amenhotep son of Hapu). However, the sequence of rulers given by Josephus: Sethos (Seti I) – Rampses for 66 years (Ramesses II) – Amenophis/Amenophthis (Merenptah) – Sethos (Seti II) – appears to set the story at the end of the 19th Dynasty. So the civil war between Mose and King Amenophis/Amenophthis must be a quite separate tradition from the Akhenaten heresy, dated to well over a century earlier.

** Manetho's Amenophthis is almost certainly a corruption of Menophtah where the 'r' of *Mr(y)-n-Pth* ('beloved of Ptah') has been dropped in the foreign (Greek) vocalisation of the Egyptian name.

refuge under the protection of the friendly Kushite ruler. There, Amenophis and his son Sethos prepared an army to retake their rightful inheritance. These preparations apparently took thirteen years (877–865 BC).

The Egyptian usurper Amenmesse/Mose ruled for five years with the support of Asa of Jerusalem, who was now himself well into the fourth decade of his reign. The Egyptian texts refer to an Asiatic named Arsa who became 'king-maker' – in other words the man behind the usurper's throne during this troubled period. Interestingly enough, an Arsa does occur in the biblical story at this precise time. The master of the royal palace of Israel, according to 1 Kings 16:8–10, bore this name. In fact, the murder of King Elah by Zimri in 886 BC took place in Arsa's house. However, we subsequently hear no more about this individual. Did he continue in the service of the next Israelite king, Omri? Or might he have fled into the protection of Asa, king of Judah, because he was implicated in the plot to assassinate Elah? If he did become an official at the Judahite court, could he somehow have become the Asiatic ARSA, king-maker in Egypt, perhaps sent with the army of Jerusalem to support Amenmesse's revolt?

Egyptologists have often speculated that the 'Great Chancellor of the entire land' Bay, who 'established the king on his father's throne', was an Asiatic power-broker, controlling the succession in Egypt at the end of the 19th Dynasty. They suggest that Bay was an Egyptian name given to the Asiatic Arsa – a foreigner perhaps more powerful than the pharaohs (Siptah and Tausert) whom he placed on the throne, and a politician of such influence that he could order a royal tomb to be made for himself in the Valley of the Kings.

Egypt's Saviour

We might justifiably ignore the Manetho tradition of the civil war at the end of the 19th Dynasty if it were not for the fact that the contemporary Egyptian texts clearly hint at a major political disturbance at this time. The great Papyrus Harris (the funeral scroll of Ramesses III) refers to these troubled times, some forty years before the king's death, which had been caused by internal revolt supported from outside Egypt.

> The land of Egypt was overthrown from without (i.e. by outsiders), and every (Egyptian) man was denied his right. They (the people) had no leader for many years. The land of Egypt was in the hands of chieftains and of rulers of towns. Each slew his neighbour, great and small. This was then followed by the empty years when Arsa – a certain Syrian – was with them as leader. He set the whole land tributary before him. He united his companions and plundered their (the Egyptians') possessions. They made the gods like men and no offerings were presented in the temple. [*Papyrus Harris*]

This dramatic downturn in Egyptian fortunes *does* sound remarkably like the civil war and foreign invasion of Egypt as related by Manetho.* Both sources clearly indicate that Asiatics were partly responsible for plunging Egypt into civil war. It seems to me that Egyptologists have never really taken on board the significance of these words in Papyrus Harris. The events which followed the death of Ramesses the Great were apparently dramatic and had a profound effect on the history of the Nile valley civilisation. Momentous changes were taking place all over the ancient world at this time and Egypt's shining light was never to burn so brightly again.

---

* However, there are two major differences. The historical résumé given by Ramesses III from beyond the grave identifies Arsa as a Syrian not an Israelite (however we do not know if the biblical Arsa was an Israelite either – he may have been a Syrian) and the text also fails to mention the part played by Jerusalem in the invasion.

The chaos which brought about the collapse in pharaonic rule at the end of the 19th Dynasty was ended by the appearance of a saviour – the war-hero Setnakht, founder of the 20th Dynasty and the father of Ramesses III.

> He (Setnakht) set the entire land which had been rebellious in order. He slew the rebels who were in the land of Egypt and cleansed the great throne of Egypt. He became ruler of the Two Lands on the throne of Atum. [*Papyrus Harris*]

A recently translated stela from Setnakht's reign (discovered at Elephantine) casts fresh light on the Egyptian recovery and expulsion of the foreign occupiers.

> [Live] the Majesty of Horus 'Mighty Bull, Great of Power', ... Lord of the Two Lands, Son of Re, Lord of Diadems, Seti-nakht-meriamun ... His Majesty is like his father Seth, who spreads out both his arms to cleanse Egypt by [expelling] those who [assail] him, having his strength as his protector. [The enemies fall] before him, because the fear of him has seized their hearts. They flee back [like little birds] when the falcon is behind them. They drop silver, gold [(and) copper – the possessions of] Egypt, which they, [as princi]pals of Egypt, desired to give to those Asiatics in order to persuade the foreign warriors to come to them in haste. Their (hostile) intentions turned out to be without success and their threats were not fulfilled. [*Elephantine Stela* of Setnakht]

This new text reflects in a remarkable way Manetho's tale of King Amenophis who came up from the south to reconquer Egypt and cast out the Asiatic mercenaries who had entered the Nile valley at the request of the usurper Mose (Amenmesse).

Amenophis advanced from Ethiopia with a large
army, his son Rampses also leading a force. And
the two together joined battle with the Shepherds
and their polluted allies, and defeated them, killing
many and pursuing the others to the frontiers of
Syria. [Josephus, *Contra Apionem*, Book I, quoting
Manetho]

However, there is one obvious difference – the Egyptian
version of the story does not attribute the expulsion of the
foreigners to Merenptah/Amenophis but rather to Setnakht.
The solution to this problem is to realise that Setnakht was
none other than Manetho's 'Sethos son of Amenophis',
who went with his father to Ethiopia (i.e. Kush) at the start
of the revolt in 877 BC and who then returned thirteen
years later, along with his son Ramesses III, to seize his
father's throne back from the usurpers. So, Manetho's King
Sethos was not Seti II, son of Merenptah, as most scholars
(including myself) have always understood, but rather the
founder of the 20th Dynasty known to Egyptologists as
Setnakht but whose name is actually written Seti-nakht ('the
man of Seth is strong') – the younger son of Merenptah
and rightful successor to the dynasty of Ramesses the Great.

During the thirteen years of turmoil (877–865 BC) there
had been three short-lived pretenders to the Egyptian
crown. Amenmesse ruled for five years before being succeeded by Ramesses-Siptah (established on the throne by
chancellor Bay/Arsa, agent of Asa of Jerusalem). The new
king (later renamed Merenptah-Siptah) was a minor and
so, during his reign, the country was ruled by his mother,
the regent Tausert, wife of the recently deceased Seti II,
son of King Merenptah and co-regent of Amenmesse.
These complex political manoeuvres are difficult to understand with such scant information to work from, but it seems
that Seti II was a contemporary (and perhaps rival) to
Amenmesse. Following Amenmesse's death in 873 BC the
powers-that-be in Egypt established Seti II's young son on

the throne. Seti II then died in the same year and Siptah's mother became co-regent with her son. While all this was going on, the country itself was in a state of anarchy. When Siptah died in 868 BC, after six short years on the throne, Tausert was left as sole pharaoh, continuing to reign for four more years before Setnakht and Ramesses III returned from exile in 865 BC to put an end to their rival's claim to the throne and rid the country of her foreign backers.

With the rule of law re-established and the foreign troops from Canaan – and in particular Jerusalem – removed, Egypt enjoyed a brief period of recovery. Setnakht (865–859 BC) ruled for seven years, crowning his son, Ramesses III, as co-regent in his third regnal year (863 BC). In the New Chronology, Setnakht may be 'the brave and noble' Thouris (also known as Polybus), king of Egypt, visited by Menelaus following the fall of Troy, according to Homeric and Manethonian tradition. His son Ramesses III – in whose accession-year the Trojan war came to an end – was the last of the great pharaohs of the New Kingdom.

The Trojan Catalyst

Far to the north, on the west coast of Anatolia, beside the Dardanelles strait, a great war had been under way for many years. In 872 BC an Achaean/Ahhiyawan confederacy of Greek city-states, led by Agamemnon of Mycenae, had invaded the land of Wilusa (Ilios) and laid siege to its capital, Troy. In Setnakht's third year (Year 1 Ramesses III = 863 BC) Priam's city was finally captured and put to the flame. A year before the fall of Troy, the legendary hero MOPSUS, king of Colophon, joined a group of Achaean warriors returning from the war. The confederacy ended up in Pamphylia on the southern coastal plain of Anatolia, where Mopsus established new cities named Aspendus and Phaselis. He then moved eastwards into Cilicia, where he founded two more cities – MOPSOU-HESTIA and Mallus.

The Trojan war had transformed the political landscape in the region with the Aegean islanders (including the Mycenaeans of Crete) siding with the Achaeans and the Anatolian states of Lydia, Caria, Lycia and Cilicia defending the Trojans. The war began the year after the Hittite empire had crumbled under constant military setbacks at the hands of Kaskan warriors from the south-east shore of the Black Sea. Indeed, for fifty years the western Anatolian states had also been in revolt against Hittite hegemony in the region. But the sudden collapse of the former world power had now left these same former vassals vulnerable and open to attack from the Ahhiyawan (Achaean) confederacy with its large fleet of black ships. The raids and encroachments had begun with Atarisiyas (Atreus) in 890 BC (during the reign of the Hittite emperor Tudhaliya IV), followed soon after by Mukshush, who established himself in Colophon around 884 BC (Year 3 of Tudhaliya's successor, Arnuwanda III). But the real onslaught only got under way with the death of the last Hittite ruler, Shuppiluliuma II in 874 BC.

Troy is remembered as the 'legendary' victim of Mycenaean military ambition following the demise of the Hittite empire. However, it was not just Priam's lofty towers which were torn down by the plundering Greeks. The whole region was cast into conflict. Agamemnon's sea-faring Achaeans indulged in decades of piracy and plunder, attacking the coastal cities of southern Anatolia and eventually destroying the wealthy trading city of Ugarit, now famed for its magnificent archive of cuneiform tablets. A series of tablets – perhaps the last to be written before the city fell – ominously presage the impending disaster. Ammurapi, the king of Ugarit, writes to his senior monarch in Alashiya (Cyprus) for assistance in repelling the sea invaders. The reply gives instructions to prepare one hundred and fifty ships to defend Ugarit and Alashiya from enemy attack. The exasperated response to this command from Alashiya's king cruelly exposes the predicament

Ugarit finds itself in, having already committed all its forces to fight on behalf of the collapsing Hittite empire.

> Does my father not know that all my forces and chariots are stationed in Hatti Land (i.e. central Anatolia), and all my ships are in Lukka Land (i.e. Lycia)? Thus the country (of Ugarit) is abandoned to itself ... seven enemy ships have appeared and inflicted much damage upon us.

These raids are represented in the Homeric poems by Odysseus' raids upon the cities of the eastern Mediterranean coast as described in the Odyssey. As we have seen, the Achaeans (the Akawasha of the Egyptian texts) had even joined the Libyans in an attack upon the Egyptian delta in the fifth year of Merenptah (884 BC) which the pharaoh had successfully repulsed. Again we read in the Odyssey of a raid upon the Egyptian shore, uncannily reflecting the events at the end of the 19th Dynasty.

The Greek hero Mopsus (mentioned in several Classical sources but not in Homer) appears in the Hittite records of Arnuwanda III (c. 886–884 BC) as a freebooting adventurer named Mukshush, thus confirming the historical existence of this legendary figure and dating his first appearance (c. 884 BC) to the last decade of Ramesses II. The Lydian historian, Xanthus, tells us that, having left Colophon and established his power base in Cilicia (south-east Anatolia) – where he founded several cities – Mopsus eventually led a mighty army down the Levantine coast all the way to the Philistine city of Ashkelon. In turn, the Egyptian records of Ramesses III tell of a great invasion by the 'Peoples of the Sea' in the Pharaoh's eighth year (856 BC).

The mortuary temple of Medinet Habu is covered in reliefs depicting two battles – one on land (somewhere on the Canaanite coastal plain) and one in the estuaries of the Nile delta. The famous poem accompanying these scenes gives a graphic account of this failed invasion attempt.

As for the foreign countries, they made a conspiracy in their islands. All at once the nations were disturbed, scattered in war. No country could stand before their arms. From Hatti (the Hittite empire), Kode, Carchemish, Arvad, Alashiya (Cyprus) – all were wasted. They [set up] a camp in Amurru (Syria). They desolated its people and land like that which never existed. They came with fire prepared before them – forward towards Egypt. Their confederacy were PILISTA, TJEUKERA, SHIKILESH, DANOYNA, and WASHOSHA. (These) lands were all united and they laid their hands upon the land as far as the circle of the Earth. Their hearts were confident, full of their plans. ... Those who reached my boundary (by land) – their seed is no more. Their heart and their soul are finished forever and ever. As for those who had assembled (in ships) before them on the sea, the full flame was in their front, before the harbour-mouths, and a wall of metal upon the shore surrounded them. They were dragged, overturned and laid low upon the beach; slain and made into heaps from stern to bow of their ships, whilst all their belongings were cast upon the water.

The collapse of the Egyptian 19th Dynasty, the fall of the Hittite empire, the rise of the Assyrians and the migration of the Anatolian peoples all came together to mark the end of a golden age – the Late Bronze Age – and heralded in a new, much more impoverished era which we call the Iron Age. The great empires and civilisations of the hero-kings were no more. There would never be another 'Ramesses the Great' or 'Solomon the Wise' to rule over Egypt and Canaan – only oppressive foreign masters from Assyria, Babylon, Persia, Greece and Rome.

What had brought about such momentous change in the ancient world? The answer once again, as in the case of the collapse of the Early Bronze Age city-states, is to be found in sudden climate change. It is clear from the ancient texts that famine was rife in the entire region from around 886 BC onwards (the year of Omri's accession in Israel). In 884 BC the Hittite emperor, Arnuwanda III, writes to Egypt asking Pharaoh Merenptah to send grain urgently so that he can feed his starving people. Similar requests come to Ugarit from Cilicia, whilst three letters found in the archive there refer to famine in the Hittite heartlands. During the years of political turmoil at the end of the 19th Dynasty, documents from Thebes present a picture of real difficulties for the ordinary Egyptian people. During the reign of Ramesses III (863–832 BC) the situation failed to improve. Indeed, the price of grain soared. A great drought is also recorded in 1 Kings 17 when, for three consecutive years, the rains failed to arrive and the land was parched. All this took place in the early reign of Ahab (*c.* 870 BC) – coincident with the Hittite grain crisis (and subsequent collapse) and the Egyptian civil war at the end of the 19th Dynasty – when 'the famine was particularly severe in Samaria' [1 Kings 18:3].

ᒪᑫᗯᔆᔀᣳᒪᣳ

Chapter Seventeen

HOW ARE THE MIGHTY FALLEN

(1 Kings 17:1 to 2 Kings 17:41 and 2 Chronicles 17:1 to
2 Chronicles 27:9)

*Resettlement in the Hill Country – The Aramaean Wars
– Destruction of the House of Omri – Egyptian
Intervention under Shoshenk I – Jeroboam II – The Fall
of Samaria*

he effect of the climate change and political unrest
was just as severe for the Children of Yahweh in
Israel as it was for the Anatolians and Egyptians.
Pressure from the Assyrians in the north, and a desperate
need to secure supplies to feed their people, had persuaded
the Aramaean rulers of Damascus to send raiding parties
south in search of livestock and food. The Israelites living
in Transjordan and in the Galilean hills were being ter-
rorised by these violent incursions which stripped them of
the meagre resources upon which they were so dependent
during the difficult years of famine. Thousands abandoned
their homes and fled towards the heartland of Israel – the
central hill country of Ephraim and Manasseh. There they
built new villages, scattered across the highlands.

Refugees from the North and East

When you pick up a modern archaeological history of Israel you will read about a major population influx in the central hills at the beginning of the Iron Age (OC – *c.* 1200 BC but NC – *c.* 880 BC). This arrival of new people from the east is invariably equated with the first appearance of the Israelites in Canaan, synonymous with – though recognised as being very different from – the events described in the books of Joshua and Judges. In other words, the new Iron Age settlements represent archaeological evidence for a very different biblical era to that which I am describing here. But we have already seen that the conquest of the Promised Land actually took place hundreds of years earlier – towards the end of the Middle Bronze Age (OC – *c.* 1550 BC but NC – *c.* 1400 BC). In this revised historical model, David and Solomon are consequently identified as Late Bronze Age kings rather than rulers of the Iron Age II-A (as in the conventional chronology). As a result, the early Iron Age falls in the time of the Divided Monarchy period. This New Chronology historical reassignment of the Iron Age I hill settlements to the era of the great famine and the subsequent Aramaean raids makes complete sense and explains one puzzling aspect raised by archaeologists concerning the cultural origins of the newcomers of Iron Age I-A.

It has recently been realised that the material culture of the new hill country settlements (that is their pottery, artefacts, lifestyle and religious practices) varied little from that of the Late Bronze Age people already living in the region. Archaeology has produced no clearly defined boundary between the two periods in terms of temple design or the type of cultic vessels in use in those temples. The incoming 'Israelites' were essentially no different to the indigenous, so-called 'Canaanite' population of earlier periods. Detailed studies of the pottery suggest that these newcomers came from northern Transjordan – in contrast to the biblical model which has the Israelites coming out of Egypt and invading the Promised Land from the southern part of Transjordan. These contradictions – and especially the absence of city destructions at the end of the Late Bronze Age – have become the principal reasons for rejecting an invasion as the means by which the Israelites arrived in Canaan. The military conquest of the Promised Land by Joshua and the Israelites simply did not happen in the orthodox chronological scheme.

Proponents of the New Chronology have resolved these difficulties by placing the conquest at the time when Middle Bronze Age Jericho was destroyed in 1406 BC. As a result, we find that the building of new settlements in the Iron Age I-A period now occurs, historically speaking, at the time of the Aramaean crisis. The newcomers, whose cultural traits were so similar to those people already settled in the hill country, were simply Israelite refugees from the tribal territories of Gad, Manasseh, Asher, Zebulun, Naphtali and Issachar fleeing into the heartland of an already existing Israelite state. This demographic shift took place during the ninety years of uncertainty encompassed by the reigns of Omri through to Jehoahaz (886 BC down to 797 BC) represented by the Iron I archaeological period.

At War with Aram

In the Northern Kingdom of Israel, the drought and famine took hold early in Ahab's rule. The king's great protagonist was the prophet ELIJAH, who warned that the lack of rain for three years was a punishment from Yahweh for Ahab's Baal-worship and abandonment of the one true god.

The Israelite prophets were rather different to the prophets of other cultures and civilisations in the ancient world. The Mesopotamians and Phoenicians had sooth-sayer priests who used astronomical portents to predict the future. In these cases prophecy was very much an institutionalised affair, with schools or colleges of prophets where the secrets of the profession were handed down through organised teaching. Israelite prophets like Elijah, on the other hand, are portrayed as individual, lone figures wandering over the landscape. However, this may not be the whole story. The Old Testament does hint at Israelite colleges of lesser prophets hidden in the shadows of the outstanding prophetic figures of the Bible. For instance, we hear of the 'brotherhood of the prophets living in Bethel' and the 'brotherhood of the prophets living in Jericho', suggesting communities of prophets in several major religious centres. And it seems that the numbers in each college were fairly large – those of the Jericho prophets who witnessed Elijah's crossing of the River Jordan before his ascent into heaven amounted to over fifty according to 2 Kings 2:7.

Elijah was responsible for the massacre of eight hundred and fifty prophets of Baal after the trial of strength between the followers of Yahweh and the devotees of Baal on Mount Carmel [1 Kings 18:20–40]. He then fled into Sinai and spent forty days on sacred Mount Horeb where Moses had received the commandments. Elijah then eventually journeyed to Damascus to stir up the Aramaeans against Ahab of Samaria. The Israelite prophets were often more dangerous to the rulers of Israel than rival states because they were able to stir up trouble from within – and the kings were afraid of their power ordained through the national god of Israel whom the prophets represented.

Elijah reawoke the Aramaean demon and the Northern kingdom of Israel found itself threatened once more from the direction of the rolling plains of Amurru. The attacks upon Israelite territory culminated in a battle outside Samaria itself when Ben-Hadad III (c. 873–843 BC = Hadadezer II, Assyrian Adad-idri*) of Damascus made his way to the very gates of Ahab's capital in 857 BC. Samaria's gallant defenders defeated the Aramaeans in a surprise

---

* The biblical name Ben-Hadad 'son of Adad' was a dynastic throne-name of the Aramaean kings.

attack on the enemy camp before they had time to marshal their forces in battle formation. But the skirmish was a close-run thing. King Ben-Hadad III of Damascus, quickly realising his predicament, abandoned his troops and escaped north on horseback vowing to avenge Aram's humiliation in the following year.

In the spring of Ahab's nineteenth regnal year (856 BC) a much larger Aramaean army headed back into Israel – but, this time, the king of the Northern Kingdom was ready for them. Ahab's forces once more overran Ben-Hadad's men at Aphek. This time there was a great slaughter and the king of Damascus was taken captive. Having humbled Ben-Hadad and annihilated a major part of his army, Ahab magnanimously sent his captive home – but first made him swear a loyalty oath to the Omrid dynasty. Included within this treaty was an agreement that the border towns and villages captured by the Aramaeans in the time of Omri were to be returned to Israel [1 Kings 20:34]. These were some of the settlements abandoned by the Israelite refugees who had fled into the central hill country in response to the earlier Aramaean raids. Even though Damascus was now a vassal subject of the Northern Kingdom of Israel, these refugees did not return to their former homes in any great numbers.

Back in Samaria Ahab wished to expand the royal compound down the western slopes of the hill to the Pool of Samaria. However, the terraces were covered by the vineyard of Naboth – a wealthy citizen of Jezreel. The viniculturist refused to sell his land to the king and so Queen Jezebel hatched a plot to have the obstinate man done away with. When the citizens of Jezreel came to Samaria to attended a fasting festival, Naboth was accused by paid troublemakers of the crime of cursing both God and the king. The people were incited to riot by these same agents and they dragged poor Naboth into his own vineyard, outside the town walls, and stoned him to death. Naboth's vineyard at Samaria, which gave access from the royal palace to the spring pool, thus passed into the hands of the king of Israel.* However, the prophet Elijah went to warn Ahab that his usurpation of the property of another man would, in the end, be the cause of his own downfall and the extinction of his dynasty.

> You have committed murder and now you also usurp. For this – and Yahweh says this – in the place where the dogs licked the blood of Naboth, the dogs will lick your blood also. ... I shall now bring disaster down upon you. I shall sweep away your descendants and wipe out every member of the House of Ahab ... [1 Kings 21:19–21]

For three years there was relative peace in Israel and its northern dependencies. Then a threat of far greater proportions arose to challenge Ahab in the guise of Shalmaneser III, king of Assyria – the nation which was eventually to become Israel's nemesis. However, in 853 BC Ahab and his coalition of allies were able to hold back the onslaught from the warrior-king of Ashur. They mustered forces from all over northern Canaan and Syria. Ahab himself contributed two thousand chariots and ten thousand infantry, whilst his Aramaean vassals numbered over sixty thousand. At the great set-piece battle of Karkar in north Syria the

---

* Most commentators reasonably argue that Naboth was killed at Jezreel. There do seem to be a number of contradictions in the biblical text as to the location of the vineyard, its association with Jezreel being quite strong. However, in order for the curse to be fulfilled, the place where the dogs licked Ahab's blood had to be the same location that dogs had licked Naboth's blood. Ahab's blood-soaked chariot was washed in the pool of Samaria [1 Kings 22:38] and so that is also where Naboth was killed. Thus, according to this reasoning, Naboth's vineyard must have been in Samaria and not Jezreel. On the other hand, there is even reason to dispute the identity of the king whose chariot was washed in the pool. Some commentators have suggested that the whole episode properly belongs in the reign of Joram (who also died following a battle at Ramoth-Gilead). In which case the error would be in identifying the washing place as the 'pool of Samaria' rather than the 'pool of Jezreel'.

two huge armies met and fought themselves to a standstill. Shalmaneser boasted of victory in his annals of Year 6 though, in reality, he had been prevented from moving south to attack Damascus and Samaria. The latter remained safe from the Assyrians for a hundred years – but the fighting was not over for Ahab. He had one last battle to wage. In the following year his fragile alliance with Damascus crumbled and he found himself once more at war with the Aramaeans.

Ahab decided to recapture the town of Ramoth-Gilead in Transjordan which had been seized by Ben-Hadad II (c. 893–874 BC) during his father's reign. He persuaded Jehoshaphat, king of Judah (whose son and heir was married to Ahab's daughter), to join him in the campaign. The combined Israelite army attacked Ramoth in the spring of 852 BC … but, this time, there was no victory. Ahab was struck by an arrow which pierced his armour. He fought on bravely until sundown in order not to panic the troops, as the blood from the wound ran down into the platform of the king's chariot. As Ahab's strength finally gave way and he collapsed, the soldiers around him realised that their leader had been killed. A shout went up. 'The king is dead. Every man back to his town, every man back to his country!' The Israelite ranks disintegrated, leaving the field of battle in the hands of the victorious Aramaeans.

Ahab's body was taken back to Samaria, where he was buried by his widow, Jezebel. The blood-soaked royal chariot was taken to be washed in the pool of Samaria, within the old vineyard of Naboth … and the dogs licked up King Ahab's blood from the pool in fulfilment of Elijah's prophecy.

The Vassals' Revolt

In 855 BC Ahab had taken his son Ahaziah as co-regent. In that year the Moabites, under their new king Mesha, revolted. The famous 'Moabite Stone' of King Mesha stands as independent confirmation of Israel's loss of Moab by the successors of the 'House of Dud' (David).

> As for Omri, king of Israel, he humbled Moab for many years, because (the god) Chemosh was angry with his land (i.e. Moab). His son (Ahab) followed him and he also said, 'I will humble Moab.' In my time he said this, but I have triumphed over him and over his house, whilst Israel has perished forever! [*Moabite Stone*, lines 4–7]

Mesha refused to pay the annual tribute to the 'House of Omri'. In the following year (854 BC) Ahaziah fell from his palace balcony and suffered serious bone fractures. And, as if this was not enough, the prophet Elijah, scourge of his father Ahab, was back on the scene, stirring up trouble for the kingship. All these problems, coming in quick succession, were too much for Ahaziah and within months he had died of his injuries. He was succeeded by his brother Jehoram – abbreviated in the book of Kings to Joram – who became Ahab's co-regent for the last two years of the senior monarch's life.

Following Ahab's fall at Ramoth-Gilead in 852 BC, the throne of the Northern Kingdom was left to Joram (853–842 BC*). The Southern Kingdom of Judah had already passed into the hands of Jehoshaphat at the death of his father Asa in 871 BC. The marriage between Jehoshaphat and Ahab's daughter Athaliah had ensured peace between the two Israelite states for a generation, after fifty years of hostility following the schism. The peace with Judah had enabled Ahab to concentrate on fighting the Aramaeans and had even allowed the king of Israel briefly to reconquer the land of Moab across the Jordan. But the fragile politics of the two Israelite kingdoms was soon to be shattered by the arrival upon the scene of another bloody usurper.

---

* It may have been Joram, rather than Ahab, whose chariot was immersed in the pool of Jezreel (not Samaria) to wash away the royal blood.

In 849 BC Jehoshaphat was succeeded in Jerusalem by his son Jehoram. Thus, for the eight years between 849 to 842 BC, two Jehorams ruled over the Northern and Southern Kingdoms. The new king of Judah's first act was to form a military alliance with Joram of Israel so that the two forces might work together to recover the Israelite tribal lands lost to the Moabites over the previous six years.

Jehoram (son of Jehoshaphat and Athaliah) and Joram (son of Ahab and Jezebel) marched to retake Moab. The combined Israelite army headed into the Arabah, south of the Dead Sea, where they retook the town of Horonen captured by the Moabites a few years earlier, as Mesha himself attests.

And the House [of D]ud (i.e. Judah) dwelt in Horonen […] and (the god) Chemosh said to me, 'Go down! Fight against Horonen.' And I went down, and [I fought against the town, and I took it] and Chemosh [resto]red it in my days. And I took up there ten […] [*Moabite Stone*, lines 32–33]

At this point the text of Mesha's decree breaks off and we do not know the outcome of the war from the Moabite perspective. However, the mere fact that the stela exists demonstrates that the Israelites failed to recapture Moab. The biblical text confirms this reality in a rather extraordinary way. The Israelite campaign began with a series of military victories which led to King Mesha being chased all the way back inside the walls of his capital, KIR-HARESHETH. There the Moabite ruler employed the weapon of last resort in these superstitious times. Mesha proceeded to sacrifice his eldest son atop the walls of the citadel, in full view of the enemy. This was the ultimate offering to his god Chemosh in a desperate plea for divine intervention. The Israelites were taken aback by this terrible drama being carried out before their eyes and feared the vengeance of the god of the Moabites. The two Jehorams retreated back across the Jordan, leaving Moab to its independence.

Needless to say, the failure to crush the Moabite rebellion was seen as a sign of weakness by the other vassal states of the old Davidic empire. The Edomites were the next to break away from the kingdom of Judah and gain their freedom. The southern and eastern tributary nations were severing their ties with the 'House of David' one by one. The annual tribute quickly dried up. The Israelites did try to recover these losses by force of arms ... but to no avail.

The prophet Elijah died at around this time (c. 847 BC) and was succeeded by his protégé, ELISHA. Once more the Levant was struck by famine and, this time, the drought lasted a full seven years. Documents from the reign of Ramesses III (863–832 BC), found at Thebes, tell of similar hardships which led to the workmen in the Valley of the Kings downing tools, going on strike and rioting because they had not received their food rations for months. The whole of the ancient world was in similar turmoil.

Once again the Aramaeans of Damascus, led by Ben-Hadad III, attacked Israel and besieged Joram and his people in Samaria. Weeks went by as the population, holed up within the walls, slowly began to starve. But then, just as suddenly as they had arrived, the Aramaeans disappeared, leaving their camp empty and abandoned. The passage in 2 Kings 7:6–7 explains this remarkable turn of events in a rather strange way. The biblical writer states that the Aramaeans heard the sound of a great army approaching. Believing that the Egyptians and Hittites were coming to Israel's rescue, they fled back to Damascus, abandoning their possessions in the confusion. I have no idea what this is about. The Hittite empire had collapsed a decade earlier and the Egyptian records are silent on any military campaigns of Ramesses III after the first twelve years of his reign (863–852 BC). But then again, according to the biblical story, the Aramaean panic was only an illusion – there really was no Egyptian-Hittite army, just the sound of a mighty host sent by Yahweh from out of the darkness of night to engender panic amongst Israel's enemies.

Elisha, just as his predecessor Elijah had done a generation earlier, went to Damascus to foment trouble in Ben-Hadad's court. He encouraged the king's servant, Hazael, to believe that it was his destiny to rule over Aram and that he would be the one to vanquish Israel.

> … what harm you will do to the Israelites! You will burn down their fortresses, put their picked warriors to the sword, dash their little children to pieces and disembowel their pregnant women. … (for) I have seen you as king of Aram. [2 Kings 8:12–13]

The next day Hazael took a blanket soaked in water and smothered the old king, Ben-Hadad. So a servant succeeded to the throne of Damascus in 842 BC. As Elisha had predicted, the usurper Hazael became the greatest of Israel's Aramaean foes, wreaking havoc and mayhem amongst the settlements of the northern tribes for the next forty years.

Coup d'État

In the sixth year of Jehoram of Judah (844 BC) the Philistines and their Arab allies attacked the Southern Kingdom. As we saw in the previous chapter, twelve years earlier, in the eighth year of Ramesses III (856 BC) a great army of 'Sea Peoples' had marched down the Levantine coast from the north, led by the Tjeukera (Greek *Teuceri*) warlord, Moksus (Greek *Mopsus*). They had reached as far as Ashkelon where their Philistine kindred had settled half a millennium earlier, towards the end of the Middle Bronze Age. This new wave of Aegean and Anatolian settlers had migrated to Philistia as a direct response to the great famine and in order to escape the turmoil caused by the collapse of the Hittite empire and the fall of Troy. But Philistia was not their intended destination. Like many refugees before them in a time of crisis, they had been heading for Egypt.

Ashkelon was as far as they got. Ramesses III met the army of Moksus near Gaza and halted the invasion of his land. Moksus was killed and the northern confederacy of Pilaset (Philistines), Tjeukera (Teuceri), Shikilesh (Cilicians), Shardina (from Sardis in Lydia), Danoyna (Danoi, Homer's Bronze Age Greeks) and Washosha (from Iasos or Ouassos) were repulsed. Many of the survivors of the battle took refuge with their brethren in the five Philistine cities of Ashkelon, Ashdod, Gath, Gaza and Ekron. Others chose to seek out a new life further afield. They took to the ships which had been shadowing their march down from Cilicia and sailed west to found colonies on the islands of the western Mediterranean (especially Sicily and Sardinia), in Italy and along the coast of north Africa. This was the beginning of the great colonising movement of Greek and Phoenician tradition, made famous by the stories of Dido

30. Shardina mercenaries in Ramesses III's defence force attack the Sea Peoples land army as it approaches the Sinai frontier. The invaders were searching for a new homeland, bringing their women and children with them, transported in ox-carts.

and Aeneas and the legends surrounding the foundations of Carthage and Rome.

It was a band of these newcomers, remaining behind on the fringes of the Negeb, which attacked Judah in the reign of Jehoram. The king's wives and children were captured by the plunderers and taken away to be sold as slaves, leaving only the youngest son to inherit his father's throne. Jehoram's eight-year reign came to an end a couple of years later in 842 BC when he died and was succeeded by his surviving son, Ahaziah.

In his very first year, the new king of Jerusalem agreed to accompany his uncle, Joram of Samaria, on a second campaign to try to recover Ramoth-Gilead from the Aramaeans. Ahab had died at the first attempt and his son (Joram of Israel) and great-grandson (Ahaziah of Judah) now fared little better. Hazael's army marched south to repulse the Israelite incursion. A long-drawn-out battle ensued with the Israelite army holding out against repeated attacks. During one of these assaults upon Ramoth-Gilead, Joram of Samaria was wounded by an arrow, just as had happened to his father, and returned to the winter palace at Jezreel to recover from the wound. Ahaziah, his young comrade-in-arms, joined the king of Israel there, leaving the senior Israelite army commanders to take charge of the campaign in Transjordan.

At the same time the prophet Elisha was making secret moves to oust the two royal allies. The series of military defeats and loss of the vassal states had made the Israelites weak and it was time for a new, strong leader to take control. Elisha sent a priest to Ramoth-Gilead to anoint one of the generals still stationed there. Jehu, a tough, uncompromising warlord, was proclaimed king of Israel by his troops and headed for Jezreel to seize the throne.

As soon as the kings of Israel and Judah came out to greet their army commander they realised they had been tricked. They tried to turn and flee back into the safety of the fortified palace … but it was too late. Jehu loosed an arrow which struck Joram between the shoulder blades and pierced his heart. The king of Israel dropped down dead in his chariot. Ahaziah was pursued to Megiddo. Having himself been struck by an arrow, he died there. The servants of the king of Judah carried the body of their master back to Jerusalem for burial. King Ahaziah, youngest son of Jehoram, had ruled the Southern Kingdom for less than a year.

In the meantime, Jehu had entered Jezreel to search out the Phoenician 'harlot', Queen Jezebel. The defiant daughter of Ittobaal, king of Sidon, prepared to meet her end, painting her eyelids with kohl and donning a golden diadem. From the upper storey of the royal apartments she railed against her son's murderer. The palace servants quickly realised that their future now lay in the hands of the usurper. The most powerful lady in the land – wife of Ahab, mother of two kings, grandmother of a third and great-grandmother of a fourth – was in no position to save herself ... or them. Better to show their allegiance to the new power in Israel than die for a lost cause.

Jezebel was hurled from the window and cast down onto the cobbled street before the chariot of Jehu, who rode over the queen to enter the palace as its new lord and master. Jezebel's body was left to the dogs in fulfilment of Elisha's prophecy.

> The dogs will eat the flesh of Jezebel in the field of Jezreel. The corpse of Jezebel will be like dung spread in the fields, so that no-one will be able to say 'This was Jezebel.' [2 Kings 9:37]

According to the biblical practice of translating foreign names into Hebrew words, the queen's Phoenician hypo-coristic nomen was changed from Yezebul ('[Baal] is exalted') to Hebrew Ayzebel (i.e. Jezebel – 'where is the piece of dung?') – a pejorative which has become synonymous with the harlot – the archetypal sinful woman whose body-parts were strewn across the fields of Jezreel, scattered amongst the cattle droppings.

Jehu, in the typical fashion of royal assassin and usurper, slaughtered the entire royal family of the House of Omri, leaving no-one alive to contest the throne. Seventy of Ahab's sons, resident in Samaria, were butchered, their heads delivered in baskets to Jehu in Jezreel.

> Jehu then killed every member of the House of Ahab surviving in Jezreel, all his leading men, his close friends, his priests; he did not leave a single one alive. [2 Kings 10:11]

As ill-luck would have it, Jehu also captured the princes of Judah on their way to pay their respects to Jezebel in Jezreel, not realising the *coup d'état* had taken place. And so Jehu

> ... slaughtered them at the storage-well of Beth-Eked – forty-two of them – he did not spare a single one. [2 Kings 10:14]

But the bloodletting was not over yet for this most bloodthirsty of Israel's rulers and the agent of Elisha's punishment for those who did not follow Yahweh's' path.

> When he entered Samaria, he killed all the survivors of Ahab's family in Samaria; he destroyed it, as Yahweh had told Elijah it would happen. [2 Kings 10:17]

Next came the priests and prophets of Baal. They were summoned to a great assembly in the temple of Baal in Samaria. Once inside, the signal was given for the slaughter to begin.

> The guards and equerries went in, putting everyone to the sword all the way to the holy of holies in

> Baal's temple. They took the sacred (Asherah) pole
> out of Baal's temple and burned it. They demolished
> Baal's image and demolished Baal's temple too,
> making it into a latrine, which it still is today. [2
> Kings 10:25–27]

According to the writer of the book of Kings, Jehu's deeds
were rewarded by Israel's state god who granted his dynasty
four further 'generations' of rule over the Northern Kingdom – made manifest in the reigns of Jehoahaz, Jehoash,
Jeroboam II and Zechariah.

> Yahweh said to Jehu, 'Since you have done well in
> carrying out what pleases me, and have done every-
> thing I required to be done to the House of Ahab,
> your sons will occupy the throne of Israel down to
> the fourth generation.' [2 Kings 10:30]

The four descendants of Jehu reigned for a total of seventy
years before being ousted by the generation which witnessed the fall of Samaria at the hands of the Assyrians.

More Murder and Palace Intrigue

With the burial of King Ahaziah in Jerusalem, the queen-
mother Athaliah (daughter of Ahab and Jezebel), having
done away with all the royal princes, seized the throne.
However, Ahaziah's sister – Jehosheba by name – had
spirited away the youngest of the dead king's sons before
he could be murdered along with his elder brothers. For
six years the baby Jehoash was brought up in secret within
the Temple of Yahweh whilst Athaliah reigned as Judah's
only female monarch. Then, in the seventh year of her
rule, the queen was overthrown and herself murdered in a
palace coup led by the high priest Jehoiada and the commander of the CARIAN royal guard. The temple of Baal in
Jerusalem was destroyed and its high priest put to the sword.

The seven-year-old Jehoash (whose name is shortened to Joash in the Bible) was established on the throne of Judah as Ahaziah's legitimate heir in 835 BC. He then reigned for forty years.

The New World Order

In the eleventh year of Joash's reign (Year 17 of Jehu in Samaria) the Egyptian priest, Wenamun, set sail for Byblos to obtain cedar wood to repair the great barque of Amun. He left Egypt in the fifth year of the 'Repeating of Births' (825 BC) – a 'Renaissance Era' when several pharaohs were established as co-rulers in the Nile valley, following another period of civil war which devastated Egypt towards the end of the 20th Dynasty.

Whilst his ship was tied up at the Canaanite port of Dor, the Egyptian envoy was robbed of the funds given to him for the purchase of the wood for Karnak's great religious barge. He then got himself embroiled in a dispute with Tjeukera pirates who had settled in the Levantine port during Moksus' invasion thirty-one years earlier. These were just the first of many trials and tribulations for the unfortunate Wenamun. Nevertheless he continued on to Byblos in the hope that the king of that city would grant his request for the wood and treat it as a gift of friendship and loyalty towards Egypt.

However, things had changed in the ancient world. This was the early Iron Age and Egypt was no longer the master of all it surveyed. The New Kingdom Bronze Age empire had withered by the end of the reign of Ramesses III. Egyptian influence in the south continued for a while, but the northern Levantine coast was lost as a result of constant attacks by the Sea Peoples of the Aegean and Anatolia, whilst the lands of the northern interior had fallen firmly under the control of the rising power in the region – Assyria.

Wenamun was humiliated by being kept waiting twenty-nine days in the port of Byblos for an audience with the king of the city. Then, after all that, the lord of Byblos refused to supply the wood without full and proper payment. Wenamun thus had to remain in Byblos for many months whilst agents of the king were despatched south to collect Egypt's part of the 'gift exchange'. Just as things were looking up, with the funds from Egypt arriving and the wood waiting by the shore for loading, a fleet of eleven ships turned up in the port of Byblos. The Tjeukera pirates from Dor had caught up with Wenamun and were demanding he be handed over to them. Egypt's accident-prone envoy managed to give his hunters the slip once more but had to endure a perilous journey home via Cyprus, where he narrowly avoided being beaten to death by an angry mob. So much for the prestige and respect given to an envoy of the mighty temple of Karnak following the demise of the Egyptian New Kingdom!

That king of Byblos, who at first rebuffed the Egyptian envoy, was Zikarbaal (Greek *Sicharbas*, called Sychaeus in the *Aeneid*), husband of Dido, who was herself the sister of Pumatos (Greek *Pygmalion*) king of Tyre (831–785 BC).

Within weeks of Wenamun's departure from Byblos, Zikarbaal was assassinated by Pygmalion. According to legend, Dido fled her murdered husband's capital by sea to found Phoenicia's most famous colony – Carthage (Phoenician *Kahardasht* – 'new city') on the north coast of Africa (in modern Tunisia). The traditional date for the founding of Carthage is 825 BC. According to the New Chronology, this is Year 5 of the REPEATING OF BIRTHS in Egypt – when Egyptian texts record the visit by Wenamun to Zikarbaal in Byblos. In the conventional scheme, Wenamun made his journey to Zikarbaal in 1076 BC – a full two-and-a-half centuries before the founding of Carthage.

Israel's Saviour

In the twenty-third year of Joash's reign in Judah (813 BC) King Jehu died in Samaria and was succeeded by his son

Jehoahaz (813–797 BC). Then, within a couple of years, the scourge of the Children of Yahweh – the Aramaeans – arose once more, this time to challenge both of the Israelite kingdoms.

First, Hazael of Damascus attacked the Philistine city of Gath in 811 BC. The Aramaeans sensed that the lowlands of the coastal plain were ripe for plunder with Egypt preoccupied with its own internal problems following the civil war of 830 BC. Gath fell and Hazael turned east, heading up into the hill country to sack Jerusalem. In a desperate move to avoid the destruction and ransacking of his capital, Joash requisitioned all the treasures of his kingdom – even the sacred offerings in Yahweh's temple dedicated by his royal ancestors – and despatched the huge bribe to Hazael before he reached the gates of Jerusalem. The king of Damascus accepted his 'gift' and went home to Aram. Judah was safe for a while.

However, the Northern Kingdom was not spared from Aramaean assaults in subsequent years. Throughout Jehoahaz's reign the Aramaeans continued to raid and plunder. The army of Israel was almost wiped out by this constant attrition. By 803 BC there were only fifty horsemen, ten chariots and ten thousand infantry left to defend Jehoahaz's crumbling kingdom. Then, quite unexpectedly, a saviour appeared, marching up from the south to take on Israel's oppressors.

Out of the confusion and political jostling of the ten-year period known as the Repeating of Births, an Egyptian pharaoh of a new and vigorous bloodline had come to the fore. He was crowned as Hedjkheperre Shoshenk I, founder of the Libyan 22nd Dynasty in 822 BC.

The Meshwesh and Libu tribes of the north African coast had begun to settle in Egypt as early as the time of Merenptah when captives from the king's Libyan wars were garrisoned as mercenaries in the delta cities to protect Egypt's eastern border. During the troubled years of the 20th Dynasty these Libyan warriors had become a powerful force in their own right and their chieftains had played a major part in the civil war which led to the political rebirth or 'Renaissance' known as the Repeating of Births (829–820 BC).

By the second decade of his reign Shoshenk, ruling from the eastern delta city of Bubastis, had come to dominate the whole country – so much so that his son was installed as high priest of Amun at Karnak in 813 BC. Shoshenk's co-rulers – Ramesses XI in Pi-Ramesse, Tjetkheperre Psusennes I in Tanis and Pinudjem I in Thebes – were all subservient to the ruler of Bubastis. The strong man of the Libyan 22nd Dynasty now sallied forth from the eastern delta with a large army to recover Canaan, relinquished by the ineffectual Ramesside rulers of the late 20th Dynasty.

In the spring of Year 21 (802 BC) Shoshenk I campaigned right across the region, pushing back the Aramaeans and seizing Israel's annexed towns wherever he went. He marched up into the hill country, along the border between the kingdoms of Judah and Israel, past Jerusalem, and headed down into the Jordan valley to flush out Hazael's troops occupying the towns in Gilead. On he went,

31. The fragment of a commemorative stela erected by Hedjkheperre Shoshenk I at Megiddo to proclaim his defeat of Hazael's Aramaean hordes occupying Israelite territory in southern Canaan. Sadly, the rest of the stela has not, as yet, been unearthed in the ongoing Megiddo excavations. If and when it does surface, it should cast fascinating new light on the campaign of Israel's 'saviour' who threw out the forces of Damascus in the reign of Jehoahaz of Samaria. It should also prove once and for all that Shoshenk I of the 22nd Dynasty was not the biblical Shishak who plundered the temple of Solomon in Jerusalem.

How are the mighty fallen! [2 Samuel 1:19]

Plate 33: Colossal head of Akhenaten from Karnak temple (Luxor Museum).

Plate 34: The superb 'trial head' of Neferneferuaten Nefertiti found in the sculptor's workshop at Amarna (Berlin Museum).

Plate 35: El-Amarna letter 252 from Labaya to Akhenaten (left); El-Amarna Letter 256 from Mutbaal to Akhenaten, giving the names of five personalities from the book of Samuel (right); both currently in the British Museum.

Plate 36: The famous golden funerary mask of Tutankhamun (Cairo Museum).

So all the elders of Israel came to the king at Hebron. And King David made a pact with them in Yahweh's presence at Hebron, and they anointed David as king of Israel. [2 Samuel 5:3]

Plate 37: General Haremheb receiving the praise of Tutankhamun following his campaign into southern Palestine (Memphite tomb of Haremheb).

Plate 38: Small artefacts (not to scale) from the Egyptian tomb complex north of Damascus Gate: 1 & 2 (ushabti and faience rosettes) from the Garden Tomb; 3 to 6 (funerary stela fragment, alabaster vases, statuette) from St Etienne monastery.

Plate 39: Egyptian palmiform column capital found by the monks of St Etienne.

Plate 40: The inner sarcophagus chamber of the Egyptian tomb at St Etienne.

Plate 41: The Merenptah stela with the name Israel (penultimate row, centre) darkened by the rubbing of tourists' fingers (Cairo Museum).

Plate 42: The famous hieroglyphs which spell out the name Israel on the Merenptah stela (Cairo Museum)

Plate 43: The upper two blocks on the right side of the Hittite Treaty wall of Ramesses II at Karnak. Above the scene of the siege of Ashkelon we see a small enemy (Israelite) chariot being overrun by the bigger horses of Ramesses II's chariot. The Israelites did not possess a chariot force until the reign of Solomon, proving that Ramesses II could not have been the Pharaoh of the Exodus.

Plate 44: A subservient Jehu of Israel grovels at the feet of his Assyrian overlord, Shalmaneser III. Black Obelisk dated to Year 18 of Shalmaneser (British Museum).

Plate 45: The famous black basalt Moabite Stone of King Mesha (Louvre Museum).

Plate 46: King Sargon II of Assyria from the magnificent reliefs in his Khorsabad palace (Louvre Museum).

Plate 47: Israelite deportees heading into exile (British Museum).

northwards into the Jezreel valley where the Egyptian army entered the cities of Taanach and Megiddo in triumph. In the old Solomonic royal city he set up a great stela commemorating his victory over the Aramaeans, a fragment of which was recovered from the excavation debris of Megiddo. In the New Chronology the Shoshenk stela fragment belongs to Stratum V-B (Iron Age I-B). The Egyptian pharaoh then cleared out more of Israel's oppressors from the western Jezreel and Galilean hills before heading through the Carmel ridge into the Sharon plain and on south back in the direction of Egypt. On his way home he despatched a battalion of troops to destroy the early Iron Age fortresses of the Negeb, occupied by the Edomites who had revolted against Judah during the reign of Joram.

By throwing out the Aramaean marauders, Shoshenk had rescued Israel from its oppressors and given the Northern Kingdom's much-beleaguered king vital respite to rebuild his forces. The Aramaeans were not annihilated but they would never be the force for chaos that they had been under Hadadezer (Aziru), Ben-Hadad II, Ben-Hadad III and Hazael.

War Between the Kingdoms

In the thirty-ninth year of Joash's reign (797 BC) Jehoahaz of Israel died, leaving his son and co-regent of three years, Jehoash (799–783 BC), to rule in his stead for the next fourteen years. In 795 BC the long-reigned Joash was murdered by his own palace retainers who placed his son Amaziah (795–767 BC) on the throne. It was during the early years of these two new rulers of the Israelite tribes – Jehoash and Amaziah – that Elisha the prophet died.

Jehoash of Israel was a strong leader and he set about capitalising on Shoshenk I's fortuitous military intervention. Hazael had died in Damascus shortly after the Egyptian campaign of 802 BC, to be succeeded by Ben-Hadad IV. Jehoash seized the initiative and recaptured many of the

Israelite towns in Transjordan and Galilee lost in the time of his father Jehoahaz. Three campaigns were launched by the king of Israel and three times he was victorious against the new king of Damascus.

Meanwhile Amaziah of Jerusalem waged war against the Edomites in the Valley of Salt to the south of the Dead Sea and killed ten thousand of the enemy troops. This victory filled Amaziah with confidence and he arrogantly challenged Jehoash of Israel to a trial of strength to determine which of them should rule as sole king over the Israelite tribes. The battle between Judah and Israel – the first in many years – took place at Beth-Shemesh. Amaziah was defeated and taken captive before being led in shackles back to his own capital city for ritual humiliation. The great wall surrounding Jerusalem was partially demolished as a warning not to challenge Israel's superiority again. The treasures of the temple and royal palace were removed to Samaria along with a substantial number of hostages. The much-chastened Amaziah was then released back to his plundered city where he continued to rule for another sixteen years beyond the death of his conqueror, Jehoash.

Jehoash was succeeded by his son Jeroboam II (782–742 BC) – one of Israel's most powerful kings and second only to Solomon as Israel's monumental monarch.

The New Builder-king

Jeroboam II ascended the throne of Samaria in the fifteenth year of Amaziah and reigned for forty-one years. Following in the footsteps of his father, he set about recovering all the remaining tribal territories lost to the Aramaeans in the previous century. The Damascenes were in no position to resist, having been smashed in the south by Shoshenk I and under the constant threat of the Assyrians in the north. Damascus had paid tribute to Adad-nirari III in 798 BC and Ben-Hadad IV was now a vassal of the Assyrian king. Jeroboam exploited Aram's weakness to the full, seizing territory from the pass of Hamath (in Syria) all the way down to the Dead Sea. These were effectively the old boundaries of the Davidic empire. Although the Bible gives scant space to Jeroboam II (just three paragraphs), this king was perhaps the greatest of the post-schism rulers of Israel. His conquests and resultant control of the trade routes provided the resources to rebuild the cities of the Northern Kingdom, returning them to something like the glory-days of the United Monarchy.

In Megiddo he built a fine governor's palace with its own fortified compound and gate. He also constructed a triple-entry gate into the city made of ashlar stone. The Iron Age II-A city of Megiddo (stratum V-A/IV-B) once believed to have been the work of Solomon is, in fact, nothing of the sort. Solomon, as we now know, was a king of the Late Bronze II-A period. In contradiction to all the tourist signs at Megiddo, the 'Solomonic' building works of the Iron Age II-A were, in reality, the achievement of Jeroboam II.

The famous Shema Seal found beside the gate into the local governor's residence at Megiddo (building 1723) is engraved with Hebrew writing of the eighth century BC (the time of Jeroboam II). The brief inscription simply states 'Shema, servant of Jeroboam'. The New Chronology finally provides the proper historical context for this famous little seal. Shema was Jeroboam II's governor ('servant') at Megiddo and not a contemporary of Solomon's successor Jeroboam I as some historians have tried to argue.

32. This famous Megiddo seal bears the very brief inscription 'Shema, servant of Jeroboam' and is recognised by many writing specialists to date palaeographically to the time of Jeroboam II (782–742 BC) and not to Jeroboam I (931–911 BC) [Illustrated by P. van der Veen].

Jeroboam II also constructed the ashlar triple-entry gates at Gezer and Hazor, the latter having been retaken following its destruction by the Aramaeans late in Solomon's reign (c. 935 BC).

The king also lavished his attention on his capital at Samaria where he built a new palace. This consisted of the solid inner wall which supported a grand terrace (Samaria Period I), later expanded by the construction of an outer casemate wall (Samaria Period II). The palace erected on this terrace was decorated and furnished with magnificent carved ivories (later found by the archaeologists in the debris of Period II). Mixed with building fill for later structures were documents written on ostraca (pottery sherds) which palaeographers have also dated to the eighth century. And, with these, they recovered an inscription bearing the cartouche of Jeroboam's Egyptian contemporary, Osorkon II (NC – 784–760 BC, but OC – 874–850 BC, i.e. a hundred years before Jeroboam II). This combination of historical synchronisms is only possible within the revised chronology model.

In his later years Jeroboam was even able to regain the allegiance of Hamath and Damascus, first established in the time of David. But these challenges to Assyria's control of Syria did not go unnoticed by Adad-nirari III's successors. The era of the Neo-Assyrian empire was drawing near when powerful warrior-kings such as Tiglath-pileser III, Shalmaneser V, Sargon II and Sennacherib swept southwards to subjugate the whole of southern Canaan.

Like the Wolf on the Fold

In Amaziah's eighteenth year, the king of Judah took his son, Uzziah (Azariah), as his co-regent. Only sixteen years of age, he reigned for fifty-two years according to the biblical text. But this last figure is almost certainly an error on the part of the biblical redactor, which has created the most complex and confusing era in the chronology of the

Divided Monarchy period when nothing seems to fit. The only way I have been able to reconstruct the timeline for this period is to reduce Uzziah's fifty-two-year reign to forty-two, and to adjust all the other regnal dates which are synchronised to his shortened reign in a like manner. Thus Pekahiah now comes to the throne in Year 40 of Uzziah, not Year 50, and his successor Pekah in Year 42, not 52. However, Menahem's accession to the throne in Samaria takes place during Year 39 of Uzziah just as 2 Kings 15:17

	Judah (A)	Judah (B)	Tirzah	Samaria
760	19 Uzziah (42)			24 Jeroboam (42)
759	20			25
758	21			26
757	22			27
756	23			28
755	24			29
754	25			30
753	26			31
752	27			32
751	27			33
750	29			34
749	30			35
748	31			36
747	32	1 – Jotham		37
476	33	2		38
475	34	3		39
744	35	4		40
743	36	5		41
742	37	6		42
741	38	7		1 – Zechariah (1)
740	39 (= 1 – Menahem)	8		1 – Menahem (10)
739	40 (= 1 – Pekahiah)	9	1 – Pekahiah (2)	2
738	41	10	2	3
737	42 (= 1 – Pekah)	11 (Uzziah dies)	1 – Pekah (8)	4
736		12	2 (= Jotham sole rule)	5
735		13	3	6
734		14	4	7
733		15	5 T-P III in Galilee	8
732		16	6	9 Pul captures Gaza
731		1 – Ahaz (16)	7 (= 1 – Ahaz)	10 Tribute to T-P III
730		2 (= 1 – Hoshea)	1 – Hoshea (9)	
729		3	2	
728		4	3	
727	1 – Hezekiah (29)	5	4 (= 1 – Hezekiah)	
726	2	6	5	
725	3	7	6	
724	4 (= 7 – Hoshea)	8	7 (= 4 – Hezekiah)	
723	5	9	8	
722	6	10	9 Fall of Samaria	

33. The complex co-regency chronology of 8th-century Israel and Judah.

states. The chronology which results from these adjustments is represented in the chart (previous page).

This is all necessary to maintain the absolute chronological synchronisms with Assyria which define the upper and lower limits of the period. These anchor points are the battle of Karkar in the time of Ahab (Year 6 Shalmaneser III = 853 BC) and the fall of Samaria at the end of the ninth year of Menahem's successor, Hoshea (Year 5 Shalmaneser V = 722 BC). The problems of this confused era are compounded by the fact that a rival line of kings to the Northern Kingdom established itself at Tirzah in opposition to Samaria, whilst Uzziah himself took a co-regent in Judah. So, in the years 739 to 737 BC there were four Israelite monarchs ruling from three capitals at the same time.

The reason for the co-regency in Jerusalem is explained in 2 Kings 15:5 where we read that Uzziah was struck by 'a virulent skin-disease' (probably leprosy) which confined the king to his apartments in the palace whilst his son, Jotham, acted as regent in his stead.

In the thirty-eighth year of Uzziah (Year 7 of his co-regent Jotham = 741 BC) Jeroboam of Samaria died and was succeeded by his son Zechariah. His reign was short-lived. After six months Zechariah was murdered by Shallum of Jabesh-Gilead whilst the king was staying at Ibleam. So ended the line of Jehu in the fourth generation as the prophet Elisha had foretold.

Civil war broke out in the Northern Kingdom of Israel. Shallum was himself slain by Menahem of Tirzah just one month after he had seized the throne. The leader of the revolt then sacked the town of TAPPUAH where he 'disembowelled all the pregnant women', because its citizens had sided with the usurper Shallum. So, in Year 39 of Uzziah (740 BC), Menahem 'son of Gadi' became king of Samaria. In the following year he placed his son Pekahiah on the throne at Tirzah as his co-regent (in Year 40 Uzziah) and ruled himself from Samaria for ten years. But the kingdom was still not secure. Pekahiah was murdered by his equerry,

Pekah, after just two years. The assassin then ruled for a further eight years in opposition to Menahem in Samaria, with the support of the northern tribes of Naphtali, Asher, Zebulun and Issachar. Following the death of Uzziah in 737 BC, Pekah allied himself with King Rezin (755–731 BC) of Damascus and the two campaigned against Jotham (now sole ruler of Judah), who thus found himself a natural ally in Menahem of Samaria.

It was during these years of civil war that the Assyrians finally made their move south to carve out a southern empire and challenge Egyptian hegemony in Canaan. The invitation to march south came from Menahem, who needed Assyria's help to put an end to Pekah's rebellion. The 'fee' for the military intervention was an astonishing one-off payment of a thousand talents of silver (three million shekels, equivalent to thirty-seven tons). Bearing in mind that the slave-price in those days was fifty shekels, this was a huge sum, collected by Menahem from landowners and merchants of Israel still loyal to him.

And so, in 733 BC the Assyrian emperor Tiglath-pileser III (744–727 BC) – the Bible calls him by his hypocoristicon 'Pul' – arrived in northern Israel. He captured all the towns of Galilee, including Hazor, deporting a large percentage of the population back to Assyria. Pekah's support in the north was utterly crushed. Pul marched on south, through the Carmel ridge onto the Sharon plain and down into Philistia where he captured Gaza on the Egyptian border. Having wreaked havoc all through northern and western Canaan, the Assyrian king returned home, leaving Menahem's Israel and Jotham's Judah untouched. Tiglath-pileser III then spent the next two years finishing off Aramaean resistance. The following spring he was besieging Damascus, which held out for a whole year before succumbing in 731 BC. King Rezin, the last Aramaean scourge of the Israelites, was executed and the whole of Syria was finally annexed into the Assyrian empire.

Meanwhile, back in Israel, Pekah was now completely

isolated. He held out for two more years but then in 730 BC was murdered by Hoshea (730–722 BC), son of Elah. In 731 BC Jotham had died in Jerusalem to be succeeded by his son Ahaz (731–716 BC) and, at the close of that same year, Menahem 'fell asleep with his ancestors', leaving Hoshea as sole ruler in the Northern Kingdom.

For a while the new king of Israel, established on the throne by his Mesopotamian masters, continued to pay the annual tribute to Assyria, now under the rule of Shalmaneser V (726–722 BC). But Hoshea was also writing to Pharaoh So, asking for his help to throw off the Assyrian yoke. According to the New Chronology, the senior monarch in Egypt at this time was the long-reigned Usermaatre Shoshenk III (758–720 BC). The biblical name 'So' is thus a hypocoristicon of Sho[shenk] (Assyrian *Su[sinku]*). The reality was that Shoshenk III was in no position to campaign in Canaan because of the growing threat on his southern border from a Kushite line of pharaohs which would soon rule Egypt as the 25th Dynasty. Hoshea was on his own.

Unfortunately, Shalmaneser of Assyria got wind of the plot to involve the Egyptians and took matters into his own hands. In 724 BC he brought the Assyrian army back south and laid siege to Samaria. Hoshea held out for two years before the royal capital fell in the year of Shalmaneser V's death. It was down to his successor, Sargon II (721–705 BC), to complete the military operation, dragging the last king of Israel off to Mesopotamia in chains, along with thousands of his Israelite subjects. The annals of Sargon add considerable detail to the story of Israel's fall.

> ... the men of Samaria with their king were hostile to me and consorted together not to carry out their vassal obligations or bring tribute to me. So they fought me ... I clashed with them and took as booty 27,280 people with their chariots and their gods in whom they trusted. I incorporated 200 chariots into my army. The rest of the people I made to dwell

within Assyria. I restored the city of Samaria and
made it greater than before.

The 'lost tribes' of Israel, deported in the disastrous years
from 732 to 721 BC, were settled in the former territory of
Mitanni (the Khabur river region), as well as in the land of
the Medes (around Mount Sahand in former Eden) and in
Assyria proper. The town of Samaria was transformed into
the capital of the Samarian governorate of the Assyrian
empire with a native Assyrian governor resident in King
Jeroboam II's old palace. As part of their policy to weaken
resistance to Assyrian hegemony, Sargon II imported
foreigners from the north (in particular Babylon and the
territory of Hamath) to settle in the empty towns of Samaria.
These newcomers eventually adopted Yahweh as their deity
and are identified in the New Testament with the people
known as the Samaritans.

ᐃᕀᐊ᙭ᔕᏀ

Chapter Eighteen

EXILE

(2 Kings 18:1 to 2 Kings 25:30 and 2 Chronicles 28:1 to
2 Chronicles 36:21)

*Hezekiah's Reforms – Sennacherib's Invasion – The Fall
of Lachish – Egypt's Retaliation – Manasseh – Josiah
and the Lost Scroll – The Fall of Jerusalem*

Although, over the centuries, the two kingdoms had
occasionally quarrelled and gone to war with each
other, the people of Israel and Judah still saw themselves as Israelites with a common heritage. Now, with the
Northern Kingdom kingless, much of its population deported and an Assyrian governor resident in Samaria, the two
co-regent rulers of Judah – Ahaz and Hezekiah – felt
isolated and alone. The forces of the Assyrian empire were
poised on Judah's borders, ready to strike at any moment.
Preparations were hastily made to shore up Jerusalem's
defences and the army enlarged for despatch to the outlying
Judahite cities. Hezekiah began work on a tunnel which
would divert the waters of the Gihon spring into the city
so that Jerusalem had access to plentiful supplies of drink-
ing-water during a prolonged siege. The tunnel survives to

this day, winding through the limestone beneath the City of David for five hundred and thirty metres (1,740 ft) from the spring below the stepped stone structure which supported the old royal palace south to the pool of Siloam, safely within the town walls. At the point where the two tunnelling teams met, as they worked their way from either end of the project, the workmen carved a commemorative inscription.

> See the tunnel. This is the story of how it was built. When the miners were swinging their axes, one miner towards another, and when there were only three more cubits to dig, a voice of one miner was heard calling to his comrades (for there was an echo in the rock) both from the north and from the south. On the day when the miners broke through, they struck one against the other, axe against axe, and the water flowed from the spring into the pool, 1,200 cubits long. The rock above the miners' heads was 100 cubits in height.

In his sixteenth regnal year (Year 12 Hezekiah) Ahaz died and Hezekiah became sole ruler in Judah. He immediately began a series of pious reforms, dismantling the high places of worship scattered about the hills outside Jerusalem. He overthrew the Asherah poles and even smashed the bronze serpent made by Moses in 1407 BC at the copper mines of Punon in the Arabah basin. This powerful standard had become an object of veneration and Hezekiah believed that it distracted from the purity of Yahweh worship. Aided by the prophet Isaiah, the king of Judah determined that only Yahweh could save Jerusalem from destruction and no false idols must be allowed to anger Israel's great god. He had witnessed how Yahweh had abandoned the Northern Kingdom. Jerusalem, with its national temple, must remain unswervingly loyal to Yahweh at the expense of all the foreign gods and fetishes to which the ordinary folk adhered. At the same time, Judah's ruler prepared his troops for war.

In Hezekiah's fifteenth year the king fell ill with a serious ulcer and was on the point of death. However, with the application of a fig poultice supplied by the prophet Isaiah, Hezekiah miraculously recovered and continued to reign for a further fifteen years. A year later, in 712 BC, King Marduk-apla-iddina II of Babylon (721–710 BC, biblical Merodach-Baladan) sent an ambassadorial delegation to Jerusalem to congratulate Hezekiah on his recovery. Behind this overtly friendly gesture lay a rather darker political agenda. The rulers of the ancient world were beginning to forge military alliances in the face of Assyria's ever-threatening expansionist policies.

The Return of the Assyrians

Eight years later (in 705 BC), Hezekiah learnt that Sargon II of Assyria had died whilst campaigning in Cappadocia (central Anatolia) that spring. The body of the great warlord – scourge of Israel and Philistia – had not been recovered from the battlefield for burial. Isaiah mocked the Assyrian ruler's undignified end in typical prophetic fashion.

> Is this the man who made the earth tremble? Who shook kingdoms? Who made the world like a desert and overthrew its cities? Who would not let his prisoners go home? All the kings of the nations lie in glory, each in his own tomb. But you are cast out – away from your grave – like loathsome carrion … [Isaiah 14:16–19]

With the surprise defeat of the Assyrian army and the death of the king in a far-off land, a political shock-wave swept across the ancient world. Great swathes of the Assyrian empire erupted in revolt. Hezekiah realised that now was his moment to seize the initiative and cast off the Assyrian yoke. He immediately led his forces down onto the coastal plain and attacked the old Philistine territory around Gaza which had remained stubbornly loyal to the empire. He also refused to pay tribute to the Assyrian governor at Samaria. The new ruler of Nineveh – Sennacherib (704–681 BC) son of Sargon – was informed of the trouble going on in his southern border zone with Egypt, but he had rebellion to take care of nearer home before he could turn his attention to the Judaean revolt. Having suppressed the uprising in Mesopotamia by defeating Marduk-apla-iddina and his allies, Sennacherib finally marched south to take care of his troublesome Judaean vassal.

In 702 BC (Hezekiah's fourteenth year of sole rule) the Assyrian army was besieging the large city of LACHISH when Sennacherib received a message of capitulation from Hezekiah. Judah would surrender, accept its vassal status and make reparation for the attack upon those Philistine cities which had been under Assyria's hegemony. The Assyrian king despatched a division of troops up into the hills, led by his chief deputy (Akkadian *rabshakeh*), to negotiate surrender terms and collect the heavy ransom. A payment of three hundred talents of silver and thirty talents of gold was handed over. Jerusalem was thus spared – but Judah's capital and its pious king had paid a heavy price for their redemption. The royal coffers were empty and even the golden panelling on the great cedar doors and jambs of Yahweh's temple had to be stripped away in order to meet Sennacherib's ransom.

Even though Sennacherib had agreed to spare the Judahite capital, the Assyrian army continued to besiege Lachish. Eventually the city (Stratum IV) fell – its citizens sent back to Mesopotamia in fetters. All in all the Assyrian annals record the deportation of more than two hundred thousand Judaeans from Hezekiah's cities.

As for Hezekiah the Judaean, who had not submitted to my yoke, I besieged forty-six of his fortified walled cities and surrounding smaller towns, which were without number. Using siege ramps and by applying battering rams, infantry attacks by mines, breeches, and siege machines, I conquered (them all). I took out 200,150 people, young and old, male and female, horses, mules, donkeys, camels, cattle, and sheep, without number, and counted them as the spoils of war. [*Taylor Prism*, British Museum]

Then, quite unexpectedly, a powerful enemy appeared on the scene to challenge Sennacherib's wholesale devastation of the southern coastal plain. News reached the king at his military headquarters in Lachish that a great Egyptian army was marching out from northern Sinai to confront the Assyrians.

Egypt was now under the rule of the Kushite 25th Dynasty (714–664 BC). Prince Taharka, son of Piankhy, had been appointed commander-in-chief of the Egyptian military forces as the representative of his aged uncle Shabaka, ruling in Memphis. Osorkon III of Thebes also contributed his soldiers to the fight, as did Pimay of Tanis. A huge contingent of Kushite troops had already marched up from Napata (in Sudan) at the behest of King Piankhy, with Crown-Prince Taharka at its head. The whole army amassed at the old city of Pi-Ramesse before sallying forth, past Migdol and across the flat desert of northern Sinai to meet the Assyrian threat head-on. The battle between the two superpowers took place at Eltekeh, where Sennacherib managed to inflict a crushing defeat upon Taharka. However, the triumph was short-lived as the Assyrian troops, having been on campaign for several months, started to come down with both bacillary dysentery and plague. Herodotus (Book II:141) explains this calamity as a plague of mice which devoured the bowstrings of the Assyrian archers – but it was almost certainly the bubonic plague carried by rats. The Greek god of pestilence was Apollo Smintheus – the mouse-god.

King Sennacherib then broke his word. Having accepted a payment to leave Hezekiah's Jerusalem unharmed, the king of Assyria reneged on the deal and sent his troops back up to Jerusalem. He intended to make an example of the leader of the southern revolt. An advanced guard surrounded the city, preparing for a long siege and, as the Assyrian annals put it, they 'shut the Judaean up in his royal capital like a bird in a cage' whilst the main Assyrian force rested from the battle against Egypt near the town of LIBNAH. However, King Sennacherib's deceit did not to go unpunished.

One morning the king awoke to find that one hundred and eighty-five of his officers had died of the plague during the night. Sennacherib could not sustain such heavy losses amongst his key commanders, given the large numbers of troops killed at Eltekeh and from the subsequent pestilence. There was nothing else for it but to retreat back to Nineveh. King Sennacherib never returned to the coastal plain of Philistia. According to later Jewish tradition, he was eventually murdered by his own sons in 681 BC whilst worshipping a plank of wood from Noah's ark in the temple of the state god, Ashur. Sennacherib was succeeded by his son Esarhaddon after his sibling royal assassins had fled into the mountains of Ararat (Urartu).

The Bible explains the deaths of Sennacherib's commanders at Libnah and the relief of the siege of Jerusalem as the act of God in protection of his loyal servant Hezekiah. In the 2 Kings 19:35 version, the Assyrians are struck down in the middle of the night by the angel of Yahweh. Jerusalem is saved from capture and destruction because the king of Judah and his prophet Isaiah had purified Yahweh's capital city and removed the pagan idols introduced in previous impious reigns.

Hezekiah continued to rule for another three years before dying in his twenty-ninth year (699 BC). He was succeeded by his son, Manasseh (698–644 BC) – one of Judah's most notorious rulers.

The Wicked Kings

King Manasseh was just twelve years old when he came to
the throne and ruled for more than half a century. He rebuilt
the high-places destroyed by Hezekiah, established new
altars dedicated to Baal in the courtyard of Yahweh's temple
and re-erected the Asherah pole in Jerusalem. The king
even sacrificed his own son as a burnt offering to Moloch,
god of fire. The prophets of Judah railed against Manasseh
for his worship of false idols, threatening Jerusalem with a
similar fate to that which befell Samaria. But Manasseh
simply silenced all opposition. The blood of many innocent
people was shed in the first decades of the king's rule –
including that of the prophet Isaiah. Political assassination
and terror ruled in Jerusalem as the warnings of Yahweh's
holy-men went unheeded.

> Yahweh, God of Israel, says this, 'Look, I shall bring
> such disaster on Jerusalem and Judah as will make
> the ears of all who hear of it tingle. … I shall cast
> away the remnant of my heritage, delivering them
> (i.e. the people of Judah) into the clutches of their
> enemies (i.e. the Babylonians) and making them the
> prey and booty of all their foes. For they have done
> what is displeasing to me and have provoked my
> anger from the day that their ancestors came out of
> Egypt until this day.' [2 Kings 21:12–15]

In Manasseh's twenty-ninth year (670 BC), King Esarhaddon of Assyria (680–669 BC) conquered Egypt with
the help of local Arab chieftains who supplied the camels
to ferry provisions across Sinai. Many city-rulers from the
southern states deemed to be Egypt's allies were taken to
Nineveh, along with the minor pharaohs and chieftains of
Egypt's petty kingdoms, for pro-Assyrian political 're-
education' – amongst them Manasseh of Judah. After two
years Jerusalem's king was returned to his capital, remaining

loyal to his new Mesopotamian masters for the last twenty-five years of his long reign. Later tradition (exemplified in 2 Chronicles 33) suggests that he even returned, somewhat belatedly, to the worship of Yahweh, following his exile.*

Egypt had been dominated by King Taharka of Kush (690–665 BC) for nineteen years since he had succeeded his father Piankhy (720–690 BC) in 690 BC.** In his invasion of Egypt, Esarhaddon had thus been confronted by Assyria's old enemy – the young prince, now king, who had battled against Sennacherib at Eltekeh thirty-one years earlier in 702 BC. Esarhaddon, like his father, at first failed to take Egypt in the campaign of 674 BC but his second attempt, four years later, was successful, thanks to the support of the local Bedouin.

Fighting began on the sands of Sinai and continued into the marshes of the eastern delta. The conflict lasted several weeks as the Assyrian forces pushed the Egyptians back in a series of battles. Taharka fought stubbornly to save his kingdom but was eventually forced to concede the old capital of Memphis and retreat south to Thebes, leaving his family, including the crown-prince, to be carried off to Assyria. The whole of the delta was now in foreign hands for the first time since the expulsion of the Hyksos in 1192 BC. The Assyrian king then placed compliant petty-kings in the principal cities of northern Egypt to govern

---

* A pseudepigraphal prayer known as the Lament of Manasseh survives in both Greek and Syriac manuscripts of early Christian times. The text was probably composed by a Jew living in the era prior to the destruction of Herod's temple in AD 70. However, it has been suggested that the prayer is based on the reference to Manasseh's confession of past sins referred to in 2 Chronicles 33:13.

** For five years the new king of Napata (ruling from Kush) had reigned in co-operation with his cousin Shabataka, king of Egypt (son of Shabaka). Then Taharka became sole 25th-Dynasty ruler of both Kush and Egypt in his sixth regnal year following the death of Shabataka in 684 BC. There were other Libyan pharaohs in Egypt (such as Shoshenk V of Tanis and Rudamun of Thebes) but they were all subservient to the Kushite king.

this new addition to the empire on his behalf.

However, almost as soon as Esarhaddon had returned to Nineveh, Taharka went back on the offensive, recapturing Memphis and causing panic amongst the Assyrian king's newly appointed vassals. Esarhaddon was marching back to Egypt in 669 BC when he died. Taharka thus gained valuable time whilst Esarhaddon's successor – Ashurbanipal (668–627 BC) – secured his position. When the Assyrians finally returned south to overthrow Taharka and capture Thebes, Ashurbanipal's huge army included troops from Jerusalem, led by King Manasseh. And so, in 664 BC, soldiers of Jerusalem took part in the devastating destruction and looting of holy Thebes. The sacred Egyptian city of Amun which had stood inviolate for over a thousand years was stripped of its treasures, never to recover its former glory. Taharka fled south into Nubia and was not seen again. Assyria became master of Egypt and all its former territories – including the vassal states of Philistia, Israel and Judah.

In 644 BC Manasseh died and was succeeded by his son Amon, who reverted to the sinful ways of his father, worshipping idols and failing to 'follow the path of Yahweh'. His short reign of two years (643–642 BC) ended with the king's assassination at the hands of his courtiers. But the murderers had failed to gauge the mood of the people. Jerusalem rose up against the plotters and they were all slaughtered. Amon's son, Josiah, was then crowned king of Judah in his father's stead.

A Reformer King

Josiah was just eight years old when he was anointed king of Jerusalem. By the time he reached his twentieth year, the young monarch had already begun a series of major religious reforms to re-establish Yahweh as the one true god, purging Judah of all its high-places, sacred poles and graven images.

He oversaw the smashing of the altars of Baal, he
broke up the incense altars standing above them,
he shattered the sacred poles and the sculpted and
cast images and reduced them to powder, scattering
the powder on the graves of those who had sacrificed to them. He burned the bones of their priests
on their altars and so purified Judah and Jerusalem.
[2 Chronicles 34:4–5]

In his eighteenth regnal year (624 BC) restoration work
was begun on the great temple of Yahweh in Jerusalem. In
the process, the high-priest Hilkiah came across an ancient
scroll which he identified as a copy of the Book of the Law
originally written by Moses. The discovery was so significant to the pious Josiah that he personally read the
scroll's contents out loud before the people of Jerusalem,
assembled in the court of Yahweh's temple. There the
congregation renewed their covenant with the god of the
ancestors and kept faith with Yahweh for the remainder of
Josiah's thirty-one-year reign (641–611 BC).

Having been on display before the people at the
covenant renewal ceremony, the Ark of the Covenant was
placed back in the Holy of Holies of the temple. The king
ordered that it should remain there, no longer to be carried
by the Levitical priests in war or ritual. The Ark of the
Tablets would be mentioned only once more in scripture
before disappearing from human knowledge. A great
Passover feast was then celebrated by the sacrifice of
thousands of bullocks, lambs and goats.

No Passover like this one had ever been celebrated
in Israel since the days of the prophet Samuel, nor
had any of the kings of Israel ever celebrated a Passover like the one celebrated by Josiah, the priests,
the Levites, all Judah and Israel who were present,
and the inhabitants of Jerusalem. [2 Chronicles
35:18]

The Book of the Law found by Hilkiah became the stimulus for the writing of a great historical and didactic narrative of the Children of Yahweh which scholars have called the Deuteronomistic History. In effect, the Deuteronomist (possibly the high-priest Hilkiah or the king's secretary Shaphan) made substantial editorial additions to the original Mosaic composition, written during the Sinai wanderings, before composing new sections and adding other works and oral traditions bringing the story of Yahweh's people up to date. And so the books of DEUTERONOMY, Joshua, Judges, Samuel and Kings were incorporated into the Tanaak (Hebrew scriptures) by the leading religious and administrative scholars of the day.

All this took place in the middle years of Josiah's reign when Assyria continued to dominate Canaan under the forceful rule of King Ashurbanipal. But by the time that the Assyrian emperor had died in 627 BC, a new and more powerful military alliance was beginning to threaten Judah's masters. During the reign of Ashurbanipal's successor, Sinsharishkun (626–612 BC), Babylon and Assyria were constantly at war. The conflict came to a head in 614 BC when King Nabopolassar (Nabu-apil-usur, 626–606 BC) of Babylon (with the help of his allies the Medes from western Iran) conquered Ashur and then, two years later, Nineveh. Assyria's great cities were left in smouldering ruins. Ashuruballit III, the last of Assyria's rulers, managed to escape and regroup his forces at Harran where Abraham had once stayed. He then called for military assistance from Assyria's old vassal and erstwhile enemy, Egypt. Extraordinary as it may seem to us today, the recently crowned Pharaoh Necho II (611–596 BC) marched north to join the battle against Babylon. Egypt's reasons for coming to the aid of its recent oppressors remain a mystery. Perhaps Necho realised that the rising power of Babylon posed a far greater threat to continuing Egyptian hard-won sovereignty than the declining state of Assyria.

In a time of confusing political manoeuvres, a fateful

decision was also made by Josiah of Jerusalem. Instead of sitting back and watching the Egyptians march up the Via Maris into Syria, on their way to Assyria's aid, the king of Judah blockaded Necho's advance in the plain below the city of Megiddo. Necho sent messengers ahead to warn Josiah to move out of the way – his quarrel was not with Judah, he had more important matters to attend to in the far north. But the Judaean monarch stubbornly refused to budge. The ensuing battle cost Josiah his life, shot in the chest by an Egyptian arrow. The king of Judah was carried away in his chariot and buried in Jerusalem, to be succeeded by his son Jehoahaz in 610 BC.

The Fall of Jerusalem

Jehoahaz lasted just three months. Upon his return from the north, Pharaoh Necho had the young twenty-three-year-old arrested and taken back to Egypt. In Jehoahaz's place the Egyptians made Eliakim, son of Josiah, king of Jerusalem. At his coronation the new ruler took the name Jehoiakim – changing the theophoric element in his birth-name from El to Yahu (Yahweh). Jehoahaz died in captivity.

Heavy taxes were levied on the citizens of Judah in order to pay the huge sums demanded by Necho in vassal tribute during the first few years of Jehoiakim's eleven-year reign (609–599 BC). Then, in 606 BC, the Egyptian pharaoh was defeated at Carchemish on the upper Euphrates by Prince Nebuchadrezzar whilst the latter's father, Nabopolassar, lay dying in Babylon. The Egyptian army was almost wiped out as it fought a bloody retreat back through Amurru and Canaan to Sinai. In the following year (605 BC) Nebuchadrezzar II (Nabu-kudur-usur, 605–563 BC), now king and emperor, marched his victorious army to the borders of Egypt to stake his claim on the last unconquered region of the old Assyrian empire. The king of Babylon succeeded in subjugating all the territories in Canaan recovered by Egypt during the Saite (26th Dynasty) revival under Psamtek I and Necho II. The Babylonians had arrived on the biblical scene.

> The king of Egypt did not come again out of his land, for the king of Babylon had taken all that belonged to the king of Egypt – from the Brook of Egypt (i.e. Wadi el-Arish) to the River Euphrates. [2 Kings 24:7]

Judah and Jerusalem submitted to Nebuchadrezzar at the behest of Jerusalem's pro-Babylonian faction – led by the prophet Jeremiah – but there were many who only grudgingly accepted their new predicament. Amongst these reluctant vassals was the king himself. Jehoiakim found the Babylonians even more oppressive and demanding than the Egyptians.

In his fourth regnal year (602 BC) Nebuchadrezzar attempted to invade Egypt, but suffered a major setback – repulsed by Necho II's replenished forces. The Babylonians retreated back to Mesopotamia and it looked as if the tide had turned in favour of the pro-Egyptian lobby in Jerusalem. Necho retook Gaza and Jehoiakim openly rebelled against Babylonian hegemony. But Judah's independence was short-lived.

In December 599 BC, the king of Babylon gathered a huge army of Mesopotamians, Aramaeans, Ammonites and Moabites – all Israel's old enemies – with the intention of putting an end to the Judaean revolt. The outcome was inevitable when the Egyptians chose not to come to Jerusalem's rescue. The Babylonian Chronicle records what happened in its customary terse fashion.

> Year 7 in the month of Kislev. The king of Babylonia mobilised his troops and marched to the west. He encamped against the city of Judah (i.e. Jerusalem) and, on the second of Adar (16th March 598 BC), he captured the city and seized its king. A king of

his choice he appointed there. He took its heavy
tribute and carried it off to Babylon.

As Nebuchadrezzar's great army was on its way into
southern Canaan, Jehoiakim had died, to be succeeded by
his son, the eighteen-year-old Jehoiakin. The new king's
whole reign was spent caged up within his capital as the
Babylonians laid siege to Jerusalem. Jehoiakin capitulated
after three months and surrendered to the mercy of King
Nebuchadrezzar. The royal family of Judah was deported
to Babylon, where the Judaean monarch remained in prison
for thirty-seven years. He was finally pardoned and released
upon the death of Nebuchadrezzar and the installation of
Evil-Merodach (Amel-Marduk, 562–560 BC), in whose
time he became a favourite of the court and ate at the king's
table.

But, back in 598 BC, the Babylonian army had entered
Jerusalem and carried off the treasures of Yahweh's temple
and the royal palace. Ten thousand men of high rank were
force-marched into exile, along with military personnel and
skilled artisans such as metalworkers. Only the poorest
citizens were left behind in Judah's capital. Jehoiakin's
paternal uncle, Mattaniah, was made king of Jerusalem by
Nebuchadrezzar, taking the throne-name ZEDEKIAH.

Zedekiah ruled for eleven years (597–587 BC). Almost
as soon as the king of Judah was crowned, Necho II died
in Egypt and was replaced by his son Psamtek II (596–
590 BC). Then, in 590 BC, Psamtek in turn was succeeded
by Pharaoh Apries (590–571 BC), known to the Bible as
Hophra. The new 26th-Dynasty Egyptian ruler immediately set out to challenge Babylonian hegemony in southern
Canaan and encouraged the city-state rulers of the region
to rebel against their Mesopotamian masters. Zedekiah
bought the Egyptian propaganda and, ignoring the vehe-
ment protests of the prophet Jeremiah, declared Judah's
independence from Babylon. He was cruelly punished for
his lack of loyalty.

Nebuchadrezzar returned to Jerusalem in January 589 BC (Zedekiah's ninth year) and laid siege to the city for two full years. The siege was lifted briefly in 588 BC when Apries mounted a counter-attack against the Babylonians, but he failed to rescue his Judaean ally. The siege resumed. In July of the following year, with the population ravaged by starvation and disease, a breach was finally made in Jerusalem's wall and the Babylonian army stormed into the city. Zedekiah fled under cover of darkness but was captured by the pursuing Babylonian troops near Jericho. He was taken to Nebuchadrezzar, camped at RIBLAH in Syria. There, in the summer of 587 BC, the last in a long line of Judahite rulers was forced to witness the slaughter of his own sons before having his eyes gouged out. Zedekiah was dragged off in chains to die in Babylonian exile.

A month later Nebuchadrezzar's top military commander, Nabuzaradan, arrived in Jerusalem to oversee the total destruction of the city. The temple of Yahweh was put to the flame. The bronze pillars and cultic furnishings were broken up and carried off. The high priest, Zephaniah, the temple priests, the Judaean military commanders and friends of the king were all rounded up and taken to Riblah where they were summarily executed. Great fires were set throughout Jerusalem. The royal palace and all the noble houses in the City of David were destroyed and the city wall demolished. The rest of the population was carried off into slavery. Little of value was left in the ruins for the few scavengers left behind. The Children of Yahweh were gone from King David's royal city.

> How deserted sits the city which once was full of people! How like a widow she has become – she that was great amongst the nations! [Lamentations 1:1]

Nebuchadrezzar appointed Gedaliah, grandson of Josiah's royal scribe Shaphan, as governor in the Babylonian province of Judah, resident at Mizpah a few kilometres north of the ruined capital. He was joined there by the prophet Jeremiah. But two months later Gedaliah was murdered, along with his Babylonian officials, by Ishmael, son of Nethaniah of the royal house of David. The remaining people of Judah, living in the scattered towns and villages, realised that retribution would quickly follow and so they fled southwards to Egypt, establishing colonies in the delta and Nile valley. The most famous of these settlements is on the island of Elephantine at Syene (Aswan) where some of the earliest Hebrew documents have been unearthed. Amongst the refugees was the prophet Jeremiah, who carried a great secret with him on the flight into Egypt – a secret which he would take to his Egyptian grave in Tahpanhes (Tell Daphne) – the Baal-Zephon of Exodus.

During the days of respite when the siege of Jerusalem had been lifted in 588 BC, Yahweh's messenger had gone to Solomon's temple and, with the help of the temple priests, removed the Ark of the Covenant and the Tent of the Tabernacle from their resting place in the Holy of Holies. He then took the temple scrolls and gave them to the people who were soon to be exiled to Babylon, saying that they should 'never forget the Lord's precepts' and urging them 'not to let the Law (of Moses) depart from their hearts'. The fate of the Ark of the Tablets is disclosed in a passage from the second book of Maccabees.

> ... the prophet (Jeremiah), warned by an oracle, gave orders for the tent and the ark to go with him, when he set out for the mountain which Moses had climbed to survey God's heritage. On his arrival, Jeremiah found a cave-dwelling, into which he put the tent, the Ark and the altar of incense, afterwards blocking up the entrance. Some of his companions went back later (in the time of Gedaliah) to mark out the path but were unable to find it. When Jeremiah learned this, he reproached them: 'The place is

to remain unknown', he said, 'until God gathers his
people together again and shows them his mercy.
Then the Lord will bring these things once more to
light, and the glory of the Lord will be seen, and so
will the cloud, as it was revealed in the time of Moses
…' [2 Maccabees 2: 4–8]

And so the Ark of the Covenant disappeared from the
world as Jerusalem fell, hidden now for more than two-
and-a-half millennia in the cave on Mount Nebo which
had already housed the bones of Moses for more than eight
hundred years. During that entire time the Israelites had
dwelt in the Promised Land – first as a disparate group of
tribes eking out a pastoral existence in tented villages
scattered amongst the ruins of the great Middle Bronze
Age fortified towns of Canaan. Four centuries later they
had become a nation under the leadership of three charismatic kings – Saul, David and Solomon – but then had
been split asunder by pretensions to grandeur and petty
dynastic rivalry. Towards the end of the eighth century BC
the once powerful Northern Kingdom of Israel had been
humbled by the Assyrians and now Judah, with its beautiful
capital, had been destroyed by the might of Nebuchadrezzar's Babylon.

Yahweh's holy shrine lay in ruins – the Israelite god no
longer present. According to prophecy, seventy years
would pass before some of the exiles were allowed to return
(during the reign of the beneficent Persian monarch Cyrus
the Great (559–530 BC)) to rebuild the temple of their
god. But the golden casket of Moses was not brought back
to its former home.

The era of the Children of Yahweh was over. The lives
of the Israelites had been changed utterly by their deportation to Mesopotamia. Generations lived and died by the
waters of Babylon before a new world order was born out
of the ashes of the old. Their Babylonian oppressor, in
turn, fell to the Medes and Persians in 539 BC.

By 518 BC the first stones of Yahweh's new temple were being laid upon the ruins of Solomon's past glory – stones upon which, one day, far into the future, the sandalled feet of a Nazarene healer and prophet would walk. The age of the Israelites was at an end and the Jewish world had begun.

EPILOGUE

I began this story with a family or small tribe living beside a rather unassuming river (today known as the Adji Chay – 'bitter waters') in a place called Eden. Five thousand years later the distant descendants of that family bring our story to its close – exiled from their homeland, languishing in captivity beside the waters of Babylon.

The Bible is recognised as the world's greatest work of epic literature, not only for its scope (spanning hundreds of generations) but also in its vivid portrayal of humanity as seen through the eyes of one 'chosen' people – the Children of Yahweh. But the Old Testament, in so many respects, does not glorify these people in the way that other documents of the ancient world do their kings and champions. The heroes of the Bible are humans with frailties and flaws. Their successes and failures are measured against their allegiance to one god – the god of the Israelites who, through time, was known by many names: Eya/Enki, El/El-shaddai, Yahweh, Adonai and simply Ya. This god Yahweh is both redeemer and executioner; a miracle-worker and yet a jealous deity who puts his chosen people through terrible trials and tribulations whenever they stray from his path (which they constantly do). Even Yahweh's heroes such as Moses, Joshua and David are sanctioned to commit what we today would regard as crimes against humanity. Life in the ancient world was bloody and cruel as different groups of human civilisation vied to control the Earth's limited resources and, in that respect, the major personalities of the Old Testament narrative were people of their time.

But is any of it true? That was the question I posed at the beginning of this book. Leading archaeologists in the field had come to the conclusion that most of the biblical story is not supported by the archaeological and textual evidence. These scholars are not anti-Bible – they simply looked at the remains from the past and saw no correlation. In a sense they have been courageous to point out the problems which have come to the fore over the last one hundred and fifty years of research. One by one the biblical eras came under scrutiny and were found wanting.

The Demise of Biblical Archaeology

Today, many archaeologists working in the Levant reject the idea of an Israelite empire under its two great kings, David and Solomon. The doyen of Israeli archaeology, Professor Israel Finkelstein, now places Solomon in what is regarded as the least prosperous archaeological era in the ancient world – the early Iron Age. Solomon, if he ever existed, could have been nothing more than a local chieftain ruling over a rustic tribal court. And Solomon's Jerusalem was far from being the great capital of a wealthy empire as described in the Bible.

> The most optimistic assessment ... is that tenth-century Jerusalem was rather limited in extent, perhaps no more than a typical hill country village.*

The only conclusion that can be drawn from Iron Age I-B archaeology is that Solomon's elevation to the status of legendary merchant prince and son-in-law of Pharaoh was

---

* I. Finkelstein & N. A. Silberman: *The Bible Unearthed* (New York, 2001), p. 133.

the work of a skilled storyteller from much later times (probably during the reign of Josiah).

The same goes for David – although he is at least generally accepted as a real historical figure thanks to the discovery of the Tel Dan stela bearing the phrase 'House of David' (Aramaic *Beit Dud*).

The Judges fare little better. In fact, the so-called Israelite tribes of Iron Age I-A to Iron Age II-A Canaan (from the Judges right down to the fall of Samaria) were apparently no different from the Late Bronze Age people they are supposed to have replaced.

> … it is difficult to insist, from a strictly archaeological perspective, that the kingdom of Israel as a whole was ever particularly Israelite in either the ethnic, cultural, or religious connotations of that name as we understand it from the perspective of the later biblical writers.*

When we turn to the Conquest of the Promised Land, we find that it simply did not happen. Only a few Christian evangelical scholars (Professor Kenneth Kitchen amongst them) still advocate a full military invasion of Canaan in the thirteenth century BC (that is the end of the Late Bronze Age in the conventional chronology). The majority of scholars recognise the numerous problems in reconciling such an event with the archaeological evidence. The facts are unequivocal. There was no city of Jericho at that time for Joshua to destroy; the city of Hazor *was* burnt to the ground – but a century before Kitchen's date of the Conquest; the settlements which sprang up in the central hill country in Iron Age I are culturally indistinguishable from settlements of the preceding period, demonstrating that there was no new influx of aliens from a different cultural background at that time. Moreover, as Finkelstein and his cowriter Silberman tellingly observe, it is hardly feasible

---

* *Ibid,* p. 194.

that the pharaohs of the 19th Dynasty would have permitted the wholesale devastation of Canaanite population centres right in their own backyard.

> ... it is inconceivable that the destruction of so many loyal vassal cities by the invaders (i.e. Israelites) would have left absolutely no trace in the extensive records of the Egyptian empire. ... Something clearly doesn't add up when the biblical account, the archaeological evidence, and the Egyptian records are placed side by side.*

There is no doubt about it. A thirteenth-century biblical Conquest by Joshua and the Israelites is simply not supported by the evidence.

When we turn to Egypt and the Israelite Sojourn we find a similar picture. Egyptologists have failed to produce any archaeological evidence of a large Asiatic (i.e. Israelite) population in the New Kingdom era (i.e. the Late Bronze Age) when the Israelites were supposedly enslaved there. The city of Pi-Ramesse (biblical Raamses) is being excavated by Edgar Pusch and his German team but, although they have made some extraordinary discoveries, they have failed to unearth suburbs of Asiatic dwellings indicative of a large foreign workforce. The stark reality is that there were no Israelites in the city identified by the Bible as a centre of the Israelite bondage. Joseph the vizier has also vanished from the archaeological record.

All this begs the question: were the Israelites ever in Egypt? The answer most historians give today is a qualified no. Finkelstein and Silberman's recent overview of the archaeological evidence in Egypt and Canaan leads them to a rather more dramatic and controversial conclusion. If the stories of the Exodus and Conquest are to be placed at the end of the Late Bronze Age (as tacitly accepted), then archaeology completely contradicts the biblical tradition.

---

* *Ibid*, p. 79.

The process that we describe here is, in fact, the opposite of what we have in the Bible: the emergence of early Israel was an outcome of the collapse of the Canaanite culture, not its cause. And most of the Israelites did not come from outside Canaan – they emerged from within it. There was no mass Exodus from Egypt. There was no violent conquest of Canaan. Most of the people who formed early Israel were local people – the same people whom we see in the highlands throughout the Bronze and Iron Ages. The early Israelites were – irony of ironies – themselves originally Canaanites!*

And so the whole foundation of Judaism is dramatically undermined. No Egyptian Sojourn means no Exodus and therefore no Passover. The fundamental birth-event of the nation of Israel – their sudden freedom from bondage – never happened.

As to Abraham and the other Patriarchs? Their hold on history has been equally tenuous since they came under archaeological scrutiny. No-one quite knows where to place them. Professor Thomas L. Thompson and his minimalist colleagues would prefer it if they remained trapped in the pages of the 'literary work' which is the Bible rather than attempting to release them into the real world of archaeological Palestine. And before Abraham? … Forget it. The first chapters of the book of Genesis have become the province of specialists in Mesopotamian mythology.

And so this is the uncomfortable position a reader of the Old Testament finds himself in today. Either you accept the biblical story as unerringly true because of your faith or you have to face up to the archaeological verity that most of this extraordinary book is fiction. However, if you are reading these words, then you now know that a new revolutionary approach to the synthesis of Bible and archaeology is on offer.

---

* *Ibid*, p. 118.

Having read *From Eden to Exile* (and perhaps the detailed chronological studies published in *A Test of Time* and *Legend* upon which this book is based), I hope you will have come to the conclusion that there is a third and middle way. The biblical stories are basically true – but only when they are placed in their correct archaeological setting. This has required an adjustment of the archaeological timeline downwards by several centuries so that the events described in the Bible find their proper historical context. That revision has become known as the 'New Chronology'.

A New Beginning

In the New Chronology – within which the story of *From Eden to Exile* is framed – the whole narrative of the Children of Yahweh comes to historical life. The people of the Bible did not live in an archaeological and historical vacuum. They existed and interacted with many ancient Near Eastern civilisations and their renowned leaders. What I hope this reworking of the biblical story has achieved is to explain and illuminate many of its events by setting them in an historical world reconstructed from the archaeological remains of our ancestral past. It is a world which is tangible, giving the biblical narrative a credible background in which to set the lives of its people.

Adam appears on the scene at the end of the Neolithic Age (*c.* 5375 BC) when the archaeological record reveals the first signs of agriculture and the domestication of animals in the Middle East. A thousand years later, in the time of Enoch (the city-builder), the earliest cities are being founded in the southern marshes of Mesopotamia. The ancient texts of this region then tell of a great flood and a hero who saves Mankind by building a ship in which to ride out the mighty storm. The story is set in the Late Ubaid period at around 3113 BC – the time of Woolley's flood at Ur.

Towards the end of the Uruk period (*c.* 2800 BC) the first ziggurat or tower-temple is erected at Eridu – the prototype upon which the legend of the biblical Tower of Babel is based. Eridu's sacred temple is built on an island of pure sand surrounded by the sweet Waters of the Abyss (Sumerian *abzu*). The island is called *Nun.ki* – the 'Mighty Place'. The builder of the tower-temple is Enmer the Hunter (Sumerian *Enmer-kar*), who is the biblical Nimrod 'a mighty hunter against Yahweh'. His generation and that of his ancestral predecessor, Meskiagkasher (biblical Cush), successfully colonise northern Mesopotamia, Canaan and the Nile valley to herald in the historical age of the great Old World civilisations. Through their religious beliefs and burial incantations the Egyptians of later times remembered the place of their ancestral homeland on the Isle of Flame in the Waters of Nun. Even as late as the Ptolemaic period temple reliefs recall the journey made by the 'Founders' who brought the secret knowledge of the primeval temple of the 'First Time' (Egyptian *sep-tepi*) from Mesopotamia to the Nile valley.

Our story then leaps forward a thousand years to the end of the Early Bronze Age when Abraham (*c.* 1855 BC) migrates down into Canaan from Harran across the River Euphrates. He enters Egypt in the time of the Heracleopolitan 10th Dynasty as a guest of Pharaoh Nebkaure Khety IV. Having been expelled from the eastern Delta for deceiving Pharaoh over his wife Sarah, Abraham settles in the hill country of Canaan at a time when the Amorite tribes are moving into the region from the north. Abraham himself is an Amorite chieftain and is a part of this historically recognised movement. He gets embroiled in a major revolt against the great superpower of the time – the Third Dynasty of Ur. Amar-Sin (biblical Amraphel) of Ur sends a great army to crush the rebellion amongst the Cities of the Plain (south of the Dead Sea). Abraham's nephew, Lot, is taken captive but then rescued by his uncle. Lot returns to the Dead Sea region to witness the great cataclysm which overwhelms Sodom and Gomorrah. The imprint of that disaster is manifest in the massive destruction of the Early

Bronze Age settlements in the Arabah basin.*

Some two hundred years later (in 1666 BC) a young man named Joseph becomes vizier in the court of Pharaoh Amenemhat III – the most powerful king of the 12th Dynasty. He saves Egypt from the worst of a terrible famine by diverting the waters from a series of massive Nile floods into the Faiyum basin via what was later to be known as the Bahr Yussef ('waterway of Joseph'). The Asiatic vizier's reward is to be given his own private estate in the eastern delta region of Goshen where he settles his Hebrew brethren (including his father Jacob). Their extended sojourn in Egypt is marked by the cultural phase known as Middle Bronze II-A (c. 1800–1440 BC). Joseph dies and is buried in a pyramid tomb furnished with its own cult-statue. The empty tomb (for Joseph's body is later removed by Moses for transportation to Israel), with its (subsequently) smashed statue, has been unearthed by Professor Manfred Bietak and his Austrian team at Tell ed-Daba within the earliest strata of the ancient city of Avaris.

Moses is born in the middle years of the 13th Dynasty (c. 1530 BC) and is adopted by the queen of Pharaoh Khaneferre Sobekhotep IV – the greatest king of that dynasty. Moses prince of Egypt, of Hebrew parentage, fights a war in Kush on behalf of his Egyptian father-in-law, but dynastic rivalries and intrigue force him to flee into exile. He remains for several decades with a community of nomadic Midianites wandering the Negeb and Sinai wilderness, marrying the daughter of Jethro, priest of Yahweh. Through his Midianite kin, Moses learns of the common heritage between the 'sons of Abraham' (through Ishmael

---

* The earthquake which destroyed the sites of Bab ed-Drah, Numeira, etc. probably occurred about a century before the time of Abraham and became a folk-memory which was later attached to the story of the Hebrew patriarch. Further research will be required to resolve the archaeological dating surrounding this issue. However, I have chosen to retain the Sodom and Gomorrah episode in the biblical story as part of the life and times of Abraham for the sake of simplicity.

and Isaac). The Israelite slaves in Egypt have forgotten their ancestral history and the god of the patriarchs – but the descendants of Abraham dwelling in the desert have retained their knowledge of the past through oral tradition. Moses, as an educated prince with language skills, is able to read cuneiform tablets which are circulating in the Middle East thanks to their wide publication during the reign of Hammurabi of Babylon (1565–1523 BC). These tablets contain the great epic poetry of the early Mesopotamian period, including the stories of Creation, Paradise, the Flood and the Tower of Babel, all of which involve Enki/Eya – the god who was 'the friend of Man'. Eya is one and the same as Ya (Hebrew *Yah*), the ancestral deity worshipped by the Midianites. Eya/Ya is the god who dwells upon Mount Horeb at the heart of the black peaks in southern Sinai. When Moses later compiles the Bible's own legendary epic – the book of Genesis – these early Mesopotamian stories relating to Eya and his followers are incorporated into the work to become one of the finest pieces of ancient literature.

Having returned from exile, Moses challenges the new pharaoh – Dudimose – to 'let his people go' out of Egypt and worship their god Ya in his Sinai abode. But Pharaoh refuses to allow his slaves to abandon their servitude. In 1447 BC a terrible disaster strikes the Egyptians – Manetho calls it 'a blast of God' – which results in the deaths of thousands. The dead are cast into makeshift burial pits (unearthed at Tell ed-Daba/Avaris within the final phase of Stratum G). The city of Avaris, in which a major part of the Israelite slave population dwelt, is then abandoned (the hiatus between Stratum G and Stratum F) as the Children of Yahweh depart into Sinai.

At Mount Horeb (probably Gebel Musa) Moses employs the recently invented Proto-Sinaitic script (Egyptian hieroglyphic signs used to represent the Semitic alphabet) to record the Laws of Yahweh. These oldest tablets of the Hebrew script are placed in a golden box known as the Ark of the Covenant and carried at the head of the army on its conquest of the Promised Land.

The Middle Bronze Age cities of Jericho, Ai and Hazor are destroyed and 'sown with salt' by Joshua and the Israelite tribes. All the cities sacked by the Children of Yahweh in the biblical text are destroyed during the Middle Bronze II-B. The great covenant ceremony is then celebrated before a gleaming white monolith erected in front of the Middle Bronze II-B migdol temple of Baal-Berith in Shechem. The Covenant Stone of Joshua is still standing in that same spot today at the heart of the modern city of Nablus. The migdol temple was later destroyed by Abimelech during the Late Bronze I period when this brutal Israelite king burnt one thousand of his citizens alive in the sanctuary of Shechem.

The Judges period spans the last part of the Middle Bronze Age through to the end of Late Bronze I. Then, in Late Bronze II-A we have the golden age of the United Monarchy period – the era of Saul, David and Solomon.

The el-Amarna letters (c. 1020–1000 BC), found in Akhenaten's royal city, attest to Saul's 'Hebrew revolt' against the Philistine lords on the coastal plain. The kings of Gath and Megiddo write to Pharaoh, informing him of the death of Saul (here known by his birth-name, Labaya – 'lion [of Yah]'), whilst other letters deal with the aftermath of Saul's death on Mount Gilboa and the rise of David (here called by his Hurrian royal title, Tadua – 'beloved [of Yah]'). Involved in all the political turmoil of Amarna-period Syro-Palestine is a king of Amurru named Aziru. This name is a hypocoristicon of the biblical Hadadezer, erstwhile enemy of King David of Jerusalem.

In Akhenaten's twelfth year the palace at Ugarit is partially destroyed by fire. Three thousand years later, a tiny clay tablet is recovered from the charred ruins of the palace archive. This tablet records a solar eclipse at Ugarit just as the sun was setting over the Mediterranean Sea. This almost unique event (occurring once in every four thousand years or so) has been calculated (using astronomy computer programmes) to have taken place in 1012 BC – nearly three hundred and thirty years later than the conventional date for Akhenaten's twelfth year – but exactly when the heretic pharaoh succeeded his father, Amenhotep III, in the New Chronology. This eclipse thus confirms Akhenaten's contemporaneity with Saul and David and the foundation of the Israelite monarchy. It was Akhenaten's flawed rule which created the political conditions for the dramatic birth of the kingdom of Israel.

David is succeeded by Solomon, son-in-law of Pharaoh Haremheb. He builds the magnificent LB II-A palaces at Megiddo and Hazor, and is portrayed on a beautiful ivory plaque originating from archaeological excavations of the Megiddo Stratum VIII palace. The Phoenician building techniques of Late Bronze Age Megiddo are identical to those employed in the construction of Solomon's palaces and the Jerusalem temple (as described in the biblical text). The copper mines at Timnah are being worked to their maximum during the LB II-A when Solomon is casting his elaborate bronze furnishings for Yahweh's temple in the Israelite capital. The mines are then abandoned during the 20th Dynasty (Iron Age I) when the now divided monarchy of Israel is under increasing pressure from Aramaean raids and when the Transjordanian states are rebelling against their once powerful Israelite masters. The fortunes of the Children of Yahweh are at their lowest ebb as the outlying tribes flock for protection into the central hill where they build refugee camps. They are the Iron I-A villages which appear throughout the central highlands at this time. As Finkelstein says, these people are no different culturally from the people already living in the region. This is absolutely true – because they are fellow Israelites from Galilee and Gilead, fleeing the Aramaean oppression of Ben-Hadad III and Hazael (c. 873–800 BC).

A new dynasty arises in the Northern Kingdom at this time. The Assyrians refer to it as *Bit Humri* – the 'House of

Omri'. Kings Omri and Ahab establish a new capital at Samaria and a winter palace at Jezreel. At both sites these Israelite rulers and their courts are represented by the Iron Age I pottery found in the fills of buildings belonging to a later king, Jeroboam II, in whose time the Northern Kingdom of Israel is reinvigorated as a powerful and wealthy state. Jeroboam constructs the fine ashlar buildings of Samaria Periods I and II. He builds the Iron Age II-A casemate walls and six-chambered gates of Jezreel, Hazor, Gezer and Megiddo. But, within twenty years of Jeroboam's death the kingdom of Israel has fallen to Sargon II and the royal capital at Samaria is in the hands of an Assyrian provincial governor.

A century later, Assyria too has succumbed to the new power in the region – the Babylonians. The kingdom of Judah had held out against the Assyrians, in spite of losing major cities such as Lachish (Stratum IV) to Sennacherib's mighty army. However, the Babylonians are another matter. Under the leadership of Nebuchadrezzar II the army of Babylon is simply too strong for the now isolated Judaean hill country state. Lachish (Stratum II) is besieged and sacked in 599 BC and Jerusalem surrenders in the following year, its new king – Jehoiakin – taken off into exile. Ten years later Zedekiah, the last ruler of Jerusalem, rebels against his Babylonian overlord and Nebuchadrezzar returns south to put an end, once and for all, to his troublesome vassal. The holy city of Yahweh falls in 587 BC and its remaining population is deported to Mesopotamia. Jerusalem and its magnificent temple are systematically dismantled by the Babylonian army and turned into mounds of rubble, fit only as the abodes for scavengers and wild animals.

* * *

That, in brief outline, is the historical model which the New Chronology makes possible when the correct timeline is superimposed upon the archaeological remains of the ancient world. It is a history satisfyingly supported by the stratigraphic record and colourfully enhanced by the contemporary texts of Israel's powerful neighbours. It provides a solid and ultimately believable historical foundation for the religious messages of the biblical text.

The lost testament of the Children of Yahweh has been retrieved from the ruins of the past, bringing the Bible story from the shadows of myth out into the light of history.

Part Six

Reference
Section

ACKNOWLEDGEMENTS

As usual I must thank my colleagues and friends for their help in completing this substantial and complex volume. Their advice and assistance has proved invaluable.

The expertise of biblical scholar Peter van der Veen has always been just a phone-call or e-mail away, and what he imparts is invariably both fascinating and academically measured. A number of the ideas in *From Eden to Exile* originated with Peter or came out of discussions we have had together relating to New Chronology research. I look forward to reading his PhD on the Iron Age II-C period in Israel with great interest. Thank you, Peter – you are a constant inspiration.

The same goes for Dr John Bimson, whose work, as you have seen, is much exploited in this volume. Dr Bernard Newgrosh has also helped by supplying his detailed New Chronology research on Mesopotamian history and checking out the parts of this book which heavily rely on detailed synchronisms with both Assyria and Babylon. Two astronomers, Wayne Mitchell and Dr David Lappin, must also be recognised for their amazing work on eclipse observations and lunar calendar sequences recorded in ancient documents. Their conclusions have been shown to strongly support the New Chronology revision proposed in *From Eden to Exile* and give me the confidence to continue with my own historical research.

Acknowledgements

My researcher, Alda Watson, has done sterling work in pulling together the piles of documents which were the basic resource for this writing project. Her trips to the British Library and hours spent on the World Wide Web have produced fascinating material which has added much of the colour to this story of Israel's origins.

The excellent satellite photographs/maps which are scattered throughout *From Eden to Exile* were downloaded from Nasa-related sites by my good friend and computer whiz, Edward Rogers. My appreciation goes to Nasa and the government of the USA for making these amazing images available to everyone copyright free. But Eddie gets a hefty pat on the back for finding so many relevant images out of the thousands available – a task which saved me days of research. I actually get the distinct impression that Eddie enjoyed the challenge and I certainly appreciated his wide-ranging internet savvy and dogged persistence.

My Web Master, Andy Gough, has also been a great supporter and I much appreciate all the work he has put in to getting Nunki.net (the official David Rohl website) up and running. I must also congratulate Cami McCraw for the fantastic achievement of inaugurating and running the tremendously successful internet discussion group devoted to New Chronology research. If you want to follow up on the ideas published in my books and get involved with like-minded people interested in ancient history and chronology, then do log on to www.group.yahoo.com/group/NewChronology and get to know all Cami's international members already there and debating hundreds of topics related to the ongoing New Chronology research.

I must also thank the people in broadcasting who have recently been working with me to bring many of my ideas to the television screen. They include: producers Richard Denton, Najat Rizk and Eli Khouri; directors Peter Minns and Mouna Mounayer; and cameramen Danny Rohrer, Keith Woods and Fouad Sleiman. Thanks guys for all your hard work.

Tony Barnes, sidekick and 'Man Friday' on so many of the expeditions and filming trips I have got myself caught up in these past four years, has been a constant source of strength and encouragement. Thanks for being there, Tony!

The same goes for all my friends at Sussex Egyptology Society – especially chairman Janet Wilton who has always been on hand to ease the pressures on a very pressured life. Janet is one of the most efficient and go-getting people I have met. Nothing is impossible in her book and she makes things happen when others wouldn't even attempt to start. Thanks, Janet, for making sure that things got done when I was up to my neck in writing or filming or heading off into the back of beyond on some wild goose chase. For information on Sussex Egyptology Society (for whom I am Honorary President) log on to www.egyptology-uk.com.

I must also mention in these despatches the sterling work and professional guiding hand of ISIS chairman, Anthony van der Elst. When I retired as chairman of the Institute for the Study of Interdisciplinary Sciences (which I founded in 1983), I knew it was going to be difficult to find someone to take over the mantle and responsibilities of an international educational charity with such specialist interests. The New Chronology academic debate has been safely passed over into Anthony's steady hands and I have been booted upstairs into another Honorary President's office. Thanks for the tie, Anthony – remind me to wear it at the next AGM. For information on ISIS and *JACF* log on to www.Nunki.net/ISIS.

Mike Rowland, Administrator and Treasurer of Legend Conferences has also been doing his usual sterling work organising the annual conference which I initiated in 1999. Mike has not only been taking care of the ISIS membership and accounts for more than fifteen years, but has carried the burden of four hugely successful conferences (two at Buckfast Abbey and two at Reading University) in which more than thirty academic speakers and a thousand delegates have participated. If you want to get onto the Legend

ACKNOWLEDGEMENTS

Conferences mailing list and join the party, then just write to Mike Rowland, c/o Legend Conferences, 127 Porter Road, Basingstoke, Hants, RG22 4JT, UK.

I would also like to thank all the people at Century and Arrow – especially my editor Mark Booth – for all their support over the years. It's not every publisher who would be so patient with an author only capable of turning out one book every three years. But, then again, not every author spends so much of his time out in the wildernesses of the Middle East gathering his research material – so I suppose I have a reasonable excuse. Thanks, Mark, for your understanding and encouragement.

As always, my wife Ditas gets the final word of appreciation because she is the rock upon which all this effort is built. Without her constant and unwavering support I could never have completed *From Eden to Exile* in the three years it has taken from concept to finished book. Ditas has once again typeset the volume and helped in so many ways to get the task done. This book is as much her work as mine.

According to tradition, it took Moses forty years in the wilderness to write the first five books of the Old Testament. It has taken me just three years to rework the eleven 'historical' books from Eden to the fall of Jerusalem. Not bad going in my opinion. I hope you enjoyed reading the result.

BIBLIOGRAPHY

A

Aharoni, Y. – 1979: *The Land of the Bible, 2nd ed.* (London).
Aharoni, Y. & **Avi-Yonah**, M. (eds.) – 1977: *McMillan Bible Atlas* (London).
Albright, W. F. – 1922: 'The Location of the Garden of Eden' in *AJSL* 39, pp. 15-31.
Albright, W. F. – 1937: 'The Egyptian Correspondence of Abimilki, Prince of Tyre' in *JEA* 23, pp. 190-203.
Albright, W. F. – 1942: 'A Votive Stele Erected by Ben-Hadad I of Damascus to the God Melcarth' in *BASOR* 87, pp. 23-29.
Albright, W. F. – 1943: 'An Archaic Hebrew Proverb on an Amarna Letter from Central Palestine' in *BASOR* 89, pp. 29-32.
Albright, W. F. – 1943: 'Two Little Understood Amarna Letters from the Middle Jordan Valley' in *BASOR* 89, pp. 7-17.
Albright, W. F. – 1956: 'Further Light on Synchronisms Between Egypt and Asia in the Period 935-685 B.C.' in *BASOR* 141, pp. 23-27.
Albright, W. F. – 1964: 'The Eighteenth-Century Princes of Byblos and the Chronology of Middle Bronze' in *BASOR* 176, pp. 38-46.
Albright, W. F. – 1965: 'Further Light on the History of Middle-Bronze Byblos' in *BASOR* 179, pp. 38-43.
Albright, W. F. – 1966: 'Remarks on the Chronology of Early Bronze IV–Middle Bronze IIA in Phoenicia and Syria-Palestine' in *BASOR* 184, pp. 27-35.
Albright, W. F. – 1973: 'The Historical Framework of Palestinian Archaeology Between 2100 and 1600 B.C.' in *BASOR* 209, pp. 12-19.
Albright, W. F. – 1975: 'The Amarna Letters from Palestine' in *CAH,* vol. II:2A, pp. 98-116.
Albright, W. F. & **Mendenhall**, G. E. (transl.) – 1950: 'The Amarna Letters' in *ANET*, pp. 483-490.
Albright, W. F. & **Lambdin**, T. O. – 1970: 'The Evidence of Language' in *CAH* I:1, pp. 122-55.
Aldred, C. – 1991: *Akhenaten, King of Egypt* (London).
Aldred, C. – 1975: 'Egypt: The Amarna Period and the End of the Eighteenth Dynasty' in *CAH* II:2A, pp. 49-97.
Amiran, R. – 1969: *Ancient Pottery of the Holy Land* (Jerusalem).
Alster, B. – 1995: 'Epic Tales from Ancient Sumer: Enmerkar, Lugalbanda, and Other Cunning Heroes' in J. M. Sasson (ed.): *Civilisations of the Ancient Near East*, Vol. IV, pp. 2315-26.
Amiet, P. – 1957: 'Glyptique susienne archaique' in *Revue d'assyriologie* 51, pp. 121-29.
Amiet, P. – 1961: *La glyptique mésopotamienne archaique* (Paris).
Amiet, P. – 1993: 'The Period of Irano-Mesopotamian Contacts 3500-1600 BC' in J. Curtis (ed.): *Early Mesopotamia and Iran: Contact and Conflict 3500–1600 BC* (London), pp. 23-30.

455

BIBLIOGRAPHY

Anati, E. – 1986: *The Mountain of God* (New York).
Arnold, F. – 1992: 'New Evidence for the Length of the Reign of Senwosret III?' in *GM* 129, pp. 27-31.
Arnold, P. M. – 1990: *Gibeah: The Search for a Biblical City* (JSOT Supplement Series 79, Sheffield).
Aston, D. A. – 1989: 'Takeloth II – A King of the 'Theban Twenty-third Dynasty'?' in *JEA* 75, pp. 139-53.
Aubet, M. E. – 1987: *The Phoenicians and the West: Politics, Colonies and Trade* (Cambridge).
Avigad, N.– 1978: in Avi-Yonah, M. (ed.) *Encyclopedia of Archaeological Excavations in the Holy Land*, vol. IV (Oxford).

B

Baillie, M. G. L. – 1991: 'Dendrochronology and Thera: The Scientific Case' in *JACF* 4, pp. 15-28.
Baines, J. R. & **Malek**, J. – 1980: *Atlas of Ancient Egypt* (Oxford).
Baldwin, J. – 1988: *I and 2 Samuel: An Introduction and Commentary* (Tyndale Old Testament Commentaries, Leicester).
Barkay, G. – 1990: 'A Late Bronze Age Egyptian Temple in Jerusalem' in *Eretz-Israel* 21, pp. 94-106.
Barnett, R. D. – 1958: 'Early Shipping in the Near East' in *Antiquity* 32, pp. 220-30.
Barsanti, A. – 1908: 'Stéle Inédite au Nom du Roi Radadouhotep Doudoumes' in *ASAE* 9, pp. 1-2.
Bartlett, J. – 1982: *Jericho* (Guildford).
Baumgartel, E. J. – 1947: *The Cultures of Prehistoric Egypt*, Vol. 1 (London).
Baumgartel, E. J. – 1960: *The Cultures of Prehistoric Egypt*, Vol. 2 (Oxford).
Baumgartel, E. J. – 1970: 'Predynastic Egypt' in *CAH*, 3rd edn, Vol. 1, pt. 1 (Cambridge), pp. 463-97.
von Beckerath, J. – 1958: 'Notes on the Viziers Ankhu and Iymeru in the 13th Egyptian Dynasty' in *JNES* 17, pp. 263-68.
Bell, B. – 1975: 'Climate and the History of Egypt: The Middle Kingdom' in *AJA* 79, pp. 223-69.
Ben-Tor, A. (ed.) – 1992: *The Archaeology of Ancient Israel* (New Haven & London).
Bénédite, G. A. – 1916: 'Le Couteau de Gebel el-Arak' in *Fondation Eugene Piot, Monuments et Mémoires* 22, pp. 1-34.
Berlin, A. – 1979: *Enmerkar and Ensuhkesdanna: A Sumerian Narrative* (Philadelphia).
Berry, A. C. & **Berry**, R. J. – 1973: 'Origins and relations of the ancient Egyptians' in D. R. Brothwell (ed.): *Population biology of the ancient Egyptians*, pp. 200-8.
Bienkowski, P. – 1986: *Jericho in the Late Bronze Age* (Warminster).
Bierbrier, M. L. – 1975: *The Late New Kingdom in Egypt* (Warminster).
Bietak, M. – 1979: *Avaris and Piramesse: Archaeological Exploration of the Eastern Nile Delta* (London).
Bietak, M. – 1984: 'Problems of Middle Bronze Age Chronology: New Evidence from Egypt' in *AJA* 88, pp. 471-85.
Bietak, M. – 1989: 'The Middle Bronze Age of the Levant: A New Approach to Relative and Absolute Chronology' in *HML?*, part 3 (Gothenburg), pp. 78-123.
Bietak, M. – 1991: 'Egypt and Canaan During the Middle Bronze Age' in *BASOR* 281, pp. 27-72.

Bietak, M. – 1991: 'Der Friedhof in einem Palastgarten aus der Zeit des spaten mittleren Reiches und andere Forschung-sergebnisse aus dem ostlichen Nildelta (Tell el-Dab'a 1984–1987)' in *Ägypten und Levante* 2, pp. 47-109.

Bietak, M. – 1992: *Tell el-Dab'a*, vol. V (Vienna).

Bietak, M. – 1996: *Avaris: The Capital of the Hyksos* (London).

Bimson, J. – 1978: *Redating the Exodus and Conquest* (Sheffield).

Bimson, J. J. – 1979: 'A Chronology for the Middle Kingdom and Israel's Egyptian Bondage' in *SIS Review* III:3, pp. 64-69.

Bimson, J. J. – 1986: 'Shoshenq and Shishak: A Case of Mistaken Identity' in *SIS Review* 8, pp. 36-46.

Bimson, J. J. & **Livingston**, D. – 1987: 'Redating the Exodus' in *BAR* 13:5, pp. 40-53.

Bimson, J. J. – 1988: 'Exodus and Conquest – Myth or Reality? Can Archaeology Provide the Answer?' in *JACF* 2, pp. 27-40.

Bimson, J. J. – 1999: 'Iron Age Palestine: A Need for Chronological Revision' in *JACF* 8, pp. 57-65.

Biran, A. & **Naveh**, J. – 1993: 'An Aramaic Stele Fragment from Tel Dan' in *IEJ* 43, pp. 81-98.

Black, J. & **Green**, A. – 1992: *Gods, Demons and Symbols of Ancient Mesopotamia* (London).

Bonnet, C. – 1986: *Kerma: Territoire et Metropole* (Cairo).

Bordreuil, P. & **Teixidor**, J. – 1983: 'Nouvel Examen de l'Inscription de Bar-Hadad' in *Aula Orientalis* 1, pp. 271-76.

Bourriau, J. – 1991: 'Relations Between Egypt and Kerma During the Middle and New Kingdoms' in W. V. Davies (ed.): *Egypt and Africa: Nubia from Prehistory to Islam* (London).

Breasted, J. H. – 1905: *A History of Egypt* (Chicago).

Breasted, J. H. – 1988: *Ancient Records of Egypt: Historical Documents from the Earliest Times to the Persian Conquest*, Part 1 (London).

Brugsch, H. F. K. – 1858: *Geographische Inschriften altägyptischer Denkmäler*, vol. II (Leipzig).

Brugsch, H. F. K. – 1884: *Thesaurus Inscriptionum Aegyptiacarum Altaegyptische Inschriften* (Leipzig).

Brugsch, H. F. K. – 1891: *Egypt Under the Pharaohs* (London).

Bryce, T. – 1998: *The Kingdom of the Hittites* (Oxford).

Burney, C. A. – 1964: 'The Excavations at Yanik Tepe, Azerbaijan, 1962: Third Preliminary Report' in *Iraq* 26, pp. 54-62.

Burney, C. – 1977: *From Village to Empire: An introduction to Near Eastern archaeology* (Oxford).

Burstein, S. M. – 1978: *The Babyloniaca of Berossus* (Malibu).

C

Cameron, G. G. – 1936: *History of Early Iran* (Chicago).

Castellino, G. – 1994: 'The Origins of Civilization According to Biblical and Cuneiform Texts' in R. S. Hess & D. T. Tsumura (eds.): *'I Studied Inscriptions from before the Flood': Ancient Near Eastern, Literary, and Linguistic Approaches to Genesis 1–11*, pp. 75-95.

Civil, M. – 1969: 'The Sumerian Flood Story' in W. G. Lambert & A. R. Millard: *Atra-hasis*, pp. 138-45.

Cohen, S. – 1973: *Enmerkar and the Lord of Aratta* (Dissertation in Oriental Studies, Pennsylvania).

Cohen, R. – 1983: 'The Mysterious MB I People' in *BAR* 9:4, pp. 16-29.

BIBLIOGRAPHY

Collins, J. J. – 1985: 'Artapanus' in J. M. Charlesworth (ed.): *The Old Testament Pseudepigrapha*, vol. II (London), pp. 889-903.

Collins, A. – 1996: *From the Ashes of Angels: The Forbidden Legacy of a Fallen Race* (London).

Coogan, M. D. (ed.) – 1998: *The Oxford History of the Biblical World* (New York).

Cooper, B. – 1995: *After the Flood: The early post-flood history of Europe traced back to Noah* (West Sussex).

Cooper, J. S. & **Heimpel**, W. – 1983: 'The Sumerian Sargon Legend' in *JAOS* 103, pp. 67-82.

Corney, R. W. – 1962: 'Achish' in K. Crim *et al.* (eds.): *Interpreters' Dictionary of the Bible*, vol. I (Nashville), p. 27.

Craigie, P. C. – 1983: 'The Tablets from Ugarit and their Importance for Biblical Studies' in *BAR* 9:5, pp. 62-73.

Crawford, H. –1991: *Sumer and the Sumerians* (Cambridge).

Crawford, H. – 1992: 'Patterns of Trade in Mesopotamia 3500–2500 BC' in *Dilmun* 15, pp. 17-21.

Cross, F. M. – 1972: 'The Stele Dedicated to Melcarth by Ben-Hadad of Damascus' in *BASOR* 205, pp. 36-42.

Curtis, J. – 1993: *Early Mesopotamia and Iran: Contact and Conflict 3500–1600 BC* (London).

D

Dalley, S. (trans.) – 1989: *Myths from Mesopotamia: Creation, The Flood, Gilgamesh and Others* (Oxford).

Davies, G. I. – 1988: 'Solomonic Stables at Megiddo After All?' in *PEQ* 120 (July–Dec), pp. 130-41.

Derry, D. E. – 1956: 'The Dynastic Race in Egypt' in *JEA* 42, pp. 80-5.

Dever, W. G. – 1984: 'Asherah, Consort of Yahweh? New Evidence from Kuntillet Ajrud' in *BASOR* 255, pp. 21-37.

Dorsey, D. A. –1991: *The Roads and Highways of Ancient Israel* (Baltimore).

Dunham, D. & **Janssen**, J. M. A. – 1960: *Semna Kumma* (Boston).

Dussaud, R. – 1925: 'Dedicace d'une statue d'Osorkon I par Eliba'al, roi de Byblos' in *Syria* 6, pp. 101-17.

Dyson, R. & **Cuyler Young**, T. – 1960: 'The Solduz Valley, Iran: Pisdeli Tape' in *Antiquity* 34, pp. 19-28.

E

Edelman, D. – 1985: 'The 'Ashurites' of Eshbaal's State' in *PEQ* 117 (July–December), pp. 85-91.

Edwards, I. E. S. – 1980: 'The Early Dynastic Period in Egypt' in *CAH* 1:2, pp. 1-70.

Edwards, M. – 1986: ''Urmia Ware' and Its Distribution in North-Western Iran' in *Iran* 24, pp. 57-78.

Eigner, D. – 1995: 'A Palace of the Early 13th Dynasty at Tell el Dab'a' in *Ägypten und Levante* 5.

Eissfeldt, O. – 1975: 'The Hebrew Kingdom' in *CAH*, vol. II:2B, pp. 537-605.

Emery, W. B. – 1952: *Saqqara and the Dynastic Race: An Inaugural Lecture delivered at University College London* (London).

Emery, W. B. – 1961: *Archaic Egypt: Culture and Civilization in Egypt Five Thousand Years Ago* (London).

458

Engelbach, R. – 1943: 'An Essay on the Advent of the Dynastic Race in Egypt and Its Consequences' in *ASAE* 42, pp. 193-221.

F

Fairbridge, R. W. – 1963: 'Nile Sedimentation above Wadi Halfa during the last 20,000 years' in *Kush* 11, pp. 104-07.
Faulkner, R. O. – 1969: *The Ancient Egyptian Pyramid Texts*, 2 vols. (Oxford).
Faulkner, R. O. – 1972: *The Ancient Egyptian Book of the Dead* (New York).
Finkelstein, J. J. – 1963: 'The Antediluvian Kings: A University of California Tablet' in *JCS* 17, pp. 39-51.
Finkelstein, J. J. – 1966: 'The Genealogy of the Hammurapi Dynasty' in *JCS* 20, pp. 95-118.
Finkelstein, I. (ed.) – 1993: *Shiloh: The Archaeology of a Biblical Site* (Jerusalem).
Finkelstein, I. & **Na'aman**, N. (eds.) – 1994: *From Nomadism to Monarchy: Archaeological & Historical Aspects of Early Israel* (Jerusalem).
Finkelstein, I. & **Silberman**, N. A. – 2001: *The Bible Unearthed: Archaeology's New Vision of Ancient Israel and the Origins of its Sacred Texts* (New York).
Fisher, W. B. (ed.) – 1968: *The Cambridge History of Iran Volume 1: The Land of Iran* (Cambridge).
Flanagan, J. W. – 1983: 'Succession and Genealogy in the Davidic Dynasty' in H. B. Huffman *et. al.* (eds.): *The Quest for the Kingdom of God: Studies in Honor of George E. Mendenhall* (Winona Lake), pp. 35-55.
Foster, B. R. – 1995: *From Distant Days: Myths, Tales, and Poetry of Ancient Mesopotamia* (Bethesda, Maryland).
Frankfort, H. – 1944: 'A Note on the Lady of Birth' in *JNES* 3, pp. 198-200.
Frankfort, H. – 1948: *Kingship and the Gods: A Study of Ancient Near Eastern Religion as the Integration of Society and Nature* (Chicago).
Frankfort, H. – 1951: *The Birth of Civilization in the Near East* (London).
Freedman, D. N. – 1992: *Anchor Bible Dictionary* (New York).
Friedman, R. & **Adams**, B. (eds.) – 1992: *The Followers of Horus: Studies dedicated to Michael Allen Hoffman 1944–1990* (Oxford).
Fuchs, G. – 1989: 'Rock engravings in the Wadi el-Barramiya, Eastern Desert of Egypt' in *The African Archaeological Review* 7, pp. 127-53.
Fuchs, G. – 1991: 'Petroglyphs in the Eastern Desert of Egypt: new finds in the Wadi el-Barramiya' in *Sahara* 4, pp. 59-70.

G

Gadd, C. J. – 1937: 'The Infancy of Man in a Sumerian Legend: An Assyrian Parallel to an Incident in the Story of Semiramis' in *Iraq* 4, p. 33-4.
Gardiner, A. H. – 1944: 'Horus the Behdetite' in *JEA* 30, pp. 23-60.
Gardiner, A. H. – 1961: *Egypt of the Pharaohs* (London).
Garstang, J. – 1930: 'Jericho. Sir Charles Marston's Expedition in 1931' in *PEFQS*, pp. 129-32.
Garstang, J. & **Garstang**, J. B. E. – 1940: *The Story of Jericho* (London).
Gelb, I. J. – 1994: 'The Name of Babylon' in R. S. Hess & D. T. Tsumura (eds.): *'I Studied Inscriptions from before the Flood': Ancient Near Eastern, Literary, and Linguistic Approaches to Genesis 1–11*, pp. 266-69.
George, A. – 1999: *The Epic of Gilgamesh: A New Translation* (London).
Gifford, E. H. (transl.) – 1903: *Eusebius Pamphilis: Evangelicae Preparationis*, book XV (London).
Goedicke, H. – 1994: 'Exodus: Myth or History?' in M. Rowland (ed.):

BIBLIOGRAPHY

Exodus: Myth or History. The ISIS Seminar Meeting of 19th October 1993 Held at the Institute of Archaeology, London (ISIS Occasional Publications, vol. II, Basingstoke), pp. 1-15.

Goff, B. L. – 1963: *Symbols of Prehistoric Mesopotamia* (New Haven).

Gottwald, N. K. – 1979: *The Tribes of Yahweh* (London).

Grant, M. – 1984: *The History of Ancient Israel* (London).

Graves, R. & **Patai**, R. – 1989: *Hebrew Myths: The Book of Genesis* (London, 1st ed. 1964).

Grayson, A. K. – 1972: *Assyrian Royal Inscriptions, Volume 1: From the Beginning to Ashur-resha-ishi I* (Wiesbaden).

Grayson, A. K. – 1976: *Assyrian Royal Inscriptions, Volume 2: From Tiglath-pileser I to Ashur-nasir-apli II* (Wiesbaden).

Greenberg, M. – 1955: *The Hab/piru* (New Haven).

Greenfield, J. C. – 1984: 'A Touch of Eden' in *Orientalia J. Duchesne-Guillemin Emerito Oblata* (Hommages et Opera Minora 9, Leiden), pp. 219-24.

Griffith, F. Ll. – 1898: *Hieratic Papyri from Kahun and Gurob*, vol. II (London).

H

Habachi, L. – 1954: 'Khatâ'na – Qantir: Importance' in *ASAE* 52, pp. 443-559.

Hall, H. R. – 1922: 'The Discoveries At Tell el-Obeid In Southern Babylonia, And Some Egyptian Comparisons' in *JEA* 8, pp. 241-57.

Hall, H. R. – 1923: 'Ur and Eridu: The British Museum Excavations of 1919' in *JEA* 9, pp. 177-95.

Hallo, W. H. – 1971: *Encyclopaedia Judaica* (New York).

Hallo, W. W. & **Simpson**, W. K. – 1971: *The Ancient Near East: A History* (San Diego).

Hamza, M. – 1930: 'Excavations of the Department of Antiquities at Qantir (faqûs Distnet), (Season, May 21st–July 7th, 1928)' in *ASAE* 30, p. 31-68.

Harpur, J. (ed.) – 1987: *Great Events of Bible Times* (London).

Hawkins, J. D. – 1979: 'The Origin and Dissemination of Writing in Western Asia' in P. R. S. Moorey: *The Origins of Civilization*, pp. 128-66.

Hayes, W. C. – 1970: 'Chronology: I, Egypt – To The End Of The Twentieth Dynasty' in *CAH* I:1, pp. 173-193.

Hayes, J. & **Miller**, M. – 1986: *A History of Ancient Israel and Judah* (Philadelphia).

Healey, J. F. (trans.) – 1991: *Pliny The Elder: Natural History: A Selection* (London).

Healy, M. – 1993: *Qadesh 1300BC* (London).

Heide, M. & **van der Veen**, P. G. – 1999: '*A Test of Time* and Comparative Semitism' in *JACF* 8, pp. 31-42.

Heidel, A. – 1942: *The Babylonian Genesis: The Story of Creation* (Chicago, 2nd edition 1951).

Heidel, A. – 1946: *The Gilgamesh Epic and Old Testament Parallels* (Chicago).

Helck, W. – 1978: 'Ein indirekter Beleg für die Benutzung des leichten Streitwagens in Ägypten zu ende der 13.Dynastie' in *JNES* 37, pp. 337-40.

Heller, J. – 1958: 'Der Name *Eva*' in *An. Or.* 26, pp. 636-56.

Henrickson, E. F. – 1985: 'An Updated Chronology of the Early and Middle Chalcolithic of the Central Zagros Highlands, Western Iran' in *Iran* XXIII, pp. 63-108.

Henzberg, H. – 1965: *Die Samuel Bucher* (Gottingen).

Herrman, G. – 1968: 'Lapis lazuli: the early phases of its trade' in *Iraq* 30, pp. 21-57.

Herzog, C. & **Gichon**, M. – 1978: *Battles of the Bible* (London).

Hess, R. S. – 1993: *Amarna Personal Names* (Winona Lake).

Hess, R. S. – 1994: 'One Hundred Fifty Years of Comparative Studies on Genesis 1-11: An Overview' in R. S. Hess & D. T. Tsumura (eds.): *'I Studied Inscriptions from before the Flood': Ancient Near Eastern, Literary, and Linguistic Approaches to Genesis 1–11*, pp. 3-26.

Hess, R. S. – 1994: 'The Genealogies of Genesis 1–11 and Comparative Literature' in R. S. Hess & D. T. Tsumura (eds.): *'I Studied Inscriptions from before the Flood': Ancient Near Eastern, Literary, and Linguistic Approaches to Genesis 1–11*, pp. 58-72.

Heyerdahl, T. – 1980: *The Tigris Expedition: In Search of Our Beginnings* (London).

Hobbs, J. J. – 1906. *Mount Sinai* (Cairo).

Hoffman, M. A. – 1984: *Egypt Before the Pharaohs* (New York).

Hoffmeier, J. K. – 1996: *Israel in Egypt: The Evidence for the Authenticity of the Exodus Tradition* (Oxford).

Horowitz, W. & **Shaffer**, A. – 1992: 'A Fragment of a Letter from Hazor' in *IEJ* 42, pp. 165-66.

Huehnergard, J. – 1995: 'Semitic Languages' in J. M. Sasson (ed.): *Civilisations of the Ancient Near East*, Vol. IV, pp. 2117-34.

Hughes, J. – 1990: *Secrets of the Times: Myth and History in Biblical Chronology* (Sheffield).

Hughes, D. R. & **Brothwell**, D. R. – 1970: 'The Earliest Populations of Man in Europe, Western Asia and Northern Africa' in *CAH* I:1, pp. 156-172.

I

Ibrahim, M. & **Rohl**, D. M. – 1988: 'Apis and the Serapeum' in *JACF* 2, pp. 6-26.

Irving, C. – 1979: *Crossroads of Civilization: 3000 Years of Persian History* (London).

Ishida, T. – 1977: *The Royal Dynasties in Ancient Israel* (New York)

Izady, M. R. – 1992: *The Kurds – A Concise Handbook* (London).

J

Jacobsen, T. – 1939: *The Sumerian King List* (Chicago).

Jacobsen, T. – 1980: 'Sumer' in A. Cotterell (ed.): *The Penguin Encyclopedia of Ancient Civilizations*, pp. 72-108.

Jacobsen, T. – 1994: 'The Eridu Genesis' in R. S. Hess & D. T. Tsumura (eds.): *'I Studied Inscriptions from before the Flood': Ancient Near Eastern, Literary, and Linguistic Approaches to Genesis 1–11*, pp. 129-42.

James, P. *et al.* – 1991: *Centuries of Darkness* (London).

Jansen-Winkeln, C. – 1999: 'Dating the Beginning of the 22nd Dynasty' in *JACF* 8, pp. 17-21.

Jelinkova, E. A. E. – 1962: 'The Shebtiw in the temple at Edfu' in *ZÄS* 87, pp. 41-54.

Johnston, P. – 1980: *The Seacraft of Prehistory* (London).

Jones, A. – 1990: *Jones' Dictionary of Old Testament Proper Names* (first published in 1856) (Grand Rapids).

Jones, T. B. (ed.) – 1969: *The Sumerian Problem* (New York).

Jones, W. H. S. (trans.) – 1980: *Pliny, The Elder: Natural History,* Book VI (Cambridge, Massachusetts).

BIBLIOGRAPHY

Jonsson, C. O. – 1987: 'The Foundations of the Assyro-Babylonian Chronology' in *C & C Review* 9, pp. 14-23.

K

Kammenhuber, A. – 1968: *Die Arier im Vorderen Orient* (Heidelberg).

Kantor, H. J. – 1944: 'The Final Phase of Predynastic Culture' in *JNES* 3, pp. 110-48.

Kantor, H. J. – 1949: Review of Baumgartel (1947) in *AJA* 53, pp. 76-79.

Kantor, H. J. – 1952: 'Further Evidence for Early Mesopotamian Relations with Egypt' in *JNES* 11, pp. 239-50.

Kantor, H. J. – 1954: 'The Relative Chronology of Egypt and its Foreign Correlations Before the Late Bronze Age' in *Chronologies in Old World Archaeology*, pp. 1-46.

Keel, O. – 1978: *The Symbolism of the Biblical World: Ancient Near Eastern Iconography and the Book of Psalms* (London).

Kelley, A. L. – 1974: 'The evidence of Mesopotamian influence in Pre-dynastic Egypt' in *Newsl. Soc. Study Egypt. Ant.* 4, pp. 2-22.

Kelley, A. L. – 1983: 'A review of the evidence concerning early Egyptian ivory knife handles' in *The Ancient World* 6, pp. 95-102.

Kemp, B. J. – 1967: 'The Egyptian 1st Dynasty royal cemetery' in *Antiquity* 41, pp. 22-32.

Kemp, B. J. – 1989: *Ancient Egypt: Anatomy of a Civilization* (London).

Kempinski, A. – 1974: 'Tell el-Ajjul – Beth-Aglayim or Sharuhen?' in *IEJ* 24, pp. 145-52.

Kempinski, A. – 1983: *Syrien und Palästina (Kanaan) in der letzten Phase der Mittelbronze IIB–Zeit (1650–1570 v. chr.)* (Wiesbaden).

Kempinski, A. – 1988: 'Jacob in History' in *BAR* 14:1, pp. 42-47.

Kenyon, K. M. in J. W. Crowfoot *et al.* – 1957: *The Objects from Samaria* (London).

Kenyon, K. M. – 1957: *Digging up Jericho* (London).

Kenyon, K. M. – 1960: *Archaeology in the Holy Land* (London).

Kenyon, K. M. – 1963: 'Excavations in Jerusalem, 1962' in *PEQ* 95, pp. 7-21.

Kenyon, K. M. – 1965: 'Excavations in Jerusalem, 1964' in *PEQ* 97, pp. 13-14.

King, L. W. – 1969: 'History of Sumer and Akkad' in T. B. Jones (ed.): *The Sumerian Problem*, pp. 50-62.

Kitchen, K. A. – 1971: 'Punt and how to get there' in *Orientalia* 40, pp. 184-207.

Kitchen, K. A. – 1973: *The Third Intermediate Period in Egypt* (Warminster).

Kitchen, K. A. – 1982: *Pharaoh Triumphant* (Warminster).

Kitchen, K. A. – 1987: 'The Basics of Egyptian Chronology in Relation to the Bronze Age' in P. Aström (ed.): *HML?*, pp. 35-55.

Kitchen, K. A. – 1992: Discussion of the Exodus in D. N. Freedman (ed.): *Anchor Bible Dictionary*, vol. II (New York), pp. 702-07.

Kitchen, K. A. – 1993: 'The Land of Punt' in T. Shaw *et al.* (eds): *The Archaeology of Africa*, pp. 587-608.

Kitchen, K. A. – 1993: 'Genesis 12 to 50 in the Near Eastern World' in R. S. Hess *et al.* (eds.): *He Swore an Oath: Biblical Themes from Genesis 12 to 50*, pp. 67-92.

Knudtzon, J. A. – 1915: *Die el-Amarna Tafeln* (Leipzig, 2nd ed., 1978).

Kovacs, M. G. (trans.) –1985: *The Epic of Gilgamesh* (California).

Kramer, S. N. – 1952: *Enmerkar and the Lord of Aratta* (Philadelphia).

Kramer, S. N. – 1956: *From the Tablets of Sumer (History Begins at Sumer)* (Indian Hills, new enlarged ed.: Philadelphia, 1981).

Kramer, S. N. – 1963: *The Sumerians: Their History, Culture, and Character* (Chicago).

Kramer, S. N. – 1968: 'The 'Babel of Tongues': A Sumerian Version' in *JAOS* 88, pp. 108-11.

Kramer, S. N. – 1969: 'Sumerian Myths and Epic Tales' in J. B. Pritchard (ed.): *ANET*, 3rd ed., pp. 37-59.

Kramer, S. N. & **Maier**, J. – 1989: *Myths of Enki, the Crafty God* (New York).

Kramer, S. N. – 1948: 'New Light on the Early History of the Ancient Near East' in *AJA* 52, pp. 156-64.

Kuhrt, A. – 1995: *The Ancient Near East* c. *3000–330 BC*, Vol. 1 (London).

Külling, S. R. – 1996: *Are the genealogies in Genesis 5 and 11 historical and complete, that is, without gaps?* (Riehen).

L

Lambert, W. G. & **Millard**, A. R. – 1969: *Atra-hasis: The Babylonian Story of the Flood* (Oxford).

Landstrom, B. – 1970: *Ships of the Pharaohs* (London).

Lang, D. M. – 1980: 'Urartu and Armenia' in A. Cotterell (ed.): *The Penguin Encyclopedia of Ancient Civilizations*, pp. 117-22.

Langdon, S. H. – 1921: 'The Early Chronology of Sumer and Egypt and the Similarities in Their Culture' in *JEA* 7, pp. 133-53.

Langdon, S. H. – 1923: *Historical Inscriptions, Containing Principally the Chronological Prism, W-B. 444* (Oxford Editions of Cuneiform Texts, II, London).

Langdon, S. & **Fotheringham**, J. K. – 1928: *The Venus Tablets of Ammizaduga* (London).

Leclant, J. & **Yoyotte**, J. – 1952: 'Notes d'Histoire et de Civilisation Éthiopienne' in *BIFAO* 51, pp. 1-39.

Legrain, G. – 1897: 'Deux steles trouvees a Karnak en fevrier 1897' in *ZÄS* 35, pp. 13-16.

Legrain, G. – 1914: *Catalogue Général des Antiquités Égyptiennes du Musée du Caire: Statues et Statuettes*, vol. III (Cairo).

Lehmann, J. – 1977: *The Hittites* (London).

Lenzen, H. J. – 1968: *Uruk-Warka*, Vol. XXIV (Berlin).

Lichtheim, M. –1973: *Ancient Egyptian Literature, Volume I: The Old and Middle Kingdoms* (Berkeley).

Lichtheim, M. –1976: *Ancient Egyptian Literature, Volume II: The New Kingdom* (Berkeley).

Lloyd, S. – 1984: *The Archaeology of Mesopotamia: From the Old Stone Age to the Persian Conquest* (Revised edition, London).

Luckenbill, D. D. – 1926: *Ancient Records of Assyria and Babylon*, vol. I (Chicago).

Luckenbill, D. D. – 1927: *Ancient Records of Assyria and Babylon*, Vol. II (Chicago).

M

Mackenzie, D. A. – 1915: *Mythology of the Babylonian People* (London).

Magnusson, M. – 1977: *BC: The Archaeology of the Bible Lands* (London).

Majer, J. – 1992: 'The Eastern Desert and Egyptian Prehistory' in R. Friedman & B. Adams (eds.): *The Followers of Horus: Studies dedicated to Michael Allen Hoffman 1944–1990*, pp. 227-34.

BIBLIOGRAPHY

Malamat, A. – 1958: 'The Kingdom of David and Solomon in its Contact with Aram Naharaim' in *BA* 21:4, pp. 96-102.

Malamat, A. – 1994: 'King Lists of the Old Babylonian Period and Biblical Genealogies' in R. S. Hess & D. T. Tsumura (eds.): *'I Studied Inscriptions from before the Flood': Ancient Near Eastern, Literary, and Linguistic Approaches to Genesis 1–11*, pp. 183-200.

Mallowan, M. E. L. – 1964: 'Noah's Flood Reconsidered' in *Iraq* 26, pp. 62-82.

Mallowan, M. E. L. – 1970: 'The Development of Cities From Al-Ubaid to the End of Uruk 5' in *CAH* I:1, pp. 327-462.

Mazar, B. – 1963: 'The Military Élite of King David' in *VT*, 13 (Leiden), pp. 310-20.

Mazar, A. – 1986: *The Early Biblical Period* (Jerusalem).

Mazar, A. – 1990: *Archaeology of the Land of the Bible: 10000–586 BCE* (New York).

Mazar, A. (ed.) – 2001: *Studies in the Archaeology of the Iron Age in Israel and Jordan* (Sheffield).

McCall, H. – 1990: *Mesopotamian Myths* (London).

McCarter, P. K. – 1984: *II Samuel: A New Translation with Introduction Notes and Commentary* (Anchor Bible, New York).

McCarter, P. K. – 1986: 'The Historical David' in *Interpretation* 40:2, pp. 117-29.

McGovern, P. *et al.* – 1993: 'The Late Bronze Egyptian Garrison at Beth Shan: Glass and Faience Production and Importation in the Late New Kingdom' in *BASOR* 290/91, pp. 1-28.

Mellaart, J. – 1970: 'The Earliest Settlements in Western Asia from the Ninth to the End of the Fifth Millennium B.C.' in *CAH* I:1, pp. 248-303.

Mellaart, J. – 1979: 'Early Urban Communities in the Near East, *c.* 9000–3400 BC' in P. R. S. Moorey (ed.): *The Origins of Civilization*, pp. 22-33.

Mendenhall, G. – 1973: *The Tenth Generation* (Baltimore).

Meyers, E. M. – 1997: *The Oxford Encyclopedia of Archaeology in the Near East* (New York).

Michalowski, P. – 1995: 'Sumerian Literature: An Overview' in J. M. Sasson (ed.): *Civilisations of the Ancient Near East*, Vol. IV, pp. 2279-91.

Millard, A. R. – 1984: 'The Etymology of Eden' in *VT* 34, pp. 103-6.

Millard, A. R. – 1994: 'A New Babylonian 'Genesis' Story' in R. S. Hess & D. T. Tsumura (eds.): *'I Studied Inscriptions from before the Flood': Ancient Near Eastern, Literary, and Linguistic Approaches to Genesis 1–11*, pp. 114-28.

Miller, J. M. – 1974: 'Saul's Rise to Power' in *Catholic Biblical Quarterly* 36, pp. 160-64 & 173-74.

Miller, J. M. – 1975: 'Geba/Gibeah of Benjamin' in *VT* 25, pp. 145-66.

Miller Jr., P. D. – 1994: 'Eridu, Dunnu, and Babel: A Study in Comparative Mythology' in R. S. Hess & D. T. Tsumura (eds.): *'I Studied Inscriptions from before the Flood': Ancient Near Eastern, Literary, and Linguistic Approaches to Genesis 1–11*, pp. 143-68.

Mitchell, W. A. – 1990: 'Ancient Astronomical Observations and Near Eastern Chronology' in *JACF* 3, pp. 18-20.

Moorey, P. R. S. – 1993: 'Iran: A Sumerian El-Dorado?' in J. Curtis (ed.): *Early Mesopotamia and Iran: Contact and Conflict 3500–1600 BC*, pp. 31-43.

Moran, W. L. – 1992: *The Amarna Letters* (Johns Hopkins, Baltimore).

Moran, W. – 1995: 'The Gilgamesh Epic: A Masterpiece from Ancient Mesopotamia' in J. M. Sasson (ed.): *Civilisations of the Ancient Near East*, Vol. IV, pp. 2327-36.

Morkot, R. G. – 2000: *The Black Pharaohs: Egypt's Nubian Rulers* (London).
Moscati, S. – 1973: *The World of the Phoenicians* (London).
Mullen Jr., E. T. – 1980: *The Divine Council in Canaanite and Early Hebrew Literature* (HSM 24; Chico, Cal.).
Murnane, W. J. – 1977: *Ancient Egyptian Coregencies* (Chicago).

N

Na'aman, N. – 1986: 'Habiru and Hebrews: the Transfer of a Social Term to the Literary Sphere' in *JNES* 45:4, pp. 271-88.
Naville, E. – 1885: *The Store-City of Pithom and the Route of the Exodus* (London).
Naville, E. – 1887: *The Shrine of Saft el-Henneh and the Land of Goshen* (London).
Negev, A. (ed.) – 1986: *The Archaeological Encyclopedia of the Holy Land* (New York).
Newberry, P. E. – 1943: 'Co-regencies of Ammenemes III, IV and Sebeknofru' in *JEA* 29, pp. 74-75.
Newgrosh, B. *et al.* – 1994: 'The el-Amarna Letters and Israelite History' in *JACF* 6, pp. 33-64.
Newgrosh, B. – 1999: 'The Chronology of Ancient Assyria Re-assessed' in *JACF* 8, pp. 78-106.
Newton, I. – 1728: *The Chronology of Ancient Kingdoms Amended* (London).
Nissen, H. J. – 1987: 'The chronology of the proto- and early historic periods in Mesopotamia and Susiana' in O. Aurenche *et al.* (eds.): *Chronologies du Proche-Orient*, pp. 607-14.
Nissen, H. J. – 1993: 'The Context of the Emergence of Writing in Mesopotamia and Iran' in J. Curtis (ed.): *Early Mesopotamia and Iran: Contact and Conflict 3500–1600 BC*, pp. 54-71.
Noth, M. – 1928: *Israelitische Personennamen* (Stuttgart).
Noth, M. – 1938: 'Die Wege der Pharaonenheere in Palästina und Syrien; IV. Die Schoschenkliste' in *ZDPV* 61, pp. 277-304.
Noth, M. – 1958: *The History of Israel* (London).

O

Oates, J. – 1960: 'Ur and Eridu, the Prehistory' in *Iraq* 22, pp. 32-50.
Oates, J. – 1969: 'Ur and Eridu; the Prehistory' in T. B. Jones (ed.): *The Sumerian Problem*, pp. 126-34.
Odelain, O. & **Séguineau**, R. – 1981: *Dictionary of Proper Names and Places in the Bible* (London).
Oldfather, C. H. (trans.) – 1933: *Diodorus Siculus* (London).
Oppenheim, A. L. – 1969: 'Texts from the Beginnings to the First Dynasty of Babylon' in J. B. Pritchard (ed): *ANET*, pp. 263-317.

P

Papke, W. – 1993: *Die geheime Botschaft des Gilgamesh: 4000 Jahre alte astronomische Aufzeichnungen entschlüsselt* (Augsburg).
Pardee, D. & **Swerdlow** – 1993: 'Not the earliest solar eclipse' in *Nature* 363, p. 406.
Parker, R. A. – 1950: *Calendars of Ancient Egypt* (Chicago).
Partridge, R. – 1996: *Transport in Ancient Egypt* (London).
Payne, J. C. – 1968: 'Lapis lazuli in early Egypt' in *Iraq* 30, pp. 58-61.
Peet, T. E. – 1915: 'The Art of the Predynastic Period' in *JEA* 2, pp. 88-94.

BIBLIOGRAPHY

Petrie, W. M. F. – 1894: *A History of Egypt*, part 1 (London).
Petrie, W. M. F. – 1896: *Koptos* (London).
Petrie, W. M. F. – 1900: *The royal tombs of the first dynasty*, Vol. 1 (London).
Petrie, W. M. F. – 1901: *The royal tombs of the first dynasty*, Vol. II (London).
Petrie, W. M. F. – 1906: *Researches in Sinai* (London).
Petrie, W. M. F. – 1939: *The Making of Egypt* (London).
Petrie, W. M. F. & **Quibell**, J. E. – 1896: *Naqada and Ballas* (London).
Pitard, W. T. – 1987: *Ancient Damascus* (Winona Lake).
Pitard, W. T. – 1988: 'The Identity of Bir-Hadad of the Melqart Stela' in *BASOR* 272, pp. 3-21.
Poebel, A. – 1942: 'The Assyrian King List from Khorsabad' in *JNES* 1:3, pp. 247-306.
Poebel, A. – 1943: 'The Assyrian King List from Khorsabad – Concluded' in *JNES* 2, pp. 56-90.
Porada, E. – 1993: 'Seals and Related Objects from Early Mesopotamia and Iran' in J. Curtis (ed.): *Early Mesopotamia and Iran: Contact and Conflict 3500–1600 BC*, pp. 44-53.
Porter, R. – 1999: 'The Generation Game' in *JACF* 8, pp. 26-30.
Porter, R. – 1999: 'The Iron Age and the New Chronology' in *JACF* 8, pp. 66-77.
Posener, G. – 1939: 'Nouveaux Textes Hiératiques de Proscription' in R. Dussaud: *Mélanges Syriens offerts a M. René Dussaud*, vol. I, pp. 313-17.
Posener, G. – 1940: *Princes et Pays D'Asie et de Nubie* (Brussels).
Postgate, J. N. – 1992: *Early Mesopotamia: Society and Economy at the Dawn of History* (London).
Potts, T. – 1994: *Mesopotamia and the East* (Oxford).
Pritchard, J. B. –1969: *Ancient Near Eastern Texts Relating to the Old Testament* (Princeton).
Pritchard, J. B. (ed.) – 1974: *Solomon and Sheba* (London).

Q

Quibell, J. E. – 1898: *The Ramesseum* (London).
Quibell, J. E. & **Green**, F. W. – 1902: *Hierakonpolis*, 2 vols. (London).
Quirke, S. – 1990: *The Administration of Egypt in the Late Middle Kingdom* (New Malden).

R

Raikes, R. L. – 1966: 'The Physical Evidence for Noah's Flood' in *Iraq* 28, pp. 52-63.
Rainey, A. – 1978: *El Amarna Tablets 257–379 – Supplement to J. A. Knudtzon: Die El Amarna Taffeln*, 2nd edn. revised (Neukirchen-Vluyn).
Rawlinson, G. – 1889: *History of Phoenicia* (London).
Redford, D. B. – 1984: *Akhenaten: The Heretic King* (Princeton).
Redman, C. L. – 1978: *The Rise of Civilization: From Early Farmers to Urban Society in the Ancient Near East* (San Francisco).
Reeves, N. – 2001: *Akhenaten: Egypt's False Prophet* (London).
Reiner, E. – 1961: 'The Etiological Myth of the 'Seven Sages' in *Or* 30, pp. 1-11.
Renfrew, C. – 1987: *Archaeology and Language: The Puzzle of Indo-European Origins* (London).
Reymond, E. A. E. – 1969: *The Mythical Origin of the Egyptian Temple* (New York).

Rice, M. – 1985: *The Search for the Paradise Land* (London).
Rice, M. – 1990: *Egypt's Making: The Origins of Ancient Egypt 5000–2000 BC* (London).
Richards, L. O. – 1985: *New International Encyclopedia of Bible Words* (Grand Rapids).
Roaf, M. – 1990: *Cultural Atlas of Mesopotamia and the Ancient Near East* (New York).
Robins, G. – 1994: 'Women and Children in Peril: Pregnancy, Birth and Infant Mortality in Ancient Egypt' in *KMT* 5:4, pp. 24-35.
Rohl, D. M. – 1985: 'Forum' in *SIS Workshop* 6:2, pp. 21-26.
Rohl, D. M. – 1990: 'The Early Third Intermediate Period: Some Chronological Considerations' in *JACF* 3, pp. 45-69.
Rohl, D. M. – 1992: 'A Test of Time: The New Chronology of Egypt and its Implications for Biblical Archaeology and History' in *JACF* 5, pp. 30-58.
Rohl, D. M. – 1992: 'Some Chronological Conundrums of the 21st Dynasty' in *Ägypten und Levante* 3, pp. 137-39.
Rohl, D. M. – 1992: 'The Length of Sojourn in Egypt' in *C & C Workshop* 1992:1, pp. 48-49.
Rohl, D. M. – 1995: *A Test of Time: The Bible – From Myth to History* (London).
Rohl, D. M. – 1998: *Legend: The Genesis of Civilisation* (London).
Rohl, D. M. – 1999: 'Biblical Archaeology: Time to Think Again?' in *JACF* 8, pp. 7-12.
Rohl, D. M. – 1999: 'Kenneth Kitchen's Atom Bomb' in *JACF* 8, pp. 43-47.
Rohl, D. M. – 1999: 'Absence of Evidence is not Evidence of Absence' in *JACF* 8, pp. 47-49.
Rohl, D. M. – 1999: 'The Monster in Philippe Brissaud's Nightmares' in *JACF* 8, pp. 50-56.
Rohl, D. M. (ed.) – 2000: *The Followers of Horus: Eastern Desert Survey Report* (Abingdon).
Rohl, D. M. & **James**, P. – 1983: 'An Alternative to the Velikovskian Chronology of Ancient Egypt: A Preview of Some Recent Work in the Field of Ancient History' in *SIS Workshop* 5:2, pp. 12-21.
Rohl, D. M. & **Newgrosh**, B. – 1988: 'The el-Amarna Letters and the New Chronology' in *C & C Review* 10, pp. 33-34.
Ross, J. – 1967: 'Gezer in the Tell el-Amarna Letters' in *BA* 30, pp. 62-70.
Roux, G. – 1964: *Ancient Iraq* (Middlesex).
Roux, G. – 1969: *Ancient Iraq* in T. B. Jones (ed.): *The Sumerian Problem*, pp. 134-38.
Rowley, H. H. (ed.) – 1969: *New Atlas of the Bible* (London).
Rowton, M. B. – 1970: 'Ancient Western Asia' in *CAH* I:1, pp. 193-239.
Rundle Clark, R. T. – 1959: *Myth and Symbol in Ancient Egypt* (London).
Ryan, W. & **Pitman**, W. – 1998 : *Noah' Flood: The New Scientific Discoveries About the Event That Changed History* (New York).

S

Safar, F. *et al.* – 1981: *Eridu* (Baghdad).
Saggs, H. W. F. – 1984: *The Might That Was Assyria* (London).
Saggs, H. W. F. – 1989: *Civilization Before Greece and Rome* (London).
Saggs, H. W. F. – 1995: *Babylonians* (London).
Saleh, A. A. – 1969: 'The So-called 'Primeval Hill' and other Related Elevations in Ancient Egyptian Mythology' in *MDAIK* 25, pp. 110-20.
Sasson, J. M. (ed.) – 1995: *Civilisations of the Ancient Near East*, Vol. IV (New York).

BIBLIOGRAPHY

Sassoon, J. – 1993: *From Sumer to Jerusalem: The Forbidden Hypothesis* (Oxford).

Sawyer, J. F. A. & **Stephenson**, F. R. – 1970: 'Literary and Astronomical Evidence for a Total Eclipse of the Sun Observed in Ancient Ugarit on 3 May 1375 BC' in *BSOAS* 33, pp. 467-89.

Schaeffer, C. F. A. – 1948: *Stratigraphie comparée et chronologie de l'Asie occidentale (IIIe et IIe millénaires)* (Oxford).

Schley, D. G. – 1989: *Shiloh: A Biblical City in Tradition and History* (JSOT Supplement Series 63, Sheffield).

Schmidt, B. B. – 1995: 'Flood Narratives of Ancient Western Asia' in J. M. Sasson (ed.): *Civilisations of the Ancient Near East*, Vol. IV, pp. 2337-51.

S éguineau, R. & **Odelain**, O. –1978: *Dictionary of Proper Names and Places in the Bible* (London).

Seligman, C. G. – 1934: *Egypt and Negro Africa: A Study in Divine Kingship* (London).

Sethe, K. H. – 1904: 'Der Name Sesostris' in *ZÄS* 41, pp. 43-57.

Sethe, K. – 1908–1922: *Die altägyptischen Pyramidentexte*, 4 vols. (Leipzig).

Seton-Williams, M. V. – 1988: *Egyptian Legends and Stories* (London).

Shaw, I. & **Nicholson**, P. – 1995: *British Museum Dictionary of Ancient Egypt* (London).

Shea, W. H. – 1977: 'Adam in Ancient Mesopotamian Traditions' in *AUSS* 15, p. 39.

Shiloh, Y. – 1979: *The Proto-Aeolic Capital and Israelite Ashlar Masonry* (*Qedem* 11, Jerusalem).

Shiloh, Y. – 1981: 'The City of David Archaeological Project: The Third Season, 1980' in *BA* 44, pp. 161-70.

Simons, J. – 1994: 'The 'Table of Nations' (Genesis 10): Its General Structure and Meaning' in R. S. Hess & D. T. Tsumura (eds.): *'I Studied Inscriptions from before the Flood': Ancient Near Eastern, Literary, and Linguistic Approaches to Genesis 1–11*, pp. 234-53.

Singer, I. – 1985: 'The Beginning of Philistine Settlement in Canaan and the Northern Boundary of Philistia' in *Tel Aviv* 12:2, pp. 109-22.

Singer, I. – 1994: 'Egyptians, Canaanites, and Philistines in the Period of the Emergence of Israel' in Finkelstein & Na'aman (eds.), 1994, pp. 282-338.

Smith, G. – 1874: 'The Chaldean Account of the Deluge' in *Transactions of the Society of Biblical Archaeology* 2, pp. 213-34.

Smith, G. A. – 1894: *The Historical Geography of the Holy Land* (London).

Smith, H. S. – 1992: 'The Making of Egypt: A Review of the Influence of Susa and Sumer on Upper Egypt and Lower Nubia in the 4th Millennium B.C.' in R. Friedman and B. Adams (eds.): *The Followers of Horus. Studies Dedicated to Michael Allen Hoffman* (Oxford), pp. 235-46.

Smith, S. – 1922: 'The Relation of Marduk, Ashur, and Osiris' in *JEA* 8, pp. 41-4.

von Soden, W. – 1966: *Akkadisches Handworterbuch* (Wiesbaden).

Soggin, J. A. – 1984: *A History of Israel* (London).

Speiser, E. A. – 1930: *Mesopotamian Origins* (Philadelphia).

Speiser, E. A. – 1950: 'The Sumerian Problem Reviewed' in *Hebrew Union College Annual* 23, pp. 339-55.

Speiser, E. A. (trans.) – 1969: 'Akkadian Myths and Epics' in J. B. Pritchard (ed.): *Ancient Near Eastern Texts: Relating to Old Testament*, pp. 60-119.

Speiser, E. A. – 1969: 'The Beginnings of Civilization in Mesopotamia' in T. Jones (ed.): *The Sumerian Problems*, pp. 76-92.

Speiser, E. A. – 1969: 'The Sumerian Problem Reviewed' in T. Jones: *The*

Sumerian Problem, pp. 93-124.

Speiser, E. A. – 1994: 'The Rivers of Paradise' in R. S. Hess & D. T. Tsumura (eds.): *'I Studied Inscriptions from before the Flood': Ancient Near Eastern, Literary, and Linguistic Approaches to Genesis 1–11*, pp. 175-82.

Speiser, E. A. – 1994: 'In Search of Nimrod' in R. S. Hess & D. T. Tsumura (eds.): *'I Studied Inscriptions from before the Flood': Ancient Near Eastern, Literary, and Linguistic Approaches to Genesis 1–11*, pp. 270-77.

Spencer, A. J. – 1993: *Early Egypt: The Rise of Civilisation in the Nile Valley* (London).

Stager, L. E. – 1982: 'The Archaeology of the East Slope of Jerusalem and the Terraces of the Kidron' in *JNES* 41, pp. 111-21.

Stager, L. E. – 1990: 'Shemer's Estate' in *BASOR* 277/8, pp. 93-107.

Stamm, J. J. – 1960: 'Der Name David' in *Supplement to VT* 7 (Leiden), pp. 175-81.

Steiner, M. L. – 1994: 'Redating the Terraces of Jerusalem' in *IEJ* 44, pp. 13-20.

Steiner, M. L. – 1999: 'Problems of Synthesis' in *JACF* 8, pp. 12-13.

Stern, E. (ed.) – 1993: *The New Encyclopedia of Archaeological Excavations in the Holy Land* (New York).

Stevenson Smith, W. – 1962: 'The land of Punt' in *JARCE* 1, pp. 59-60.

Stock, H. – 1942: *Studien zur Geschichte und Archäologie der 13. bis 17. Dynastie Ägyptens, unter besonderer Berücksichtigung der Scarab en dieser Zwischenzeit (ÄF 12)*.

Strabo: *Histories*, book XVII.

Strong, J. – 1896: *The Exhaustive Concordance of the Bible* (New York).

Sturgis, M. – 2001: *It Ain't Necessarily So: Investigating the Truth of the Biblical Past* (London).

T

Teissier, B. – 1987: 'Glyptic Evidence for a Connection Between Iran, Syro-Palestine and Egypt in the Fourth and Third Millennia' in *Iran* 25, pp. 27-54.

Thiele, E. R.– 1983: *The Mysterious Numbers of the Hebrew Kings* (Grand Rapids).

Thompson, T. L. – 1992: *Early History of the Israelite People: From the Written and Archaeological Sources* (Leiden).

Thompson, T. L. – 1999: *The Bible in History: How Writers Create a Past* (London).

Trigger, B. G. *et al.* – 1983: *Ancient Egypt: A Social History* (Cambridge).

Tsevat, M. – 1954: 'The Canaanite God Salah' in *VT* 4, pp. 41-49.

Tsevat, M. – 1975: 'Ishbosheth and Congeners: The Names and their Study' in *HUCA* 46, pp. 71-87.

Tsumura, D. T. – 1994: 'Genesis and Ancient Near Eastern Stories of Creation and Flood: An Introduction' in R. S. Hess & D. T. Tsumura (eds.): *'I Studied Inscriptions from before the Flood': Ancient Near Eastern, Literary, and Linguistic Approaches to Genesis 1–11*, pp. 27-57.

Tsumura, D. T. – 1994: 'The Earth in Genesis 1' in R. S. Hess & D. T. Tsumura (eds.): *'I Studied Inscriptions from before the Flood': Ancient Near Eastern, Literary, and Linguistic Approaches to Genesis 1–11*, pp. 310-28.

U

Ussishkin, D. – 1980: 'Was the 'Solomonic' City Gate at Megiddo Built by King Solomon?' in *BASOR* 239, pp. 1-18.

BIBLIOGRAPHY

Ussishkin, D. – 1990: 'Notes on Megiddo, Gezer, Ashdod, and Tel Batash in the Tenth to Ninth Centuries B.C.' in *BASOR* 277/278, pp. 71-91.

V

Valloggia, M. – 1974: 'Les Vizirs des XIe et XIIe Dynasties' in *BIFAO* 74, pp. 123-34.

de Vaux, R. – 1978: *The Early History of Israel*, vols. I & II (London).

van der Veen, P. G. – 1989: *I Samuel and the Habiru-Problem* (Leuven); thesis submitted to the Evangelical Theological Faculty of Leuven in partial fulfilment of the requirements for the degree of Licentiate in Theology.

van der Veen, P. G. – 1990: 'The el-Amarna *Habiru* and the Early Monarchy in Israel' in *JACF* 3, pp. 72-78.

van der Veen, P. G. – 1993: 'The *Habiru* as the *Ibrim* of I Samuel and the Implications for the 'New Chronology'' in *C & C Review* 15, p. 33.

van der Veen, P. G. – 1999: 'The Kingdom of Labayu' in *JACF* 8, pp. 14-16.

van der Veen, P. G. – 1999: 'The Name Shishak' in *JACF* 8, pp. 22-25.

van der Veen, P. G. & **Zerbst**, U. – 2002: *Biblische Archäologie am Scheideweg?* (Holzgerlingen).

Velikovsky, I. – 1952: *Ages in Chaos* (London).

Vercoutter, J. – 1966: 'Semna South Fort and the Records of Nile Levels at Kumma' in *Kush* 14, pp. 125-64.

W

Waddell, W. G. – 1971: *Manetho*, Loeb Classical Library (London).

Walker, C. B. F. – 1987: *Reading the Past: Cuneiform* (London).

Walker, C. B. F. – 1989: 'Eclipse seen at ancient Ugarit' in *Nature* 338, pp. 204-05.

Walker, R. A. – 1987: *The Garden of Eden* (Rhyl).

Wallenfels, R. – 1983: 'Redating the Byblian Inscriptions' in *JANES* 15, pp. 79-118.

Walton, J. – 1981: 'The Antediluvian Section of the Sumerian King List and Genesis 5' in *BA* 44.4, pp. 207-08.

Ward, W. A. – 1984: in O. Tufnell: *Studies on Scarab Seals*, vol. II (Warminster).

Weigall, A. E. P. – 1909: *Travels in the Upper Egyptian Desert* (London).

Weir, J. D. – 1972: *The Venus Tablets of Ammizaduga* (Istanbul).

Weir, J. D. – 1982: 'The Venus Tablets: A Fresh Approach' in *JHA* 13, pp. 23-49.

Wenham, G. J. – 1994: 'Sanctuary Symbolism in the Garden of Eden Story' in R. S. Hess & D. T. Tsumura (eds.): *'I Studied Inscriptions from Before the Flood': Ancient Near Eastern, Literary, and Linguistic Approaches to Genesis 1–11*, pp. 399-404.

Whiston, W. (transl.) – 1960: *Josephus: Complete Works* (Glasgow).

Whitcomb, J. C. & **Morris**, H. M. – 1961: *The Genesis Flood: The Biblical Record and its Scientific Implications* (Michigan).

Wightman, G. J. – 1985: 'Megiddo VIA-III: Associated Structures and Chronology' in *Levant* 17 , pp. 117-29.

Wigram, W. A. & **Wigram**, E. T. A. – 1922: *The Cradle of Mankind: Life in Eastern Kurdistan* (London).

Wilkinson, R. H. – 1985: 'The Horus name and the form and significance of the *serekh* in the royal Egyptian titulary' in *JSSEA* 15, pp. 98-104.

Wilson, J. A. – 1950: 'The Hymn to the Aton' in *ANET*, pp. 369-71.

Wilson, J. A. – 1969: 'Egyptian Myths, Tales, and Mortuary Texts' in J. B. Pritchard: *ANET*, 3rd ed., pp. 3-36.

Wilson, J. A. – 1969: 'Egyptian Hymns and Prayers' in J. B. Pritchard: *ANET*, 3rd ed., pp. 365-81.

Wilson, J. V. K. – 1985: *The Legend of Etana* (Warminster).

Wilson, R. R. – 1975: 'The Old Testament Genealogies in Recent Research' in *JBL* 94, pp. 169-89.

Wilson, R. R. – 1977: *Genealogy and History in the Biblical World* (New Haven).

Winkler, E. & **Wilfing**, H. – 1991: *Tell el-Dab'a VI: Anthropologische Untersuchungen an den Skelettresten der Kampagnen 1966–69, 1975–80, 1985* (Vienna).

Winkler, H. A. – 1938–39: *Rock Drawings of Southern Upper Egypt*, 2 vols. (London).

Wiseman, D. J. – 1994: 'Genesis 10: Some Archaeological Considerations' in R. S. Hess & D. T. Tsumura (eds.): *'I Studied Inscriptions from before the Flood': Ancient Near Eastern, Literary, and Linguistic Approaches to Genesis 1–11*, pp. 254-65.

Wolkstein, D. & **Kramer**, S. N. – 1983: *Inanna: Queen of Heaven and Earth* (New York).

Wood, B. G. – 1990: 'Dating Jericho's Destruction: Bienkowski is Wrong on All Counts' in *BAR* 16:5, pp. 45-49 & 68-69.

Wood, M. – 1992: *Legacy: A Search for the Origins of Civilization* (London).

Woolley, C. L. – 1954: *Excavations at Ur* (London).

Woolley, C. L. – 1982: *Ur 'of the Chaldees'*, new revised edition by P. R. S. Moorey (London).

Woolley, C. L. – 1969: 'The Sumerians' in T. B. Jones (ed.): *The Sumerian Problem*, pp. 66-73.

Wright, G. E. – 1966: 'Fresh Evidence for the Philistine Story' in *BA* 29:3, pp. 70-86.

Wyatt, N. – 1981: 'Interpreting the Creation and Fall Story in Genesis 2–3' in *ZAW* 93, p. 19.

Y

Yadin, Y. – 1976: 'Hazor' in Avi-Yonah M. & Stern E. (eds): *Encyclopedia of Archaeological Excavations in the Holy Land*, vol. II (London), pp. 474-95.

Yadin, Y. – 1977: 'Megiddo' in Avi-Yonah M. & Stern E. (eds): *Encyclopedia of Archaeological Excavations in the Holy Land*, vol. III (London), pp. 830-56.

Young, D. A. – 1995: *The Biblical Flood: A Case Study of the Church's Response to Extrabiblical Evidence* (Michigan).

Young, T. C. & **Smith**, P. E. L. – 1966: 'Research in the Prehistory of Central Western Iran' in *Science* 153, pp. 386-91.

Yurco, F. J. – 1986: 'Merenptah's Canaanite Campaign' in *JARCE* 23, pp. 189-215.

Yusuf Ali, A. (transl.) – 1975: *The Holy Qur'an* (London).

Z

Zadok, R. – 1984: 'The Origin of the Name Shinar' in *ZA* 74, pp. 240-44.

ABBREVIATIONS

ÄF = Ägyptologische Forschungen

AJA = American Journal of Archeology

AJSL = American Journal of Semitic Languages and Literature

ANET = Ancient Near Eastern Texts

ASAE = Annales du Services des Antiquités de l'Égypte

AUSS = Andrews University Seminary Studies

BA = Biblical Archaeologist

BAR = Biblical Archaeology Review

BASOR = Bulletin of the American Schools of Oriental Research

BIFAO = Bulletin de l'Institute Francais d'Archéologie Orientale

BSOAS = Bulletin of the School of Oriental & African Studies

CAH = Cambridge Ancient History

C & C Workshop (also known as **SIS Workshop**) = Chronology and Catastrophism Workshop

GM = Göttinger Miszellen

HML? = High Middle or Low?

HUCA = Hebrew Union College Annual

ISIS = Institute for the Study of Interdisciplinary Sciences

IEJ = Israel Exploration Journal

JACF = Journal of the Ancient Chronology Forum

JANES = Journal of the Ancient Near East Society

JAOS = Journal of the American Oriental Society

JARCE = Journal of the American Research Center in Egypt

JBL = Journal of Biblical Literature

JCS = Journal of Cuneiform Studies

JEA = Journal of Egyptian Archaeology

JHA = Journal for the History of Astronomy

JNES = Journal of Near Eastern Studies

JSOT = Journal for the Study of the Old Testament

JSSEA = Journal of the Society for the Study of Egyptian Antiquities

MDAIK = Mitteilungen des Deutschen Archäologischen Instituts Abteilung Kairo

Newsl. Soc. Study Egypt. Ant = Newsletter of the Society for the Study of Egyptian Antiquities

Or. = Orientalia

PEFQS = Palestine Exploration Fund Quarterly Statement

PEQ = Palestine Exploration Quarterly

SIS Review = Society for Interdisciplinary Studies Review

VT = Vetus Testamentum

ZA = Zeitschrift für Assyriologie

ZÄS = Zeitschrift für Ägyptische Sprache und Altertumskunde

ZAW = Zeitschrift für die Alttestamentlische Wüssenschaft

ZDPV = Zeitschrift des Deutschen Palaestina-Vereins

472

GLOSSARY

ABD-EL: 'servant of El'.

ABEL: Hebrew *Hebel* – 'offering smoke'.

ABIATHAR: 'father of excellence'.

ABIB: the lunar month, later known as Nisan = March/April.

ABIJAH: 'my [divine] father is Yah', 2 Kings 15 calls him Abijam.

ABNER: 'the father is the lamp'.

ABRAHAM: traditionally translated as 'father of a multitude' but more likely derived from Akkadian 'the father loves'.

ACHAEAN: Homeric term for the LBA Greeks otherwise known as Mycenaeans. The Hittite texts refer to the Achaeans as the men of Ahhiyawa.

ADDA-DANU: 'Haddad has judged'.

ADONIJAH: 'my lord is Yah'.

ADULLAM: modern Odullam above the vale of Elah.

AHIJAH: 'Yah is my brother'.

AKKADIAN: the East Semitic language of Mesopotamia.

ALBRIGHT: (1891–1971).

ALUSH: the modern Wadi Mukkatab – 'valley of writing'.

AMORITES: the overall name for the pastoralist tribes who came down from the Zagros foothills and settled in Syria and Canaan (including Transjordan) during the EB/MB transition – at the time of Abraham.

AN: from Anu god of heaven.

ANBU-HAZ: Egyptological *Ineb-hedj* – 'white wall'.

APHEK: overlooking the eastern shore of the Sea of Galilee (not Aphek on the Sharon plain).

ARAM-NAHARAIM: Egyptian Naharina – the land 'between the two rivers' i.e. the Euphrates and Khabur.

ARSA: also written Arsu or Irsu. However the hieroglyph usually transcribed as 'u' was invariably vocalised as 'a' (e.g. Hut-waret = Haware; Hut-Hor = Hathor).

BAAL: 'lord'.

BAB-ILU: 'gate of god'.

BAHRAIN: the 'twin waters'.

BALU-MEHIR: 'Baal is a warrior', otherwise written Balu-*ursag*, the second element being a Sumerian logogram.

BENAIAH: 'Yah has built'.

BEROSSUS: a Babylonian priest who wrote three books on Babylonian history utilising the archives from the temple of Bel in Babylon. As with Manetho, only excerpts survive in the writings of Josephus, Eusebius and Syncellus. His *floruit* was around 260 BC.

BETHLEHEM: 'house of Lahem'.

CAIN: Hebrew *Kayin* – 'metal smith'.

GLOSSARY

CARIAN: perhaps the Carians were one and the same as the people the Egyptians called Kharu, otherwise known as Hurrians (biblical Horites).

CORVÉE: volunteer labour arranged in rotation.

DANOYNA: Danoi = Homer's Greeks.

DASHT-É KAVIR: the 'salt desert'.

DEUTERONOMY: referred to in the Septuagint as to deuteronomion touto – 'this second law'.

DIDACTIC SCHOLAR: a man who teaches by instruction based on parable.

DURBAR: from Hindi *darbar* meaning 'court'. A grand reception at which the king or governor receives ambassadors and vassal rulers.

EBENEZER: 'stone of the protector', located at Izbet-Sarta near Aphek.

EHNAS: Greek Heracleopolis, modern Ehnasya el-Medina.

EHUD: 'Ya of praise'.

EL: Akkadian *ilu* and Arabic *Allah*, simply meaning 'power'.

EL-SHADDAI: 'El the mountain-dweller' from Akkadian *shadu*.

ELIJAH: 'my god is Yah'.

ELISHA: 'El has helped'.

ELHANAN: 'El shows favour'.

EN-GEDI: 'spring of the kid-goat'.

EN-ROGEL: 'spring of the fuller' – modern Bir Ayub.

EYA: previously written Ia, more recently written Ea, pronounced Éya.

FAIYUM LAKE: the Egyptians called this large expanse of water *pa-yam* ('the sea'), from which the modern Egyptian 'Faiyum' derives.

GALENA: for kohl eye make-up.

GEBTU: modern Kuft.

GIDEON: 'hewer [of wood]'.

HABIRU: probably derived from the Akkadian verb *habaru* 'to migrate'.

HADAD-AZIRU: 'Hadad is (my) helper' or 'Hadad is (my) protection'.

HAMATH: possibly Tell el-Hammeh, 15 kilometres south of Beth-Shean, or Hamman Tabariya, south of Tiberias on the western shore of the Sea of Galilee.

HAMMAMAT: (also written Hanmamet) and archaeologically represented by the Badarian and Nakada I cultures.

HAZOR: modern Tell el-Kedah.

HELAN: modern Alma, 56 kilometres east of the Sea of Galilee.

HIERAKONPOLIS: 'city of the hawk'.

IONA: Egyptian *Iwnw*, biblical On, Mesopotamian E-anna ('house of heaven'), Greek Heliopolis; named after the sacred precinct in Uruk.

ISAAC: 'may [God] smile' – biblical *Yizhak*.

ISHMAEL: 'El hears'.

ITJ-TAWY: 'seizer of the two lands'.

JABIN: Canaanite *Ibni[-Addu]*.

JEDIDIAH: Hebrew *Yedidyah* – 'beloved of Ya', probably from older Dud-Yah, 2 Samuel 12:24–25.

JONATHAN: 'Yah has given'.

JOSHUA: 'Ya has saved'.

KI: earth, place.

KHIRBET EL-MUKKATIR: also known as Khirbet el-Makkatar – 'offering up', possibly referring to its destruction by fire as a sacrifice to Yahweh.

KIR-HARESHETH: modern Karak/Kerak.

LACHISH: modern Tell ed-Duweir.

LIBNAH: possibly Tell Bornat, at a major route junction in the Wadi Zeita.

LISHT: a corruption of el-Itjet.

LUXOR: ancient *Niwe*, Greek *Thebes*.

MAHANAIM: Khirbet Mahna in the Wadi Jabesh.

MILCAH: from Akkadian *malkutu*, 'queen'.

MIZPAH: 'watchtower' – modern Tell en-Nasbeh.

MOPSUS: Greek *Mokoso*, Lydian *Moxus*, Akkadian *Mukshush*, Luwian *Muksas*.

MOPSOU-HESTIA: 'Mopsus' hearth'.

MOTHER EARTH: Sumerian *Ninhursag* – 'mistress of the mountain peaks'.

MUTBAAL: Hebrew Ishbaal, 'man of Baal'.

NAHARINA: 'river land' – another Egyptian name for Mitanni.

NATHAN: 'he gave'.

NEFERTITI: 'the beautiful one has come'.

NINTU: an epithet for the Mother Goddess *Ninhursag* who was the 'mother of all the living'.

NINHURSAG: 'mistress of the mountain peaks'.

NINURTA: Originally Nimurda, 'lord plough' or 'lord earth'.

NUN.KI: 'mighty place'.

ONBET: known in the Egyptological literature as Nubt – 'gold town'.

OTHNIEL: 'my strength is El'.

PA-KES: the region surrounding the modern town of Fakus.

PER WADJET: 'the house of the cobra-goddess Wadjet'.

PILISTA: Philistines.

PISHON: known in the local Turkic dialect as Kezel Uzun – the 'golden Uzun'.

POENI: 'belonging to Poen'.

REPEATING OF BIRTHS: Egyptian *wehem.mesut*, meaning unclear.

RIBLAH: on the Orontes to the south of Kadesh (Tell Nebi Mend).

SAMARIA: later Roman Sebaste.

SAMUEL: 'the name [of God] is El'.

SARAH: from Akkadian *sharatu*, 'princess'.

SETH: Hebrew *Shet* 'raised up'.

SHARUHEN: either modern Tell el-Ajjul or Tell el-Farah South.

SHECHEM: named after Shechem son of Hamor.

SHIKILESH: Cilicians who, later, through their migrations, gave their name to Sicily.

GLOSSARY

SHOFARS: ram's-horn trumpets.

ST ETIENNE: home of the famous École Biblique.

SUMERIAN: the archaic language of the southern Mesopotamian region.

SUSA: Semitic *Shushan* – the 'city of the white lily'.

TANAAKH: the scriptures of Judaism or Hebrew Bible, including the Torah.

TAKHT-É SULEIMAN: 'throne of Solomon'.

TAPPUAH: modern Sheikh Abu-Zared.

TJEUKERA: Teuceri = followers of the Greek hero, Teucer, who seized eastern Cyprus and founded the city of Salamis.

TIRZAH: Tell el-Farah North.

TJENU: Greek *Thinis*, possibly located at modern Girga.

UANNA-ADAPA: Berossus gives *Oannes* in his Greek text. The name Adapa has often been equated with the Semitic name Adama, the biblical Adam – the original 'red earth man'. It is therefore possible that Adama was a tribal name born by the descendants of the eponymous founder of the clan. We could then understand the legendary name of the great sage and priest of Eya as Uanna (of the clan) Adama or, in biblical terms, Enoch (of the line of) Adam.

UGARIT: modern Ras Shamra.

UR: modern Urfa.

UR OF KALDU: biblical 'Ur of the Chaldees' and the Kardu of later times – from what is today modern Urfa, not Sumerian Ur.

URAEUS: the image of the cobra-goddess Wadjet which was attached to the forehead of royal crowns and headdresses. Its mythological function was to protect the king by spitting flames at those who might try to harm the person of Pharaoh.

VIA MARIS: 'way of the sea'.

WADI HAMMAMAT: named after the ancient Hammamat desert hunters.

WASHOSHA: Iasos or Ouassos in south-west Anatolia, part of later Caria.

WELLHAUSEN: (1844–1918).

WRIGHT: (1909–1974).

YANOAM: possibly Tel Yinaam in eastern Galilee.

YASENAT: 'she belongs to you'.

ZADOK: 'the just'.

ZENDAN-É SULEIMAN: 'prison of Solomon'.

ZEDEKIAH: 'Yahweh is my righteousness'.

ZION: Hebrew *Tsiyon*, perhaps based on Canaanite *Tianna* – a city which, according to EAs 284, 298 & 306, was apparently at war with the rulers of the coastal plain.

INDEX

INDEX

**Order further Arrow titles
from your local bookshop, or have them delivered
direct to your door by Bookpost**

Free post and packing
Overseas customers allow £2 per paperback

Phone: 01624 677237

Post: Random House Books
c/o Bookpost, PO Box 29, Douglas, Isle of Man IM99 1BQ

Fax: 01624 670923

email: bookshop@enterprise.net

Cheques (payable to Bookpost) and credit cards accepted

Prices and availability subject to change without notice.
Allow 28 days for delivery.
When placing your order, please state if you do not wish to receive any
additional information.

www.randomhouse.co.uk/arrowbooks

arrow books